AMERICAN TERRORIST

AMERICAN TERRORIST

TIMOTHY McVEIGH & THE OKLAHOMA CITY BOMBING

LOU MICHEL AND DAN HERBECK

ReganBooks
An Imprint of HarperCollinsPublishers

To our wives,

Barbara Michel and Joyce Herbeck,

whose love and patience made this work possible

All photographs in this book, unless otherwise credited, are courtesy of the McVeigh family.

AMERICAN TERRORIST. Copyright © 2001 by Lou Michel and Dan Herbeck. All rights reserved. Printed in the United States of America. No part of this book may be used or reproduced in any manner whatsoever without written permission except in the case of brief quotations embodied in critical articles and reviews. For information address HarperCollins Publishers Inc., 10 East 53rd Street, New York, NY 10022.

HarperCollins books may be purchased for educational, business, or sales promotional use. For information please write: Special Markets Department, HarperCollins Publishers Inc., 10 East 53rd Street, New York, NY 10022.

FIRST EDITION

Designed by Paula Russell Szafranski

Printed on acid-free paper

Library of Congress Cataloging-in-Publication Data

Michel, Lou, 1955–
American terrorist : Timothy McVeigh and the Oklahoma City bombing / Lou Michel and Dan Herbeck.—1st ed.
p. cm.
Includes index.
ISBN 0-06-039407-2
1. McVeigh, Timothy. 2. Terrorists—United States—Biography. 3. Right-wing extremists—United States—Biography. 4. Oklahoma City Federal Building Bombing, Oklahoma City, Okla., 1995. I. Herbeck, Dan. II. Title.

HV6430.M28 M53 2001
976.6'38053'092—dc21
[B]

2001016094

01 02 03 04 05 BVG/RRD 10 9 8 7 6 5 4 3 2 1

CONTENTS

ACKNOWLEDGMENTS

This was not an easy story to tell. We needed—and received—much help. First and foremost, we would like to thank God for lifting us up, removing obstacles, and showing us the way forward so many times during the five years it took us to research and write this book.

We dedicate this work to our loving and supportive wives and children— Barb, Chris, Brian, and Amy Michel; and Joyce, Rich, and Chris Herbeck. As husbands and dads, we couldn't be luckier or more proud.

We are in deep gratitude to the people in the book business who were willing to take a chance on a controversial book by two new authors. We thank our agent, Noah Lukeman of Lukeman Literary Management Ltd. in New York City, and everyone at ReganBooks and HarperCollins, especially publisher Judith Regan, our brilliant and levelheaded editor, Calvert D. Morgan, Jr., his assistant, Jamilet Ortiz, managing editors Cassie Jones and Kim Lewis, and publicist Jennifer Suitor. We also appreciate the sage legal advice of our attorneys, Terrence M. Connors and Victor Kovner. It would be remiss to leave out the federal Bureau of Prisons, which allowed us many hours of access to Timothy McVeigh. For that we are deeply appreciative, and we hope that the bureau will continue to open its doors to journalists.

We are fortunate to work with a wonderful group of reporters and editors at an outstanding newspaper, the *Buffalo News*. We are especially indebted to three *News* copy editors who, on their own time, provided invaluable help and expertise—Gene Krzyzynski, Kevin Noonan, and Joseph Roland. We also appreciate the patience and cooperation of our editors, especially Margaret Sullivan, Stephen Bell, Edward Cuddihy, Stan Evans, Bill Flynn, and retired editor Murray B. Light.

The *News* staffers whose advice and encouragement helped to keep us pushing on are too many to mention, but we would like to thank David Valenzuela, Andrew Bailey, Gene Warner, Mike Beebe, Mike Vogel, George Gates, Robert J. McCarthy, Kevin Collison, Roger Durant, Jerry and Barb Sullivan, Henry Davis, Susan Martin, Donn Esmonde, Tom Buckham, Agnes Palazzetti, Pat Lakamp, Larry Felser, Karen Brady, Susan LoTempio, Charles "Bud" Anzalone, Peter Simon, Jay Rey, Jim Staas, Janice Habuda, Brian Meyer, Sharon Linstedt, Chet Bridger, Harold McNeil, Tom Ernst, Jay Bonfatti, Phil Fairbanks, Charity Vogel, Elizabeth Gaughan, Randy Rodda, Mark Sommer, Carolyn Raeke, Bruce Andriatch, Rod Watson, Laura Winchester, Margaret Kenny, Richard Baldwin, Mary Muzyka, Bobbie Rein, Dick Bradley, Tom Dolan, Jean Westmoore, Dom Catalano, Jim and Sue Kelley, David Robinson, Mary Kunz, Andy Galarneau, Lauri Githens, Margaret Hammersley, James Heaney, Jerry Zremski, Dave Condren, Jim Brennan, Tony Cardinale, Gerald Goldberg, Vic Carucci, Jack Connolly, Louise Continelli, Jeff Simon, Paula Voell, Ed Kelly, Bob Summers, Dick Haynes, Paul Price, Lonnie Hudkins, Scott Thomas, and Rick Stanley.

So many others, from so many walks of life, have also helped us, including: Alice Holland, Lou and Mary Michel, Bill Michel, Patricia Muscarella, Maryanne Cox, Jacqueline Michel, Regina Barone, Rosemary Michel, Bobby Michel, Anthony Michel, Tommy Quigley, Fran and Eleanor Malczynski, Roy and Maryann Tripi, Mary Yeskoot, Peter Yeskoot, Susan Muchow, Rosemary Johnston, Esther and Lionel Barrick, Jim and Diane Thompson, Father Stephen Collins, Father Jerome Machar, Monsignor James Campbell, Sister Noreen McCarrick, Jimmy Breslin, Lee Brown, Leo Damore, Marshall Brown, Joe Mombrea, Marc Lacey, Juan Forero, Carmen Granto, Lynn Hemming, Lew Jeckovich, Richard Kloch, Phil Kiefer, Gary Luczak, Bob

Calabrese, Charles W. Beinhauer, Maryanne Murphy, James Giammaresti, Edward Hempling, Joseph Riga, Lauren and Matt Krzyzynski, Harry and Mary Lou Herbeck, Joe and Dawn Herbeck, Patty and Bill Charles, Betty and Ray Reformat, Larry and Betsy Hertel, Anne Marie Gorlewski, Richard "Duke" Abbott, Jeff Balsom, Richard and Nancy Holland, Corky Cray, Leo Garrison, Thomas H. Burton, Lisa Flynn, Thomas Eoannou, Frank Clark, Don and Nancy Flaig, Peter and Sandy Cammarata, Craig Toth, Joe Flaig, Dick Flaig, Bob Schreck, Cate McCauley, Doug and Paulette Pagano, Greg Zoerb, Bill Bodkin, Matt Murphy III, Gabe DiBernardo, Glenn Murray, John Molloy, Mike Taheri, Joseph Terranova, Mary Murray, Tom Beilein, Denise O'Donnell, Paul Moskal, Bernard Tolbert, Norman Toy, Father Pete Brophy, Dennis Vacco, Father Paul Seil, Dave Gorlewski, Monica Roland, Bob Penders, George Maziarz, Rocco J. Diina, Larry J. Baehre, Paul Cambria, Lee Coppola and the Russell J. Jandoli School of Journalism and Mass Communication at St. Bonaventure University, the mass communications program at Buffalo State College, all the judges and staffers at U.S. District Court in Buffalo, and the men and women of the Buffalo Police Department.

More than 150 people were interviewed by us during the course of our research, and we thank them all, from Timothy McVeigh and his family to the cops who cracked the bombing case to the people in Oklahoma City who opened their hearts to us when we visited there last summer. In that regard, we especially thank Jane Thomas, archivist at the Oklahoma City National Memorial, and H. Tom Kight, a kind and decent man who took us under his wing during the Oklahoma visit.

INTRODUCTION

Who is Timothy McVeigh?

The editors at the newspaper I work for, the *Buffalo News*, wanted to know. So did the entire world.

It was April 21, 1995, two days after a truck bomb had destroyed the Alfred P. Murrah Federal Building in Oklahoma City, killing 168 people and injuring hundreds more. McVeigh, a decorated U.S. Army veteran who had grown up in the Buffalo area, was in police custody. The news hit western New York like a thunderbolt. No one wanted to believe that a young man from our community could have been responsible for what looked to all the world like the attack of a foreign terrorist.

Who is Timothy McVeigh? My editor, Stan Evans, wanted me to find out. A member of the *News*'s Niagara County Bureau staff, I had lived for fifteen years in rural Niagara County, about twenty minutes from the McVeigh family's home in Pendleton. I'd never heard of McVeigh or his family.

Before long, I was dispatched to McVeigh's neighborhood to find out whatever I could. The McVeighs' ranch home was swarming with reporters from all over the world, and more were arriving each minute. Five New York State Police cars guarded the home, making sure none of us got anywhere near the door. The FBI was inside with Bill McVeigh, the accused bomber's father.

I began knocking on doors in the neighborhood. Every neighbor said the same thing: they could not believe that the quiet, polite, unassuming Tim McVeigh could have had anything to do with a terrorist bombing. After I called the quotes into rewrite man Mike Vogel, Evans again took the phone.

"You're going to Michigan," he said. Decker, Michigan, was once the hometown of the second bombing suspect, Terry Nichols; McVeigh had lived there for a time with Nichols's family. I stopped at home to pack. Our two young sons were petrified; if the bomber lived so close by, would he blow them up, too? My wife, Barbara, and I tried to calm the boys' fears, gathering them in a circle to pray for protection. Then I was off, on a long drive through the night, on my way to Michigan.

When I arrived I met another *News* reporter, Jerry Zremski, and together we headed into the geographical "thumb" of the state. A half-mile from the Nichols farmhouse we encountered a police roadblock, along with another huge encampment of journalists. Brothers Terry and James Nichols, like McVeigh, had already been arrested. Federal agents from the FBI and the Bureau of Alcohol, Tobacco and Firearms (ATF) were turning the property inside out. Jerry and I took to the countryside, scrounging for tidbits of information.

Several locals recalled McVeigh staying at the Nichols farm after the Gulf War. One man, a massive bearded farmer who was acquainted with the Nichols clan, invited me inside his rustic home. The farmer recalled an odd tale McVeigh had once told him: the government, he claimed, had injected a computer chip into his buttocks before the Army shipped him over to Desert Storm.

Two FBI agents knocked on the farmer's door as the interview was winding down; a few minutes later, an Associated Press reporter showed up. I kept my fingers crossed that the farmer would keep quiet about the computer chip. No such luck. Outside the house, I heard the AP man calling his bureau and shouting into the cell phone that McVeigh was telling people the government had put a computer chip in his butt.

So much for my scoop.

Other than learning that McVeigh and the Nichols brothers embraced the same antigovernment views—and that folks on the Nichols farm sometimes amused themselves making homemade bottle bombs—there was little information to be had in Michigan.

Who is Timothy McVeigh? Heading home to New York, I wondered if I would ever find out.

Over the next few days, I began taking the long way to and from work in order to swing past Bill McVeigh's house in Pendleton. Each day the horde of reporters and satellite trucks dwindled a little further, until finally there were none.

At dawn on Wednesday, May 3, 1995, the state police broke camp outside the house. A couple of hours later I parked in front of the home and walked up the driveway, figuring that my footsteps would be less intrusive than a set of tires rolling up the driveway. A moment after I knocked on a doorway entrance to the garage, a hulking man with reddish-brown hair appeared: Bill McVeigh.

I introduced myself, and apologized for intruding.

His blue eyes, squinting in the sunshine, studied me cautiously. I could hardly blame him. For days police had kept the media away from his front door; now, finally, the media had made it to his doorstep. Looking for common ground to make small talk, I noticed that Bill had a big vegetable garden in his yard. I was also a gardener, and I told him about an elderly farmer who had lived with my wife and me for years, and taught me how to garden. We talked about early peas and the uncertainties of growing sweet corn.

"I've planted peas, corn, and onions, and if the corn doesn't come up, I'll plant it all over again," Bill McVeigh said. "That's the way corn is. Sometimes it comes up and sometimes it doesn't."

Then in my eagerness to connect, I blundered: fertilizer often worked for me, I mentioned, in making sure the corn stalks sprouted.

Bill McVeigh shot me a wary glance. His son had been accused of building a truck bomb out of fuel oil and fertilizer, and my innocent, stupid remark seemed like an artless trick to try and get him to talk about the bombing. I shook my head and said I was sorry.

"I don't want to talk no more," the father said, looking out to the road as if to show me which way to leave.

It seemed the interview was over. But then something remarkable happened. An older woman barreled up the McVeighs' driveway, her car kicking up dust and stones. When the car door swung open, Wilma Donahue, a neighbor, hurried over to Bill McVeigh. "You remember, Bill, we don't have any control over our children when they grow up," she told him. "If you need anything, anything at all, you call me for help." She left as quickly as she had arrived.

I took a chance. "How do you feel about what she said?"

Bill McVeigh dropped his guard for a moment. "You still have feelings for your children," he said, clutching a fist to his chest.

We spoke a few minutes more. When I mentioned the woman's thoughtful gesture once more, Bill told me about the quiet outpouring of love and compassion his friends and neighbors had sent his way since the bombing. His son's arrest had forced him to take a leave of absence from his job, he said, and the other day he'd even let a friend talk him into nine holes of golf to take his mind off things. His life was slowly getting back to normal, he said, but he could not talk about his "Timmy." "I can't get into any of that," he said earnestly.

After the interview I hurried to a pay phone and called Dan Herbeck, a veteran *News* reporter and close friend. The few thoughts Bill McVeigh had shared with me were his first public comments about the bombing. A lead slipped from Dan's lips into the telephone receiver: "Even if millions of Americans hate his son, Bill McVeigh still loves him." Our story ran the next day on page one, and the wire services soon carried it across the country.

In the following days and weeks I took that long way to and from work again and again, stopping to talk with Bill whenever I saw him out puttering in his garden. The relationship started slowly. I filled the air with stories about myself: how I came from Long Island to Buffalo State College and met my future wife; how I fell in love with the peaceful countryside of Niagara County; how, like Bill, I was the father of three children. I was selling myself, I knew, and yet there was nothing about my interest in Bill McVeigh that was insincere. I could see he was the salt of the earth, that all he wanted was to be left in peace. His wife had left him. He'd worked hard to build himself a new life. And now he was caught in the eye of a firestorm.

Friendly as he was, Bill remained reluctant to talk about his son. As I spoke dozens of times with Bill outside and sometimes inside his house, I couldn't help but think that my presence reminded him of the horrible turn his life had taken. And yet we continued to talk.

From the start, I knew that the story of Timothy McVeigh, of his life and his deeds, could not be told thoroughly in the context of a newspaper. To understand his transformation from average American boy to decorated soldier to mass murderer would require a venue of far greater breadth and depth.

I wanted to find a way to open the door into the childhood world from which Timothy McVeigh had emerged. It was, to be sure, a deeply ambivalent compulsion; at times, when I chatted with Bill, I could hear an inner voice chiding that I was nothing more than a carnivore, picking at the bones of a broken man. Only when Bill told me he understood that I had a job to do, and that he wouldn't hold it against me, did I reach a real level of comfort with the assignment. Without his consent, this project would never have succeeded.

His daughter Jennifer, a college student who lived with him, was a different story. At every opportunity she had during my visits, she defended her brother fiercely, criticizing the media for convicting him before trial. Her anger was also directed at federal investigators, who she claimed refused to pursue leads that might vindicate her brother. Jennifer herself was for a time the target of federal agents; letters her brother had sent her before the bombing, hinting that "something big" was about to happen, had momentarily led agents to suspect that she'd had advance knowledge of the plot. Of all the McVeighs, Jennifer would prove her brother's most vigorous defender. But she was also, in many ways, a typical college student. Sometimes, when she would return home from a day of classes and find me talking with Bill at the kitchen table, she would join in, complaining that college life seemed to last forever. She wondered when she would get on with life, find a boyfriend and marry. It would not be easy to win her confidence. But little by little the McVeighs were growing accustomed to my presence.

On Monday, June 2, 1997, a federal court jury in Denver reached its verdict in McVeigh's bombing trial. It was my day off; I was out mowing the lawn when Stephen Bell, my city editor at the time, called to tell me that the verdict would be announced on TV within the hour. I hurried over to Bill McVeigh's house.

Reporters crowded the end of the driveway. Motorists driving by called them vultures, telling them to leave the McVeighs alone.

Taking another gamble, I walked up to the house and knocked. Bill answered. I asked if I could come inside and watch the verdict with him, and Bill let me in.

I took a seat on the living room couch, hoping to remain inconspicuous. But Jennifer, who was seated nearby, looked over at me with obvious displeasure and asked me to leave.

I was about to plead my case when another knock came on the door. Monsignor Paul Belzer, pastor of Pendleton's Good Shepherd Catholic Church, was welcomed inside by Bill. Jennifer's protests subsided.

Smoking one cigarette after another, Jennifer flicked the remote control from station to station as the networks awaited the verdict. Bill paced back and forth, then grabbed a chair from the dining room and straddled it in the entrance to the living room. He and Jennifer seemed to know what the verdict would be; there were no tears or outbursts of anger when CNN announced that the jury had found McVeigh guilty. For five minutes the McVeighs simply watched the television in silence, as crowds in the street in front of the Denver courthouse celebrated the conviction. Finally Jennifer spoke.

"All we can do now is save Tim's life."

The McVeighs issued a brief written statement after the verdict. They maintained that they would stand by Timothy McVeigh until the end; Jennifer asked that people pray for her brother. In a matter of days, the jury would sentence him to death.

In August 1997, two days before his formal sentencing, Timothy McVeigh called me at home from his prison cell to issue a statement accusing his lawyer, Stephen Jones, of putting up an inadequate defense. Bill McVeigh had given his son my name and phone number. Before our telephone conversation ended, I asked McVeigh if I could have a face-to-face interview with him after his court appearance, and he agreed.

That first interview lasted just under an hour; it took place in the confines of the country's most secure prison, the Supermax facility, in Florence, Colorado. In this conversation McVeigh refused to acknowledge any role in the bombing; he was appealing the verdict, he explained, though he considered his chances of overturning the conviction "slim to none." But McVeigh did share his general thoughts on the trial and the aftermath of the bombing. Before leaving, I asked if he would consider telling me his story for use in a book.

"I wouldn't want it to be just about the bombing," McVeigh said.

"Absolutely not," I said. "Your whole life."

He agreed to consider the request, although he pointed out that a number of journalists—some of them nationally known—had already asked.

In the months that followed, I wrote McVeigh with some frequency, passing bits of local news in an effort to keep the channel open. From time to time he wrote back, but offered no explicit encouragement on the idea of a book. At one point, he asked me to stop writing him. He was convinced that no one would ever give him a fair break in telling his story. And, in truth, there was a part of me that felt relief at McVeigh's request. His was a disturbing story with a horrific culmination. My life might be better off without it.

But in April 1999, McVeigh changed his mind. He wrote to say he'd reconsidered my request. He had grown tired of reading thirdhand accounts of his life, and he wanted to give someone else a chance to do better. I was from the place he called home, and would have easy access to the people who'd been closest to him for most of his life. He said he felt able to trust me, because I had treated his family fairly and with dignity in previous stories. Among other things, his letter made clear that the publication of *Others Unknown*—a conspiracy-theory-ridden memoir of the case by his own lawyer, Stephen Jones—had enraged McVeigh to the point of action. Jones's search for a scapegoat had been a bone of contention between the two from the start. McVeigh had lost patience with his defense. He was ready to talk.

Well, almost.

As I prepared to visit him again at the Supermax prison, I received a second letter from McVeigh. He was writing to say that for the moment he would only talk about the bombing in "hypotheticals"; after his court appeals were over, he said, we could convert the hypotheticals to reality. My gut told me this wasn't going to work. If the book was to be taken seriously, McVeigh had to give up the real story.

My gut was also sending me another message: writing the Timothy McVeigh story was not a journey I wanted to make alone. The immensity of the project, and its very emotional weight, would be too difficult to bear alone. A number of people involved in the case had suffered breakdowns and divorce; some of the bombing survivors themselves had even committed suicide. I wasn't suicidal, but I knew that a prolonged period of immersion in this story would tax anyone's strength.

So once again I turned to the *News*'s federal courts reporter, Dan Herbeck, for help. Dan had been my mentor at the paper. His experience in dealing with the judicial system, cops, crime victims, and Buffalo's most notorious criminals would prove invaluable. As a team, Dan and I were able to secure extensive access to McVeigh through the U.S. Bureau of Prisons, which would be crucial to the project. Together we spent weeks preparing for a series of interviews over four days. Each sitting would be a nonstop session lasting at least seven hours. In more than twenty years of reporting I had always taken word-for-word notes during interviews, but I knew these circumstances would require recording equipment, and I spent hours on practice drills setting up and breaking down the equipment so that there would be no delays in starting the interviews. Dan and I pored over every scrap of material we could find on the bombing case, from newspaper articles to court transcripts to books. By the time we left for Colorado, we had compiled thirty typed pages of questions.

When I walked into the prison visitors' booth, split by a partition of thick, bulletproof glass with a steel doughnut hole in the center, McVeigh placed his hand against the glass to "shake hands," and I raised my hand to meet his. He unleashed a disarming smile, and watched intently as I set up the recording equipment. Once more looking for common ground, I mentioned that despite my French last name I was another Irish Catholic like him. We probably even shared some of the same hang-ups, I ventured.

"That's probably why you're sitting across from me right now," McVeigh said.

Early on, I decided not to push him about the hypotheticals, at least not this first day. Instead I let the interview take its course, and that afternoon I left the prison knowing more about his childhood, his relationship with his family, his thoughts of school, and details of his Army service than the public had learned in the years since the bombing. Still, as Dan and I discussed the material that first night, there was no mistaking that he shared my concern over whether we'd ever succeed in getting what we wanted from McVeigh.

The next morning, after a few pleasantries were exchanged, McVeigh asked me if I thought the book would be a success. Here was an opening. I explained that we'd probably have trouble trying to market a book based purely on hypotheticals. It was an answer McVeigh almost seemed to be expecting.

"Okay," he said. "I've decided I'm going to tell you everything. And if anything leaks out before the book is published—well, it's on you." His meaning was clear: if word got out that he was divulging his role in the bombing, it would destroy his legal appeals and hasten the death penalty.

By 10:30 A.M., my head was spinning.

He spoke rapidly, providing detail after detail; nothing in his manner gave the slightest suggestion that he was holding anything back. He spoke with intensity and painful candor. He explained that, if he seemed devoid of feelings and sensitivity, that was because he was a soldier, a man who was used to carrying out missions that brought pain to others. The depth of detail, the way his answers often perfectly fit the scenario raised by FBI investigators and prosecutors, and jibed with witness testimony, convinced Dan and me that McVeigh was telling the truth. He made no attempt to exonerate himself from guilt; indeed, his testimony sometimes had the effect of deflecting blame from others onto himself. To McVeigh, we would learn, telling the truth—even if it means saying brutal and hurtful things that put him in the worst possible light—is a matter of both honor and calculated purpose. He was perfectly blunt and never shied away from expressing his beliefs, even when he knew full well that his statements would only exacerbate the passionate hatred of those he had wronged. In the months ahead, we never caught him in a lie.

I emerged from that second day of interviews in the cavernous Supermax with a far keener sense of the importance—and disturbing nature—of the story McVeigh had to tell. As I sat on a small decorative boulder outside the prison, waiting for Dan to arrive, I felt almost numb. At one point an odd thought crossed my mind: for a moment McVeigh's story seemed like some dark contemporary revision of *The Grapes of Wrath,* in which the young man unable to find a place in society heads for Oklahoma, not away from it, and visits a vengeance upon society as near to the Dust Bowl's wrath as any one man could produce.

During the day, Dan had reviewed the previous day's tapes, as he would throughout our stay. In the days that followed, he and I established a pattern: after each session I spent with McVeigh, I rejoined Dan for a factual and emotional debriefing; that was followed by a walk, and then a visit to a chapel located in an abbey near our motel, where we joined in evening prayer with the monks.

In January 2000, we traveled to the federal death row in Terre Haute, Indiana, where McVeigh was awaiting execution. There we conducted a second series of interviews over three days, this time with Dan participating directly in the interviews. McVeigh's extraordinary candor continued, even under our repeated and detailed questioning. His matter-of-fact narration of events was difficult to listen to; at various times both Dan and I experienced feelings of horror and outrage. Yet there was one thought that helped us retain focus: the specter of the unresolved story of John F. Kennedy's assassination, a wound that remains unhealed nearly forty years later because Lee Harvey Oswald died before he could tell his story. McVeigh, at least, had lived through his trial. Yet his silence had left room for wild speculation about the true story of the bombing, from incidental rumors about a second bomber to broader conspiracy theories involving foreign terrorists and militia groups. Securing McVeigh's account of his own involvement in the bombing—an account that would constitute, he knew well, his long-awaited confession—was the only way to bring closure to the story.

This book, in many ways, could not have been written without McVeigh's cooperation—which, it must be stressed, was given without condition, compensation, or any right of review or approval. But neither could it have been completed without the cooperation of scores of others who have figured in his life. Whenever possible, we have sought out corroborating information that would either support or dismiss McVeigh's claims, and many people have been helpful in clarifying aspects of the case that have heretofore remained obscure. Terry Nichols and Michael Fortier, the two other men convicted in the bombing, were at the top of our list of desired interviews from the start, but a number of attempts to obtain their cooperation proved unsuccessful; McVeigh remains the first and only principal involved in the bombing to cooperate with journalists. Still, in the countless hours of interviews we conducted with law-enforcement officials; relatives of McVeigh, Nichols, and Fortier; and friends and acquaintances of the suspects and bombing victims, we found that each new piece of the puzzle meshed with the rest, and with McVeigh's own self-portrait, into a coherent and consistent picture of the man who finally, with the publication of this book, becomes the confessed bomber of the Murrah Building in Oklahoma City.

Who is Timothy McVeigh? We finally have the answers. What our society does with this information remains to be seen. Surely we can learn from this tragedy; surely a better understanding of the mind behind this act can help us all come to terms with humankind's capacity for evil—and our even more remarkable capacity for healing.

—Lou Michel

Dawn

April 19, 1995.

Two hundred and twenty years to the day after Lexington and Concord; two years to the day after Waco.

He awoke with the sun on this Wednesday, yawning and stretching in the cab of the Ryder truck. He'd slept like a baby in the rental, two feet in front of a seven-thousand-pound bomb—nearly three-quarters the weight of the device that devastated Hiroshima.

He needed no alarm clock on this of all days. His finely tuned biological clock had served him well for years. He never needed a wake-up call when there was something important to do.

The padded seat in the big yellow truck had been like a fine hotel bed compared with many of the places where he'd slept in recent years. Back in the Army, he could catch his shut-eye in the rigid steel gunner's seat when he needed to, hunkered down within a cramped Bradley Fighting Vehicle. He had learned in the Army how to sleep without being comfortable.

He'd also learned how crucial sleep was when you were preparing for action, and there would be plenty of action today.

Timothy McVeigh was preparing to teach the government a lesson. He was preparing to strike back for Waco, for Ruby Ridge, for U.S. military actions against smaller nations, for no-knock search warrants. It was a list of grievances he'd been amassing for years: crooked politicians, overzealous government agents, high taxes, political correctness, gun laws.

Dirty for dirty, he thought. *You reap what you sow. This is payback time.*

He reached down below the seat and pulled out an envelope made of thick brown plastic, roughly the size of a license plate. He peeled open the plastic, pulled out the food packet inside, and tore it open. This was breakfast—a spaghetti MRE, or military meal-ready-to-eat. With a white plastic spoon he scooped the gooey mix of noodles and red sauce into his mouth. Cold spaghetti wasn't his favorite breakfast, but it met his needs today. Specially formulated for soldiers on the move, it was high in calories and carbohydrates. Energy food. He would need every ounce of it to steel himself for what was to come.

He got out, stretched again, and examined his truck. He gave it a thorough walk-around, checking the tires, making sure that the rear and side doors to the cargo box were securely locked. He made sure that nothing looked out of the ordinary.

All this came naturally to him. He was a detail man—meticulous and tireless. As a kid, he woke up in the morning with restless energy, ready to take on the day, and as an adult he retained that quality. One thing that had attracted him to the Army was its famous recruiting slogan "We do more before 9 A.M. than most people do in an entire day."

In many ways, Timothy McVeigh was like tens of millions of young, middle-class American men. His childhood was unremarkable. He had grown up the son of a factory worker. He was in love with TV, movies, and the outdoors. He loved pro football and comic books about superheroes.

Like millions of other young men throughout American history, he had also gone to war, seen tragedy, and tasted victory. But he had left the military in bitter frustration.

He was not, those who knew him would agree, a violent or nasty person. The concept of hurting others did not come easily to him. It bothered him to see anyone pushed around or hurt. As a child he had stood by helplessly as a neighbor cast a burlap bag full of kittens into a pond to drown; he himself stopped shooting frogs with his BB gun because it pained him to see the creatures suffer. Later, when he killed men in battle, he found it difficult to suppress his sense of the injustices of war.

Yet here he was, four days shy of his twenty-seventh birthday, preparing to use a truck bomb to destroy an office building filled with people he had never met—a mission he considered an act of war.

He checked the .45-caliber Glock semiautomatic handgun he carried close to his heart, in a leather holster across his chest. It could fire sixteen bullets without reloading, and he was prepared to use it to kill anyone who interfered with his task. Then he checked his wristwatch. He didn't want to reach the target too early. He wanted to be sure that there were plenty of people in the nine-story building—enough people to make President Clinton, Attorney General Janet Reno, and other government leaders pay attention.

The T-shirt he chose to wear on this occasion said it all. On the front of the shirt was a drawing of Abraham Lincoln. Underneath the drawing was the Latin refrain that John Wilkes Booth had screamed after he assassinated Lincoln—SIC SEMPER TYRANNIS, or "Thus ever to tyrants."

On the back of the shirt was a picture of a tree dripping blood, bearing a quotation from Thomas Jefferson: THE TREE OF LIBERTY MUST BE REFRESHED FROM TIME TO TIME WITH THE BLOOD OF PATRIOTS AND TYRANTS.

A lot of blood will be shed today, he thought. *Innocent people will suffer. But there is no other way.*

He looked at himself in the rearview mirror and adjusted his plain black baseball cap. He was ready.

Thus ever to tyrants!

The truck was in good running order. He'd checked all the fluid levels the night before, when he stopped for gas in southern Kansas, topping off the tank with forty dollars' worth of unleaded.

Timothy J. McVeigh turned the key in the ignition, threw the Ryder into gear, and headed for Oklahoma City.

I
GROWING UP

1

The Boy Next Door

I struggle with the question: Do I love my parents? . . . I have very few memories of my childhood, of interaction with my parents. I can't blame them for anything that's happened to me. I was often by myself or with neighbors. Most of my memories focus on that.

—TIMOTHY MCVEIGH

At 11:45 P.M. on April 22, 1968, a phone call cut short Bill McVeigh's night shift at Harrison Radiator in Lockport, New York.

"You better go home. Your wife's going to have a baby," his foreman called out after hanging up with Mildred Noreen "Mickey" McVeigh. Mickey had called the plant to summon her husband home. Ignoring the predicted due date of April 25, the second of the McVeighs' children was arriving ahead of schedule.

Bill McVeigh, a tall, lean man with a mop of reddish-brown hair, came from a family of hard workers with strong backs. He was second generation at Harrison, the factory that supplied General Motors with car radiators. As he hurried away from his post, he wondered whether he was about to welcome the family's third Harrison worker into the world.

A natural mathematician able to tally long columns of numbers in his head, McVeigh looked up into the night sky outside the plant. Crystals of snow tumbled through the air. April was almost over, but the snow was nothing shocking to Bill. He'd wintered in western New York his whole life. What interested him was the statistical contrast in temperatures. Earlier that day, the temperature had risen to almost seventy degrees. Now, the mercury had plunged low enough to speckle the night air with snowflakes.

As Bill McVeigh strode on long legs toward his car, parked with thousands of others in a massive lot, he was consumed by nervous excitement. He was anxious to know whether this time Mickey would give birth to a son. A boy would give them one of each. In the long term, of course, it didn't really matter; Bill and Mickey dreamed of having a big family, and at some point, they reasoned, the odds were bound to yield a son.

Bill jumped into his car. He hadn't far to drive. He sometimes walked to and from work in those early days, when the McVeighs were a one-car family. From his backyard on Junction Road, across a sweeping field of grass, you could see Harrison. Others might have been put off by the idea of looking out upon their place of employment during off-hours, but Bill didn't mind at all. He was a devoted company man, always glad to have the work. He would punch the time clock for thirty-six years without a grain of resentment.

The wheels of McVeigh's 1966 Chevrolet Biscayne—he was always a GM man—crunched as they rolled up the gravel driveway to his tiny three-bedroom ranch. In a moment McVeigh swept his wife into the car and the two got back on the road, barrelling toward Lockport, a city split in two by the murky waters of the Erie Canal. When they arrived five minutes later at Lockport Memorial Hospital, it was a familiar sight: they'd made the same journey for their daughter Patty two years before, nine months practically to the day after Mickey and Bill's wedding on August 28, 1965.

For all their enthusiasm about having a big family, Mickey had married reluctantly. Part of her wanted motherhood. The other part had wanted to pursue a career as a stewardess. It was only after she met and married Bill McVeigh that she had settled down, taking a job as a travel agent.

Bill McVeigh's family had for generations lived a peaceful life as farmers beside the Erie Canal. But by the time Bill was born, only fragments of that life remained. As a boy, Bill and his brother Jim worked on their grandfather Hugh McVeigh's eighty-acre farm at Bear Ridge and Robinson Roads in Lockport, helping to harvest the hay that fed the handful of cattle their grandfather raised. When Hugh McVeigh died in 1955, the family's farming tradition came to an end.

Bill's father and mother, Edward and Angela McVeigh, reared Bill and Jim in a farmhouse Ed had helped build at 5940 Bear Ridge Road, on a plot from Hugh's old farm. The house faced the Erie Canal, which to the boys and their friends was known as "the hills" because of the waterway's steep banks. The brothers were careful to stay out of the water. Neither of them knew how to swim, and one of their companions had drowned in the channel's fifteen feet of water.

Ed McVeigh was the brick and mortar of the McVeigh family, a lifelong auto worker who kept his family going in the face of tragedy. In 1942, after Angela fell down a flight of stairs shortly after giving birth to Jim, she was diagnosed with multiple sclerosis; she would never walk again. Angela was forced to rely on Ed's strong arms and back to lift her from bed and keep things running in the house. Yet Ed resolved to make sure his two sons had as close to a normal childhood as possible. At night, after Ed went to work, his elderly mother, Wilhamina, and her daughter Helen, who lived next door, would stop by to give Angela a hand.

Bill's young life was brightened by occasional summer trips to the Crystal Beach amusement park; Uncle Hugh, Ed's brother, also taught Bill how to golf. But the real focus of the family's entertainment was the South Lockport Fire Hall, where Ed was a charter member. Ed, Bill, and Jim passed their summers marching in the fire company's drum corps at countless firefighters' parades and field days. On Saturday evenings Angela would sit in the family car and watch with pride as her husband and two boys marched to patriotic songs with volunteers from neighboring fire companies. "This was our entertainment. We'd go at six o'clock every Saturday night," Bill McVeigh recalls. "There were parades all summer long and we went to all of them."

After Catholic grammar school, both Bill and his brother attended De-Sales Catholic High School. Bill was never eager to attend college. His teachers encouraged him, but the quiet young man never told his parents of their enthusiasm, and Ed never raised the question. A scholarship greased the way for Jim to attend college, but Bill seemed destined stay behind in Lockport. Bill often recalled the words of his old high school guidance counselor, Father William A. Kenney.

"Why don't you go to Cornell, the farm college?" the priest prodded.

Bill, who loved flower and vegetable gardening, wasn't interested.

"You'll end up at Harrison," Father Kenney predicted, "like everybody else."

He was right. Bill opted to lead the hardworking life of a Harrison Radiator employee. The work was steady, despite occasional threats of layoffs and labor unrest, and the pay was respectable. Bill didn't need much more than that.

Bill McVeigh met Mickey Hill in a Catholic bowling league in March 1963, the same month he started at Harrison. Bill was hardly a ladies' man. Mickey was five years younger than he was, but the slender, vivacious girl caught his eye. One day he found himself unable to resist the temptation to stop by her house when he was in her hometown of Pekin, a hamlet on the Niagara Escarpment about ten miles east of Niagara Falls. When Bill knocked on the door of the Hills' modest home, he was greeted by Mickey's parents. He explained that he was stopping by on bowling league "business." Mickey was out, but her parents invited him inside, and took an instant liking to the nervous young man.

Mickey's father, Bill Hill, was a quiet, easygoing man. An auto mechanic at a Niagara Falls Cadillac dealership, he could fix just about anything—a talent that helped to keep the marriage purring evenly for more than five decades. His domain was the garage and the basement workshop. Her mother, Dorothea "Dot" Hill, exercised absolute authority in the kitchen and throughout the rest of the house. She was something of a hypochondriac, but considering that she had spent years in a painful battle with uterine cancer, nobody blamed her.

Dot was also a woman who believed in the traditional way of life. Marriage, motherhood, homemaking—Dot couldn't imagine a woman wanting anything else. When Bill McVeigh came into her daughter's life, she was as encouraging as possible. "Look, he's got a good job and he's stable, and you want a family," Dot reminded Mickey. Their first official date was a bowling banquet.

Bill and Mickey's courtship was in full swing by the end of spring 1963, despite Bill's shyness and Mickey's reluctance to settle down. In Mickey's high school yearbook, her bowling friend Judy Rignel wrote, "Best of luck in everything you do (Bill). Don't forget all our good times." Two evenings a week, Mickey would watch Bill play softball on a team sponsored by a tavern in Pendleton. To outside observers, they might have seemed like a mismatch. He was shy; she was boisterous. He was quiet; she loved to swap stories and jokes with friends. Bill's high school yearbook didn't contain a single note from an excited classmate. For such an introverted fellow, going steady with Mickey Hill was quite a coup.

Mickey had always dreamed of being an airline stewardess, and after Bill was drafted on August 22, 1963, she left for Hartford, Connecticut, where she attended Hartford Airline Personnel School for several months before returning home to Pekin. She and Bill wrote each other; whenever he was on leave during his two-year hitch in the military, they dated. Her mom's words of wisdom resonated in Mickey's head. Bill had a *good job*, he was *stable*, and Mickey wanted a *family*. He was dependable and ruggedly handsome. In his quiet way, he could turn a young lady's head. Mickey was sure she loved him, though not wildly.

And so when Bill McVeigh proposed to her on Christmas Day 1964, while on leave from the Army in Fort Campbell, Kentucky, Mickey answered yes.

On a late August morning in 1965, Mickey made her grand entrance at Immaculate Conception Catholic Church on North Ridge Road in the town of Cambria. She wore a dazzling full-length bridal gown borrowed from her aunt Noreen, who lived in nearby Niagara Falls. A pearl-and-sequin crown held her veil in place over her wavy light brown hair; in her hands was a missal adorned with white carnations. As the red-brick church filled with organ music, Mickey walked up the center aisle of the country church with her father, Bill Hill; she was a head-turning beauty.

After honeymooning for six days in the Adirondack Mountains and New England, Bill and Mickey set up residence at a small apartment in Lockport and settled into the quiet life of newlyweds. It was 1965; there was a restless spirit in America. But Bill McVeigh felt no kinship with the rebellious side of his generation. Though others were starting to talk of dropping out of society, smoking pot and protesting against the government, Bill harbored no feelings of resentment toward his country. He was proud of his way of life, of the simple tranquillity Lockport represented.

Falling into the rhythms of domestic life wasn't as easy for Mickey. Gone were the laughs of high school, where she was remembered for her quick wit; gone were her carefree days as a young woman who went bareback riding on her girlfriend's horses. The birth of her first daughter, Patricia, so soon after her wedding, had shelved her dreams of a career as a stewardess; now she was slipping into a hospital gown and being wheeled into a hospital delivery room for the second time in less than three years.

At 8:19 A.M. on Tuesday, April 23, 1968, after enduring more than eight hours in labor and the difficulty of a breech birth, Mickey McVeigh gave birth to her first son, Timothy James McVeigh. She gazed in wonder at her newborn son's full head of waxy, brownish-red hair. He looked just like his father, though at six pounds, fourteen ounces, and nineteen inches in length, Timmy was nothing more than a peanut next to his father.

When Bill stepped quietly into Mickey's room in the maternity ward to see his new son, he found her gazing at him with amusement. "On the way home," she joked, "we're going to have to stop and get him a haircut."

That was what Bill loved most about his willowy wife—her sense of humor. Four days after Tim was born, Bill brought his wife and new son home from the hospital. Timothy's downy head of baby hair grew for more than nine months before Mickey followed through on her plans to get him a haircut. She was struck by the change in her blue-eyed baby's appearance. In a journal she kept to chronicle his first few years, she wrote, "Timmy had his first haircut at 9½ mos. He seemed to change from a baby to a little boy right away. He has quite a temper and is very stubborn, but is almost always happy and smiling."

The McVeighs were a middle-class family with simple tastes. Each Monday evening, Mickey and Dot headed off to bingo at the Pekin Volunteer Fire Hall. Bill was happy to stay at home and busy himself in the garden, while watching the children. Tim wandered about on wobbly toddler legs, and Bill would have to break away from weeding his vegetable patch periodically and fetch his son before he strayed too far. Junction Road was busy with tractor-trailers coming and going from Harrison.

One evening, Bill found his son standing on the front steps to the house. At his feet lay an earthworm—or, to be more precise, half an earthworm. Chuckling, Bill realized that the other half had to be in his son's belly. "That's just the way Tim was from the start," Bill remembers. "Always getting into things, always on the move."

Once, while his mother was visiting with another mother who lived next door, Tim walked out into the road. The next thing anyone knew, a truck driver was knocking on the neighbor's front door.

Tim, wearing a baseball cap, stood beside the trucker.

"Lady, is this your kid?" he asked.

"Yes, it is," said Mickey.

"Well," said the trucker, "he was out in the road swinging his baseball bat."

Bill smiled when he came home from work and heard the story. What use was there in having a panic attack? he figured. That's the way kids are.

Mickey continued to document Tim's toddler years in her journal, often writing in the first-person voice of the little boy. At seven months old, Tim suffered his first spanking, though there was no reason listed for it. His first spoken words were "Da-Da." His first Christmas, she wrote, "was spent at Grampa McVeigh's. Aunt Helen, Uncle Jim, Aunt Pat and Aunt Mag were also there. Patty and I got a fire truck that has a real noisy horn on it. . . . Santa left a big horse on springs for us and a farm, a little train, giant rings and lots of toys."

Tim McVeigh celebrated his first birthday on Wednesday, April 23, 1969. "Daddy is working nights this week, so can't be home for the ice cream and cake, but Mommy is taking a lot of pictures so Daddy can see everybody," the journal reported.

Tim's early childhood was marked by a love for paging through catalogs and his parents' yearbooks and wedding album; he also loved watching *Gumby* and *Truth or Consequences* on TV. Under "Mother's Notes," Mickey wrote, "at age 1½, seems to be getting into a lot of trouble. A typical Dennis the Menace." On his second birthday, "Gramma and Grampa Hill gave me a gun and holster set and a hat and cowboy suit," Mickey wrote in her son's voice.

At three years old the boy was introduced to bicycling, a passion that would continue long into his adolescence. Next to the McVeighs' house on Junction Road, Harrison Radiator began building a private road for access to a new section of the plant. On his days off, Bill used the completed portions of the road to teach his son how to ride a bike. As Tim caught on he began to ride it by himself, though at first the boy lacked endurance for long rides. But his father found a way around the problem. He tied a rope from his bike to his son's, and spent weekend afternoons towing Tim happily along behind him. From time to time a plant guard would come out and order them off the property, but Bill and Tim would return.

Bill also practiced golf, chipping and driving balls while Tim watched. Too young to golf, Tim took swings at an inflatable punching dummy his parents had given him. With sand for ballast at its base, the dummy always wobbled back for another whack.

In October 1972, the McVeighs moved from their starter home to a new and more spacious three-bedroom ranch at 5321 Hinman Road in Lockport. Then, on March 5, 1974, the McVeighs' third and final child, Jennifer Lynn McVeigh, was born. After the delivery, the doctor warned Mickey that for medical reasons she could no longer bear children safely.

There was no shortage of doting grandparents nearby to help with the children. The McVeighs' new home was less than a mile from Mickey's parents' house, and Ed McVeigh lived only a few minutes away on Bear Ridge Road. Angela, Tim's paternal grandmother, had died in August 1972. Family members saw the death as a blessing in some ways; bedridden for the last eight years of her life, she had required professional nursing care that Ed paid for out of his own pocket. With that financial burden lifted, he retired in March 1973 and turned his full attention to his grandchildren.

Tim charged forward into boyhood on Hinman Road. One of his first friends was Todd Carter, his new next-door neighbor.

Their childhood games were familiar: cowboys and Indians, cops and robbers, make-believe wars pitting right against wrong. Tim relished the role of the good guy. "I'm gonna be the sheriff," he'd announce to Todd, who was nine months his senior. Or he'd lay claim to the role of cowboy over Indian. In war games, Tim always succeeded in beating down the invading force.

In their elaborate games, forts and jails were set up in the garage attached to the McVeigh home. Using toy handcuffs, Tim incarcerated Todd. Todd was so impressed by his friend's vivid imagination that he hardly minded getting stuck playing the bad guy. An old boat stored behind their homes served as the setting for the action, or they would clamber up into a tree fort in the woods. This was serious business. The two boys would pick wild berries and devour them as "rations."

Beyond the woods were ten acres of grapes. In the autumn Tim roamed through the field, breathing in their sweet, earthy fragrance. Sometimes he and Todd would harvest bunches of grapes and race back to their fort, frightened of getting caught by the grouchy owner of the vineyard. She also was their school-bus driver, an intimidating woman with a loud and gruff voice.

The bus driver's harsh exterior crumbled one morning, though, after Tim and Patty were nearly killed while waiting to board her school bus. As the brother and sister stood at the end of their driveway, a dump truck filled with asphalt from a stone quarry rounded a blind curve. The truck flew around the bend, and there was no time to take evasive action when the driver noticed the flashing yellow lights of the school bus. Todd, sitting inside the bus, watched in horror as the truck swerved from left to right. The squealing tires drew neighbors from across the street to their front window. A gale of blacktop heaved off the top of the load, but miraculously the driver managed to avoid the two McVeigh children. The truck missed them by three feet.

Tim was shocked. His sister was so upset that she started stammering. James Donner, a neighbor who witnessed the incident, jumped into his car and took off after the trucker, who hadn't bothered to stop. Donner, a Lockport firefighter, chased the runaway truck for three miles before he was able to convince the driver to pull his truck to the side of the road.

The driver jumped out, in hysterics. "I'm sorry! I'm sorry!" he screamed. The police arrived and charged him with reckless driving.

The incident threw a scare into Mickey McVeigh. "We had to pick the blacktop out of Timmy's shoes, and his clothes," she told neighbors. "Patty's too."

Tim escaped that brush with death, but he was hardly immune to the more common injuries of childhood, which frequently resulted in trips to Lockport Memorial Hospital for stitches and bandages. He had more than his share of bumps, bruises, and ailments. When he was barely a year old, he smashed his head against a doorway. "Had four stitches over my right eye," Mickey wrote, again in his voice. "Didn't seem to slow me down."

Several months later, on January 19, 1970, another injury was noted: "Dropped can on cheek. Took three stitches. Very calm and unconcerned about the whole incident," she noted in the journal. And two months after that, Tim toppled out of a bunk bed and fractured his right wrist. "Dr. Muscato put cast on. Will be on five to six weeks," Mickey recorded dutifully. Tim amused himself with the cast, chasing his older sister and whacking her with it. At age four, the accident-prone boy contracted pneumonia and spent a week in the hospital. One year later, he missed a week of kindergarten with a mild case of scarlet fever.

One Saturday morning, in the summer of 1973, Tim and Todd Carter were playing their war games when Tim stepped up on a metal milk box in his garage, lost his balance, and toppled backward, landing hard on his head.

Blood began to spurt from a nasty wound. Todd screamed for Bill McVeigh, who came running.

"What happened?" asked Bill.

"He lost his balance and fell backwards," Todd answered, noticing that Tim was much calmer than he was.

"I want to see how bad this is," said Bill.

He parted the cut section of scalp to get a better look at the cut. When Todd looked over his shoulder, he could see the white of Tim's skull. Amazingly, Tim didn't scream, though he let a few tears trickle down his cheeks as he dealt with his pain. There was even a small upside to the accident: the game, Todd thought, had suddenly taken on a touch of realism—a bloody war wound. Bill gathered up his son and took him, once again, to Lockport Memorial Hospital. A couple of hours after returning with five stitches in his scalp, Tim was back at play.

(A faithful chronicler of childhood accidents in her baby journal, Mickey was just as painstaking in her notes under the title "Memorable Events in the Family," including one especially detailed and strange account: "Mommy and Daddy were in three-car accident Jan. 26, 1969. Mommy had four stitches in her eye, one in her neck and contussions [sic] of her ribs and knees. Daddy cut his leg and hurt his back. The car was wrecked. We got a new 1969 Chevelle and Mommy and Daddy like it very much.")

Tim and Todd were inseparable. When stuck indoors, they would build forts, especially on sleepover nights. Fashioning safe and comfortable outposts from couch cushions and blankets, they hunkered down to watch their favorite horror movies on TV. Todd loved his neighbor like a brother. Tim's energy, his easy ability to take life's ups and downs in stride, deeply impressed him.

If there was anything odd about young Tim McVeigh, it was his habit of drinking pickle juice. He would invite Todd over for pickles, encouraging him to help polish off the whole jar. Then, Tim would guzzle down the salty brine with a satisfied smile.

The boys helped each other through the difficulties of childhood. When Todd was eight, his father told him that their beloved poodle, Jolly, would have to be put to sleep because of a painful throat ailment. Todd walked back to Tim's house weeping.

"What's wrong?" Tim asked.

"My dad's taking Jolly to be put under," Todd sobbed.

Tim put his hand on his friend's shoulder. "Everything's okay," he said. "Don't worry about it. You'll get another dog."

Tim had endured his own childhood introduction to animal euthanasia, one far less tidy than Todd's. It occurred at a small fishing pond across the street from his house on Hinman Road. Tim was playing near the pond when he noticed one of the older neighborhood boys carrying a burlap sack. The sack was weighted down with rocks, but the curious Tim could see there was something else wriggling around in the sack. He watched as the older boy pitched the sack out into the pond, where it quickly sank to the bottom.

"What was that?" Tim asked, running around to the far shore of the pond where the neighborhood boy stood.

"Those are kittens my cat had," the boy answered in a matter-of-fact tone. "We had to get rid of them."

For Tim, who loved animals and especially kittens, the realization of what he had witnessed hit him hard. He cried about the incident for days.

Not long afterward, Tim walked into his garage and noticed that his own cat had cornered a frightened baby rabbit. The cat went for the back of the rabbit's neck, fatally wounding the little animal.

Tim let out a scream of shock and terror and ran for his parents in tears.

"Please," he screamed. "Take the rabbit to the veterinarian! He's hurt!"

His parents said they couldn't. After all, they said, it was just a wild rabbit, and the house cat was only doing what came naturally.

The thought of the dying rabbit was equally agonizing for Tim; in later years he would point to both incidents as landmarks in his growing awareness that life is about "difficult decisions."

In January 1977, Todd and Tim experienced one of their most memorable childhood adventures: the Blizzard of '77. The worst snowstorm in western New York history piled snow all the way up to the roofs of many homes. Twenty-nine people died, some of them freezing to death in cars buried in the snow. Thousands of families were stranded for days, and the situation was so bad that the National Guard was called in to help people dig out.

The snowstorm caused western New York to be declared a disaster area, but for Tim and Todd it was pure fun. To their delight, school was closed for a week. The towering snowbanks provided all kinds of opportunities for the construction of forts and tunnels. One day, they gleefully found the roof of a Volkswagen as they dug down into one of the piles of snow.

For the McVeigh family, though, the blizzard may have been the first sign of a chill in Bill and Mickey's marriage.

Mickey, still enjoying her career as a travel agent, had started for work when the snows were just starting to fall about 12:40 P.M. By the time she arrived at the Lockport agency, she and the other workers were told to go home. The blinding snows made travel along the rural roads impossible. The agency's workers took shelter at a motel in the city, where they spent several days with other stranded travelers. There were rumors of drinking and "fooling around" among those stuck at the motel. Mickey denied that she had done anything improper, but she would acknowledge that she was beginning to sour on her marriage.

There was much about her husband that she liked and admired; he was a great provider and a caring father. But she and Bill were very different. Mickey loved travel and excitement, while Bill was reserved, a homebody. Try as they did, it was a difference they would never be able to reconcile.

When the warmer weather came, Tim and Todd put aside their toy guns to shoot targets with a pump-action BB rifle Todd had received. He and Tim spent some time picking tin cans they'd set up in the backyard, but the game was old hat for Tim, who had already been introduced to guns at age seven by his grandfather Ed McVeigh. Later, Ed would allow him to shoot his .22-caliber rifle in what amounted to an extended course in gun safety and responsible citizenship.

A year after the Blizzard of '77, the boyhood friendship between Todd and

Tim began to fade. The McVeighs moved to yet another new house, this one bigger and better than the last. The new house on Meyer Road in neighboring Pendleton had four bedrooms, three bathrooms, and a fireplace. The move to the last house the family would share was made on Mickey's birthday in January 1978. The two-story colonial, which had cost fifty-five thousand dollars to build, was located in a township founded by Sylvester Pendleton Clarke, an early nineteenth-century tax protester who hated the federal government and had tried to start his own republic on nearby Grand Island in the Niagara River.

The McVeighs' new neighborhood had plenty of children. An art assignment from his fourth-grade teacher led Tim to befriend Vicki Hodge, a new neighbor. Tim had drawn a picture of the house his family was building, and was explaining to the class that there was a pond beside it. Recognizing the description, Vicki interrupted to let Tim know she lived across the street. She and her brother, Steve, would become two of Tim's closest friends in adolescence.

At ten, Tim had his first bad encounter with a bully. The incident occurred in late spring 1978 at Little League baseball practice. Tim's team, the Senators, were practicing in their green uniforms at the town ball diamonds across from Brauer's Tavern, which sponsored the adult fast-pitch softball team for which Bill was a pitcher.

Small and scrawny for his age, Tim took the field under the watchful eyes of his father and his father's best friend, Art Braunscheidel, who served as the team's coaches. With two adults looking out for Tim, it was surprising that another child would go after him. But his size made him an easy target.

The bully walked up to Tim and grabbed his baseball cap. Tim tried to retrieve the hat and wound up in a tugging match with the bigger youngster. Then, without warning, the bully walloped Tim.

Stunned, Tim ran to his father's station wagon and hid in the backseat and wept. He was scared and embarrassed: the men of the McVeigh family were not supposed to cry. Never once had Bill or Tim's grandfathers shed a tear in front of him. Now here he was, bawling his eyes out in public. Tim felt humiliated in front of the other kids on the team, who had seen Braunscheidel comfort him.

There was something else eating at Tim's self-esteem. He felt like a failure in the eyes of his father, who was an accomplished softball player. Tim lacked the aggressive jock mentality, the muscle coordination, and the size to be a star athlete; he would come to be known as "Noodle McVeigh" because he was as thin as a noodle. And Tim was certain that his father was disappointed by his lackluster performance.

In adolescence, when size and coordination finally caught up with Tim, what little desire he had to pursue sports had long ago died. But that humiliation on the Little League field—at the hands of a bully—was something he would remember forever. Over time, he would develop a seething hatred of bullies—of any person, institution, or even nation that seemed to be picking on the weak.

Bill somehow managed to overlook his son's deep hurt. He loved sports, and tried to share his enthusiasm with Tim by example. Twice a week he pitched for the local tavern's softball team, and he wanted his son to share his enjoyment of the game. But when Bill would try to enlist him for a game of catch, his son would shudder inside. He didn't need another opportunity to be humiliated. Bill had a strong arm, and the ball sizzled in Tim's mitt, when he managed to catch it at all. Often the ball got past him or, worse, hit him. With each pitch, Tim would think, *He's scaring the heck out of me, whipping that ball at me.*

Tim tried, but was never able to share his dad's love of baseball.

Bill wished that maintaining the happy family life he cherished was as simple as whipping his arm around and firing a softball into the mitt of his catcher. But his marriage was unraveling. The fundamental differences between his personality and Mickey's had begun to grate on them both. Mickey threw herself into her work at the travel agency, but she felt herself losing her foothold in family life. She loved her children, but was coming to the painful realization that she could no longer say the same about their father.

The truth is, Mickey McVeigh was bored with Bill. He worked long hours, and when he was around it seemed that all he wanted to do was play softball and putter in the garden. At times, despite his congenial nature, he had a nasty temper. He could explode in anger about something as minor as misplacing his car keys. The marriage just hadn't been what Mickey was expecting. Mickey began to wonder what would happen if she left him. It would have been easier if not for their three young children; the last thing she wanted to do was hurt them.

But finally, in 1979, Mickey realized she couldn't stand it anymore. She decided to be honest with Bill. When she broke the news—"I'm not in love with you anymore"—she could see the hurt in his face.

Bill was a reasonable man. He agreed with Mickey that they should split up if she was unhappy. They would obtain a legal separation. What was the point of prolonging something that seemed beyond repair? Bill offered to raise all three children; he didn't like the idea of splitting them up. Trying to make the best of a difficult situation, Bill and Mickey agreed to let the children decide for themselves where they wanted to live.

The girls wanted to stay together. They chose their mother. But Tim cast his lot with his father. "I don't want Dad to be alone," he said. Tim cared for his mother, but in later years he would insist that it didn't bother him much when she left. The real problem, he said, was that he never really felt that close to his parents in the first place. He wished they spent less time at work and more time with him and his sisters. With both his mother and father working full time, he felt like he never had a parent to talk with when he came home from school in the afternoon.

Reflecting on his boyhood, Tim McVeigh would angrily deny that his parents' split was in any way responsible for the shocking events in his later life. He would insist his childhood was no better or worse than those of millions of other sons and daughters of divorced couples. But he would also lash out—repeatedly and emotionally—at the concept of working mothers and two-income families, which he considered a major cause of problems in American society. "In the past thirty years, because of the women's movement, they've taken an influence out of the household," he said.

> When I came home from school, I looked for something to do. Years ago, there [would have been] a mom there who said, "Do the dishes," or "Let's talk about what happened at school." Maybe even there was a dad there. Maybe the mom said, "Well, your dad will be home in two hours. If you're having trouble with bullies, why don't you talk to your dad?"
>
> I can't attribute anything I am now to any lack of my parents' presence in the home. I don't know why I go off on that, but I do say that I have very few memories of interactions with my parents.
>
> I am not looking in any way, shape, or form to blame any-

thing on my parents or my upbringing. All in all, from birth to age eighteen, I emerged pretty much a functional person in the real world, and that's all that counts.

Tim never showed any deep outward wounds from the split, but his father was sure it must have marked him.

In 1979 Bill and Mickey obtained a legal separation, and Mickey packed her car. She, Patty, and Jennifer would make a new start down in Pensacola, Florida, where her brother lived. Mickey said goodbye to Bill and her eleven-year-old son. She got no farther than the end of Meyer Road before she pulled the car off to the shoulder and started sobbing uncontrollably. Her conscience was crushing her. How could she do this to her children? But at the same time, she yearned to leave. She put the car into drive and headed south.

Six weeks later, on the very day she was to begin a new job as a bank secretary, Mickey received a phone call from Bill. He sounded flustered.

"Tim's real sick," said Bill; he thought it might be pneumonia. "I don't know what to do."

Mickey decided there and then to return home. She hung up with Bill and gathered her daughters. "Okay, kids. I guess we're going back."

Then she called the bank. Instead of beginning her new job, she would be packing the car again for a return trip north. "I'm really sorry, but my son's taken ill," Mickey told a bank worker.

On the long drive home, Mickey thought, *I'm going to try to make this marriage work.*

Reunited, Mickey and Bill began the first of several efforts to patch up the relationship. Mickey returned to her travel agency job; in the months to follow, her work would take her across the world more than once as a tour guide. Mickey had her pick of free trips: she'd jet off on a junket to Las Vegas, or lead a group of Lockport senior citizens on a trip to London. She loved travel, and Bill wanted to see her happy. He never perceived her work as a means for her to separate herself from the duties of motherhood. It was just her job. Friends of the couple say that during that time Mickey carried on with other men, upset that her husband could not satisfy her. It is a claim she adamantly denies.

What is known for sure is that Bill and Mickey just weren't strung the same way. The children were always on Bill's mind, along with his job, with its long and profitable hours of overtime, which paid for family vacations and dinners out. Sometimes Bill worked twelve hours a day, and Tim could tell by his dad's testy temper on those days that he needed more sleep.

Among the things Bill noticed about his son was that he was blessed with some of Grandpa Hill's fix-it abilities. Whenever Bill brought something new into the house, Tim would take it apart to find out how it worked. Flashlights, in particular, piqued his curiosity, which sometimes landed him in trouble. Like his father, Tim was impressed with Grandpa Hill's mechanical aptitude. The old man put Tim in mind of the TV character MacGyver; he could take a pile of scrap iron and make it into a windmill. His resourcefulness made quite an impression on Tim. Yet Tim could never quite bring himself to say he loved Grandpa Hill or, for that matter, his parents and sisters. He felt fondness for all of them, but expressions of love eluded him. In all his life, there was only one person whom Tim could actually and unabashedly say he loved—his paternal grandfather, Ed McVeigh. A life of devotion to an ailing wife had well prepared the graying and bespectacled McVeigh for the role of grandfather, and Tim was devoted to his father's father with an affection otherwise absent from his life. The boy's feelings were met with the unconditional love that only a grandparent can offer, from a sphere that lies beyond the tighter, weightier world of parenting. Ed's presence provided a constant ray of sunlight in Tim's growing years.

As grandson and grandfather walked beside the Erie Canal to a small ravine where they practiced target shooting, Grandpa McVeigh offered bits of wisdom his grandson would long remember. This was better than school—his grandfather never took on the formal tone of a teacher, allowing room for a loose, friendly camaraderie to build between them instead. And their relationship revolved around an interest the two had in common: their mutual enjoyment of guns.

"When you're carrying a gun on the road, the ammunition is always in your back pocket," Ed would say as they walked along the canal. "The barrel is not pointed at traffic. When you're shooting, you make sure you have a backstop and consider the possibility of a bullet ricocheting."

Ed taught by setting an example, always checking to make sure that everything was safe before letting his .22-caliber, bolt-action rifle crackle to life as the bullets knocked down the empty soft-drink cans. Ed's sharp aim impressed Tim no end; many a woodchuck had fallen dead on raids into Ed's vegetable patch. From inside the back window of his garage, Ed had waited in secret to pick off the varmints, protecting his crop of beans, tomatoes, and corn. He rarely missed. And when he placed the gun in his grandson's hands, the boy's spirit soared. Tim determined to prove himself worthy of this crowning display of confidence in his character. It was liberating to know that he could be counted on to handle a weapon properly.

For Tim, the gun was nourishment for his self-esteem. He absorbed every detail of the rifle: the long and slender barrel, the clip that fed seven bullets into the belly of the firing chamber. *I wonder if Grandpa will give this to me,* Tim thought.

Ed's tutelage went beyond gun handling. After target shooting, they'd gather up the punctured soft-drink cans and put them in a sack to carry out. If they saw other cans carelessly littered in the grass and brush, Ed would direct his grandson to pick those up, too. Eager to please, Tim snatched them up.

Often the old man and the boy would dawdle, straying off the path to pick wild cherries on the land that McVeigh feet had trod for four generations. As a treat at the end of their walks, Ed allowed Tim to carry out the biggest rock he could hold. Halfway across the bridge leading to home on Bear Ridge Road, Tim would drop the rock into the canal waters below, checking first on both sides of the bridge for approaching boats. Ed wanted his grandson always to consider the safety of others, whether firing a gun or dropping a rock into the water to see how high a splash it could make.

Ed taught the boy all aspects of domestic life, from counting and rolling loose change to washing and drying dishes. The bond that might have formed between Tim and his parents leaped back a generation to his grandfather. At Ed's house there was always something going on, whether it was cooking on the grill, learning to drive a lawn tractor, or operating a weed whacker. For Tim—a boy otherwise starved for interesting pastimes—visiting Ed's house was the best kind of tutorial.

When Ed would declare a moment of rest, Tim dug into the old man's pile of *Popular Mechanics* magazines. And the boy could always explore Ed's basement, a workshop that seemed to contain every tool known to man. Tim watched in awe as wooden rocking horses, picnic benches, and the notched

timbers of swing sets emerged from that underground wonderland. If boredom appeared on the horizon, Ed would take his grandson and granddaugh-
ters up to Summit Park Mall in Wheatfield. They'd start out browsing in
Sears, then Waldenbooks, before drifting down the main concourse, drawn
to the indoor fountain and reflecting pool scooped into the center of the mall.
Ed would slip coins into the hands of Tim and his sisters, who would toss
them into the water for luck. At the end of each month, maintenance workers drained the blue-bottomed pool, swept up the coins, and sent the money
on to charities. A volunteer driver for the Lockport Red Cross, Ed had a soft
spot for do-gooders.

Again and again, Tim saw things in his grandpa that he wished he could
see in his dad. Bill McVeigh loved his only son, but the words "I love you"
never rolled easily off the shy man's tongue. So long as he provided the ne-
cessities—a good home, food, and a few of the extras—Bill felt his actions bespoke love. He always believed his son was living out a happy and
uncomplicated childhood.

Bill was glad to have Mickey back; he wanted desperately for their marriage to work. Several summers in a row Mickey arranged family trips to
Toronto, a two-hour drive north, where they hiked around the sprawling me-
tropolis, making stops at the science museum and other cultural centers.
There were summer excursions to the amusement park at Darien Lake and
to Lake George, several hours east in upstate New York; there were visits
with Mickey's Aunt Frances, deep in the Adirondacks.

But for all these efforts to promote family togetherness, Tim was just as
happy alone as in the company of family. In the long summers of his early
adolescence, he explored the solitary country roads of Niagara County on a
ten-speed bicycle his father had bought him. He would often make the ten-
mile trip to the Lockport travel agency where his mom worked. But before
stopping by the agency, he might catch an early afternoon matinee at the
Palace Theater, get his fill of comic books at the variety store, or stop by the
local army surplus outlet.

Tim enjoyed visiting his mother at the travel agency; indeed, his most
pleasant memories of his mother would be of her at work, rather than at
home. When her business was finished, Mickey, who had begun coloring her
hair blond, would go out of her way to make Tim feel at home, often intro-

ducing him to new clients, taking time to trade stories. From time to time Tim would go to work replacing outdated travel brochures with new ones in the office display rack, eager to please his mother.

On days when it was just too hot to go bicycling, the McVeighs' above-ground pool made Tim the most popular kid on Meyer Road. On any given afternoon there might be ten kids splashing up a storm in the pool, sometimes even more. One particularly hot afternoon when Bill arrived home from work, he counted twenty kids—the entire neighborhood—up on the red-stained deck timbers munching on chips and sipping soft drinks.

Bill was happy to share his good fortune with his neighbors. In the evenings, next-door neighbor Liz McDermott's husband, Jack, would throw on his swimming trunks and bring his two children, six-year-old Mollie and infant son Paul, over for a dip. The McVeighs' youngest child, Jennifer, was also six, and she and Mollie became as close as sisters. Watching over them was Tim. Liz McDermott was impressed with the amount of patience and care he showed; rare qualities, she thought, for a young adolescent. It wasn't long before he was watching her children.

Tim McVeigh's imagination was infectious. When Liz McDermott and her husband would come home from an evening out, they'd find their house transformed into an imaginary battleground filled with GI Joe action figures. *It's like having another kid,* Liz thought happily. Along with the elaborate action-figure battles he engineered were games of flashlight tag. He would draw down all the shades and turn off all the lights; then, stealthily, Mollie, Jennifer, and Tim would move about the house, each trying to catch another with the flashlight beam. "We'd fall on the floor and freeze for a while," Jennifer recalls, adding that their games often focused on superheroes. "I'd run around as Wonder Woman." When the *Star Wars* craze hit, Tim crafted his own lightsabers, binding flashlights and plastic golf club tubes together with duct tape. What seemed to attract him was the battle of good and evil; whether it was in the Old West or in the new frontiers of the galaxies, Liz McDermott noticed, he always took the side of the good guys.

At other times, Tim turned from the routine amusements of childhood and found contentment for hours on end in the solitude of the basement of his family's home. One day he found a set of crystal glasses in a box packed away in the basement; unaware of their value, he thought that they might make excellent gifts for a homemade carnival he was planning. When Mickey learned that her prized glasses had been given away as carnival prizes, she sent Tim out to go house to house to retrieve them. And he dreamed up other schemes in his solitary moments, building a candy machine out of cardboard that found a ready market among his neighborhood pals. He even went into business with Vicki and Steve Hodge to sell compost mixed from rotting leaves and household garbage.

To Liz McDermott, Tim was an extraordinary young man; she saw in his behavior signs that he was growing into as fine a man as his father. He volunteered to run the children's game booth at the parish picnic each summer, and insisted on going with Liz to the store to pick out the penny candy given away at the booth. You couldn't trust that job to just anyone, especially an adult, he told her. You needed just the right kinds of candies.

At the picnic, he happily followed her advice that no child should walk away from the booth crestfallen. "Oh, you did win after all," he'd say if a child's aim was off in tossing the ball into the muffin tin. Everyone walked away with a generous handful of candy.

When Liz's son Paul celebrated his sixth birthday, he wanted to invite Tim to his party at Chuck E. Cheese's, a pizza parlor and computer game emporium for kids. Liz doubted that Tim would want to spend time with children so much younger than himself, but Tim was happy to go. He seemed to take pleasure in doing the unexpected to please people.

Blessed with a high IQ, Tim knew how to get along with his teachers and stay out of trouble in the classroom. But he learned early that the world outside could be less predictable, more painful. Tim had another run-in with bullies in seventh grade at Starpoint Central School. After getting permission to leave class to go to the lavatory, Tim encountered two high school students smoking a joint; he had no idea what it was at the time, only that it smelled sweet. The boys had walked over from the attached secondary school wing seeking the privacy of the elementary school bathroom, which was rarely checked by the faculty. Tim was tiny for his age, and no match for the two when they grabbed hold of him. Before he knew what was happening they flipped him upside down and carried him over to a stall, headed for what the other kids called a "swirlie"—plunging a person's head into a flushing toilet.

Strong and wiry for his size, Tim managed to resist being dunked. When they finally released him, Tim hurried back to class, thinking, *Never again use that bathroom during that time.* He would never forget the attack.

In junior high school, Tim's grades began to tumble. The advent of puberty, without the long-anticipated growth spurt; the pain of finding his place in the world, of trying to seem normal and not a misfit—it was a difficult, if typical, passage. Then, unexpectedly, Tim caught a fleeting glimpse of what it would be like to truly excel when he joined an intramural basketball team. Though he fared poorly at most sports, Tim McVeigh was amazed to find he was able to handle a basketball: in one intramural game he scored an amazing forty-two points. It was as if the game were being played in slow motion; he dribbled around others like they were standing still. When the game ended, Tim's teammates carried him off the court chanting his name.

In eighth grade, he took a chance at wrestling. The intensity of the sport intrigued him, and he was attracted to its sense of civility, with referees close at hand to blow the whistle on unbecoming conduct. But his illusions were shattered at a regional wrestling match, when he was pitted against a fierce competitor who was more than willing to bend the rules. Before Tim could get his footing, his opponent slammed his skull into Tim's nose. Tim was sure his nose had been broken—blood gushed from both his nostrils—but the other boy didn't seem to care; he made short work of Tim, pinning him while he was still dazed from the blow. The winner marched off the mat, taking second place in the tournament. Tim walked away, giving up on the sport. *I don't have that in me,* he thought.

Tim was content to pedal his bicycle on the long solitary roads of Pendleton, or hop on a smaller bike he used for hot-dogging. Flying up and down a wooden ramp in his backyard, he would push his bike stunts to the limit. One evening his front wheel came flying off and Tim sailed over the handlebars; he landed on his head on the grass, hard enough to knock himself silly. Steve Hodge, who was with him, ran to get Bill McVeigh. When Tim came to on the living room couch, he didn't recognize Steve or his father.

"You had an accident with your bicycle," Bill said.

"I don't have one," Tim answered. He was diagnosed with a mild concussion.

He would test fate again by wrapping a rope around his waist and climbing out the window of his second-floor bedroom to scale down the side of the house. Fastened to furniture, his lifeline never gave out, though it ruined the windowsill. Everything was fine as long as he stuck to his own bedroom window, but when he decided to descend from another bedroom he found himself in danger of crashing through a pair of sliding glass doors below. Tim was left stuck in midair, calling out for help.

"Okay, Tim, just drop and we'll catch," Mickey coaxed, as she and Patty, his older sister, held out their arms below him. He let go of the rope and fell into their arms, which helped to break the fall and spare him a more severe injury than the sprained ankle he suffered on impact.

A devotee of action heroes in comic books, Tim began filling his bedroom with boxes of superhero comics. His neighbor Jack McDermott introduced Tim to a friend who owned a comic-book store in Niagara Falls. Each Saturday, Tim would take his five-dollar allowance and head to the Falls with Jack or Bill to buy the latest editions. The comic-book adventures were a welcome distraction from the furious words he heard more and more often coming from his parents' bedroom, which was right next to his. Some nights he would lie in bed frightened by their voices; some nights his parents were so angry he feared they might kill each other.

Before too long, Tim graduated from the fantasy of comic books to the more cerebral world of science fiction and the supernatural, dredging the library for books on the Loch Ness Monster, Bigfoot, and the Bermuda Triangle, and devouring the works of Isaac Asimov. The TV series *Star Trek* and its sequel, *The Next Generation,* proved equally compelling. Science fiction challenged Tim to penetrate beyond the everyday conventions of life, to think his own thoughts and question the world around him.

Tim pursued a wide path toward social acceptance. He skated from one group of friends to the next, making many acquaintances but building close connections with only a few. As he grew older and more self-confident, Tim began finding it in himself to stand up to bullies. His old childhood friend, Todd Carter, marveled at Tim's growing confidence; the bullies still knew him as skinny "Noodle McVeigh," but Tim had learned how to back them off with an angry look or a few well-chosen words. "Go fuck yourself!" Tim would scream, and it usually worked. Carter found it amazing: somehow his friend Tim seemed to know where the fine line lay between words and fists.

When the McVeighs' marriage hit another rough spot, Tim was shipped off to stay at the rural Genesee Valley home of his aunt Jean Zanghi and her husband, Lou. When his uncle Lou took him out to shoot his fancy new semi-automatic Ruger 10-22 rifle, his parents' failing marriage was the furthest thing from Tim's mind.

Even after his parents split for the third and final time in 1984, Tim seemed to take it in stride.

"Are you sure you want to do this?" Liz McDermott asked when Mickey confided in her at a church gathering that year that she was seeking a divorce from Bill.

"Yes," Mickey said.

Though rumors were circulating that Mickey had been on the hunt for men at the local bowling alley, Mickey denied it, and Bill believed her. Still, their marriage had all but disintegrated. They had tried to make it work, mostly for their kids' sakes, but their problems were insurmountable. Ultimately, they both realized, they were not meant to be together.

One summer morning, about 5:30, Liz was awakened by the sound of something going on at the McVeigh household. She looked out her bedroom window and saw Mickey and the girls, packed up and ready to move out. Bill, as usual, was being a gentleman to the last.

"Is there anything else I can get for you?" Liz heard Bill ask. "You call me if you need anything, okay?"

As he watched his wife and daughters drive away, Bill's heart ached.

At a church outing later that day, Liz and Tim worked the penny-candy game booth. Tim laughed it up. The casual observer would never imagine he had just been abandoned by his mother. But Liz had the feeling the boy she liked so much was trying his hardest to hide his pain.

After Mickey left, Bill sold the family dream house in May 1985 for seventy-two thousand dollars. Collecting a modest profit of seventeen thousand dollars, he shared the money with Mickey, helping her to buy a house trailer in Lockport. Bill hired a builder to construct a tiny two-bedroom ranch on a narrow strip of land off Campbell Boulevard, several miles away from the house on Meyer. Bill was anxious to do a good job raising his son as a single parent; he didn't want Tim to have to raise himself, though at sixteen his son was already extremely independent.

Reluctant to leave Tim unsupervised for hours at a stretch during the afternoon, Bill transferred to a permanent graveyard shift. Working nights allowed him to get home in time to get Tim off to school and to be there when he got home. Father and son ate dinner together, and Tim often had friends over in the evening before Bill left for work. Bill trusted his son, and took comfort in knowing that Tim was home asleep while he worked through the night. Together, Bill figured, they would weather this family breakup.

Tim had other things on his mind: girls, money, and cars. Two weeks before his seventeenth birthday, in April 1985, he approached Bill with a request as he was getting ready to go bowling.

"Dad," Tim asked, "if I ever get enough money, can I buy a car?"

"Okay," Bill said. When he returned home later that night, he was surprised to see an old blue car—a 1978 Dodge Monaco—sitting in the driveway. *Sure didn't waste much time,* Bill thought with a chuckle. Tim had bought the car with two hundred dollars he had saved from his allowance and baby-sitting jobs; he wanted the car to drive back and forth to a new job Mickey had arranged for him, cleaning up at a local convenience store.

On May 20, 1985, Tim received the sacrament of confirmation at Good Shepherd Catholic Church. Tim honored his dad by picking William as his confirmation name, though he continued to share a stronger bond with his grandfather, Ed McVeigh. Knowing how much his first car meant to his grandson, Ed designated a special spot off his driveway as Tim's parking space. So long as Ed was alive, Tim knew he had a place to go. Mothers and fathers may walk away from each other, but a grandfather was someone you could count on.

Tim's older sister, Patty, was now attending a nursing school in Florida. Jennifer, the youngest of the three, took the separation and divorce hard. She had wept when her mother moved them away from Tim and Bill: though the trailer park was only a few miles away, for Jennifer—forced to transfer into the tougher Lockport school district—it might as well have been a thousand.

Everything in Jennifer's world was changing—even her beloved big brother. Tim, who'd spent so many endless hours entertaining her and Mollie on Meyer Road, now spent most of his time either working—he had advanced to a job at Burger King—or holed up in his bedroom: the boy who used to show off for them, bouncing up and down the driveway on a pogo stick, had become captivated by computers.

Tim had converted his bedroom into a makeshift computer lab. Long before the Internet became common in American homes, he owned not one but two Commodore 64s; with Bill's blessing, he had his room outfitted with extra electrical outlets and phone jacks. Among his cyber-friends, Tim became known as "The Wanderer," a handle borrowed from the old rock-and-roll song by Dion.

Tim and some friends organized a primitive chat room in the bowels of a school computer and spent long nights learning to put their computers and phones to use hacking their way into computer systems from afar. They hacked into school computers at the Orleans-Niagara vocational high school, then a Defense Department computer system at the White Sands Missile Range in New Mexico. The teenage hackers found the nascent Internet technology fascinating—and, for Tim at least, a welcome respite from a family life from which he felt increasingly disconnected.

The group typed away happily until one day, out of the blue, an unexpected message appeared on their monitors. Tim's eyes bulged. It was a message from "SYSOP," the universal code for the computer system operator. YOU ARE ALL ON THIS SYSTEM ILLEGALLY, the message read. WE HAVE TRACED YOUR PHONES AND THE AUTHORITIES HAVE BEEN NOTIFIED. Tim scrambled to shut down his computer, convinced that some all-powerful government agency was out to get him. The next day he was so nervous he refused to take out the garbage, afraid that the authorities monitoring his house were lying in wait to arrest him. For days, it took all his courage to leave the house and go to school—until one of his hacker friends confessed that it was all a prank.

In his senior year, Tim's programming skills were recognized by Starpoint officials when he was named the school's "Most Promising Computer Programmer." But Bill was starting to hear from teachers who said Tim wasn't working as hard as he should, and he was growing concerned about Tim's commitment to the rest of his schoolwork. *It's the teachers' fault,* Tim would insist. He couldn't stand teachers who stressed memorization over true learning. He resented the kind of teacher who felt it was sufficient to inform the class that $E = mc^2$ without explaining what it meant. Without any way to grasp the practical logic behind the symbols, he found himself more and more inclined to gaze out the classroom windows and daydream. "I hated classes with rote memorization," McVeigh later remembered. "Sit down with me and in a practical way show me."

Tim did enjoy science. From the moment he had first experimented with a red, bubbly potion he used to astound the neighborhood children in a basement haunted house one Halloween, he was drawn to the rational enlightenment of science—and, conversely, the shadowed invitation it cast to explore the unknown. He spent plenty of time reading science fiction, but when it came to poetry or Shakespeare, he was befuddled and impatient. But Tim never missed a day of school, despite his misgivings about some of the teachers; he worked long hours at Burger King to keep a series of gas-guzzling clunkers on the road, and found time for computers and socializing along the way. No one close to him thought he was anything but perfectly normal.

From time to time, like any teenager's father, Bill would lose his temper at Tim. *Tim doesn't worry about the next day until it's here,* he thought. But his frustrations never lasted long. Tim's willingness to help around the house, his ability to get along with anyone, impressed Bill.

Tim's closest friends, those from his childhood, remained at the center of his universe. Todd Carter, Steve Hodge, and Vicki Hodge would jump into Tim's old car and cruise the back roads. Tim was a showman; he loved everything about driving—the instant freedom, the high speed, the feel of control when his outsized hands gripped the steering wheel. Tim willingly headed in to work anytime they needed him at the Burger King. He enjoyed earning his own money and the independence it gave him.

On Thanksgiving Day 1985, Bill rose at 7 A.M. to put the turkey in the oven. It was the first Thanksgiving in the new home, and the first without Mickey and the girls, but Ed McVeigh and some other relations were coming over at noon to join Bill and Tim for the feast. (The early Thanksgiving dinner was a family tradition.) Bill poked his head into Tim's bedroom to check on him, but his bed was empty. By ten o'clock, Bill was on edge. Where was Tim? Finally, at 10:30, Tim's Dodge crunched its way up the dusty gravel driveway.

"Where ya been?" Bill asked anxiously. "We got company coming in an hour."

"Burger King needed somebody to paint the ceiling, and they aren't open today," Tim said. "So I stayed all night and painted."

Flipping hamburgers began to pay off in some unexpected ways for Tim, who had grown into a handsome young man with wavy brown hair. In the winter of 1985 he began flirting with a woman he'd met at the restaurant. She was married, and at least ten years his senior—but her husband worked nights, she told him, and their flirtations soon heated up. One night after Tim finished work, they started fooling around, and Tim finally worked up the nerve to invite her over to his house.

"My dad goes to work at ten-thirty," he told the woman. Invitation accepted.

Inside the Campbell Boulevard house, Tim offered a confession. "I don't know what to do," he admitted.

"Well, first turn on some music," she said. She relished the job of teacher.

They whipped off their clothes and climbed into his bed. She climbed on top of him and showed him exactly what to do. "I love to fuck!" she said—words Tim never forgot.

"I'm on the pill," she told him later, as they lay together. She complimented him on his endurance, which caused Tim to suspect that her husband must be an older man. That was all right with Tim: he would play the young buck.

After that relationship fizzled, Tim turned his attention toward a young woman who worked at the restaurant, one much closer to his own age. A senior at the nearby Sweet Home High School, she became Tim's first real girlfriend.

Sarah found Tim "loud and goofy" sometimes, like a lot of boys she knew, but she also found that he could be nice and thoughtful. By this time he had acquired an old Ford Thunderbird, and he drove it very fast, which both scared and thrilled Sarah. For six months they became very close, going steady, and attending the Starpoint senior prom together.

Like Tim, his girlfriend had endured the divorce of her parents. Tim took Sarah to his mother's house trailer to introduce her to Mickey, and Mickey allowed Tim to use her flashy sports car to take his sweetheart to the prom. But the observant young woman felt that his parents' divorce had left Tim feeling "lost" and she sensed the anger he harbored toward his mother. So often, Sarah noticed, he was the only person at his house. *It's almost like Tim is raising himself,* she thought.

Her family took to Tim; her mother treated him like a son, trusting him enough to teach her own son how to drive. She even trusted him enough to let Tim sleep over.

On a sun-splashed June 29, Tim and the other 179 members of the Starpoint Class of 1986 headed to Artpark, an outdoor theater overlooking the spectacular Niagara River Gorge, for their graduation ceremony. Tim wore a bright red shirt that his girlfriend's mother had bought for him. Tim had never been much for fancy clothes. When she saw that he was wearing sneakers to the ceremony, the mother told him, "I would have found you a pair of shoes."

Tim was more interested in exploring Artpark than worrying about his attire. Along with Vicki, the class salutatorian, and a few others, he hiked about the natural setting, only a few miles north of Niagara Falls. Walking to the edge of the 160-foot cliff above the Lower Niagara River, they looked down into the rocky rapids.

At last, the ceremony started. Award after award was given out, including one for perfect attendance. When Tim heard another student's name called out and not his, he was upset, vowing to call the school district and point out the oversight. When the ceremony was over, there was a modest party for Tim at Bill McVeigh's. In one of the snapshots taken that day, Tim and Sarah stand together in his Campbell Boulevard living room. She is wearing a special blue summer dress for the occasion. The collar of Tim's red shirt juts out from the black graduation robe. In the background of the snapshot, the bright afternoon sun pours through the picture window. This must have been a special day for Tim: his family had come together to surround him in a shower of attention. His mother and Jennifer; Mickey's parents, Bill and Dot Hill; most important, Edward McVeigh—his fractured family had reunited around him.

Less than four months earlier, the McVeighs' marriage had officially ended at last. A judge issued the divorce decree on a wintry March 5, Jennifer's twelfth birthday. But for this one spring day in June, Mickey and Bill had come together to celebrate their son's accomplishment.

Not long after his graduation, Tim abruptly broke off his relationship with his first girlfriend. "I'm not ready to get serious," Tim explained.

To Bill's surprise, Tim had qualified for a modest college scholarship award from New York State. Yet the inscription Tim chose to have printed under his Starpoint yearbook photo suggested that academic pursuits weren't weighing heavily on his mind:

take it as it comes, buy a lamborghini, california girls

2

Real World

In the long summer days after graduation, Bill McVeigh noticed, Tim seemed to fall into a funk. He quit his Burger King job, sold his two computers, and spent the money on his car. He also spent a lot of time lying around the house, doing nothing. This was a far cry from the get-up-and-go Tim that Bill had always admired.

But what may have seemed like laziness was really a period of deep reflection. For the first time in his life, Tim was reading widely, and really beginning to think about himself and his place in the world. He knew he loved guns, the outdoors, and heading off in his car to explore things. And it must have been around this time that he fixed upon the idea of freedom—as his guiding principle, as the value he loved most of all. He began researching the Second Amendment, reading about the rights of firearms owners. Thinking back to the Blizzard of '77, Tim now decided to become a survivalist. If ever there was a calamity in America—whether a nuclear war or some huge weather disaster—he wanted to be ready for it.

All that was fine, Bill said, but he counseled his son to take a closer look at the bread-and-butter issues of life. The McVeighs were a working family, and Tim's encampment on the living room couch didn't set well with Bill. He urged Tim to take advantage of the five-hundred-dollar-a-year college scholarship he had won: after all, if Tim didn't use the money for college, he didn't get it.

Bill convinced Tim to investigate going to Bryant & Stratton, a two-year business college twenty minutes from Pendleton. Tim agreed to check it out. A recruiter at the school sold him on the idea of studying to be a computer systems analyst, and Tim bit. It was a decision that satisfied Bill; he knew Tim shared the McVeigh family's hardworking attitude, but it was hard to picture Tim slaving away in a factory setting. His mind was just too active. And in western New York in the mid-1980s, the big plants like Harrison just weren't hiring.

Tim entered Bryant & Stratton expecting to devote himself entirely to a computer-programming curriculum. But the school had other plans. Bryant & Stratton was upgrading its academic standards; incoming students were now required to add core academic courses—English, math, and the like—to their course load.

Tim felt misled. He had come here to learn about computers. The last thing he wanted was to delve back into the same old subjects that had bored him in high school. He started wondering whether this was all a big mistake. *I'm smart*, he thought. *I don't need a piece of paper to tell me I'm smart. I don't need to pay for a diploma.*

The school required all new students to take a lengthy math aptitude exam. Another waste of time, he thought. But he would show them. He breezed through the test in twenty minutes, amazed at how simple the questions were. When he went up and turned in the test and his allotment of scrap paper, the teacher asked whether he had to go to the bathroom.

"No," he said, "I'm done."

How could that be? The teacher looked at the sheet of scrap paper. It was empty.

A week later, the instructor announced the results to the class. "There's one person who got a ninety-nine on the test," she said. "Nobody else got over eighty." Tim sunk down in his seat. Maybe he shouldn't have rushed through the test so quickly.

The teacher went on to explain that the student with the 99 had failed to reduce a fraction from eight-sixteenths to one-half. The student, by a hair, had missed a perfect score—something no student in the history of the school had ever achieved on the test. After a buildup worthy of a drumroll, the teacher finally identified the math whiz: "And the student with the ninety-nine . . . is Mr. Tim McVeigh."

It pained him to think he had come so close to 100 and missed.

Before long, Tim quit Bryant & Stratton and went back to work at another Burger King. "Classes are just too boring," he told his father. "I know more than the teachers." It was a stance he would later come to regret. He had missed the deeper message from his father and the Bryant & Stratton recruiter—no matter how smart you are, or think you are, employers want to see a college diploma.

But there was another motive behind Tim's decision to drop out of college. Always careful about money, he felt sorry for his father, who had given him eight hundred dollars to cover the balance of tuition not covered by the modest scholarship. With long hours of overtime, Bill earned about fifty thousand dollars a year; but with so many financial obligations—the mortgage on the house he had built, alimony to Mickey, and child support—he was strapped. Tim told his father he didn't want to burden him further; Bill assured Tim he didn't mind, that he would always open his wallet to help his family, but Tim just didn't feel right about his dad's expenditures.

With formal schooling set aside, Tim redoubled his own efforts at self-education. And for material he turned to the literature of the rugged, fiercely independent gun culture. He read gun magazines voraciously and ordered books from small ads in the back pages. One that captivated him was a volume entitled *To Ride, Shoot Straight and Speak the Truth*, by Jeff Cooper, a military man and a world-renowned expert on self-defense and firearms. The book was in essence a training manual, but its broader messages resonated in the fertile ground of Tim's young mind. He liked the idea of going through life in a combat mind-set, with a constant awareness of his surroundings. Every page reinforced what he already felt: *Speak the truth and be an honorable man. Be a John Wayne type of guy. Don't BS people.*

The Turner Diaries was another book that hit a nerve. The novel by for-

mer American Nazi Party official William L. Pierce (under the pen name Andrew Macdonald) had become a kind of bible for a loose movement of gun
collectors, militia groups, and government protesters after its publication in
1978.

The two-hundred-page book related the story of Earl Turner, a gun en-
thusiast who reacts to tighter firearms laws by making a truck bomb and destroying the FBI headquarters building in Washington. The book described
gun laws as links in a chain. The links form slowly, one by one, until finally
citizens find that their individual rights have been choked off. A voracious
reader of newspapers and watcher of network news programs, McVeigh
thought that he saw the same thing happening in real-life America. He felt
that most Americans were ignoring the warning signs.

The Turner Diaries had other agendas: the novel's narrative is sympathetic to Adolf Hitler, suggests that blacks and Jews are inherently evil, and
advocates killing them.

Tim, who bought the book by mail order after seeing it advertised in *Soldier of Fortune* magazine, maintains that it was the book's strong advocacy of
gun rights, rather than its racist content, that captured his imagination. He
gave the book only to friends who seemed to share his feelings about gun
ownership. For him, the selling point of *The Turner Diaries* was a question
he often saw posed in ads for the book: "What will you do if the government
comes for your guns?"

The possibility that Congress and federal agents might take guns away
from law-abiding citizens suddenly seemed a very real threat to Tim. He began to circulate the book among his friends, asking them to consider: How
could an individual survive without a gun if chaos ever came upon the land?

He thought back to the duck-and-cover drills he had participated in at
school as a boy, exercises in which old movie reels of nuclear blasts were followed by the ritual of crawling beneath a desk and covering one's head with
one's arms. The threat of nuclear attack seemed real to Tim; his old neighbors on Meyer Road, Liz and Jack McDermott, had lived in a house constructed at the height of the Cold War, its concrete foundation walls eight
feet thick so the basement could serve as a fallout shelter.

The nuclear-alert mentality wasn't entirely surprising. Not far from
Pendleton was a military base, its underground silos filled with antiaircraft

missiles. But there were other threats, less remote yet still dramatic, on Tim's mind. He remembered hearing about the gasoline shortage of the early 1970s, when a neighbor of the McVeighs went up and down Hinman Road late at night stealing gas from the tanks of cars. The Blizzard of '77 was another memorable crisis in upstate New York: people unable to get out of their homes ran out of food and had to depend on others to bring it.

To Tim McVeigh, all the signs pointed in one direction: survivalism. *People have to protect themselves,* he thought. *We can't just depend on the government to protect us.*

Even within the gentle parameters of network television, Tim found support for his way of thinking. The 1970s and the 1980s saw the last stand of the old-fashioned Wild West frontier dramas, with their emphasis on overcoming the elements to survive. Back then, the shows suggested, a man could depend on his gun and wits to live free. Rugged frontiersmen had little need for government bureaucrats. Tim was especially taken by *Little House on the Prairie,* Michael Landon's frontier drama about a family making a life for itself in the wild. His favorite episode carried a snippet of anti-tax sentiment: A group of people stood in line to speak with the property tax assessor, grousing as they waited. You think this is bad? one of the pioneers predicted; I'll bet one day they'll tax a man's income! Others in the line laughed at the preposterous thought.

Tim had seen the same pioneer spirit in his grandfather. At harvest time, like millions of other rural Americans, Ed McVeigh busily canned vegetables and stored them in his basement; he kept a sizable stockpile of canned foods and drinks, Tim noted, just in case. Tim became convinced of the importance of stowing away at least a year's worth of food and water, and found further support for his survivalist beliefs at the movies: *The Omega Man, Logan's Run, Red Dawn,* and the *Planet of the Apes* films—stories about humans making a stand in a world decimated by some apocalyptic event—all fascinated him, and he took their lessons to heart.

It never occurred to Tim that there was anything unusual about wanting to prepare for the worst. In many ways survivalism was a pastime for him, no more unusual than collecting baseball cards or studying batting averages. He even felt a kinship with the simple, self-sufficient, agricultural lifestyle of the Amish; he had no pity for people who didn't bother preparing for catastrophes.

When power outages hit Pendleton, and his father's basement flooded because the sump pump was without electricity, Tim asked Bill if he could buy a gas-powered generator—not coincidentally, a staple item of the survivalist movement. The price tag for such an item—more than five hundred dollars—seemed too steep to Bill. Determined to prevent another flood, Tim went out and bought a twelve-volt-powered sump pump for emergencies. In a pinch, he figured he could use the battery in his car to energize the pump. The only kind of water that belonged in the basement was an emergency supply of potted water. To accomplish that, Tim bought two fifty-five-gallon drums and filled them. Just in case.

Tim made another decision in his first year after quitting college—he would start investing in guns. If a man had a gun, he could defend hearth and home, even hunt for his food. If he had many guns he could barter, particularly if the monetary system collapsed. Guns, some in the survivalist movement predicted, would take the place of money. Even in stable times guns usually appreciated in value—and there was always a ready market if you needed to sell one.

Guns would certainly be a better investment than his comic-book investment, which had ended in disaster. After spending years of allowance and odd-job money on hundreds of comic books, he found that the only person who would buy them back was the same Niagara Falls dealer who'd sold them to Tim in the first place. After spending a thousand dollars or more on his collection, he wound up getting only seventy-five dollars for nearly the entire collection. It was a lesson in personal finance McVeigh would never forget.

In order to finance his appetite for expensive firearms and other survivalist gear, Tim realized that he needed more cash than his job at Burger King could provide. He decided to become an armed security guard. In the months before his nineteenth birthday, he applied for a pistol permit, approaching his old neighbors to vouch for his character and sign the permit application—even though one of them ardently opposed guns.

"Would you sign my application for a gun permit?" Tim asked Liz McDermott, his old friend and Sunday school teacher from Meyer Road.

"You don't need a gun," Liz responded. "Guns only kill people."

Tim smiled and explained his reasons. He wasn't planning to kill anyone, he reassured her. He just wanted to get a job as an armed security guard. Armed guards made more money than those without pistol permits. It was a career move. Liz caved in. How could she refuse to sign? Tim had always been a model citizen.

A background check on Tim by the Niagara County Sheriff's Department caught Bill McVeigh by surprise. He was lost in the Sunday pages of the *Buffalo News* when there was a knock at his front door. Who could that be on a Sunday morning? Bill wondered. Peering out the living room window, he noticed a sheriff's car in the driveway. Had Tim found his way into some kind of mischief? No, his son was still in bed, and Bill had never known Tim to do anything that might get him into trouble with the law.

When he learned the visit was just a permit checkup Bill happily cooperated, though he remained surprised that the Sheriff's Department would conduct this kind of business on a Sunday morning.

After his permit was granted, Tim set to work improving his shooting skills, setting up a target range in the backyard. Following his grandpa's advice, he built a backstop out of logs and sandbags to keep his bullets from endangering anyone else in the neighborhood.

To Tim, it seemed perfectly natural to use the big open yard for shooting practice. He practiced his aim on groundhogs that were raiding the greens in Bill's garden: Whenever he would catch sight of one of the hungry rodents heading for his father's vegetables, Tim would grab his .22-caliber rifle, lean out the kitchen window, and take aim. But not everyone in the neighborhood appreciated Tim's efforts to hone his shooting skills. One day, an angry neighbor from Mapleton Road came charging up at Tim from the woods.

"What's going on?" Tim asked, setting down his gun.

"What the fuck are you doing, you little prick?" roared the neighbor. "Has that been you shooting all summer? Do you know how goddamn close my house is back there? That round can travel two and a half miles."

Tim was angry, too. He felt he had every right to shoot in his own backyard, especially after he'd gone to the trouble of building a backstop. The neighbor kept up his ranting until he'd finally blown off enough steam, then turned to leave. He had burst into the yard so swiftly that he hadn't noticed Bill McVeigh watching in silence from the garden, where he'd been pulling out weeds. Bill figured the neighbor had a right to his anger. It was his land behind their property, and Bill knew he had young children to protect. When the neighbor walked past him their eyes met, but Bill McVeigh said nothing.

When the neighbor was gone, Tim looked over at his father and thanked him for not intervening. To Tim, it was the ultimate compliment that his father thought he was old enough to handle his own battles. Tim headed straight inside the house and called the Sheriff's Department. He told the dispatcher that he had a question on the discharge of firearms. Could they send a deputy out to the house right away? Tim wanted to show the deputy his pistol range and find out whether he had violated the law.

A deputy came out and took a look around. He told Tim he hadn't broken any laws, but advised him that it would make sense to avoid conflicts with his neighbor, and suggested that Tim join a shooting club. Tim decided to be a good neighbor, joining the Tonawanda Sportsmen's Club in Pendleton. He resented having to pay a membership fee to have a place to shoot, but it was more important to keep the peace and not give guns a bad name.

Tim was now eager to get a fresh start in the working world. He'd been looking forward to landing a job as an armed guard, and with his pistol permit in hand he set his sights on job openings with an armored car service in Buffalo. The work required individuals who were trustworthy and honest enough to transport millions of dollars; it was a position of responsibility and respect.

In the fall of 1987, he landed a job with the Burke Armored Car service in Buffalo. The job would give Tim his first chance to explore beyond the insulated world of Pendleton and Lockport; it frequently took him through Buffalo's inner-city neighborhoods, with their impoverished conditions and large minority populations. And his older, tougher co-workers didn't hesitate to share their hardened views of the world with the newcomer.

Growing up in a community where brown and black faces were about as common as Martians, Tim McVeigh, at age nineteen, got his first exposure to racism during those armored-car runs through the city. On runs to check-cashing shops on the East Side of Buffalo, his white co-workers spared little sympathy for the shop's heavily minority clientele and the minorities who lived in the area.

"There they are—the porch monkeys," one co-worker, much older than McVeigh, jibed one day.

"Why do you call them that?" McVeigh asked.

"Because they sit out on their porches all month," the worker said, "waiting for the welfare checks to come in."

As the months passed, this casual attitude of scorn for Buffalo's black community was adopted by McVeigh. It was his first prolonged exposure to African-Americans, and the vision of so many of them lined up in front of the check-cashing shops made them a cheap target for McVeigh and his co-workers. It became a constant refrain among them all: *Here we are, busting our butts, inhaling exhaust fumes, driving around in this armored car all day long, and these people just wait for the government checks to come in. They probably get more money than we do.*

The narrow-minded attitudes of the workplace didn't keep McVeigh the country boy from fast becoming a star employee. His friends called him "The Kid," as in "Billy the Kid." Once, as a joke, he showed up at work dressed like a gunslinger, a bandolier filled with shotgun shells strapped across his chest. But it was more than just image that earned McVeigh his outlaw nickname. He could outshoot just about everyone at work; his hours of practice had given him a deadeye aim.

McVeigh advanced quickly, receiving high-profile assignments. In the middle of the night the phone would ring at his home, summoning him to drive out to the airport and transport millions of dollars from the runway to the Federal Reserve Bank in Buffalo. For security purposes, these runs were always unannounced until the last possible minute, which added a sense of intrigue. Still shy of his twentieth birthday, he was impressed that his employers trusted him enough to put him in charge of multimillion-dollar cash deliveries.

The Kid's reputation for honesty grew one day when he discovered a bank bag filled with eight thousand dollars in the back of the armored car. In an instant, he and his partner were headed back to the bank, where they had just made a cash drop. Tim sought out the bank worker who had forgotten to remove the money, a woman who had caught his eye earlier; honesty was its own reward, he'd always felt, but the bonus of seeing her again was not to be dismissed.

In another incident, when a woman backed into the armored car during a cash pickup at a shopping plaza, Tim found himself trying to calm the offending motorist, whose emotions had run away with her. He pointed out that there was no real damage to the armored vehicle, but when that failed to settle her, he tried harder, reassuring the woman he would say the accident was his fault, not hers.

At the end of his long workdays in the armored car, Tim climbed into his own decaying rust bucket and raced home at top speed. Bill knew his son loved to drive fast, and it worried him; Tim was investing thousands of dollars in high-powered rifles, but Bill wanted him to spend his money on something a little more prudent.

"Tim, you have a fairly decent job. Why don't you get yourself a halfway decent car?" Bill urged. "I can get you a discount through General Motors."

Tim was sold. He went to a Lockport dealership at the end of 1987 and purchased a Chevrolet Geo Spectrum, equipped with a powerful turbo engine. When the salesman handed him the keys to his first new car, Tim asked, "How fast will it go?" His father had told him that the engines in new cars required a breaking-in period.

"These engines are broken in before they're put in the car," the salesman said. "You can drive as fast as you want."

Tim pulled out of the dealership and headed home on Lockport Road, a straightaway; within a few minutes of taking ownership he was racing along at 100 mph. It was like an instant love affair.

Bill was relieved that Tim finally had a dependable set of wheels, but his son's appetite for speed continued to worry him. The senior McVeigh had been in a couple of bad accidents himself, but he knew it was useless to lecture his son—and a twist of fate soon occurred to make the point for him. On Christmas morning 1987, he and Tim heard a sound like a thunderclap outside their house.

Tim ran out. A car had slammed into a utility pole.

"Dad," he shouted, "call 911!"

Bill picked up the phone to call, but the line was dead. He jumped in his car and drove to a neighbor's house to make the call. By the time Bill returned, Tim had already pulled the dazed driver from his car. He had fallen asleep at the wheel, and only miraculously escaped serious injury. When an ambulance crew arrived, the motorist was reluctant to go to the hospital.

"Do you think I should go?" he asked Tim.

"Yes," Tim said, looking the man in the eye. "I think you should."

Bill was awed by the connection his son seemed able to make with perfect strangers. In the instant it had taken to help the injured man from his wrecked vehicle, Tim had forged a bond. The stranger had put his fate in Tim's hands, and Tim had answered with calm assurance. A few minutes later, an ambulance crew whisked the stranger away.

Tim learned another lesson on the road one morning, on his way to work in the predawn hours. He had just crossed from Pendleton into the neighboring town of Amherst when he happened to notice deer off in the distance, on both sides of the road. The headlight beams flashed in their eyes.

Oh, shit, Tim thought, *we're in a herd of deer.*

Just as he feared, some of the deer darted across the road. Tim swerved his new car into the empty lane for oncoming traffic and jammed his brakes. His light little car obeyed and stopped abruptly. He saw a pickup truck in front of him buck up into the air as it struck one of the deer, then screech to a stop. Tim pulled his car onto the shoulder, turned on his emergency flashers, and got out to take a look.

"Hey, man, are you all right?" Tim asked the pickup driver, a young man like himself.

"Man, I just bought this truck," the pickup driver lamented. "I can't believe I did that." His new vehicle was demolished.

Looking down into a drainage ditch alongside the road, Tim caught sight of the mangled deer, barely alive. Its ribs had been crushed, one of its hind legs so badly damaged that it was nearly severed. An awful gasping sound drew Tim's attention to the animal's head. The deer's skull had cracked through a sheet of ice covering the ditch. Tim watched the animal sucking water through one of its nostrils each time it tried to breathe; the other nostril was submerged.

Tim began to reach for his holstered 9mm Taurus handgun. *Somebody needs to shoot this deer,* he thought. But just as quickly, he remembered a roadside sign he had passed moments before the accident: DISCHARGE OF FIREARMS PROHIBITED. There was no way he could let the deer suffer like that—paralyzed, sucking in water, obviously in terrible pain. And yet he knew the penalties for firing a gun in a no-discharge zone: he could lose the pistol permit that was so important to his job and his self-esteem. He could hear the words his father and grandfather had drummed into his head since he was a boy: *No matter what, always respect the law. Never break it.*

The deer's agonizing gasps continued. Tim looked at the pickup driver. Perhaps there was a way out of this turmoil.

"Here," he said, offering his pistol to the pickup driver. "You hit the deer. Do you want to kill it?"

"No," said the driver, who wanted no part of this business.

Tim looked over at two other motorists who had stopped. They didn't want to shoot the deer, either.

Tim knew what he had to do, law or no law. He walked up to the deer and fired a single shot into the base of its skull. The animal twitched and then let out its final breath, its agony over.

Tim drove the pickup driver to a gas station and headed off to work. He knew he had done the right thing, but for weeks thereafter he worried that the Amherst police would show up at his door and charge him with illegally firing his gun. One of the other motorists could have given his description and license plate number to law enforcement; the police themselves might have discovered the deer carcass and gone looking for the shooter. In his mind, he debated the written laws of man and the unwritten laws of nature and common sense. This was one of those times, he concluded, that "natural law" was more important than man's law.

Still annoyed about having to pay to shoot at the local sportsmen's club, Tim decided it was time to buy a piece of land out in the middle of nowhere. That way he could shoot in peace, with no membership fees to pay and no complaining neighbors to worry about.

McVeigh and an old high school buddy, Dave Darlak, decided to become partners on a ten-acre parcel in the back hills of western New York's Southern Tier. For a down payment of four hundred dollars, and a series of regular payments totaling sixty-six hundred dollars, they became landowners in the rural town of Humphrey. Tim gleefully spent his time in Humphrey testing a forty-round magazine that Steve Hodge had given him for his AR-15 rifle. The only way to fully test a new magazine was to cycle it through, and that meant a lot of gunfire. But Tim soon found that the land wasn't quite as isolated as he thought.

Humphrey residents were used to hunters, but there was so much racket at the McVeigh-Darlak property that some wondered whether war was breaking out over there. One day, a man who lived nearby appeared on an all-terrain vehicle. He told Tim he was concerned that poachers were attacking a nesting ground for blue herons at the top of the property.

Nope, that's not it, Tim assured the man. "We're just popping rounds."

Soon afterward, Tim and some friends were cleaning their guns, which were laid out on the hood of Tim's car, when a farmer drove up on his tractor.

"Is that you shooting up there?" the farmer demanded. "My chickens are laying eggs and can't hatch them."

"Sorry, sir," Tim said. "This is my land."

The farmer rode off in a huff. A retired state trooper appeared in short order and informed the shooters his neighbors were concerned. He wanted to know what kind of guns they were using and whether they had permits. Tim cooperated but again mentioned that he and Darlak owned the land.

"It's your property?" the ex-trooper asked. "Okay, then I guess there's nothing here for me."

Tim noticed a look of surprise in the man's face. He felt a sense of pride, figuring the ex-cop was impressed that a man as young as Tim had the money and responsibility to own ten acres of property.

Tim enjoyed his new car, his guns, and his land. But he was restless, convinced that something was missing from his life. He was itching to move on, to see more of the world. A family friend had suggested joining the Army. Tim hadn't given it much thought at first, but now the idea took hold. Of all the organizations in the world, after all, there was a group that wouldn't complain if he fired weapons.

One day in May 1988, with no warning, he made an announcement to his father.

"Dad," he said. "I've decided to join the Army."

"When are you going?" asked Bill McVeigh, who was accustomed to his son's independent ways.

"Tomorrow."

3

"A Hundred Tim McVeighs"

There was a knock at the door of the Drzyzga home one afternoon in late May 1988. Richard and Linda Drzyzga were happy to see it was their former Meyer Road neighbor, Tim McVeigh.

"Guess what?" McVeigh told Richard Drzyzga. "I joined the Army."

Drzyzga was pleased to hear it; it was he who had suggested the idea in the first place. He had always liked Tim and considered him a smart young man, but as a financial planner Drzyzga found it frustrating to watch Tim give up on business school, moving from one dead-end job to another. It was he who'd first mentioned the military to McVeigh months before, believing it might give his life some focus. At the very least, he told McVeigh, he'd get to try out all kinds of weapons.

So, on May 24, McVeigh had driven by himself to the military recruiting office in nearby Lockport and signed up.

As on the math exam in business school, he missed only one question on the military vocational aptitude test that recruiters use to screen walk-in candidates. Recruiters from the Navy, Air Force, Marines, and Army all showed interest in him. With that kind of a test score, the Navy man told him, he could become a nuclear-propulsion specialist, working on a nuclear submarine or a carrier.

That offer interested him, but McVeigh chose the Army. He liked the idea of joining the infantry, becoming a combat soldier. He knew the experience would buttress his survival and shooting skills—and he thought it might give a sense of purpose to his restless energy. If he'd lived in a big city, McVeigh would reflect much later, he might have joined a street gang. Instead he joined the Army.

McVeigh's impressions of military life had been formed by the action movies of the Reagan era: *First Blood,* the first of Sylvester Stallone's Rambo adventures, and *Missing in Action,* with Chuck Norris as the hero rescuing prisoners of war. These were men's men, in McVeigh's eyes, and he wanted to be like them. The Army was the big time: unlike college, where big tuition payments earned you nothing more than a piece of paper, the military offered a paying job in the real world, a first-rate education in practical skills—and all the free ammunition you could use.

There was one more reason. McVeigh wanted to see the world outside Pendleton. To say the least, for his first twenty years he had led a sheltered existence. His rides in the Burke armored car to pick up State Thruway tolls in Rochester and Syracuse were almost as far from home as he'd ever been. He could not recall meeting a single African-American in all his years in the Starpoint school system. Tim McVeigh had grown up in a rural, white-bread culture; in his world, different points of view were rare as skyscrapers.

In one of his first dealings with the Army, McVeigh found himself being invited to participate in a lie.

The Army recruiter who handled him needed infantrymen badly. As an enticement to join, he told McVeigh that, if he agreed to go into the infantry, the recruiter would arrange for Tim to get credit for helping to sign up two other young men who had joined in Lockport on that same day. McVeigh didn't even know the two young recruits; he had nothing to do with their decision to join the Army. But taking credit for their recruitment would entitle him to a little boost in his starting pay, so he agreed.

Several days later, when McVeigh went to the Buffalo recruiting station for some additional physical tests and paperwork, officials there started asking him questions about his two fellow recruits.

"Did you really know those two guys?" a skeptical recruiter asked McVeigh.

McVeigh felt awkward. Here he was, joining the Army, which he wanted to believe was an institution based on honesty and integrity. He didn't feel right, lying to his superiors to get a raise, before even his first day at boot camp. But he also wanted the raise. He didn't quite know what to say.

"Well, I . . . their names are on the form with mine," McVeigh stammered.

He lost his raise. It was a minor incident, but disillusioning.

Looking ahead, McVeigh set his sights on one of the Army's special operations units—either Special Forces or the Army Rangers, the elite fighting forces that trace their roots to before the American Revolution. He thought about wearing the Green Beret, becoming a new Rambo, battling his way through the jungles with the fiercest fighting force in the world.

His first stop was Fort Benning, Georgia, where he arrived on May 30 for three months of basic and specialized training.

Fort Benning, "the home of the U.S. infantry," has a long and storied history. The base is named for General Henry Lewis Benning, a feisty lawyer who recruited and led the 17th Georgia Volunteers regiment of the Confederate Army during the Civil War. A staunch supporter of states' rights, Benning was an advocate of Georgia's secession from the Union; nicknamed "Old Rock" for his composure under fire, he served directly with Robert E. Lee. Benning died in 1875 after a postmilitary career as a state judge.

Opened in 1918, Fort Benning calls itself the most influential infantry center in the world, the incubator for the world's finest combat soldiers. Some of the most famous military leaders in American history were trained there, including Dwight D. Eisenhower, Omar N. Bradley, George C. Marshall, George S. Patton, and Colin L. Powell. Since its inception, hundreds of thousands of infantrymen—the heart of America's fighting forces—have been trained at Fort Benning. Its programs include infantry and Ranger training, an engineers group, and a course in the operation of the Bradley fighting vehicle, an armored personnel carrier armed with a 25mm cannon.

Until December 15, 2000, the fort was also home to a controversial bilingual academy, the U.S. Army School of the Americas, which has taught American combat techniques to sixty thousand military, police, and government civilian personnel, mostly from Latin American countries. The Army says that the school helped the U.S. share its knowledge with allies, in the hopes of furthering democracy. But critics, including the *New York Times* and human-rights groups, say some graduates—including former Panamanian dictator Manuel Noriega—have used what they learned there to commit murder, torture, and other cruelties in their homelands.

The post is a few miles southeast of the prosperous city of Columbus, Georgia, on the Alabama border. The rolling Chattahoochee River cuts through the north end of the 182,000-acre Army post. The land is flat and sandy, framed by Georgia pines. The Army says the local climate is well suited for training infantry—which means, in other words, that the heat and humidity are wicked enough to push recruits to the breaking point. Temperatures often reach one hundred degrees. Recruits who try to beat the heat by taking a rest in the sand have to worry about nasty red fire ants crawling up the legs of their pants.

Into all this walked McVeigh, part of a nervous contingent of 112 new soldiers in Company E, 4th Battalion. After getting haircuts, shots, medical checkups, and gear at a processing station, the bleary-eyed recruits were loaded into white trucks with wooden benches—the Army calls them cattle cars—and driven to infantry school for the first day of training.

"You pussy motherfuckers! Get off my motherfucking bus!" screamed a drill sergeant. "Get into the sawdust pit, pussies! Give me some push-ups." After that, it was sit-ups. Next, recruits had to drag themselves up and start running in place. Then back down into the sawdust for more push-ups. The Georgia sun glared down on the recruits. Some of the kid soldiers vomited, some passed out, but the Army had no sympathy for quitters.

McVeigh lay in the sawdust, his muscles quivering, unable to continue. A drill sergeant leaned over him. "You want to go back to your mother, you pussy?" He put a heavy hand on McVeigh's back, making it all the harder for him to push himself up off the ground.

As the storm of profanity raged around him, McVeigh did his best, straining to get every last push-up out of his skinny arms. Finally, he could do no more. He lay in the pit, exhausted, but somehow resolved not to give up.

His reaction that first day was sheer terror, but within a few days McVeigh was catching on to the Army's head game. Yes, all the screaming was scary, but he came to realize that most of it was an act: for all their threats, he knew that the sergeants were legally prohibited from physically attacking the recruits. He could see the plan that was being played out before him: tear the recruits down, word by angry word, push-up by push-up, mile by mile. Browbeat the kids into fighting men. Destroy any notions of individuality. Make them think, and hate the enemy, as a team.

During dawn runs and their long, exhausting marches over the Georgia sand, their sound-offs revolved around killing and mutilating the enemy, or violent sex with women.

"Blood makes the grass grow!" recruits were taught to chant. "Kill! Kill! Kill!"

"I can't hear you!" barked the sergeant.

"Blood makes the grass grow! Kill! Kill! Kill!"

"I *still* can't hear you!"

"Blood makes the grass grow! Kill! Kill! Kill!"

"Kill them all," another verse went. "Let God sort it out!"

As he caught on to the game, McVeigh sometimes had to fight to keep from smirking as the recruits around him got whipped into a frenzy. But he never thought about rejecting the Army. He chose to embrace it and all of its ways, violent or otherwise.

McVeigh had never really felt like he fit in back home in Pendleton, but he felt comfortable here. He threw himself into Army life with everything he had. Military life gave him structure—a code of honor, a sense of purpose—that he'd never felt before. He enjoyed it all—the frantic 5 A.M. wake-ups, the rushed meals in the chow hall, the crass jokes, even the uniform inspections. He thrived in the outdoors, the smell of sweat mingling with the scent of Georgia pine. Most of all, he loved anything to do with firearms. The Army's cache of weapons made him feel like a kid in a candy store.

At the start of basic training, McVeigh was assigned to a COHORT unit. COHORT was an acronym for an experimental Army program called Cohesion, Operational Readiness and Training. The idea was to put new soldiers into small teams, to encourage lasting friendships. The cohorts would work together as teammates, pushing and helping one another through their first three years in the Army. Teamwork was the key. At inspection time, if your cohort didn't have his underwear folded just the right way and displayed in the upper-right corner of his top dresser drawer, you'd *both* have all your clothes thrown on the floor. And you *both* had to do twenty push-ups.

McVeigh's assignment to a COHORT unit meant that he was prohibited from breaking away on his own and trying out for Special Forces or the Rangers for at least three years. It was a disappointment, but one he accepted as stoically as any other aspect of Army life.

One member of his COHORT unit was William David Dilly, a West Virginia native. The jovial Dilly had joined the Army as a career move, after losing a job in the restaurant business; at twenty-seven, he was one of the older recruits in the company. Dilly liked McVeigh; the two would wind up rooming together for more than a year.

Dilly saw potential in McVeigh, who had struck him as frail and meek when he first got to Fort Benning. He noticed all the attention McVeigh paid to detail, and his desire to perform his duties better than anyone else. McVeigh seemed to revel in the things that other recruits seemed to hate most—long marches in the scorching sun, crawling on his belly under barbed wire. The hot weather didn't seem to bother him, but what he really loved was pulling night guard duty, when he could be alone with nature, gazing in silence at a sky so rich and black that he could see the outlines of the Milky Way.

At Fort Benning, a bastion of American patriotism, McVeigh would meet two buddies who would become an indelible part of his life story.

Dilly and other soldiers observed the powerful bond that McVeigh quickly formed with Terry Lynn Nichols, thirty-three, a Michigan native who was the oldest recruit in the company. An intense, oddly compelling man, Nichols had failed in a number of jobs and business ventures; when he lost his small farm and wound up in court, he walked away cursing the government.

Seeking a new start and a military pension, Nichols joined the Army at a recruiting office in Michigan on the same day McVeigh signed up in Lockport. Command officers made a quick assessment of Nichols's life experience and maturity level and made him a squad leader in the second platoon, which included McVeigh. With his spectacles and slight build, Nichols looked no more imposing than Woody Allen in an Army uniform. But Nichols was no pushover. He was a leader and a commanding presence, a man of strong opinions, and those who got to know him soon learned of his intense anger at the federal government about gun laws and the financial problems of farmers. It struck some as strange that a man who despised the federal government would enlist in the Army, but Nichols carried himself with an air of maturity that made McVeigh and others look up to him unquestioningly.

As senior platoon leader, Nichols was the liaison between the drill sergeant and recruits in the platoon. A few recruits made fun of his age, calling him "Pops," but not McVeigh; as the leader of a six-man squad within the platoon, McVeigh worked closely with the older man.

"Two days into training, Tim and Terry were like brothers," Dilly said. "They were drawn to each other. It was almost like Tim idolized Terry."

McVeigh recalls the communal atmosphere of the platoon: "You live in an open-bay barrack. You all live as one, so all get to know everybody at once.

"[Nichols] was older, and had more respect, in general, from the men because of his elder status. There's a chain of command. When he was told by the drill sergeant to get something done, he would come to the squad leaders and say, 'I need to get this done.' "

McVeigh didn't have much time at Benning to socialize with Nichols or anyone else. In basic training, he was getting three or four hours of sleep each night, and wolfing down his meals in the chow hall.

"Don't look at my fuckin' food," a hard-assed soldier would tell the recruits as they sat down to eat. "Stuff it into that hole under your nose!"

Nichols's bunk in the barracks was close to McVeigh's, though, and the two found some time to trade their feelings on weapons, the government, and other subjects. He was glad to find in Nichols another ardent believer in the Second Amendment. He heard Nichols lived on a farm, and McVeigh always respected people who were from the country.

About seven weeks into basic training, McVeigh was so exhausted he didn't even know which day of the week it was. One sweltering afternoon, the recruits were out on a long march when they stopped for a rest. McVeigh and a recruit, a powerfully built black man who weighed around 250 pounds, got into a quarrel. The recruit gave McVeigh a shove and brought up his fists.

McVeigh didn't call for his drill sergeant. He called for Nichols.

"Nichols came running over, got right into the middle of it, and broke it up right away," Dilly recalled. "Nichols was a leader. He was not a wimp."

Nichols commanded respect as he led the platoon through their marches and maneuvers. One day, when the heat and humidity had driven his men to the breaking point, Nichols stood up and convinced them to push on.

"Yeah, I know it's bad," he said. "You know, I got a son at home, and I want to see my son. Just suck it up, and let's drive on."

McVeigh was thriving in basic training. As they completed basic training and moved into more specialized infantry drills, his fellow recruits noticed that McVeigh was growing up, in more ways than one. He was putting some beef on his six-foot-one, 155-pound frame, and carrying himself with more confidence—his head up, his piercing eyes always on the lookout.

The Army experience beats some men down. Timothy McVeigh would come to consider his first two years in the military as the finest period of his life.

The enthusiastic McVeigh reminded one soldier, Bruce Williams, of "Iron Mike," the twelve-foot bronze statue of the ultimate soldier at the center of the Fort Benning grounds. "Follow me," the inscription at the base of the statue read, and to Williams and others, McVeigh exuded the same kind of unstoppable warrior fervor. "He was more or less, to me, the epitome of infantry," Williams said of McVeigh. "You know, the extremist, 'follow me' kind of guy."

What made you join the Army? Williams once asked McVeigh. "I like weapons," he answered. Another time, Williams asked McVeigh why he always carried his rifle as he walked around the base. Most of the soldiers Williams knew carried their guns in a sling, draped over their shoulders. "An infantryman always carries his weapon in his hand," said McVeigh.

As much as he enjoyed Army life, though, McVeigh never liked the slogans about killing that recruits were taught to chant as they ran or marched. "Twenty times a day, it would be, 'Blood makes the grass grow! Kill! Kill! Kill!' You would be screaming that until your throat was raw," he said. "If somebody put a video camera on that, they would think it was a bunch of sickos."

William Dilly took another view. Laid-back infantrymen chanting slogans about love and peace wouldn't do the Army much good if the bullets started flying. He believed in the power of combat soldiers unified by their hate for the enemy. "Our job was to kill people," Dilly says; "it's as simple as that. They had to make you aggressive. That was their job." But McVeigh's reservations bespoke an internal conflict about killing that would resurface later in his Army career.

At Fort Benning, McVeigh also had his first exposure to the nightmare of CS gas, a low-grade chemical weapon that causes tearing, coughing, and nausea. As a training exercise, he and nine other soldiers were instructed to put on gas masks and sent into a small, enclosed room, and the gas was pumped into the room.

Once the room was filled with gas, recruits had to take off their masks and yell out their names and Social Security numbers. They held their breath as long as they could—some for two or three minutes—but ultimately, each of them was forced to draw the dry, peppery gas into their lungs. The soldiers coughed wildly; some vomited. The gas slammed their eyes shut, made them cry, made their noses run; in some cases it even burned their skin. They felt as if their heads were going to explode.

Once the instructors were satisfied that all had been exposed to the gas, the gasping GIs were led out of the room. For many, it took several minutes before they could open their eyes.

McVeigh hated the CS gas as much as anyone, but he learned the secret of dealing with it—which was not to panic. He often wondered how horrible the experience would be for a child, or indeed anyone who'd had no training with the gas.

Dedicated as he was, McVeigh had a bit of mischief in him. On Sunday mornings, the recruits were required to either attend church services or spend an hour cleaning the barracks. McVeigh, an agnostic, chose to clean the barracks until he found out that nobody took attendance at church.

One Sunday, he signed up for church and just slipped away from the rest of his platoon. He found a field of tall grass and lay there, a little worried about snakes, but enjoying the opportunity to relax in solitude.

The following Sunday McVeigh signed up for church again. This time, he sneaked into an old abandoned barracks to kill time. He was looking around on the second floor when he heard footsteps downstairs. Someone was entering the building. McVeigh took a peek down the stairs. It was a sergeant major, one of the highest-ranking noncommissioned officers on the base. Somehow, he must have spotted McVeigh sneaking into the building.

Tiptoeing in his Army boots, McVeigh silently found an overhead air duct. He pulled himself up onto the air duct and hid there as the sergeant major came up the stairs. The officer checked around the second floor and then went back down the stairs.

McVeigh heard the front door slam. Relieved, he climbed down from the air duct. *That was close,* he told himself. *I won't try anything like that again.*

Just then, he heard the footsteps running up the stairs. The slamming door had been a ruse; McVeigh was caught cold.

"I'm sorry, sir," he said, snapping to attention. "I know I'm not supposed to be here." McVeigh got off with a lecture and some push-ups.

As his Fort Benning experience wound to a close in August 1988, McVeigh achieved the maximum test score for an infantry trainee. The following month he headed off to Fort Riley, Kansas, for more specialized training.

Opened in the 1850s as a safe haven for travelers hoping to avoid being scalped along the Oregon and Santa Fe Trails, Fort Riley had been the home base of General George A. Custer, the famed Buffalo Soldiers, and other cavalry units. After World War I, Fort Riley gradually changed from a cavalry training school to one that trained infantry and armored divisions. Today, soldiers brought to its desolate Kansas prairie environs are trained to operate the Army's war machines on the ground—mainly tanks and Bradleys.

On his arrival at Fort Riley, McVeigh joined Company C, 2/16 Infantry Battalion, part of the First Infantry Division that has been memorialized in books and movies as "The Big Red One." Among the soldiers who accompanied him from Fort Benning to Kansas were Nichols and Michael J. Fortier, a recruit from Arizona who shared many of McVeigh's political views, though not his zeal for Army life.

McVeigh, a straitlaced guy who rarely drank and had never experimented with drugs, made an odd match for Fortier, who smoked pot and gobbled amphetamines on a regular basis. They had met briefly while serving in Terry Nichols's platoon at Benning, but didn't become pals until the move to Riley.

Members of the same eight-man squad at Riley, McVeigh and Fortier spent a lot of time together. They found that they shared an interest in target shooting, and they would sometimes hook up with Nichols to practice at a farm near the base. Nichols had won a coveted assignment as driver for the unit commander. But in the spring of 1989 Nichols abruptly left the Army, receiving a hardship discharge to allow him to help out with family problems at home. And in his absence McVeigh and Fortier forged a bond.

Fellow soldiers at Fort Riley were surprised by McVeigh's fierce, and growing, devotion to gun collecting and gun owners' rights. He kept dozens of books on firearms and gun laws stacked neatly next to his bunk. McVeigh wasn't the most talkative soldier on the base, but when the subject of gun rights came up his blue eyes would flash in anger, and he would launch into intense speeches about guns, Revolutionary War patriots, and the Declaration of Independence. McVeigh was especially fascinated by Patrick Henry, the great orator of the Revolution, and by the small band of Americans who took on the British army at Lexington and Concord on April 19, 1775. For McVeigh, these Revolutionary heroes had a very specific significance: they stood for liberty and freedom from government oppression—no matter what the cost.

McVeigh's hyperactive mind was forever exploring. He was reading a lot of literature about a supposed conspiracy between the United Nations and the United States to limit individual freedom and, ultimately, take over the world—a plot that seemed all too real to devotees of books like *The Turner Diaries*.

One day, McVeigh handed a paperback copy of *Diaries* to Fortier. "You should read this," he said. To the fictional Earl Turner, it seemed that most Americans couldn't care less about losing their individual freedoms, as long as their TV sets were functioning and they had a six-pack of beer in the refrigerator. McVeigh felt the same way, and he thought he might find an ally in Fortier.

Another soldier at Fort Riley, Sergeant Albert O. Warnement, also recalls McVeigh giving him a copy of *The Turner Diaries*. Warnement skimmed through the book, noticed the racist content, and gave it right back to McVeigh. There were already enough racial problems at Fort Riley, Warnement knew; there had been complaints that whites and blacks seldom hung out together, and racist slogans—both antiblack and antiwhite—had been found scrawled on bathroom walls.

Warnement was several years older than McVeigh; he liked the young man and admired his abilities as a soldier. The two were target-shooting companions and Warnement even allowed McVeigh to store some of his personal guns at his off-base home. Warnement didn't want to see his young buddy screw up his career by getting caught circulating racist literature. "I'd get rid of this," he advised McVeigh.

McVeigh received the same advice from Sergeant Jose Rodriguez, Jr., another soldier who liked McVeigh and tried to steer him away from *The Turner Diaries*. "You can't keep this in the barracks," Rodriguez said. But McVeigh didn't heed the advice. He kept trying to turn his friends on to the controversial novel and other progun, antigovernment books.

He also kept up his survivalism hobby. He rented a storage shed in nearby Junction City, and just as he had done at his father's home back in Pendleton, he kept one hundred gallons of fresh water there, along with guns, ammunition, MRE rations, and other supplies. If all hell broke loose in the world, McVeigh figured, he would be ready. And if anyone thought his behavior was weird, screw them; he'd have the last laugh.

Some at Fort Riley did consider Tim McVeigh an oddball. Some were put off by his political views. But even his harshest critics were impressed by McVeigh's dedication to Army life. He was devoted—fanatically, some would say—to becoming the best soldier on the entire base. At 5:30 every morning, soldiers had to fall out for a uniform inspection. Most soldiers would drag themselves out of bed and throw on their uniforms "around five-twenty-eight," his roommate William Dilly recalled. But not McVeigh. "Tim would be up at four A.M., not only getting himself ready, but cleaning up the barracks," Dilly said. "He kept a separate uniform, which he had starched and dry-cleaned, just for inspections. He even had a separate pair of new boots. Right after inspection, he'd run back to the barracks and change into another uniform, which he would wear for the day."

There were also regular equipment inspections, where soldiers had to lay their gear—canteens, rucksacks, eating utensils, and sleeping bag—out on their bunks. "It must have cost him hundreds of dollars, but Tim had a separate set of gear, which he kept in immaculate condition, just for the inspections," Dilly said. "The man was a perfectionist."

Some rolled their eyes when, after a hard day of training, McVeigh would load up his rucksack with eighty pounds of sandbags and go out for another long march. But McVeigh had his reasons. Although his assignment to a COHORT unit would delay him, he still had his eye on joining one of the elite special operations units. He still hoped to wear the Green Beret someday, and to do that, he knew he'd have to look sharper and train harder than anyone else.

Sergeants noticed that when they asked for a volunteer to demonstrate some new technique, McVeigh was the first to step forward. He virtually memorized weapons and procedures manuals, and had little regard for those who didn't show the same dedication. He was not afraid to correct other soldiers—even sergeants—when they failed to follow procedures to the letter. Some officers at Fort Riley saw a healthy arrogance in his manner, a quality they found in only the best soldiers. He had the ability to lead by actions, rather than words. "Any captain or lieutenant would gladly take a hundred Tim McVeighs in their platoon," Dilly would say.

Many of McVeigh's pals would spend their weekend nights out drinking, chasing women, and gawking at strippers in nightspots near the base. Some would come back so drunk they would be urinating on one another. McVeigh rarely went out, and when he did—occasionally trying to score with women—his clumsy approach rarely served him well. "Okay, we've just met," McVeigh would tell a woman he met in a bar. "We could sit here for three hours, wasting money on drinks, or we could just go now and get laid." It worked once or twice, but not often.

That was all right with McVeigh. The bar scene held little interest for him. He preferred to use his spare time to get himself and his weapons ready for the next challenge. Friday or Saturday night would find him alone in the barracks, checking equipment, or with his nose buried in *Soldier of Fortune* or some manual on guns, sniper tactics, or explosives.

While McVeigh didn't spend much money partying, he found a way to make a few bucks off the many soldiers who did. He became the company moneylender, at whatever interest rate McVeigh considered reasonable. He also hired himself and his speedy little Spectrum out as a taxi service.

McVeigh made a profit, but he maintains he wasn't trying to take advantage of his friends. "I was the only one with a car, the only one who didn't drink," he said. "You'd get paid once a month. After week number two, guys would ask, 'Tim, can I borrow twenty? Can I borrow fifty?' I said, 'You got to pace yourself.'

"We were in a high-risk environment. I could have been out money. I was worried I would lose out. They were paying me to assume the risk they wouldn't pay me back. A first-time borrower, I would charge a hundred-twenty dollars on a hundred-dollar loan. After that, a hundred-ten dollars on a hundred dollars."

One day McVeigh crammed seven other soldiers into the Spectrum, taking them to the bank so they could cash their checks and pay off what they owed him.

McVeigh made no more than gas money, he says, when soldiers paid him for rides. He'd get calls at 3 A.M. from inebriated soldiers looking for rides home from the local watering holes: "Tim, buddy . . . I'm at Ma's Lounge. Can you pick me up?"

Largely out of friendship, McVeigh would roll out of bed and go, charging the soldier a couple of dollars. He charged only five dollars for a ride to Topeka, which would cost sixty dollars by taxi.

And the entrepreneur of Fort Riley found another way to make money—playing poker. Like his father, McVeigh was a first-rate card player—so good that he started feeling guilty and ultimately stopped betting with soldiers. "It's too easy," he told Bill McVeigh on one visit back home.

Drug use by soldiers bothered McVeigh; he didn't like the idea that someday he might have to depend on a stoned soldier for his life. He once noticed two lines of cocaine on a mirror, with a razor blade beside it, on a soldier's desk. Risking trouble for himself, he did not report the incident, because he liked the soldier and had never seen drug use affect his job performance.

"Don't smoke pot in my car," McVeigh told fellow soldiers, "because we have to take urine tests."

McVeigh even suspected some command officers of drug use. One day McVeigh and Fortier were standing in a field when a sergeant walked up and told McVeigh to start digging a trench. The sergeant directed Fortier to take a walk with him.

"They went off into the woods to smoke pot, and there I was digging a ditch," McVeigh recalls. "There is a real big drug problem in the Army."

Sergeant Major Robert Harris was another who saw personnel problems in Charlie Company 2/16. Harris tried to instill more pride in the men by starting a new award system. Each day, he would honor the most exemplary soldier in terms of appearance and military knowledge. The winner would get a day off.

McVeigh won the award three times in the first week. Harris discontinued the award.

In April 1989, McVeigh's company was sent to Heidelberg, West Germany, where the German army ran a renowned training camp specializing in combat in an urban setting. The elaborate training exercise was a rush for McVeigh, Fortier, and the rest of their unit. They learned to fight their way through houses and barns, ducking into alleys and climbing up chimneys. Like the heroes in his favorite war movies, McVeigh learned how to "clear" a house of enemy soldiers by tossing in a grenade and then spraying the place with automatic-weapon fire.

In competition at Heidelberg, McVeigh won the German equivalent of the Army's Expert Infantry Badge. And, for the first time, he felt a sense of real bonding with his fellow soldiers. He called them his battle buddies.

Returning to Kansas, McVeigh shined again on the weapons range. When he first got to Fort Riley, he was trained as a light-infantry gunner, specializing in the use of a light machine gun called the M249 Squad Automatic Weapon, or the SAW.

McVeigh loved firing the SAW. During a marksmanship exercise one day, he strung several ammunition belts together until he had one seven hundred rounds long. He kept firing and firing until the barrel of the SAW turned red hot, then white hot. McVeigh had never put a gun through its paces like that, but the SAW was up to the task. He would have no qualms about taking that weapon into battle.

When the tanklike troop carrier called the Bradley fighting vehicle was introduced at Fort Riley in June 1989, McVeigh was assigned a new specialty, a new title, and a new array of weapons to master. His new role would be in the mechanized infantry, and he began training as a Bradley gunner. The move wasn't his choice, but it was an honor, and McVeigh took the challenge; he racked up a higher score than anybody in his battalion in the Bradley gunner tryouts.

For McVeigh, sitting in the turret of the camouflage-colored Bradley, peering into the padded viewfinder was like being turned loose in the world's greatest video parlor. The twenty-five-ton Bradley was designed to transport troops, but with three highly effective guns it was also an effective battle machine. The gunner's job involved more than sharpshooting; a gunner also had to recognize targets, learn about the weak spots on certain enemy vehicles, and make split-second decisions on which gun to use in a certain situation.

The biggest of the guns fired deadly TOW (tube-launched, optical-tracked, wire-command-link-guided) missiles at tanks and other targets more than a mile away. The smallest was a 7.62mm machine gun that fired one thousand rounds a minute. But the weapon favored by most Bradley gunners, including McVeigh, was a versatile 25mm cannon that fired both antiaircraft and antiarmor shells.

"The twenty-five-millimeter gun could really get your adrenaline pumping," said Dilly, who also became a Bradley gunner. "Each round is a little more powerful than a stick of dynamite, and you're able to fire ten of those in a second."

Much of the training for the Bradley gunners was done on a simulator, but the live firing exercises and competitions really put the sharpshooters to the test.

"You're rolling along, sometimes up to twenty-five miles an hour, sometimes at night, using the night vision. You're confronted with different combat situations, and you have to react to them," Dilly said. "A target will pop up, like a Russian troop carrier, or a silhouette of some troops, and you have to pick your weapon and fire. Sometimes the pop-up will be a friendly target, like one of our own tanks, so you have to hold back. You have to memorize the shapes of our tanks.

"I was a good gunner," Dilly said. "Tim was unreal."

In one live-fire competition, McVeigh dropped jaws all over the base when he scored 998 points out of a possible 1,000. The competition scored gunners on more than just accuracy; points were also awarded for speed in recognizing targets and for following proper firing procedures.

Eventually, McVeigh would top his own score, nailing a perfect 1,000.

His superiors at Fort Riley picked McVeigh as the top gunner among approximately 120 Bradley gunners on the base. McVeigh's Bradley was designated as the Division Display Vehicle; when government officials or other big shots came to Fort Riley to look over the latest hardware, beaming Fort Riley commanders showed them McVeigh's Bradley. McVeigh was proud. He and Warnement kept the Bradley looking and performing like new.

Pumped up by all the recognition, McVeigh reenlisted in the Army for another four years in September 1990. At the tender age of twenty-two, he was on a fast track for a promotion to sergeant. He had vaulted forward farther and faster than virtually anyone in his company. Then, finally, came the news he'd been waiting for: the Army wanted him to try out for Special Forces. He received orders to report for a Special Forces evaluation and tryout at North Carolina's Fort Bragg. He was told to be there in mid-November 1990. If he did well, McVeigh could earn the coveted Green Beret.

McVeigh began training harder than ever for the challenge, going on ten-mile marches by himself, using his free time for push-ups and sit-ups. But Uncle Sam and world events were moving him in another new direction. A couple of weeks before the date of his Special Forces tryout, McVeigh found out he was going to war.

Iraq's dictator, Saddam Hussein, had invaded Kuwait, a wealthy American ally and oil supplier, and the whole world was on alert. McVeigh and the rest of his company were told to prepare for combat duty in the Persian Gulf.

McVeigh had conflicted feelings about the brewing conflict in the Middle East. He did not like to see the United States meddling in the affairs of smaller nations. He felt that the U.S. military should stick to its own backyard, unless Americans were directly threatened.

"I took an oath to defend the Constitution against all enemies, foreign and domestic," McVeigh explained later. "I don't like going to other nations. I thought the principle was defending yourself."

At the same time, Saddam appeared to be the kind of leader McVeigh hated the most—a bully, brutally attacking a smaller and weaker neighbor, as Hitler had done five decades earlier. Someone has to stand up to bullies, McVeigh figured. If President Bush and the Army wanted him to go to the Persian Gulf, McVeigh would set his personal misgivings aside and go. It was a matter of duty.

Before going overseas, McVeigh found time for two quick trips back home in December 1990. First he dropped off his Spectrum, asking his dad to watch over it while he was away. The second trip was hastily arranged when an opportunity came up for McVeigh to see his favorite team, the Buffalo Bills, in the National Football League playoffs. McVeigh was one of thousands of Bills fans who rushed onto the field and tore down a goalpost to celebrate the team's victory over the rival Miami Dolphins.

Just before embarking for the Gulf, McVeigh made a brief visit to the Amherst home of his old friends, the Drzyzga family.

The visit was a troubling one for Richard and Linda Drzyzga. They could see this was not the happy-go-lucky Tim who used to play with their son, Scott, and raid their refrigerator. McVeigh was clearly worried about going to war. Just before leaving, McVeigh stood on the Drzyzgas' front porch, gazing at Linda with the one of the longest faces she'd ever seen.

"Mrs. D," he said. "I'm coming home in a body bag."

It was the first time she ever saw McVeigh with tears in his eyes.

McVeigh and the men of Charlie Company, 2/16, arrived in Saudi Arabia in early January 1991 and settled into the barracks at Al Khobar to await their marching orders.

The thirty-seven men in McVeigh's platoon did not know what to expect, and they feared the worst. They were part of a huge force of Allied ground, air, and naval troops sent to the Persian Gulf to halt the advances of Saddam Hussein, universally viewed as a bloodthirsty dictator bent on taking over all the oil-producing countries of the Middle East. A half-million troops, mostly from the United States, but also from Saudi Arabia, Britain, Egypt, Syria, France, Italy, and other countries, had arrived to push Saddam out of Kuwait. His takeover of Kuwait had given him control of nearly one-quarter of the world's oil wells, and it was feared that the neighboring, oil-rich nation of Saudi Arabia would be his next target. The American troops were ready, but they had been prepared to expect a nightmare: the twin threats of chemical weapons and long-range Iraqi Scud missiles loomed large in every soldier's mind.

But there was something else weighing on McVeigh's mind. The Army's own battle plan—and his platoon's role in it—had given him reason to worry about coming home in a body bag. More than the threat of Iraqi fire, he feared the prospect of being shot by friendly fire from an American helicopter or buried alive by one of his Army's own tanks during the ground invasion of Kuwait and Iraq.

McVeigh, his platoon leader, Second Lieutenant Jesus Rodriguez, and the seven other soldiers assigned to their Bradley had been given an unusual and dangerous assignment. They and three other Bradley crews were detached from Charlie Company and assigned to ride into battle in front of a unit of eight M-1 tanks. McVeigh and other soldiers riding in the Bradleys worried that the battle plan made them sacrificial lambs, sure to draw the first enemy fire in any conflict.

When the unit began rolling into the desert, Rodriguez's platoon would follow a heavily armored vehicle that would overturn the sand, looking for land mines. Once the mine-search vehicle had cleared out a safe avenue through the sand, the command Bradley, with Rodriguez in charge, was to be the first through the breach. Other Bradleys would follow, with the tanks behind them. The M-1 Abrams tanks were heavily armored and they weighed sixty-four tons, more than double the weight of a Bradley. McVeigh thought it made more sense for the tanks to go first. Yet he defended his commander's strategy.

"The Bradley has much less armor and is more susceptible to fire than the tank," McVeigh would explain later. "The tank commander reasoned that . . . if the Bradley goes first and blows up, the Abrams can come up behind and push it through, with its horsepower, and ignite any other mines that might not have been taken out by the mine vehicle.

"In other words, he sent us in first as a sacrificial lamb. It happened to be my vehicle. You have the driver, gunner and commander, and six troops in back. That's one of the decisions a military commander has to make, without regard for life. He decides those nine lives in the Bradley are worth doing it this way." McVeigh didn't particularly like the commander's decision, but he respected it.

As a gunner, McVeigh faced further pressures. He held the lives of all the men in his Bradley in his hands. If an enemy missile came soaring toward the Bradley, it would be his job to detect the smoke trail in the air, swiftly estimate its range, and punch up his machine gun, throwing up a wall of lead bullets that, with luck, would detonate the missile in the air. And if McVeigh noticed an enemy vehicle preparing to fire on his Bradley, it was his job to blow up the enemy first. "If I slack off, I'm not only killing myself," McVeigh explained. "I'm letting down everyone in that vehicle."

As the soldiers spent an edgy seven weeks waiting for the ground war to begin, McVeigh felt it was best to talk about their fears in the open. "I think we're all going to die," McVeigh told his friend Sheffield Anderson in the barracks one night. "We're going to get pushed through by the fuckin' tank."

"Jesus, McVeigh," said Anderson. "You didn't have to say that."

The Bradley used by Rodriguez's platoon was designated as "Charlie 11," but McVeigh gave it a catchier nickname. He called it "Bad Company," after the song by the 1970s rock group of the same name. The song's lyrics were tailor-made for McVeigh:

> *Behind a gun, I make my final stand . . .*
> *Bad Company, till the day I die.*

McVeigh related to the song, and not only because it mentioned guns. He loved the last few lines of the song, including the phrase "dirty for dirty"—giving back to people what they give you. It was a theme that became McVeigh's philosophy. And those who knew him came to understand that there were two sides to that coin. On the positive side was the Golden Rule—"Do unto others as you would have them do unto you." Most of the time, McVeigh adhered strongly to that rule. But the dark side was this: anyone who mistreated McVeigh—or made him think he was being mistreated—was making a formidable enemy with a long memory.

McVeigh had BAD COMPANY painted on the turret of the Bradley, and he used his Walkman radio to pump the hard-rocking song into his unit's intercom system. From time to time, he plugged in other motivational rock tunes, from Queen's rock anthems to "White Rabbit" by Jefferson Airplane—an odd choice for the still-antidrug McVeigh.

As Iraq and the Allies used bombs and long-range missiles to pound away at each other, McVeigh and his fellow soldiers hunkered down in the desert and waited for G-Day, for President Bush's go-ahead to begin the ground war. The armored assault force, nicknamed Task Force Iron, had set up camp near the southern border of Iraq in early February 1991 and waited for orders to move in. The waiting was taking its toll on McVeigh, but it brought a smile to his face one day when his commanding officer called him out in front of the chow line and announced his promotion to sergeant. The impromptu ceremony was held in Saudi Arabia, about thirty miles from the impending war zone.

At night, most of the soldiers from McVeigh's unit huddled in sleeping bags in tents they set up near the Bradleys. McVeigh sometimes chose to sleep at his guns, in a rigid steel seat in the cramped turret of the fighting vehicle. McVeigh didn't like trusting anyone else to stay awake on guard duty. He didn't want anyone fussing with the gun sights in his Bradley. If a fire-

fight broke out in the middle of the night, he didn't want to waste a millisec-
ond before joining the battle. The weather was not what the American soldiers expected. It was surprisingly cool during the day, with several nasty
sandstorms and rainstorms; at night it sometimes got so cold that some men
found ice in their canteens the next morning.

McVeigh found that he had little drive to keep up his physical training in
the desert. Most soldiers worked out only fifteen minutes or so a day, doing
jumping jacks or other exercises. Some put on weight during their service in
Operation Desert Storm. But the Bradley gunners worked hard, spending up
to three hours a day cleaning and greasing their guns—an especially difficult
task with the 25mm cannon. The barrel of the gun, which had to be removed
for each cleaning, weighed one hundred pounds. Cleaning and greasing the
inner workings of the gun—especially the heavy link chain that moved the
gun into position—was an arduous job that left the gunners tired and filthy.
As a sergeant, McVeigh could have assigned a lower-ranking serviceman to
clean the gun, or at least to help him. He chose to do the job himself. "It was
a very unpleasant part of the job. It was almost impossible to keep that gun
clean, with all that sand blowing around," William Dilly said. "But Tim took
it as a challenge, a competition."

Some nights, the faraway rumble of explosions made soldiers wonder
what they would face in the days ahead. The men of Bad Company passed
the time by practicing for the ground assault, playing cards and doing their
best to monitor the latest war developments.

They didn't always get the full story, or the accurate story. On February
13, U.S. Air Force bombers dropped a pair of thousand-pound laser-guided
"smart bombs" on the al-Amira bomb shelter in Baghdad. The blasts crumpled the roof of the shelter, ten feet of steel-reinforced concrete. About three
hundred people, mostly women and children, were killed. Air Force officials
explained that they'd thought the shelter was being used by the Iraqi military. McVeigh didn't hear about the tragic error until after the war was over,
and he would often cite the incident as evidence of the government's bad
faith.

The ground war was yet to begin, but the Army was already suffering
some casualties due to friendly fire. On February 16, an Apache helicopter
crew mistakenly fired on a Bradley and a U.S. armored personnel carrier,
about three miles into Iraqi-held territory.

"This Bud's for you," cracked the Apache commander as he fired a missile that rocked the Bradley, killing two soldiers.

A second missile hit the armored personnel carrier, and now the Apache gunner trained his machine-gun fire on Americans running away from their damaged vehicles. The gunfire injured six more American GIs. The attack stopped only after an Army commander on the ground radioed that the Apache had been firing on Americans. The lieutenant colonel in charge of the Apache group was relieved of his command.

The next morning, a tank commander called McVeigh and other officers together for a meeting about the incident. In somber tones, he told the soldiers that the personnel carrier had been the target of a surprise attack by an Iraqi "hit team."

There's another reason to hate the Iraqi ragheads, McVeigh thought. *Let's kill the Iraqis, kill them all.* Again, it wasn't until months later—well after the war—that McVeigh learned the truth about the Apache attack.

A couple of days before the start of the ground war, McVeigh's platoon was sent out with an Abrams tank crew to check on what appeared to be a small oil-pumping station on the Iraqi side of the border. A truck was found at the location, and McVeigh watched with amazement as the Abrams fired on the truck, virtually disintegrating it before McVeigh's eyes. Later that day, there was a news briefing at the encampment of McVeigh's company. McVeigh said he and other soldiers were strictly ordered not to speak to the press. One command officer was designated as the sole spokesman.

McVeigh couldn't believe his ears as he listened to the commander talking to the press about the day's activities. No, the commander said, there were no incursions into Iraqi territory today. No, none of our people fired any shots at Iraqi installations. If you heard rumors to the contrary, they were false.

McVeigh hated to hear the Army lie, to soldiers or the public. He saw a reporter after the news briefing, and for a moment he thought about telling him what really happened. But he didn't. He was still a soldier.

The Desert Storm ground war finally began on February 21, 1991. Saddam Hussein had ignored President Bush's demand to pull out all of the Iraqi forces that had invaded Kuwait, and now, after thirty-eight days of relentless aerial bombardment by the Allies, the ground war was starting.

In the predawn hours, a huge explosion told Army Sergeant Timothy J. McVeigh that he was about to get his chance to fight. The Americans fired a massive charge called a "daisy chain" at the Iraqi troops, setting off a blast that turned darkness into daylight and lifted McVeigh an inch off the ground.

After that came a series of earth-shaking blasts—one of them so loud that some of the soldiers wondered whether it was a nuclear weapon. "This is it, guys," McVeigh told fellow members of the First Infantry Division (Mechanized), the famed Big Red One. "Get ready. We're going today."

McVeigh jumped into the turret of Charlie Company's Bradley fighting vehicle as the Big Red One mobilized. It was a key element of the crucial "left hook" flanking attack from the west, designed to cut off and kill the Iraqi invaders. As the first morning light touched the desert, he looked around him and saw an imposing display of armored might. It was a blitzkrieg force. As far as the eye could see, Abrams tanks lined up next to Bradleys, with Apache attack helicopters hovering behind them. The noise from all those engines was deafening.

General H. Norman Schwarzkopf, commander of the Allied forces, thought the Allies would need every one of these fighting machines to rout Saddam's battle-tested army and vaunted Republican Guard. There were estimates that the ground war could last as long as seven or eight months, that a thousand or more American lives could be lost.

But after four days of slaughter, the battle ended with an Iraqi surrender. Some military experts called it the most impressive hundred hours of ground combat in American history.

The action was heated and hectic, with sand and thick black smoke swirling everywhere. For McVeigh there were some moments of genuine fear, but nothing like what he had expected.

The ride from the American encampment to the battle at the Iraqi trench lines took about thirty minutes. But to McVeigh, peering out the turret for signs of the enemy, ready to start firing at any moment, it seemed like hours.

The American soldiers pictured their adversaries as bloodthirsty zealots, slashing throats and firing chemical weapons. Instead they found a bedraggled horde of Iraqis, poorly trained, organized, and equipped. While the Allied armor and infantry were biding their time, waiting for orders to attack, the Iraqis had watched in horror as the Allies' superior missiles and "smart" bombs blew their comrades to bits. Demoralized Iraqis deserted by the hundreds. Those caught trying were arrested, and in some cases executed on the spot.

The ground fighting in which McVeigh would be engaged was more of a high-tech turkey shoot than a war. The American tanks could fire farther and more accurately than the obsolete Soviet-made tanks used by the Iraqis. McVeigh and other gunners were even able to use night-vision viewfinders to help them find targets in the daylight smoke and blowing sand of the desert landscape.

Many of the Iraqi troops had been ordered into military service and had no great desire to tangle with the world's most powerful army. Some didn't even know what war they were fighting in; they thought they were involved in an extension of the Iran-Iraq war.

The Iraqis were so weakened and rattled by airstrikes that some American soldiers called them "crunchies" as they rolled right over their bodies in what was the largest tank attack since World War II.

"On the first day, one of our tanks fired one round into an earth berm, thinking there was a tank behind it," McVeigh recalls. "As soon as he fired that shot, everybody in the Iraqi trenches surrendered. There was no tank back there. All these people were surrendering with their hands up."

The First Infantry Division, part of VII Corps, the main attack force, pushed steadily north into Iraq. The men in McVeigh's platoon were told to keep charging ahead at the enemy. "If it's in front of us, it dies" was the motto of one company.

As McVeigh had feared, Charlie Company encountered not only enemy but friendly fire. Mortar rounds exploded dangerously close to the Bradley, no more than five yards away. As they forged ahead, the company also kept encountering large groups of scared, frantic Iraqis, carrying white flags or raising their hands sky-high as they emerged from their trenches. The Americans didn't quite know what to do with tens of thousands of surrendering Iraqis.

Searching the horizon for enemy tanks and machine-gun emplacements, McVeigh could spare no time for compassion. "We told them, 'Keep walking, you stupid fucking Iraqis,'" McVeigh remembers. "'We don't have time to deal with hostages right now. Just walk to the mass of armored vehicles coming up our ass. Just keep moving.'"

The Americans found countless weapons abandoned by the shell-shocked Iraqis. They would pile up the weapons and ammunition in trenches, and blow them up.

According to his platoon leader, Lieutenant Jesus Rodriguez, McVeigh may have saved one of his fellow platoon members from bleeding to death. The soldier fired his grenade launcher at a bunker from too close range, and the round struck a hard surface, sending shrapnel flying back at the soldier. Jagged metal pierced the man's hand and arm, near an artery. He was lying in the sand, bleeding at a life-threatening rate, and screaming for help.

Rodriguez told McVeigh, who had special training in combat lifesaving, to get out and help the soldier. The assistant gunner took McVeigh's seat in the Bradley while McVeigh calmed the man down and dressed his wounds.

The platoon leader insisted that McVeigh pull the shrapnel out of the soldier's hand right away. But McVeigh, worried that the soldier might bleed to death, decided to bandage the hand up—shrapnel and all—until a combat surgeon could work on it. Rodriguez was enraged with McVeigh at the time for going against his directions, though later he would write up a glowing commendation of McVeigh's handling of the medical emergency.

McVeigh saw the dispute with his lieutenant as a classic illustration of one of the things he despised about the Army. In the Army's eyes, orders were always orders. The command officer was always right, even in a situation such as this one, where McVeigh knew far more about combat lifesaving than his superior officer.

McVeigh put his gunnery skills to good use in the desert assault. On the second day of the ground war many of the Iraqis were still surrendering, but off in the distance McVeigh's crew spotted a dug-in enemy machine-gun nest. It was more than a mile away, but Rodriguez knew McVeigh could hit it. He gave the order to fire.

McVeigh saw a flash of light, the apparent source of some Iraqi gunfire. He pressed his forehead against the padded viewfinder, zeroing in on the target. He knew he'd have to adjust his shot slightly to allow for the movement of the rolling Bradley.

An Iraqi soldier popped his head up for a split second.

From his position roughly nineteen football fields away, McVeigh fired, hitting the soldier in the chest. The man's upper body exploded.

"His head just disappeared . . . I saw everything above the shoulders disappear, like in a red mist," McVeigh recalls.

The same shot, a 25mm high-explosive round with the power of a small grenade, killed another Iraqi soldier who was standing a few feet away from the man whom McVeigh was targeting.

"The guy next to him just dropped," McVeigh says. "In the military, you're always supposed to stay at least five meters from anybody, at any time. That's the minimum fragmentation distance for some weapons."

It was an astonishing shot.

"Did you see that?" another gunner exclaimed over the radio. "Great shot!"

Sergeant William Dilly, another member of McVeigh's unit, was looking through his own viewfinder two Bradleys away when he saw the Iraqi soldier "just vaporize before my eyes." To Dilly, McVeigh seemed like a golfer with the ability to step up to the tee and nail a hole in one without even a practice swing.

"After that, we all began firing on that bunker," Dilly recalled. "The amazing thing about that shot is, in a situation like that, the first round you fire is usually to help you zero in on the target. You watch where the first round lands, and then you adjust the second shot to hit the target. Tim hit this guy dead-on with the first shot. That's unheard of."

McVeigh credited the shot to his training, his gunnery skills, and a bit of luck. "I was scanning back and forth. I saw a muzzle flash. That's where instinct takes over. If you're trained enough, you do things by instinct that you later attribute to luck."

Army combat procedures called for McVeigh to fire again. But this time he decided not to follow the book. In his viewfinder, he saw nothing but barren desert and a few surrendering Iraqis.

He stopped shooting. Once again, his lieutenant was not pleased.

"Why'd you stop firing? Keep firing!" Rodriguez said.

"I got 'em, sir," McVeigh said. "I got 'em."

Finally, to satisfy the lieutenant, he fired off a few more rounds, far off into the desert.

"The white flag came up. They all surrendered," McVeigh remembers. "There was an Iraqi officer there. He later told one of our interpreters that when they first saw us coming, they thought we were either British or Egyptians. They don't like Egyptians. They fired on us, thinking they could engage us. But when a single shot took out their main gun, they just gave up. It was like, 'Two guys get taken down with one shot. Fuck this!' It was then they realized they must be fighting Americans, because no one else could have done that."

McVeigh received the Army Commendation Medal for taking out the Iraqis. Lieutenant Colonel Anthony Moreno wrote that McVeigh had inspired members of his platoon by "destroying an enemy machine-gun emplacement, killing two Iraqi soldiers and forcing the surrender of 30 others from dug-in positions." McVeigh also received four other medals for his service in the Persian Gulf.

But the would-be Rambo was emotionally torn about what he had done. Though he'd been around weapons since he was a boy, this was the first time he had fired at a human being. The two Iraqis were the first lives he had taken. In a way it had been a great thrill, putting his skills to the test and succeeding. But later, as he reflected on his actions, McVeigh found that his first taste of killing left him angry and uncomfortable.

The carnage and the sadness he saw in the hundred-hour war left him with a feeling of sorrow for the Iraqis. He saw the faces of broken Iraqi POWs, some of them so scared by bombing raids that they had become addicted to Valium. He saw unspeakable carnage—hideously charred bodies, some of them with their heads or limbs blown off. Some of the Iraqi corpses were bloated to the size of cows as they rotted in the sun.

As they rolled through the desert, members of McVeigh's platoon saw horribly wounded enemy soldiers, some of them without arms or legs, trying to crawl along the sand. They saw stray dogs chewing on severed body parts.

At one point, members of McVeigh's unit were told to help bury the Iraqi dead in the sand. Later, without explanation, they were told to stop the burials and leave the bodies out where they could be seen.

Saddam, with his belligerent ways, had started this conflict. But now, as part of the massive Allied fighting force, McVeigh felt as if he were one of the bullies, one of a type he had reviled since childhood. Beating the Iraqis was almost too easy.

It still bothered McVeigh to be part of a war that involved no direct threat to the United States. It rankled him further to be part of a United Nations force that, he feared, was eventually planning to take over the world. Though he tried to justify his killing of two Iraqis by telling himself that the Iraqis were trying to fire on Americans, he knew the enemy machine guns had been too far away to do any damage.

"What made me feel bad was, number one, I didn't kill them in self-defense," McVeigh says now. "When I took a human life, it taught me these were human beings, even though they speak a different language and have different customs. The truth is, we all have the same dreams, the same desires, the same care for our children and our family. These people were humans, like me, at the core."

At one heated moment in the fighting, McVeigh noticed that one of the Bradley crews was still firing at surrendering Iraqi soldiers. He could not make radio contact with the crew, and briefly considered firing a few machine-gun rounds off the armor of their Bradley "just to try to wake them up."

McVeigh thought back to one of his favorite war movies, *The Big Red One*, about the proud division in which he was now serving, featuring Lee Marvin playing a grizzled World War II combat sergeant. When a young soldier tells Marvin he doesn't think he can kill enemy soldiers, Marvin snaps back, "These are your enemies. They're animals. We kill animals."

McVeigh had loved that line in the movie; now he'd begun to reconsider.

In a letter to Vicki Hodge, a lifelong friend back in Pendleton, he expressed his regret about the killings. McVeigh said he wished he'd had an opportunity to fight Saddam face-to-face, instead of the ragtag band of soldiers the Iraqi dictator sent into battle. "Saddam, if he ever showed up," McVeigh wrote from the desert. "Chickenshit bastard. Because of him, I killed a man who didn't want to fight us, but was forced to."

There had been some very tense moments during this hundred-hour war. One pitch-black night, the men in Rodriguez's crew were ordered out on a scouting mission to determine whether a vehicle appearing in the distance was carrying enemy soldiers. But the unidentified vehicle turned out to be a British minesweeper. "You boys have just driven into a minefield!" one of the Brits told Rodriguez. The lieutenant ordered his driver, a soldier named Jay Smith, to back out of the minefield on the exact same path as they had driven in. It was a nerve-racking little excursion.

Their closest call came one day when they were rolling through the desert at about thirty miles per hour. A soldier who was supposed to be watching out for trouble had fallen fast asleep. McVeigh, half-dozing himself, glimpsed a metal object partly buried in the sand, directly in the path of the Bradley.

"Smith!" McVeigh yelled into the intercom. "Left! Hard left!"

The driver made a sharp turn, narrowly missing an unexploded Iraqi bomb.

"It was the biggest bomb I ever saw, maybe two thousand pounds," McVeigh recalls. "We were so close, I'll bet we scraped some of the paint off it as we went by."

McVeigh's nerves were also rubbed raw by his role as an intermediary between Rodriguez and the rest of his platoon. McVeigh said he repeatedly found himself in the role of calming Rodriguez, a dedicated but excitable platoon leader.

Rodriguez was a "butter bar," a new lieutenant. Like many new command officers, he sometimes drove his men crazy with his insistence on doing things by the book, regardless of the situation. McVeigh admired Rodriguez as a man, but his refusal to improvise or break rules in service of an obvious goal rankled McVeigh.

Other soldiers concurred. One, Bruce Williams, described Rodriguez as a hothead—"kind of a wild man"—and remembered McVeigh as the only person in the platoon who could settle him down when he "went off the deep end."

Some of the thirty-seven soldiers in the platoon were so angry with Rodriguez that they talked about fragging him—"putting a bullet in his head," McVeigh claims. But he himself seemed to understand how to deal with Rodriguez. "Lieutenant Rodriguez was wired," he says. "I would just have to calm him down with the tone of my voice. I'd have to tell him everything in a calm and slow voice, and not react to anything he said."

The situation wasn't really Rodriguez's fault, McVeigh said. He blamed it on the command structure of the Army. It made no sense to him that a new lieutenant was given total authority over sergeants, regardless of their experience. It was unfair—not only to the sergeants, but to the lieutenants, and especially to the infantrymen whose lives depended on receiving smart guidance from above.

President Bush ordered a cease-fire to end the slaughter on February 28. Fewer than 400 Americans were killed in the war, and about two-thirds of those deaths resulted from accidents, not combat. No accurate casualty figure was ever compiled for the Iraqis. The *Army Times* later said estimates of Iraqi deaths ranged from "150,000 to 15,000 to 1,500." About 80,000 Iraqis were taken prisoner.

One thing was clear, though: the Iraqis were crushed. They had been forced out of Kuwait after one of the most one-sided wars in modern military history. Amid the Iraqi retreat, Saddam defiantly ordered his troops to torch hundreds of Kuwaiti oil wells, and to dump thousands of gallons of crude oil into the Gulf. One night, McVeigh counted the fires from more than fifty oil wells. The next morning, a coating of black soot covered the sand for acres. Soldiers stepping over it left white footprints.

The Allies, though, had failed in one regard. Their hundreds of airstrikes were unable to destroy their main target—Saddam himself. President Bush, fearing international criticism if he allowed the slaughter to continue after having made clear that the mission was to liberate Kuwait, halted the troops from marching all the way to the Iraqi capital of Baghdad.

Like many Allied soldiers, McVeigh felt that the job had not been finished, because Saddam was still in control of his death machine. He wanted to march through the doors of Saddam's palace and personally put a bullet between his eyes.

Charlie Company spent several weeks on security details near Iraqi towns and villages that were decimated by the war, and during this period McVeigh continued to witness disturbing incidents that made him sympathize with the Iraqis and question his own role in the conflict.

A few days after the cease-fire, a member of his platoon engaged in some looting near a small town in southern Iraq. Considering it the spoils of war, the soldier took a big chest of old tools from an Iraqi farmer. The farmer turned out to be a feisty character. He approached an American commander, screaming and arguing in his native language. Many Iraqis were intimidated by Americans, who were taller and heavier than most Arabs. With their Kevlar helmets, bulky uniforms, and thick-soled Army boots, the Americans were like larger-than-life creatures from another planet. But this farmer wasn't backing down. The only problem was, the commander had no idea what the farmer was talking about. He did not know about the theft, and couldn't understand the language.

"This ballsy farmer, I give this guy credit," McVeigh says. "The guy's going nuts. His friend comes over, and he's screaming, too. The situation is about to get out of control; there's going to be armed conflict. The commander says, We gotta get an interpreter. It took five hours to get the interpreter because we were so far forward. We finally found out the driver had stolen his toolbox, and we said, 'Give it back. You can't do that.' "

The American soldiers witnessed some heartbreaking poverty in Iraq, but they were sternly told not to give any supplies to Iraqi citizens. McVeigh decided to violate that rule one day after observing a poor family.

"They had nothing to eat but prunes and tomatoes," McVeigh said. "I saw a family walking down the road. It was a mother, a girl, maybe twelve years old, and a little boy, maybe four or five. I made sure no one was around, except my driver. I took a case of MREs, one of those big cans of fruit cocktail, and a gallon can of applesauce."

McVeigh figured the nervous Iraqi mother would "freak out" if he approached her with the cases of food. So he gently placed the cases down on the road and slowly backed away, gesturing at the woman that it was all right to take the food.

"They were afraid of the 'evil' American soldiers. They didn't know if I was ordering them to take it, or I would shoot them, or if it was a booby trap. Eventually, they walked over, they looked at it. They took it and walked away, nodding, like, 'Thank you.' "

In that brief moment, McVeigh felt as if he had made a connection with people from another culture. In a letter written to Vicki Hodge later, he joked about giving more food away. "Since I'm in charge, I gave the locals six cases of MREs," McVeigh wrote. "Is that good or bad, you ask. I just hope they didn't get sick eating something their stomachs aren't used to. I know they'll definitely be farting a lot."

And in a letter to another friend, Liz McDermott, McVeigh said the Iraqis begging for food reminded him of sad-eyed puppy dogs, trying to get a snack at the dinner table. But this, he said, "is much worse.

"A major six-lane highway runs through here, and we've set up a blockade to deter the movement of supplies from south to north," he wrote from his encampment in southern Iraq. "It's not like the movies, where a car comes crashing through the middle to get through. Try crashing a Toyota pickup through two M-1 tanks."

In early March, the soldiers in McVeigh's company were sent to act as part of a security force at Safwan, Iraq, while the victorious General Schwarzkopf dictated the terms of the pullout to Iraqi military leaders. McVeigh was one of a select group of soldiers assigned to the inner perimeter while Schwarzkopf and the Iraqis signed an armistice.

Despite his misgivings, McVeigh was proud of the Allied victory and caught up in the anti-Saddam sentiment.

I wish Saddam would show up here, McVeigh thought, *so I could shoot him.*

McVeigh got an opportunity to meet briefly with NBC News anchor Tom Brokaw, an exciting moment for the small-town news junkie from western New York. He also snapped some photos of Schwarzkopf, surrounded by members of the elite Special Forces, striding toward a group of Iraqi generals.

And in late March, the Special Forces reached out for McVeigh. He received orders to travel back to the good old USA and report to the Special Forces Selection and Assessment Course at Fort Bragg, North Carolina.

McVeigh's future was brimming with promise. At twenty-two, he was already a highly respected noncommissioned officer. He had just been part of a triumphant war effort, and was headed home to be greeted as a hero.

Better yet, he was now on track to become the Army's ultimate warrior: a Green Beret.

4

War Hero

The next few days, in late March of 1991, were some of the most frantic and enjoyable of McVeigh's life.

He and Mitch Whitmire, a buddy from Fort Riley who had also gone to the Gulf War, had some hustling to do. The Army had directed them both to be at Camp McCall, the Special Forces training facility at Fort Bragg, North Carolina, by April 5. They were told to stop in at Fort Riley first to report in and pick up their gear.

How were they supposed to get to Kansas from Iraq, half a world away?

You figure it out, the Army told them.

Because he outranked Whitmire, McVeigh took on the responsibility of conniving, cajoling, and improvising their way through the travel plan. First they managed to get a chopper ride to a post in the middle of the desert and find a major to sign their transfer orders. The two soldiers hitched a ride on an Army C-130 transport plane to Spain; from there McVeigh found them seats on a military flight to Connecticut, with a brief stopover in Newfoundland.

On the flight with them was a group of Air Force "flyboys" in their dress blues. McVeigh and Whitmire wore rumpled Army uniforms, stained with the sweat of combat. McVeigh had washed when he could in the desert, pouring bottles of water over himself and scrubbing down with a washcloth. But he hadn't had a proper shower in a month.

Because they had been sent back early for the Special Forces tryout, McVeigh and Whitmire were two of the first combat veterans to return home from Desert Storm. The two scruffy soldiers found themselves being treated like heroes, though, at a red-carpet reception at the airport in Connecticut, and then on a commercial flight toward Fort Riley. "We're as dirty as hell, we haven't seen a woman in months. We looked like the combat troops," McVeigh remembers. "We got so many, what I would call 'grinding' hugs, it was driving us crazy. Grinding thighs, women hanging over the ropes of the red carpet. It was an amazing welcome home. And it didn't end there."

At the moment, America was giddy with patriotic pride over its Desert Storm victory. Many Americans recalled, with some guilt, the way Vietnam War veterans had been treated on their return, and they wanted to do much better this time. Lee Greenwood's patriotic country song, "God Bless the USA," was riding the top of the music charts. For those on the home front, this was the first feel-good war in a long time.

They stopped at Fort Riley for a couple of days. McVeigh was happy to see Fortier, who had stayed behind because of a back problem while his cohorts went to war. Whitmire, Fortier, and McVeigh went out to celebrate at a bar near the base.

For the first time in his life, McVeigh picked up the prettiest woman in the bar. Noticing her sexy clothes, McVeigh sidled up to her and uttered a line he'd heard a friend use.

"Hey," he said, "do you need some kind of special license to wear an outfit like that?"

It wasn't exactly James Bond, but it was better than McVeigh's usual clumsy approach. And for one of the first guys home from Desert Storm, it was good enough. They chatted awhile, and McVeigh left with the woman, giving his car keys to Fortier and Whitmire. McVeigh and his new friend went to her place and made love—just like in the movies.

On the flight from Kansas to North Carolina, civilian passengers noticed

McVeigh's clothes and brush cut. "Hey," one man asked, "were you over there?"

"Yes, I was," McVeigh replied, beaming.

An off-duty stewardess was sitting next to him, and she went up and told the pilot that two Desert Storm vets were aboard the plane.

The pilot announced, "We would like to honor Sergeant McVeigh and Specialist Whitmire, who have just come back from the Gulf War."

What followed was a show of adulation the likes of which Americans usually reserve for their top athletes and movies stars. As the plane soared over the American heartland, passengers got out of their seats and stood in line in the aisle to shake hands with the soldiers. McVeigh, probably because of his obviously military haircut, drew most of the attention.

The passengers had a hundred questions. "What were those Apache helicopters like?" one man wanted to know. "Were they breaking down like they said on TV?"

"No way!" said McVeigh. "They were with us every step of the way."

"Did you see Saddam?"

"No, sir, I didn't," McVeigh said.

"Did you kill anybody?"

"Yes, I did," McVeigh answered, with a solemn nod.

McVeigh spoke to people for half an hour, answering the questions one by one, accepting kisses, handshakes, and slaps on the back. It was a taste of hero worship that most people never get to experience in their entire lives.

Then the plane touched down in Fayetteville, North Carolina, and the high times were over. There were no slaps on the back from the men of Special Forces, the most elite fighting force in the Army.

The Army gives many of its toughest and most dangerous jobs to Special Forces, more widely known as the Green Berets. The Army calls its prototype Special Forces soldier "a breed apart, a cut above the rest . . . mature, highly skilled, superbly trained . . . a fighter of uncommon physical and mental caliber, ready to serve anywhere at any time."

Special Forces soldiers are the Army's cutting edge. If a job calls for parachuting a small cadre of men into some remote jungle teeming with enemy soldiers, or rescuing American hostages in hostile territory, Special Forces, with their unique training in weaponry and guerrilla warfare, get the call.

Like their colleagues in the Army Rangers, the Green Berets trace their proud history all the way back to 1670, when Captain Benjamin Church of the British army organized the first organized Ranger unit on American soil to protect a British settlement from Indians. In the Revolutionary War the tradition continued with several different units of guerrilla fighters, including one in South Carolina headed by Colonel Francis Marion, the "Swamp Fox." Ranger units fought on both sides of the Civil War, and the Green Berets have played major roles in World War II, Korea, Vietnam, the Iranian hostage crisis of 1979–81, Operation Just Cause in Panama in 1989, Desert Storm, and the mission in Somalia in 1993.

Since the day he enlisted, McVeigh had been hoping for a chance to join one of these elite units as a weapons specialist. The men in Special Forces had his kind of expertise, dedication, and cohesiveness.

He had grown frustrated with the changes he'd seen in his unit after they started using the Bradleys in 1989. There were jealousies in the platoon between the "dismounts," whose assignment was to get out of the Bradleys and engage in hand-to-hand combat, and the "mounted" forces, the drivers and gunners who stayed in the vehicle. Morale had suffered. McVeigh was tired of serving with men who really didn't want to be in the Army. And although he loved firing the guns in the Bradley, he didn't like being cooped up in the turret. He missed the outdoors, the solidarity he felt with his buddies, working up a sweat, marching through the pine woods back in Fort Benning. He loved the idea of being part of a tight-knit, no-nonsense fighting unit.

Soldiers who qualified for Special Forces were assigned to a twelve-member unit called an SF Operational Detachment-A, nicknamed the A-Team. That was the kind of teamwork McVeigh was looking for. But there was a problem when McVeigh reported to Camp McCall, the Special Forces Assessment and Selection facility that is part of Fort Bragg.

He wasn't ready.

The three months he spent in the Persian Gulf had broken McVeigh down, physically and emotionally. He was out of shape; worse yet, he'd endured a period of pure, unrelieved stress, time he spent searching constantly for enemy gunners, worrying that the Bradley could be blown to bits at any moment. And he was still frazzled from playing peacemaker between Rodriguez and others in the platoon.

When he arrived at Camp McCall, McVeigh was breaking in a new pair of combat boots. He may as well have been hiking in wing-tipped dress shoes.

Commanders at Camp McCall immediately recognized the difficulty faced by McVeigh and others just getting back from Desert Storm. They called all the Gulf War veterans together and offered them an opportunity to defer their tryouts, to come back another time when they were better prepared for it.

"No way," one of the proud Desert Storm vets yelled out, "we're ready!"

Peer pressure took hold. None of the others spoke up. *Asking to delay the tryout might be seen as a sign of weakness,* McVeigh thought. He decided to go ahead with the tryout.

It was a mistake—and a turning point in his life. Special Forces designed their assessment program to weed out all but the toughest and fittest soldiers. The twenty-four-day program was designed to tear men down both physically and emotionally, to push them much further than anything they had seen in basic training. Physical requirements for the assessment program included a 50-meter swim with boots and battle uniform, and more than 150 miles of marches with a rifle and a fifty-pound rucksack. At the start of the assessment program, McVeigh was questioned and analyzed by a psychologist. He then began a week of physical evaluation.

He got through the first requirement, doing fifty-two push-ups in two minutes without much trouble. But he felt the first signs of weakness in the fifty-meter swim. Pushing his waterlogged boots through the water as fast as he could, McVeigh felt like he weighed a ton. By the time he completed one length of the Fort Bragg pool, most of the other soldiers had already done two. He worried that his cardiovascular system was not up to the challenge.

Something is wrong here, he thought.

He then did a two-mile run, recording his slowest time since basic training. He did better on the Special Forces obstacle course, climbing trees, crawling through tunnels and under barbed wire, jumping onto a log, landing on his belly. Sixty-one soldiers started the obstacle course before McVeigh, and he passed almost fifty of them.

Maybe I can cut this, he thought.

But then, after a quick lunch, the soldiers were told to get ready for a long march, and weren't told how far they would be traveling. This time McVeigh found no joy in the exercise. He already had blisters on the heels of both feet.

He tried the old soldier's remedies, putting on fresh socks and spraying antiperspirant on his feet, but a mile into the march they were killing him.

The march went on for five grueling miles. The day was hot and muggy. Much of the march was through sand, which made McVeigh feel like he was wearing lead weights on his legs. The sweat pouring off his body puddled and dried on his new boots, leaving white salt marks.

I'm not going to make it, McVeigh finally admitted to himself.

McVeigh was one of the last to finish. He dragged himself to the barracks, feeling as demoralized as one of those shell-shocked Iraqi servicemen. Now, just two days into the assessment program, it was his time to surrender.

He was still a couple weeks short of his twenty-third birthday, but McVeigh felt like a tired old man. He spoke to Whitmire, who was having the same problems. They decided to go to the commander and pull themselves out of the program.

The Army sends its very best soldiers for Special Forces assessment, and about half of those don't make it through. One thing the program teaches soldiers is how to make honest evaluations of their own capabilities. It's a self-assessment program. Soldiers don't get booted out; they withdraw.

Through his disappointment, McVeigh was thinking logically. He realized he had made a mistake by trying out for Special Forces so soon after his return from the Persian Gulf. "The rucksack march hurt more than it should," McVeigh told the commander. "I just can't hack it." The official told McVeigh and Whitmire he understood, reassured them that they could try again sometime, and wished them good luck.

Tim McVeigh would never get a second chance at Special Forces. His three years in the military had seen one success after another, but now his star was falling.

McVeigh insisted to friends that he was not devastated by what happened at Fort McCall. But Army life would never be the same for him again.

He received approval to visit home for several weeks before going back to Fort Riley. These visits to his hometown, especially with his grandfather, helped McVeigh calm down, and he went whenever he could arrange it. He loved getting behind the wheel of his little Spectrum, opening up the engine, and seeing how fast he could make the 1,200-mile drive from Kansas to western New York. His speed record for the trip was a torrid fourteen hours—an average speed of nearly 85 miles per hour, accomplished with the help of a radar detector. It wasn't unusual for McVeigh to tear down a country road at more than 110 miles per hour.

After visiting with his family McVeigh returned to his old post at Fort Riley. Battle buddies quickly sensed that something had changed in McVeigh. He didn't seem like the same guy. He still excelled in his duties, especially gunnery. But his gung-ho attitude was slowly giving way to bitterness, anger, and a desire for isolation. Bruce Williams, the soldier who'd seen McVeigh as the second coming of "Iron Mike," noticed that the sergeant was spending a lot of time alone in his room, playing video games.

McVeigh was growing disenchanted with Army life. More and more, he was disgusted with the lack of cohesion, the absence of a commitment to excellence in those he worked with in Charlie Company. He was especially bothered by what he saw as a lack of commitment, and respect for authority, among some of the younger black soldiers in the company. He felt some of the blacks resented him because he'd made sergeant at such a tender age. And he convinced himself that the blacks were getting special treatment.

A series of incidents led to racial tension on the base. A young black private threatened another soldier with a gun, demanding to see his commanding officer. Some black soldiers walked around the base in BLACK POWER T-shirts, and casually addressed their sergeants as "Sarge"—unacceptable behavior to McVeigh.

And some of McVeigh's actions prompted talk around the base that he was a racist. On occasion, soldiers heard him refer to blacks as "niggers"—a term he'd first used back in his days as an armored-car driver, sneering at "porch monkeys" on the East Side of Buffalo. Some black soldiers resented his habit of assigning them to sweep up the motor pool.

McVeigh admits today that he disliked a few blacks in the company, but he claims that racism had nothing to do with it. He cites several black soldiers—Williams, Sheffield Anderson, sniper Howard Ian Thompson, and Derrick Bunch—whom McVeigh considered some of his closest "battle buddies," about the highest compliment McVeigh would pay to a fellow soldier. And on the flip side, there were plenty of white soldiers he did not like.

But McVeigh has also admitted that, on occasion, he used the N word in anger, that at times he'd laugh heartily at what he considered a "good nigger joke."

McVeigh believes that the rumors about him were fueled by an incident that involved him, Thompson, and another black soldier one day when McVeigh couldn't get into the trunk of his car. Perhaps one of the black guys could teach him how to break into a car trunk with a screwdriver, McVeigh joked.

"You white cracker," one of the black men said to McVeigh.

"You nigger!" McVeigh fired back.

McVeigh said it was all in fun, but another soldier overheard the exchange and was upset enough to report it to a superior. McVeigh later had to explain to his commander what had happened.

While he swore he never embraced racism, McVeigh actively explored the racist point of view. He had already begun selling copies of *The Turner Diaries* at gun shows, and because of the racist content of the book, McVeigh wound up on a mailing list for the Ku Klux Klan.

McVeigh claims he had virtually no idea what the KKK was all about the first time he received literature from the racist group. He was impressed by one of its pamphlets, which expressed concerns about the loss of individual rights in American society, and a desire to go back to the way things were in the days of the Founding Fathers.

McVeigh sent twenty dollars for a trial membership to KKK headquarters in North Carolina. One of the enticements for joining was a WHITE POWER T-shirt that McVeigh planned to wear around Fort Riley. Why would a non-racist want a WHITE POWER T-shirt? McVeigh maintains it was intended to protest what he saw as a growing double standard in the army. He says today that he never did wear the shirt, but he made no apologies for buying it, then or now. "I wanted to make a point," he said. "Black guys were wearing 'Black Power' T-shirts on the base. They weren't supposed to. I wanted to see what would happen if I wore the 'White Power' T-shirt."

McVeigh didn't renew his KKK membership when his first year was up. He had joined the KKK, he says, because he thought the Klan was fighting for the restoration of individual rights, especially gun rights. But the more research and reading he did, the more he realized that the Klan was almost entirely devoted to the cause of racism. McVeigh's enemies weren't blacks;

they were the politicians who were pushing more gun laws. He decided that the KKK material was "manipulative to young people." He was looking for a way to get to patriotism, but the KKK seemed like the wrong way.

Still, McVeigh's extreme political views were ruffling feathers among some of his fellow soldiers at Fort Riley.

In May 1991 he moved off-base, to a house in nearby Herington, with Sergeant Rick Cerney and Corporal John Kelso. McVeigh didn't hit it off with his two housemates, and he left after a month. Kelso said McVeigh was a great soldier, but "weird, strange . . . a racist." He was also annoyed by McVeigh's driving. Herington was forty minutes away from Fort Riley, and sometimes Kelso would catch a ride with McVeigh.

"He drove very, very fast," Kelso said of McVeigh. "No conscience for laws at all."

Later McVeigh moved to another house in Herington, this time with Sergeant Royal Witcher. Witcher was a protégé of McVeigh's, and he looked up to McVeigh so much he once took him on a trip to meet his family in the Ozark Mountains of Missouri. Witcher appreciated the way McVeigh patiently taught him about weapons and Army procedures, never moving on to the next point until he was sure Witcher understood the last one.

When Witcher had a problem, he would confide in McVeigh; he found McVeigh to be honest and sympathetic, a good listener.

The humble decor in McVeigh's room reflected his lifestyle at the time. Instead of cheery curtains, he had the drab liner of an Army poncho hanging in his window. A laundry bag lay on the floor next to the bed. And on the bed was a set of Garfield the Cat sheets that McVeigh—always careful with his money—had received for free from a friend. For Tim McVeigh, Gulf War veteran and survivalist, fancy curtains and bed linens were not a priority.

Much as he liked McVeigh, Witcher saw some oddities in his friend's behavior. To him, it seemed that McVeigh kept guns "all over" the little house, from the bathroom to a little ledge above the stairs. Witcher noticed that whenever McVeigh went out, he always kept a gun in his car. Out of all the hundreds of men he met in the military, many of them ardently pro-gun, Witcher never met anyone who had such a fascination with firearms.

Why do you always carry a gun? Witcher once asked.

"You never know," McVeigh said.

McVeigh was attending more and more gun shows. He'd gotten back in touch with Terry Nichols, who was living in Decker, Michigan, at his brother James's farmhouse, which was owned by their mother, Joyce. More and more, McVeigh found that he shared Terry Nichols's disgust for the federal government.

Not everything was going sour for McVeigh. He continued to be the top Bradley gunner at Fort Riley, scoring a perfect 1,000 in a competition in September 1991. He kept getting excellent evaluations from his superiors. Every week, it seemed, they were giving some new responsibility to the young sergeant, showing their confidence in him. If McVeigh wanted to make the Army his future, he could have.

Two of his sergeant friends, Charles Johnson and Theodore Thorpe, figured McVeigh would be a career soldier and wind up with a good military pension. Johnson belonged to the Audie Murphy Club, a select group of the Army's very best sergeants. Only about 1 percent of all sergeants are invited to join, but Johnson thought McVeigh had the credentials to get in someday.

McVeigh had a uniform full of medals and a drawer full of commendations. He wore the patches of the Presidential Citation, the Unit Citation, and the Meritorious Citation. On his left shoulder he wore the Big Red One patch, showing he had gone to war with the First Infantry Division. He displayed, among other awards, the Bronze Star, the Combat Infantryman's Badge, the Army Commendation Medal, the Army Achievement Medal, the National Defense Service Medal, the Expert Rifleman's Crest, and the Southwest Asian ribbon.

Despite the recognition, though, McVeigh couldn't escape the feeling that something was missing. The military just didn't seem the same after Desert Storm and his Special Forces fiasco. He was starting to find Army life one hassle after another.

He became upset because he thought he was entitled to a monthly allowance for off-post housing, and didn't get it. (McVeigh was making one thousand dollars a month at the time.) He was annoyed when the Army tried to charge him eighty dollars after finding a urine stain on the mattress he had used in the barracks. McVeigh insisted he was no bed-wetter—the stain was already on the mattress when he got it—and the Army ultimately backed off.

After his perfect score in the shooting competition, word got back to McVeigh that the battalion commander wanted to make him his personal gunner. The job entailed much more than firing guns in a Bradley; it would make McVeigh something of a big shot at Fort Riley. He would be a confidant to the commander, somebody soldiers would approach to hear out their problems or ask favors—an honor that usually went to a soldier with more experience.

On the negative side, McVeigh knew the job would mean spending more time with officers—desk soldiers, the people he considered the politicians of the Army. McVeigh was a field soldier. He liked being outdoors, in the woods or on the firing range—not sitting in the garrison with paper-pushers.

In late 1991, McVeigh was summoned to a meeting in the battalion commander's office. Nervously, he thanked the commander for the offer to become his gunner. But he could not accept. Furthermore, McVeigh blurted out, he was leaving the Army altogether.

The commander was taken aback. One of his best and most dedicated sergeants, leaving the Army? Was McVeigh still upset about his housing allowance?

McVeigh was surprised, and a bit flattered, that the commander even knew about that issue. "No, sir, it wasn't that," McVeigh said. "It's just . . . It's other stuff."

Standing before the colonel's desk, McVeigh just couldn't find the right words. He hesitated. He felt his eyes welling up with tears, the last thing he wanted to happen in front of a high-ranking officer.

"I, I just feel I need to leave," McVeigh stammered. He could barely get the words out.

The commander was disappointed, but he decided not to push the young sergeant any further.

"Okay," the commander said. "I respect your decision."

No one, McVeigh included, will ever know what would have happened if he had made it into Special Forces. Or if he had decided to take his commander's offer, and commit to a long military career.

McVeigh saluted, turned, and walked out of the office. He said goodbye to his friends and left the Army at the end of 1991, driving back to his father's home in Pendleton.

His forty-three months in the Army had been the best of McVeigh's life. At times, his accomplishments there had made him a star, a feeling he'd never experienced before.

And yet, as he looked back, the disappointments somehow overshadowed the good times. Bit by bit—starting with the recruiter who offered him false credit for enlisting two other soldiers, continuing with the lies he heard in the Persian Gulf—McVeigh had lost faith in the Army and, at the same time, in his country.

Much more than his failure to make Special Forces, his war experience had soured him on the military. The more he thought about it, the worse he felt about the killing he had done for the American government.

He no longer felt comfortable serving a government that, in his opinion, pushed the values of political correctness at the expense of individual rights. McVeigh felt he could no longer stomach being part of a government that fought so hard against the sacred Second Amendment rights of gun owners.

He no longer wanted to work for a government he was beginning to hate.

II

ADRIFT

5

Nothingness

Despite the waning satisfaction of his final months in the service, McVeigh had high expectations for his future as he returned home to Pendleton. He felt he had a lot to offer the world. After all, he had gone off to war and come back a hero. He had shown his dedication and his leadership abilities, coming back with a chestful of medals. He figured his years of military service would carry the same weight in the job market as a four-year college degree. *Surely,* he thought, *some employer in western New York will be happy to have me.*

But it didn't work out that way. Western New York, its economy still struggling as it had been when he went off to the Army, didn't have much to offer McVeigh—a realization that hit him hard. The next thirteen months back in Pendleton would turn out to be the most disappointing time of his life, and it would drive him into a deep depression.

McVeigh quickly learned he was wrong in his assumption that employers would give the same respect to his Army record that they would accord to a four-year diploma. There was no big position at a computer software company—or even a decent-paying factory job—awaiting the decorated veteran. The only door that swung open was in the security industry, the very line of work he'd left behind when he joined the Army. A disappointed McVeigh soon found himself trading in his Army uniform, with its crisp green dress jacket and pressed pants, for the dull shirt and slacks of a security guard: he became a rent-a-cop for the Buffalo-based Burns Security.

To supplement his low-paying position he enlisted in the reserves, joining an antitank missile squad with the National Guard's 174th Infantry in the city of Tonawanda, a fifteen-minute drive from home. The reserves paid $150 a month. All of a sudden he found himself back in security work and back in the military. McVeigh wasn't moving forward, he was going backward. And the realization stung.

McVeigh hadn't entirely given up; he took civil service tests and scored well. But it seemed he had even slipped from his short-lived glory days as an armed guard for Burke before the war. McVeigh looked around at the people with whom he was now working and couldn't help thinking that some of them were the "dregs of the earth." When he heard that Burns was negotiating to provide armed security to some of its customers, McVeigh jumped at the opportunity to advance. Being an armed guard would pay a little more. It might help him recapture some of the dignity he'd felt back at Burke, where he was trusted with shipments of millions of dollars and known to his co-workers as The Kid.

McVeigh and three other guards from Burns were sent to the pistol range to demonstrate their shooting abilities. McVeigh was aghast at what he witnessed. *These three guys couldn't hit the broad side of a barn if they were standing beside it,* he thought. *How did they ever manage to get pistol permits?* As for McVeigh, he drilled forty-eight of fifty rounds into the target from twenty-five feet away. His marksmanship bought him an occasional spot on armored-car duty, collecting deposits from the booming Galleria Mall, just east of Buffalo. In an armored car, at least, McVeigh felt he was doing something of value. But most of his assignments for Burns were routine guard duty.

He made the best of it, starting first at the Buffalo Zoo, where he supervised the guards and worked the graveyard shift. The job had its good points. Animals had always fascinated McVeigh, and here was an opportunity to ob-

serve them during the wee hours when nobody else was around. As he patrolled the long, empty corridors of the "big-cat house" one night, McVeigh
spotted a large cougar watching him from inside its cage. McVeigh had loved
cats ever since he was a kid. And like the small house cats he kept as pets,
the powerful cougar proved affectionate. The big cat was named Cory, and
she was the caring mother to a couple of cubs. Soon, he and Cory had
reached a meeting of the minds. When the cougar heard the jingle of
McVeigh's keys as he made his rounds, she would temporarily push aside the
cubs and press against the bars of the cage. McVeigh rewarded the four-year-
old cougar with his trust, slipping his hand between the bars and petting her
behind the ear.

It wasn't the worst job in the world, but one persistent annoyance confronted McVeigh during the time he worked midnights at the zoo. Someone
kept calling the telephone in the guards' shack and then hanging up as soon
as he answered. McVeigh could hear loud rock music on the other end of the
line, but the caller never said a word. It drove McVeigh crazy, but he had to
answer the phone every time, for fear that it might be one of his supervisors
calling.

He mentioned the situation to Andrea Peters, an office-worker friend at
Burns on whom McVeigh had developed a crush. He asked Peters to give
him the names and phone numbers of former Burns employees who had
worked at the zoo. He dialed a few of the numbers; sure enough, when a man
answered at one of them, he heard loud rock music on the other end.
McVeigh hung up.

A day later, he called the number again. The former employee's mother
answered.

"Who's this?" the woman asked.

"An old friend of your son's from school," McVeigh said. "Can I talk to
him? I'm just in town for a couple of days. I'd like to catch up with him."

The woman paused. McVeigh was sure he heard the woman talking to her
son, relaying his request to talk with the former employee.

"Well, he says . . ." the woman began. But McVeigh started talking again,
and this time, his deadly serious tone made her stop and listen.

"Listen very carefully, ma'am," McVeigh said. "You think about this—why
would your son have you screening his calls for him? What's going on?"

McVeigh abruptly hung up, and then called the number again a moment later. The woman answered again.

"Listen very carefully, ma'am," he said, the same frightening tone in his voice. "If your son doesn't stop this shit—and he knows what I'm talking about—I know where you live. I'm going to burn your fucking house down."

McVeigh hung up. He never received another annoyance call at the guardhouse; later, he learned that the former Burns employee had changed his telephone number.

He got along well with most people he met at the zoo, but McVeigh's feisty behavior with the caller hinted at a deeper anger. He developed a lingering resentment for a zoo official who tried to get him fired for helping out a fellow employee, even as the official regularly left work with a trunk full of premium dog food for his own use. McVeigh's disenchantment with authority figures was growing by the day.

He channeled some of his anger into handwritten letters to a local newspaper and his congressman. His letter to the Lockport *Union Sun & Journal* was published on February 11, 1992. McVeigh spouted off about a variety of issues, ranging from government and its leaders to crime, taxes, and racism. The words came out in a rush from a young man who was becoming more and more disenchanted, as it became clearer to him that his hometown was not going to be where he would find the American Dream.

"Crime is so out of control. Criminals have no fear of punishment," McVeigh wrote.

> Prisons are overcrowded, so they know they will not be imprisoned long. This breeds more crime in an escalating cyclic pattern. Taxes are a joke. Regardless of what a political candidate "promises," they will increase. More taxes are always the answer to government mismanagement. They mess up, we suffer. Taxes are reaching cataclysmic levels, with no slowdown in sight. The "American Dream" of the middle class has all but disappeared, substituted with people struggling just to buy next week's groceries. Heaven forbid the car breaks down. Politicians are further eroding the "American Dream" by passing laws which are supposed to be a "quick fix," when all they

are really designed for is to get the official re-elected. These laws tend to "dilute" a problem for a while, until the problem comes roaring back in a worsened form (much like a strain of bacteria will alter itself to defeat a known medication).

Politicians are out of control. Their yearly salaries are more than an average person will see in a lifetime. They have been entrusted with the power to regulate their own salaries and have grossly violated that trust to live in luxury.

Racism on the rise? You had better believe it. Is this America's frustrations venting themselves? Is it a valid frustration? Who is to blame for the mess? At a point when the world has seen communism falter as an imperfect system to manage people, democracy seems to be headed down the same road. No one is seeing the "big" picture.

Maybe we have to combine ideologies to achieve the perfect utopian government. Remember, government-sponsored health care was a communist idea. Should only the rich be allowed to live longer? Does that say that because a person is poor he is a lesser human being and doesn't deserve to live as long, because he doesn't wear a tie to work?

What is it going to take to open the eyes of our elected officials?

America is in serious decline.

We have no proverbial tea to dump. Should we instead sink a ship full of Japanese imports?

Is a civil war imminent?

Do we have to shed blood to reform the current system?

I hope it doesn't come to that, but it might.

Timothy McVeigh

Five days after the newspaper published that letter, Rep. John J. LaFalce, a moderate Town of Tonawanda Democrat whose district includes Pendleton, received another one from McVeigh sounding off about the arrest of a Niagara Falls resident for "possession of a noxious substance"—namely, Mace. McVeigh thought it was outrageous.

"It is a lie if we tell ourselves that the police can protect us everywhere at all times," he wrote. "Firearms restrictions are bad enough, but now a woman can't even carry Mace in her purse?!?!"

McVeigh's disgust with government grew deeper. He came to believe that his racial status as a young white male counted against him. He viewed himself as a victim of reverse discrimination, and grew certain that government affirmative-action guidelines were blocking his way to civil service jobs with the state and federal governments. He and his old friend Jack McDermott had taken the toll collector's test for the New York State Thruway Authority. Sometime later, they received their test results. Even with McDermott's veteran credits, he had ranked low among the thousands who had taken the exam. McVeigh was right at the top. He scored 100, and the addition of his veteran's points gave him a ranking of number two on the list. When he received a letter asking where he would like to work along the Thruway system, he answered almost anywhere except the New York City area. He expected that he would be hired soon, but when weeks passed, then months, he convinced himself that he was not being hired because he was white.

"The equal-opportunity shit bothers me," McVeigh said years later. "The job should go to the most qualified person, regardless of race. You can't tell me that within a year's time, two slots wouldn't open. As a white male, I got put out of a job."

He became convinced that the same discrimination was afoot after taking the federal civil service test for the U.S. Marshals Service. Again, he scored high; McVeigh thought he would make a great deputy marshal, and figured that his chances of appointment were strong. He was the right age, clean-cut, and physically strong. He had a glowing military record, and was already working in a quasi-law-enforcement position. The idea of working as a deputy marshal—guarding prisoners, protecting federal judges, hunting for dangerous fugitives—interested McVeigh enough that he was even willing to set aside his negative feelings about the government.

But Uncle Sam never called, and neither did anyone else. In better economic times, Bill McVeigh might have been able to pull a few strings and find his son a job at the Harrison Radiator plant, where good wages and benefits were the standard among the unionized auto workers. McVeigh might have followed in the footsteps of his father and grandfather. But the idea of repetitive factory work never interested him: he would have liked the money, but McVeigh doubted that he could handle the monotony.

In addition to his long hours as a security guard, McVeigh took on a part-time job at Johnson's Country Store in Lockport, one of the biggest gun suppliers in the region. A mecca for sportsmen with its shelves of guns, knives, and ammo, it seemed like a perfect fit for McVeigh. But he didn't get along with one of the established workers there, and instead of trying to work things out, McVeigh backed off. He quit his job at the gun shop after just a few weeks.

McVeigh realized that it was more than just a personality clash that kept him from sticking with the gun-shop job. The long hours of working—eighty hours some weeks on the security job alone—were taking a toll. While on guard duty one day at Niagara Falls Convention Center, he was accused of snapping at a young woman who lacked proper identification to go into a restricted area. The woman complained that McVeigh had told her to "get the fuck out of here." He denied using such language, but McVeigh knew he wasn't himself. His job was making him angry and sullen. He began to request guard posts that would give him the least possible exposure to the public, asking for out-of-the-way stations when he had to work World Wrestling Federation matches, Monster Truck competitions, and other such events. "Working the crowd is a pain in the ass," he would complain. "People coming at you from all directions."

Tim was back living with his father, and he lived like a gypsy, usually sleeping on the living room couch. When his father was at work, he'd crawl into Bill's bed. Even with just three people living there—Bill, Tim, and his younger sister, Jennifer, who had left Florida to rejoin her father—the little house on Campbell Boulevard felt crowded. McVeigh's old bedroom had been taken over by Jennifer while he was off in the Army. Unlike her older sister, Patty, who moved to Florida to complete nursing school, Jennifer had experienced hard times since her parents' divorce. Mickey had been determined to make a new start as a travel agent in Tallahassee, but when that fell through she stayed in northern Florida, connecting with her brother in Pensacola. And so began a nomadic lifestyle for mother and daughter; they would move at least three times in those years, each time forcing Jennifer to settle into a new high school. A former A student, Jennifer saw her grades

plunge in Florida, and even at sixteen she was astute enough to know she
needed a change. Under her father's roof she knew she could find structure,
a chance for her life to settle down a bit. Yet even at Starpoint, Jennifer's
grades continued to lag; not until college was she truly able to regain her
footing.

Meanwhile, Tim McVeigh was growing irritable. Unable to get enough
rest shuttling back and forth from the living room to his father's bedroom, he
was chronically overtired, and soon he was showing signs of aggravation at
work. At home, he felt out of place.

A disheartening realization finally hit him: *I don't fit in here anymore.*

One cold and snowy winter day, within three months of returning from the
Army, McVeigh bottomed out. Dressed only in sweatpants, not even bothering to throw on a shirt, shoes, or socks, he hurried out of his father's house
in a state of panic and despair. He climbed into his Spectrum. He had to get
away—but where? The speedy little car carried him to the one place on
earth where he had always found comfort: the home of Ed McVeigh.

Tears streaming down his face, McVeigh knocked on his grandfather's
door. If Ed was out, McVeigh knew he could find the spare house key hidden on the porch. He was always welcome there.

"Timmy, what are you doing? It's the middle of the winter," Ed said, ush-
ering him inside.

The old man noticed the tears. His grandson was having a breakdown.

"Tim," Ed said gently. "What's wrong?"

"Grandpa . . . I can't tell you," McVeigh answered.

"Are you in trouble with the law?" inquired Ed. "Do I need to call someone?"

"No." McVeigh searched in vain for the right words to explain what was
going on inside him. "Just leave me alone. I'll get through it."

Ed took him at his word. "Why don't you lie down for a while," he suggested.

Tim headed upstairs to the room he had often stayed in while visiting his
grandfather. As he lay there, he was overcome by dark thoughts. He considered killing himself, and only stopped himself because he knew how much it
would hurt his grandfather. Finally, his anxiety subsided, he fell into a deep

sleep. When he awoke, Ed was no longer there. He had left his grandson alone to sort things out. The young man appreciated beyond words the compassion the old man had shown just by opening his door, welcoming him inside, and leaving him alone to think.

It always bothered McVeigh that he never got around to explaining this episode to his grandfather. "I couldn't tell him what was wrong with me. He may have been thinking the craziest things," he said later. "Maybe he thought I was raped or something. He really showed how much he cared by asking those questions and by letting me be, when I didn't want to tell him what the problem was. I knew I always had a place in his home."

It was all crashing down on McVeigh—the long hours in a dead-end job, the feeling that he didn't have a home, his failure to establish a relationship with a woman. For the first time, he began trying to ease the stress by gambling on Buffalo Bills games and other sporting events; for a guy making a paltry salary, the gambling only made things worse.

Later McVeigh would come to believe he was suffering from post-traumatic stress disorder, brought on by his Gulf War experiences. Whatever the cause, though his life as a civilian seemed busy enough on the surface, something was missing. Nothing compared with the thrills Army life delivered.

In the turret of his Bradley, he'd been the undisputed top gun at Fort Riley. Now, in his new life, he was just another bored and unhappy rent-a-cop. The boredom, at times, was so acute he could sense himself start to slip, growing listless and depressed. Despite all his misgivings about Desert Storm, he could not deny that war had brought him to an intensity civilian life could never match.

He identified with the famed soldier-author David Hackworth, a Vietnam War hero whose book *About Face* helped crystallize some of McVeigh's feeling. War indeed had been an elevating experience for McVeigh.

"And when you come back to the world, everything is different," McVeigh observed:

> You've seen the extremes, experienced the ultimate highs, lows, and realities. Who gives a shit about conversation about the weather, or about who's late for work, or who stubbed their toe? The daily grind, all of a sudden, has gotten much more intolerable. Normal coffeepot conversation becomes intolerably

boring. You separate yourself from these encounters, and from people, to escape. Who wants to settle down, get married, buy a house, go to work nine-to-five, back home? Back to the same old trivialities at home, get up the next day, back to the same old job—it's all just so routine.

Having hit bottom that day at his grandfather's, McVeigh eventually regrouped and marched forward. He might not have a bed to call his own and he might never climb his way up the corporate ladder, but he found he could still enjoy the things about life that invigorated him. With winter winding down, he took to the notion of becoming a hunter—not just any hunter, but one who could kill his quarry with a single long-range shot. McVeigh drove out to a field near the Attica State Correctional Facility, the scene of the bloodiest prison riot in the nation's history, about forty minutes southeast of Buffalo.

McVeigh had been hunting in the field before with his friends, with the blessing of the farmer who owned it; the woodchucks who ravaged his land were a costly nuisance, burrowing holes in the pasture where the farmer's cattle grazed. Sometimes the cattle stepped into the holes and snapped their legs; the owner was more than happy for a little free help in running them down.

Now, unexpectedly, McVeigh found himself standing directly over one of the holes, looking down at a woodchuck. *Just coming out of hibernation,* McVeigh thought. *It's groggy, that's why it doesn't realize I'm standing up here.*

McVeigh held his AR-15 rifle in hand. This wasn't the long-range hunting he had in mind. He reminded himself that he'd be helping out the farmer, protecting his cattle.

The woodchuck raised its head out of the hole, still unaware of the man with a gun standing above him. McVeigh wanted a clean kill. Practically on top of the animal, he aimed the rifle, slowly and carefully at what looked like the woodchuck's skull, and fired. An instant after the muzzle flash, McVeigh saw that the bullet had creased the animal's frame and bloodied its little front paw. The woodchuck threw its head back and saw McVeigh. Its mouth opened and hissed, as though it were begging for mercy. The animal's paw hung limply. Blood drooled from a gash in its side.

I gotta hit him again, McVeigh thought.

The rifle roared again, blasting the woodchuck in the head. This time, the animal dropped down in its hole, out of sight. McVeigh lingered a moment.

I'm out here to help the farmer, he thought. *But this did not feel right.*

The incident left him unsettled for days.

But McVeigh's feelings on hunting were mixed, as evidenced by a second letter to the Lockport newspaper, which was published on March 10, 1992. This time he defended the right to hunt for sustenance, and lashed out at the inhumane conditions endured by animals raised in captivity for the slaughterhouse:

"Since the beginning of his existence, man has been a hunter, a predator," McVeigh wrote.

> He has hunted and eaten meat to insure his survival. To deny this is to deny your past, your religion, even your existence.
>
> Since we have now established that about every human being on this planet consumes meat, we (in America) are left with two choices, buy your meat from a supermarket, or harvest it yourself.
>
> We will, for now, not discuss the fact that in many areas of the world, there is no "supermarket." We know the choice these people make; their lives, or the lives of meat-providing animals. To harvest his own meat, a good hunter enters the woods and kills a deer with a clean, merciful shot. The deer dies in his own environment, quick and unexpected.
>
> To buy your meat in a store seems so innocent, but have you ever seen or thought how it comes to be wrapped up so neatly in cellophane?
>
> First, cattle live their entire lives penned up in cramped quarters, never allowed to roam freely, bred for one purpose when their time has come. The technique that I have personally seen is to take cattle, line them up side by side with their heads and necks protruding over a low fence, and walk from one end to the other, slitting their throats with either a machete or power saw. Unable to run or move, they are left there until they bleed to death, standing up.

Would you rather die while living happily, or die while leading a miserable life? You tell me which is more "humane."

Does a "growing percentage of the public" have any pity or respect for any of the animals which are butchered and then sold in the store?

Or is it just so conveniently "clean" that a double standard is allowed?

Sincerely,
Timothy McVeigh

When spring arrived, McVeigh took a security assignment working next door to an Amherst women's clinic targeted by hundreds of abortion protesters. Reciting prayers and singing hymns, the protesters charged the lines of police officers surrounding the medical office of Dr. Barnett Slepian. McVeigh guarded property owned by a bank, and worked to keep it clear of protesters. He favored free choice when it came to abortion; yet he also favored the protesters' rights to free speech, and it unsettled him to see government so deeply involved in the issue. To McVeigh, government had no role in the dispute. He saw it strictly as an issue of individual rights.

The protests, which became known as the "Spring of Life" demonstrations, ended after several days with six hundred arrests. Seven years later, Slepian, an outspoken pro-choice physician with four sons of his own, was killed in his kitchen by a sniper's bullet. His alleged killer, a radical activist named James C. Kopp, escaped and seemingly vanished.

McVeigh had other things on his mind, and not least among them was romance. Tumbling back to a routine civilian life might have been easier to handle if a woman had been there to catch him. He spent some time pursuing Andrea Peters, the office worker at Burns who'd helped him with the list of former employees; after his promotion to scheduler at the security firm, he had ample opportunity to talk with her, and in the evening they continued their conversations by phone from their homes, often for hours on end. He sometimes mentioned his mother, Mickey, calling her a "whore" and a "bitch," and blamed her for breaking up the family. "He was so mad at her and he felt bad for his dad," Andrea recalled years later. In sounding hard, McVeigh claims, he was trying to impress Andrea. When McVeigh learned that she was fond of strawberries, he even headed out to Bill's garden and

Bill and Mickey McVeigh at their wedding, August 1965.
(inset) Timothy McVeigh with his older sister, Patty.

RECORD OF ILLNESSES AND INJURIES

- June 1, 1969 - Admitted to Lockport Hosp. with sister Patty. Bacterial germ (ear, throat, stomach ache, diarrhea) Was in for 4 days.

- Oct. 1969 - banged my head into doorway and had 4 stitches over my right eye. Didn't seem to slow my doing on cheek.

- Jan. 19, 1970 - dropped can Took 3 stitches. Very calm and unconcerned about the whole incident.

- March 17, 1970 - fell off top bunk. Right wrist fractured. Dr. Muscato put cast on. Will be on 5 to 6 weeks.

- Feb. 1973 - in hospital 7 days with pneumonia

- Feb. 1974 - Scarlet Fever - home from school 1 week - mild case

- Summer of 1973 - Fell on back of head - 5 1/2 yrs. - took 5 stitches

early playmates

AGE 1½   REMARKS
_____
_____
_____
_____
_____

VORITE GAMES

WARD PLAYMATES
_____
_____
_____
_____

CHARACTER INDICATIONS IN PLAY

Characteristics	2 years	3 years	4 years	5 years	6 years	7 years
Natural						
Friendly	X ☒					
Hostile	X					
Aggressive					X	
Shy						
Fearful	X					
Brave					X	
Indifferent	☒					
Happy						
Serious	X				☒	
Affectionate						
Jealous	☒					
Selfish					☒	
Generous	☒					
Truthful	X					
Imaginative						
Sensitive						
Confident	X ☒					
Wants to lead						
Desires leader						
Easily lead						
Enjoys a crowd	X ☒					
Likes being alone	X					
Alert	X					
Timid					☒	
Self conscious						
Cooperative	X ☒				☒	
Uncooperative						

[35]

Mickey McVeigh kept a baby journal throughout her son's childhood, sometimes writing entries in her son's voice. One page chronicles a series of childhood illnesses and injuries, including several blows to the head. Another records sides of his personality: "confident" and "jealous" at two, "aggressive" and "brave" at six.

Tim McVeigh *(back row, third from right)* with his childhood baseball team. His father, Bill *(back row, left)*, had expectations Tim felt hard-pressed to meet.

McVeigh with his grandfather, Ed McVeigh, the only person he could ever say he loved: high school graduation, 1986.

McVeigh with his sister Jennifer, early '90s: she was among his few close confidants, a status that would later cast a cloud of suspicion over her head.

GNR SPC Timothy McVeigh (sitting on tank) with "battle buddies," October 1990. The back of the photograph identifies him as " Tim 'Jew' McVeigh," which he believes to be a reference to his loan-sharking activities in the Army.

"**B**ad Company," McVeigh's Bradley fighting vehicle.

McVeigh at attention in his dress uniform.

The "Road Warrior": McVeigh's Chevrolet Geo Spectrum, his home on the road.

Carl E. Lebron, Jr., a fellow security guard who became a reluctant sounding board for McVeigh's antigovernment diatribes.

McVeigh (right) with his Army buddy Terry Nichols and Nichols's son, Josh, on a 1992 trip to Niagara Falls. (AP)

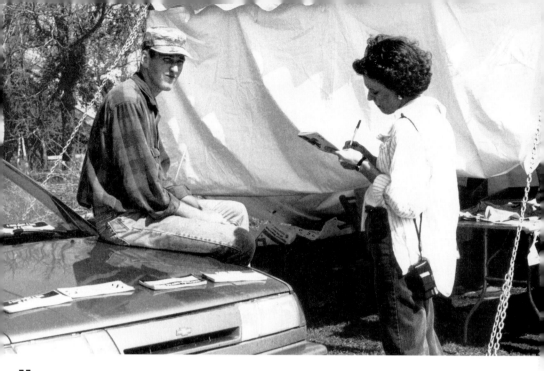

McVeigh being interviewed by a reporter while hawking bumper stickers on his visit to the seige at Waco, March 1993. *(Laurence Merville/Gamma Liaison)*

04-19-95 WED
08:57:05 24

A surveillance camera photograph showing McVeigh's Ryder truck passing the Regency Towers Apartments in Oklahoma City minutes before the Murrah Building was bombed. *(AP/Justice Dept.)*

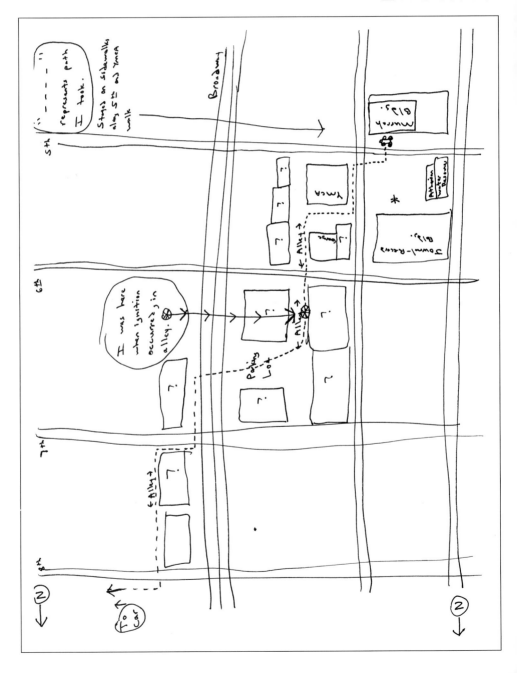

In the fall of 2000, McVeigh sent the authors this hand-drawn map of the route he took on foot after the bombing of the building (*lower right*).

raided the berry patch; the next day Andrea found a bucket of berries beneath her desk. But unlike McVeigh, Andrea was interested only in friendship.

Undaunted, McVeigh drove down to visit his boyhood friend Scott Drzyzga at Geneseo State College, in the rolling hills of the Genesee Valley between Buffalo and Rochester, and try his luck with coeds. On the way, he stopped in at the home of his mother's sister, Jean Zanghi, who lived several miles from the college.

He told her that the military reserve unit he had joined in Tonawanda was disbanding and that he was looking into the possibility of transferring to a "mechanized reserve unit" stationed near her home. Unabashed, he added, "My friend is in a fraternity at Geneseo, and we're going to go to the bars and check out the babes."

Aunt Jean was glad to see her only nephew. He'd always been conscientious, stopping by to spend a few hours with her before he left for the war, lending a hand when she and her family were moving. Now she wished she'd spent more time with her nephew when he was growing up. He had become a man in the blink of an eye.

On May 16, 1992, the day of her daughter's wedding, Aunt Jean briefly saw her nephew for the last time. He had decided to stop by after another visit to Geneseo. The front door of Aunt Jean's home opened up to a living room full of young women dressed in their bridal-party gowns, and McVeigh peeked in nervously. At the center of all the fuss was his cousin Tammy in a wedding dress. Aunt Jean tried to coax him inside, to get him to come along to the wedding. They offered to find him a dress shirt to replace the plaid one he was wearing. He was wearing jeans, but it didn't matter; they simply wanted him to be at the wedding, to join the family in the celebration.

McVeigh felt uncomfortable. He had no use for dress-up affairs. His only words, before hopping back in his car, were "Oh, shit. I'm outta here."

Two weeks after shying away from his cousin's wedding, McVeigh ended the one relationship in his life that had given him glory and satisfaction. He resigned from the Army reserve unit in Tonawanda, three months ahead of its deactivation date. He cited "employment conflict" as his reason for leaving. In addition to his office job as a scheduler at Burns, he often worked long hours of overtime as a guard. Something had to give, and cutting the last vestiges of his connection to the United States government seemed like a good place to start.

McVeigh's disdain for the government was building. With his sister Jennifer he started sharing stories he'd read about the Rockefeller family, and how U.S. currency was once backed by gold until the gold standard had been scuttled in favor of paper money that McVeigh viewed as worthless. On top of that, he said, there was the mountain of spent credit called the national debt. The brother and sister's discussions sprawled in myriad directions, from the Bible to the pyramid and its crowning all-seeing eye on the back of the dollar bill.

McVeigh was reading more antigovernment books and pamphlets, and he shared them with his inquisitive younger sister. He wanted to expand her perspective, though some of the claims in the literature seemed bizarre and inconceivable to Jennifer—including one writer's contention that the government was building massive crematoriums and 130 concentration camps to exterminate individuals who disagreed with federal policies.

The authors of the pamphlets, anticipating skepticism, warned that Americans risked becoming victims of the "it-can't-happen-here syndrome" when it came to government usurping power from the people. Jennifer wasn't sold on everything she read, but just as McVeigh hoped, the literature got her thinking about the government and individual rights. She looked up to her older brother, flattered that he thought enough of her to engage her in political discourse.

McVeigh believed the federal government intended to disarm the American public gradually and take away the right to bear arms under the Second Amendment. In the summer of 1992, he pointed to the events in Ruby Ridge, Idaho, as proof positive that his theory was correct. On August 21, federal agents attempted a raid on the remote hillside cabin of Randy Weaver, a white separatist accused of selling an illegal sawed-off shotgun to a police informant. Agents had tried to pressure Weaver into becoming an informant against a racist group called the Aryan Nations, but Weaver had refused.

A gun battle broke out when federal marshals arrived at the cabin to arrest Weaver. His fourteen-year-old son, Sammy, and U.S. Marshal William F. Degan were killed. The next day, Weaver's wife, Vicki, was fatally shot by an FBI sniper while standing in the doorway with her infant daughter in her arms. The FBI sniper swore he was shooting at Kevin Harris, a Weaver family friend who had fired at Degan. After Vicki Weaver's death, federal agents and marshals laid siege to the cabin for eleven days before Weaver surrendered.

The killings at Ruby Ridge became a rallying cry for militia and survivalist groups, and a wake-up call for millions more Americans who were growing increasingly concerned about the issue of overzealousness by law enforcement. The incident reinforced McVeigh's deepening fears that America was becoming an overtaxed police state. The evidence was all around him—he only had to read the newspaper or turn on the television news to hear more reports about the government cracking down on people, like Weaver, who tried to resist.

Unlike Jennifer, who hung on her brother's every word, Bill McVeigh had little interest in his son's antigovernment views. The American flag proudly flying from a pole in the center of his front lawn left no question where Bill stood: my country, right or wrong. He, too, had honorably served in the military before carving out a comfortable life for himself and his family. He had no complaints about the government; he'd done just fine under the Stars and Stripes.

It was alarming for Bill McVeigh to watch his son turn from a highly successful soldier to a harsh critic of the very government he had served so heroically. Nowadays, whenever Tim saw a newscast detailing some inept government operation, or any example of faltering leadership, he'd shout and throw things at the TV. Bill, who rarely said an unkind word about anyone or anything, did little to reproach his son. "Timmy is strong-willed" was all he could find to say.

Despite McVeigh's outbursts, he respected his father and realized it would serve no purpose to try to convert him to his point of view. Bill McVeigh was from a different era. In his mind, anything less than patriotism was treason. In contrast, his son thought that modern-day leaders were intentionally convoluting the beauty of America and its intended freedoms. The more he dug his nose into history books and militia pamphlets, the more he was convinced he was right.

McVeigh had spent years reading about the Founding Fathers and the American Revolution, and he had become convinced that if George Washington and Thomas Jefferson could climb into a time machine and travel to

America as it approached the year 2000, they would be horrified. He imagined them becoming "physically ill" at what they saw and immediately calling for a "full revolution" against the United States government.

Oddly enough, McVeigh did have one experience during this time that helped him see that not everything about the American government was bad. When a persistent and painful wart kept returning to his toe, he called the Veterans Affairs Medical Center in Buffalo and found out that he qualified for free treatment because he was a veteran earning less than twelve thousand dollars annually. Lacking health insurance, he decided to take advantage of the government benefit. He had already spent eighty dollars of his own money on a Lockport physician, but the laser treatment he received had failed to remove the growth, which had first appeared during the Gulf War.

Each week, while an acidic cream was applied to his wart, he schmoozed the VA doctor. "You get back from people what you feed them," McVeigh would say. After two months of treatment, the wart vanished. The hospital's medical staff also checked him for the mysterious malady known as Gulf War syndrome. But McVeigh exhibited no signs of fatigue, headaches, memory loss, or other symptoms associated with the illness; he was issued a clean bill of health.

Struggling to find his place in the world, McVeigh began breaking ties with the past. He gave up his survivalist dream of someday building a fallout shelter on the wooded land south of Buffalo he had purchased with his high school buddy Dave Darlak, and he and Darlak sold the land in September 1992 to a couple from the Buffalo suburb of Kenmore. The nine thousand they received barely allowed McVeigh and Darlak to break even on their initial investment after adding up the property taxes, but the cash provided McVeigh with a financial cushion as he struggled to regain his emotional footing.

McVeigh had known for months that he would have to find his own apartment. Shifting from room to room, trying to catch some shut-eye in his father's house—it just wasn't working out. He was a grown man who had fought in a war; he needed his own space. Even his sister, who'd graduated from high school in June of 1992 and gotten a job as a waitress, had rented an apartment in Lockport. He owed it to himself to take that final step toward adulthood.

For about $250 a month, McVeigh finally rented a second-floor, one-bedroom apartment in a complex off Dysinger Road in Lockport. Intent on living within the modest means of his minimum-wage job at the guard agency, McVeigh ruled out the luxury of a telephone, which had the added benefit of raising a fire wall between him and work. At last, he would be un-reachable when Burns needed someone in a hurry to work overtime. He had been a dependable worker to a fault, never saying no when asked to pinch-hit, but his reliability had come at a price—sleep deprivation. From now on he was determined to live a normal life, working five days a week, eight hours a shift.

McVeigh knew that it seemed strange to some people that a young man in the 1990s would have no telephone, but to him it was strictly a financial decision. He was usually careful with his money. It astonished him to see other young people he knew spending their cash on luxuries like ski trips to the slopes south of Buffalo. Affluence among young people had always per-plexed McVeigh. While he was busy pulling himself up by the bootstraps, they were slipping on ski boots.

While young people in the fantasy world of TV sitcoms were endlessly pursuing fun, McVeigh was canceling his membership in the National Rifle Association to save twenty dollars. In all honesty, it was twenty bucks he hardly minded trimming. The NRA, as far as he was concerned, was a weak warrior in the fight to save the Second Amendment. He thought the organi-zation should take a much harder line. He considered his own beliefs on the gun-rights issue, by contrast, to be solid, absolutely unshakable.

When McVeigh felt he was burning out in his office job as scheduler at Burns, he transferred back to guard duty, which turned out to be a blessing. He was assigned a post at Calspan, a high-tech research company in the Buf-falo suburb of Cheektowaga. Calspan researchers were always working on projects for the government and the military, and from the moment he set foot on the property, he was intrigued. At every opportunity, McVeigh asked Calspan workers about their work. And when a directive came down in-structing the night watchmen to steer clear of certain portions of the plant, McVeigh took it as a personal invitation to poke around. Unable to contain his curiosity, he prowled the wind and shock tunnels at night, looking in on the latest research. How could he not disobey the directive? For McVeigh, it was like telling a kid not to peek into his parents' closet where the Christmas gifts were hidden.

In one of the Calspan buildings, McVeigh discovered that the federal government was renting out space for a secretive law enforcement project called Operation North Star. The project was housed in an ultra-secure area, with entry by special code. McVeigh had caught a glimpse of some paperwork that led him to believe that the U.S. military, federal marshals, and Drug Enforcement Administration agents were occupying the space.

One night, he noticed an oddly written memo on a desk. It read like an old-fashioned telegram, with the word "STOP" following each sentence of the message. It mentioned the possibility of a two-man submarine penetrating rivers in the United States, but failed to say why. McVeigh wondered whether the government suspected drug dealers of using such subs in sophisticated smuggling operations. (His guesses weren't far off: years later, the government would confirm that it had operated a secret drug-interdiction program from office space at Calspan.)

McVeigh told a fellow guard, Carl E. Lebron, Jr., about the secret memo, explaining that it could not be copied because it was printed on special paper that resisted reproduction. But that wasn't all he and Lebron discussed. In the long, quiet hours of the night, they speculated about the New World Order, a phrase coined by President Bush in 1990 but later used by fringe groups to refer to a consolidation of free governments throughout the world into a single, tyrannical global power. McVeigh expressed anger about the killings at Ruby Ridge; he believed that a cover-up was under way to hide the deeds of trigger-happy federal agents. The discussion even veered into a dissection of McVeigh's favorite TV show, *Star Trek: The Next Generation*. Still a devoted Trekkie, McVeigh saw something of himself in each of the show's characters:

> Picard—the most respected man in Star Fleet, knows all systems, highly skilled diplomat, yet lonely man. Keeps his emotions in check; no quality I dislike or don't understand.
>
> Worf—the consummate warrior. I do consider myself a warrior.
>
> Data—android, so no emotion. Logic rules. He's the Spock equivalent. Access stored memory on command—highly retentive.
>
> LaForge—chief engineer. Just look at the pride he takes in knowing his shit. Engineering section is "his." And he takes

> pride in knowing it like the back of his hand. Highly proficient
> in his field. I absolutely relate to the pride and care he takes in
> the upkeep of his systems.

McVeigh watched the show religiously. To him, the series represented a utopian model for the future.

One day, McVeigh came into the Calspan security office during his day off and handed out some white-supremacist pamphlets. Sometime later, he made an odd observation to Lebron: "It would be easy for two people to steal firearms from a military base."

Lebron's reaction: "Uh-oh."

Sometimes a tremor of rage seemed to cross McVeigh's face when he spouted off to Lebron about the government, and Lebron began to suspect that his co-worker was trying to recruit him for some kind of antigovernment action. It worried Lebron to the point that, a couple of weeks later, he began bringing in a pocket-sized tape recorder to keep a record of some of his conversations with McVeigh.

If McVeigh kept making remarks like that, Lebron figured, he would take the tape to Calspan officials and let them know what kind of man they had guarding their secret projects. All the security workers at Calspan had clearance from the Defense Department. He was worried that McVeigh might try something crazy.

With the recorder running in his pocket, Lebron did attempt to draw McVeigh out, rehashing old subjects. But he could never get him to revisit the theft of guns from a military installation.

Lebron wasn't the only person at Burns Security to notice McVeigh's extreme political views. McVeigh gave Brian Profic, a supervisor, a book on how to avoid paying taxes and a white-supremacist publication called *The White Patriot*. Unlike Lebron, Profic never suspected that McVeigh could be capable of a drastic act. Many people who knew McVeigh were well aware of his strident antigovernment views, but nobody dreamed he would ever put his words into action.

In the latter part of 1992, McVeigh received a visit from his Army pal Terry Nichols. Nichols drove in from Decker, Michigan, with his second wife, Marife, and her infant child, Jason. Josh—Nichols's adolescent son from his first marriage, to Lana Padilla—also made the trip. McVeigh admired Nichols for the great lengths he had gone in pursuing a second marriage. Enlisting the help of a mail-order bride service after leaving the Army, Nichols had traveled to the Philippines in search of a mate. His journey led him to Marife.

Unlucky in love, McVeigh could understand why Nichols traveled so far to find it. McVeigh was beginning to believe American women were sexually shortchanging the opposite sex. For McVeigh, sex was a kind of release, and he grew angry and frustrated when he wasn't getting any. He had come to see American women as "prudish and stingy," but in the Army he had heard tell that some foreign women were cut from more accommodating cloth. McVeigh was certain that Nichols and others like him were onto something big. Why not seek out a willing wife overseas?

Marife impressed McVeigh. At one point, she stayed behind and cleaned his apartment while the men stopped by Bill's house on Sunday afternoon. McVeigh, Nichols, and young Josh found Bill sprawled out on the couch watching football.

Noticing that Marife and her infant son were missing, Bill asked, "Where's Terry's wife?"

"You know what a woman is supposed to do." McVeigh grinned. "She's home cleaning my apartment. She likes to clean."

Watching football proved a much safer pastime for Josh than driving through western New York with his dad's friend Tim. Josh was convinced that he'd narrowly escaped death on a drive to nearby Niagara Falls, when McVeigh recklessly shifted into a lane of oncoming traffic to pass a truck. For his part, McVeigh felt entirely comfortable with the pass: stuck behind a slow-moving tractor-trailer, he had raced up to the rear end of the rig and swung out into the open lane as soon as two oncoming cars had passed; then, in an instant, he pulled past the truck and tucked back into his lane.

McVeigh may not have considered himself a reckless driver, but soon after the Nichols family left, he found himself careening down another perilous path: obsessive gambling. With the Buffalo Bills advancing toward their third straight berth in the Super Bowl, McVeigh began betting heavily on National Football League playoff games. Sports gambling was illegal in New York State, but bookies with organized-crime ties were easy to find.

For McVeigh, a man so cautious with his money that he wouldn't even get a telephone, sports betting provided a roller-coaster thrill. Tossing aside his spartan lifestyle, he let his gambling fever get the best of him. When he lost, he doubled the wager on the next game. When his gambling debts hit five hundred dollars, he convinced himself he could make it back with one really big bet. He called the local bookie in Lockport.

"I want a dime—a thousand bucks—on the Super Bowl for the Bills to win," McVeigh barked. It was his biggest bet so far.

Bill McVeigh was unaware of the thousand-dollar wager, but knew enough to be concerned about his son's betting activities. He called the bookie, a man he knew, and asked him to stop accepting his son's bets. Bill knew that Tim didn't have the money to cover his growing gambling debt, and he felt responsible because he had hooked him up with the bookie. But the bookie told him it was too late—his son's bet had already been placed for the Super Bowl.

On January 31 in Pasadena, California, the Bills got off to a good start, taking an early lead. But the Dallas Cowboys roared back and hammered them 52–17. McVeigh was devastated. Casting about for a way to pay off his debts, he hit upon a plan: he would use a credit card to get a three-thousand-dollar cash advance—and then stiff the credit card company. Banks, he figured, had more than enough cash to absorb the loss.

McVeigh usually prided himself as being honorable in financial matters, but he convinced himself that defrauding a bank was an acceptable solution. "Three thousand dollars is something they just write off," he said. "They don't even think about it." He'd heard about people running up credit card debts of fifty thousand or even one hundred thousand dollars and then using bankruptcy to walk away. *Compared to that,* he thought, *this is no big deal.*

He later realized that his gambling addiction was self-destructive, almost suicidal, a sign that his life had reached rock bottom. He hated his job and was arguing with co-workers. He still felt lost in his old hometown. With no prospects for romance or advancement in his life, for the first time Tim McVeigh started feeling indifferent toward life itself.

He'd tried to embrace the play-by-the-rules life that his father and so many McVeighs before him had lived, but McVeigh knew he could no longer stomach it. He had to make a change, or he'd be suffocated by the repetition of ordinary life. He needed to return to the razor's edge, which he'd known in the Gulf War.

In the days following the Super Bowl, McVeigh finally broke the news to his father: he was leaving New York State. "Taxes are too high," he said.

His growing obsession with the concept of personal freedom had convinced him that he needed to find a place where he could live without heavy government regulation or high taxes. He wanted to live under "God's law, natural law," not the constraints of man's laws. McVeigh had been studying the principle of states' rights. Not every state had property taxes, sales taxes, income taxes; not every state charged tolls on highways like the New York State Thruway. Even more important to him, some states had far less regulation on gun purchases. All this impressed McVeigh, who thought that if his future held only minimum-wage employment, he might as well find a place where his earnings were unyoked from the burden of heavy taxation.

His personal freedom could be expanded, he determined, simply by moving to a state less burdensome than New York. He would set out to find a "free state."

"Where are you going?" Bill asked.

McVeigh had to admit he didn't know.

6

Kindred Spirits

Get your motor runnin'.
Head out on the highway.

—STEPPENWOLF, "BORN TO BE WILD"

I hit the road, and my first stop was Florida.

—TIMOTHY MCVEIGH

In February 1993, two weeks after McVeigh had started his search for a state free of oppressive taxes, a form letter from the Defense Department's finance and accounting office arrived at his father's house. Bill McVeigh read it. A re-examination of his son's service record indicated that Tim had been overpaid $1,058 while he was in the Army. The government demanded full restitution, and if that weren't possible immediately, repayment at a rate of fifty dollars a month.

When McVeigh learned of the letter sent to his father's house, he was enraged. Here he was in Florida, trying to make a new life for himself; his sister Patty's husband had even arranged a construction job for him. The whole idea was to *get away* from government, and now his first bit of news from Pendleton was that the government was hounding him for money. He fired off an angry response to the Defense Department:

> I have received your notice informing me of my debt owed to
> you, as well as your threat of referring me to the Justice De-

partment (Big Brother). In all honesty, I cannot even dream of repaying you the $1,000 which you say I owe. In fact, I can barely afford my monthly rent. Assets? The only thing I own of any value is my car, a 1987 Chevrolet/Geo Spectrum. If you really want the car, go ahead and seize it.

My car is my only way to get to work to support myself. But I guess that's all irrelevant to you. Go ahead, take everything I own; take my dignity. Feel good as you grow fat and rich at my expense; sucking my tax dollars and property, tax dollars which justify your existence and pay your federal salary. Do you get it? By doing your evil job, you put me out of work.

Of course, McVeigh knew full well that the Army had overpaid him; he'd noticed the extra money in his paychecks at the time, but he never reported it. He and other soldiers deserved the extra money, he told himself, considering the sacrifices they had made. He also justified his lack of honesty by reminding himself of all the waste and inefficiency he had witnessed in the military.

He imagined the petty bureaucrat sitting in a government office somewhere whose job it was to send out letters like this to McVeigh and other soldiers. It was another detail added to McVeigh's image of a bloated, greedy government, using its vast powers to bully people—veterans, no less—who were down on their luck.

These guys waste millions every day, McVeigh thought, *and they're coming after me for a thousand bucks. Okay, let the fuckers take my car, I'll go on welfare, bleed the system myself.*

Writing the letter gave him some satisfaction. It allowed him to blow off some steam, to spit back in the face of the federal government. But two weeks after he mailed it, he read about a situation in Waco, Texas, that made him so angry that all the letters in the world would never calm him down.

On February 28, 1993, federal agents raided the Mount Carmel home and church of a religious group known as the Branch Davidians. Seventy-six agents from the Bureau of Alcohol, Tobacco and Firearms arrived beneath covered cattle wagons to execute a search warrant for illegal weapons. A shootout erupted, taking the lives of four agents and injuring dozens more.

Fatalities were higher on the Branch Davidians' side. Six lives lost, and more were wounded, including their strange and charismatic leader, David Koresh.

After the shootout the ATF retreated; Koresh and his followers held their ground inside their home, refusing to come out. The ensuing standoff—like the siege at Randy Weaver's cabin in Idaho—would become a rallying cry for the antigovernment crowd nationwide.

Nobody in America followed the developments any closer than Timothy McVeigh. Day after day, he devoured every article and broadcast account he could find. After a few weeks of following the events from Florida, he couldn't take it any longer. He had to go and see for himself. He loaded up his car with a supply of antigovernment pamphlets and bumper stickers and headed for Waco. He finally came to rest in an area near the site; onlookers and protesters gathered there were selling T-shirts, one woman marching among them carrying a cross.

But McVeigh hadn't come all this way just to sit on the sidelines; he came to see the action firsthand. He began driving, but was stopped at a checkpoint about three miles from Mount Carmel. About six federal agents immediately surrounded his car. Another eight, he noticed, stood off to the side. McVeigh sensed in them what he had felt in the Gulf War—that underlying rush of excitement that comes from taking risks. It was a spectacle he was alarmed to witness on his own soil.

"What are you doing?" one of the agents asked McVeigh.

"I'm turning onto this public road, and I'm going to visit the compound."

"Are you press?"

"No."

"Well, you can't visit it."

"Well, this is a public road."

"Turn around."

As McVeigh reluctantly turned his car around, his mind swung into military mode. The checkpoint resembled a military cluster. The agents were armed to the teeth. They had an Army tent erected, an old military truck for personnel transport, and government cars parked all over the site.

Incredulously, McVeigh watched as the agents gathered in a circle. Apparently convinced that McVeigh posed no real threat, they dropped their alert.

I could take out the whole group of them with one hand grenade, McVeigh thought.

Before leaving Waco, McVeigh agreed to an interview with a student journalist from Southern Methodist University. Michelle Rauch, a senior, had driven to Waco on her spring break in search of a behind-the-headlines story. She noticed McVeigh selling bumper stickers. The slogans left little doubt about his political beliefs: "FEAR THE GOVERNMENT THAT FEARS YOUR GUN," read one. There were others: "POLITICIANS LOVE GUN CONTROL," "A MAN WITH A GUN IS A CITIZEN, A MAN WITHOUT A GUN IS A SUBJECT." And one of McVeigh's favorites: "WHEN GUNS ARE OUTLAWED, I WILL BECOME AN OUTLAW."

Rauch had found her story. McVeigh told her he felt sorry for those on both sides who had been injured or killed, but that in his view the ATF had no reason to be there. The local sheriff, he said, was the proper authority to execute the search warrant.

"It seems the ATF just wants a chance to play with their toys, paid for by government money," said McVeigh, warming to the topic as he sat on the hood of his car. "The government is afraid of the guns people have because they have to have control of the people at all times. Once you take away the guns, you can do anything to the people. You give them an inch and they take a mile.

"I believe we are slowly turning into a socialist government. The government is continually growing bigger and more powerful, and the people need to prepare to defend themselves against government control."

Speaking calmly, McVeigh said ATF agents were merely pawns, acting under government orders. The government thought that it had to spend taxpayer dollars on something, he believed; they saw Waco as an opportunity and seized it. In the process, the government had broken constitutional laws. America's armed forces should not be used against civilians, yet here they were being used against Koresh and his followers. McVeigh also scorned the Brady Firearms Control Bill, and predicted that this standoff was only the beginning. People should watch the government's role here at Waco, he warned, and heed the signs.

On March 30, 1993, Rauch's article appeared in the college newspaper, along with a photo of McVeigh taken by Lauren Aldinger. Those who saw it as just another gun nut spouting off would, in two years, learn differently.

. . .

McVeigh left Waco after a couple of days. The time he'd spent working construction in Florida was hardly enough to lure him back; he had to move on. And so he packed up his car and took off—on an odyssey that would take him to forty of the fifty states within the ensuing twenty-six months.

The gun shows that had fascinated him during his time in the Army would now take a greater hold on his life. He would travel from show to show, selling books and survival items, meeting people who shared his preoccupation with the Second Amendment and the federal government's efforts to crack down on gun ownership. In all, he would attend about eighty gun shows, communing with dealers by day and tuning in Patriot movement talk shows on his shortwave radio by night.

McVeigh found kindred spirits everywhere; the land was teeming with people with antigovernment views, especially in the western states. The farther west he drove, he noticed, the less respect people seemed to have for the federal government—at least until you got to what McVeigh called "The People's Socialist Republic of California." It wasn't hard to trace the reasons for the Patriot movement's western orientation: many of the westerners McVeigh met perceived the federal government as an eastern body with no rightful jurisdiction over their lives. McVeigh could hardly believe his eyes one day as he looked at a map showing federal government land holdings throughout the nation. Black dots designated the sites. The East Coast was relatively clear, but to McVeigh's eyes, the area west of the Rockies was black like a cancer—more black than white.

He thought about some private land he had once considered buying out in Seligman, Arizona. He had checked out the property with his Army buddy Michael Fortier after a 1988 Thanksgiving visit to Fortier's family in Kingman, Arizona, about an hour's drive away. During the Kingman visit, McVeigh had shown Fortier's girlfriend, Lori Hart, who was still in high school, a road atlas with his hand-drawn designations of the most likely places for nuclear attacks. Seligman, McVeigh determined, was in a nuclear-free zone.

McVeigh never got around to buying the land, but he liked what he saw in Kingman. The little desert town of more than twenty-five thousand was one hundred miles southeast of the blazing lights of Las Vegas, yet well off the beaten track. He liked its easygoing ways. The rugged terrain, beyond the town limits, appealed to the survivalist in him.

On the road after leaving Waco, McVeigh headed back to Kingman to renew contact with Fortier. Now out of the Army, Fortier was living in a mobile home with Lori and their daughter, Kayla, born a few weeks earlier, on Valentine's Day. It didn't take long for McVeigh and Fortier to find that they were still on the same philosophical page. United in their opposition to gun control, they agreed that the continuing siege at Waco was all about the government taking guns away from citizens. They shared their concerns about the New World Order, of a United Nations takeover and establishment of a single world government designed to place severe limits on individual freedom. McVeigh even suspected that the overthrow might come from the ranks of U.S. government officials unfaithful to the nation's founding beliefs. Fortier wore his defiance on his sleeve: Outside his mobile home he flew both the Stars and Stripes and the yellow flag, with its image of a coiled snake and the words "DON'T TREAD ON ME," that was raised as the first official American flag by naval hero John Paul Jones.

McVeigh was set up in a spare front bedroom in the Fortier home. Before long he'd become like family, so much so that when Mike and Lori married on July 25, 1994, he was their best man.

In the Army McVeigh had made no secret of his contempt for recreational drugs. But he was growing restless, dissatisfied by daily life, increasingly eager to set his own rules. He wondered what it was that Mike and Lori experienced when they smoked marijuana or crystal methamphetamine. Halfway through his twenties, McVeigh realized that civilian boredom was getting to him.

McVeigh found in Fortier a willing guide for his brief excursion into the drug world. But before sampling pot and speed, McVeigh opened up an encyclopedia to learn more about what he was planning to put into his system. He wanted to make sure he wasn't going to kill himself.

"Could I lose my mind?" McVeigh asked Fortier. "Could I die?"

Nah, Fortier said confidently, you'll be fine.

McVeigh was satisfied. After all, Fortier had been smoking the stuff like crazy and hadn't dropped dead. Still, McVeigh took a final precaution after they bought the drugs.

"You first," McVeigh said. "You know the guy we bought them from."

Marijuana proved a hollow high for McVeigh, but methamphetamine seemed to energize his brain. Soaring on the crystallized speed, McVeigh found himself suddenly recalling obscure high school physics formulas he thought he'd never learned at all. He and Fortier took to gazing at the stars in the black desert sky, trading stoned insights like Wayne and Garth from *Saturday Night Live.*

But it wasn't long before McVeigh began to perceive the downside of drugs. To him, it seemed as if Lori couldn't start her day without speed, and the drug slowly but surely seemed to be taking a toll on Mike's brain. Fortier often appeared washed-out and tuned-out; McVeigh considered his friend an intelligent guy, but all too often Mike Fortier seemed to be cruising through life in a daze. After returning home from his job at a True Value hardware store in Kingman, Fortier slipped into what McVeigh called "wife-listening mode," tuning out whatever was going on around him. At times, McVeigh found himself vying awkwardly with Lori for Mike's depleted attention span.

There was something else about drugs that bothered McVeigh—the money. Why should he shell out ten dollars each time for a high that had once come free on the surf of adrenaline? McVeigh soon realized that he wasn't getting the same high from the Fortiers' regimen of pot and meth; he'd always prided himself on being his own master, and now his experience confirmed the belief he'd held since his teenage years—that only a soft-minded weakling would fall under the spell of drugs.

McVeigh didn't altogether dislike the laid-back desert lifestyle of Kingman. He made himself useful, earning his keep by helping out around Mike and Lori's home. McVeigh washed dishes, took out the garbage, and handled minor household repairs, and Lori welcomed the help; she would jokingly say that she patterned herself after the character Peg Bundy of the TV show *Married . . . With Children. She'd rather buy new dishes than wash the old ones,* McVeigh thought. When a parade of fire ants invaded the Fortiers' kitchen, McVeigh blitzed through a stack of dirty dishes in five minutes; he was glad to see the place clean at last—though in the end the domestic arts were no more thrilling than an evening spent zoning out with Mike Fortier.

In early April 1993, McVeigh headed east to Tulsa, Oklahoma, to visit Wanenmacher's World's Largest Gun and Knife Show. The annual show, much anticipated among gun enthusiasts nationwide, was more than a great place to buy and sell firearms. Here McVeigh would find men and women like himself, eager to trade opinions about the rights of gun owners and the government's perceived conspiracies to abolish them.

He headed for Tulsa at the suggestion of Roger E. Moore, a dealer he'd met at a Fort Lauderdale gun show, shortly after moving away from Pendleton. Moore ran a weapons-supply business he called the American Assault Company. McVeigh was impressed. The fifty-eight-year-old man described his gun-show business as a candy store of exotic ammunition. Moore also went by the name "Bob Miller," he told McVeigh, to discourage thieves who might seek out his home address and rob him.

Moore had a lot to lose. He was a millionaire several times over, he said, after starting and selling five successful boat-building businesses in Florida, and investing his money carefully in stocks and bonds. He lived on a $250,000, ten-acre ranch in Royal, Arkansas. The ranch was secluded, set seven hundred feet back from the road, but Moore was concerned that anybody could walk onto the property. He lived there with his longtime girlfriend and business partner, Karen Anderson, though he was also married to a woman who lived in Florida.

In the winters, Moore would head for Florida while Anderson stayed in Arkansas, tending the animals she and Moore kept at the ranch. The livestock included horses, ducks, cats, and parrots. Moore also owned a collection of eighty to ninety guns, and he kept gold and silver at the Arkansas home because he had his doubts about the country's banking system.

Moore and Anderson traveled to several gun shows a year to display the wares of the American Assault Company. But Moore happened to be alone at the south Florida gun show when he met McVeigh in early 1993. McVeigh wore his sand-colored Desert Storm uniform, Moore later recalled, right down to polished boots; to Moore, he looked ready to march in a military parade. McVeigh, who was operating his own sales table at the gun show, claims he never wore the complete uniform to such shows; afraid he'd be accused of impersonating an active-duty soldier, he says he generally wore only his camouflage Army pants.

McVeigh's sales table at the Florida gun show caught Moore's interest. It was stocked with T-shirts, camouflage pants, canteens, duffel bags, a couple sleeping bags, and copies of *The Turner Diaries.* They struck up a conversation, and Moore was taken with the younger man and his passionate Patriot rhetoric.

Moore later called Karen Anderson and described the encounter with McVeigh. Thinking that Anderson might be able to use some of McVeigh's Army pants around the ranch, Moore asked what size she wore. Before he and McVeigh parted company, Moore told him about the Tulsa gun show in early April. If McVeigh were heading west, Moore advised, he should check it out.

McVeigh was making himself a fixture on the gun-show circuit, and he was in his element. Walking around the big county fair buildings or rented halls where the shows were held, he encountered all kinds of items for sale, from guns to turkey calls to anti-Clinton bumper stickers to Adolf Hitler wall clocks and Hitler Youth posters.

Although he never aligned himself with the stranger elements of the gun culture, McVeigh was always interested in listening. Every new show was a chance to meet new people who shared his views, to pick up on the latest rumors about the government. In the company of gun loyalists, he never felt forced to justify his positions, or to explain how important guns had been in his life.

According to some of the rumors making the rounds, it was only a matter of time before the United Nations and the New World Order put their plan into action, with American gun owners their prime targets. McVeigh thrived on the us-against-them spirit of the gun shows. If the New World Order is coming, the gun owners vowed, we'll be ready for them.

The hard-core members of the gun community shared a perspective and lifestyle that would have seemed alien to most Americans. What the average citizen might consider an excessive number of guns for personal use, for example, seemed perfectly reasonable to them. Consider the number of screwdrivers the average American man keeps in his toolbox, McVeigh would argue. Big, small, mini, micro; standard and Phillips; short-handled and long. It was the same way with guns, McVeigh explained. The survivalist in him felt the need to have the right tool for each potential job—even if the job was killing people.

At the very least, he concluded, five guns were essentials:

- A semiautomatic, magazine-fed rifle for home and self-defense. (To those who might disagree, McVeigh would reply, "Ask those storekeepers in the L.A. riots if this is unreasonable!")
- A bolt-action, hunting/sniper rifle useful for killing large game if the normal food supply were ever interrupted, and for defense against an entrenched marauder.
- A shotgun for fowl hunting.
- A .22-caliber rifle to hone shooting skills and bag small game.
- A pistol for close-in self-defense.

A true survivalist had to stockpile more than food and water, McVeigh believed. If the land were in chaos, he would need his guns to protect his supplies from desperate people who might try to steal them. The goal of a true survivalist was to achieve personal freedom—in other words, total independence from government. Like the Ingalls family in their little house on the prairie, McVeigh wanted to achieve complete independence from the rest of the world. And, in his mind, he couldn't do it without guns. They were, to him, the first tool of freedom.

The Wanenmacher show in Tulsa, in some ways, was the Super Bowl of gun shows. Sponsored since 1955 by the Indian Territory Gun Collectors Association and held in a sprawling eleven-acre building on the Tulsa Fairgrounds, the show calls itself the largest true gun show in the world. Some gun shows allow exhibitors to hawk everything from candy to spas, but Wanenmacher organizers boast that merchandise at their show is "98 percent gun-related."

McVeigh was awestruck when he arrived at the show on the first Friday in April and began scoping out its more than four thousand sales tables. Noticing a woman setting out inventory on the American Assault Company table, he made a point of introducing himself.

"Are you Anderson?"

"Yes, I am."

"I'm Tim McVeigh."

"Oh, nice to meet you."

McVeigh told her how impressed he was with the size of the gun show, and then moved on to take the rest of it in. On Saturday morning he returned and asked Anderson whether she and Moore could spare some table space so that he could set up shop. He had a cot, a sleeping bag, some shirts, and a couple of books for sale. Anderson agreed, clearing off a spot on a card table at the end of their regular display area.

Moore came by, and soon he and McVeigh were discussing the New World Order. You watch, McVeigh said: there'll be a single currency, a single police force—one all-powerful central government for everyone on the planet.

> People need to understand New World Order is a metaphor, not just a paranoid belief. When you look around, it's happening. It means one superpower, which is going to morally lead the world into a new age. People on the other end of the gun see it as one superpower forcing others. You will agree with us or we're going to bomb your ass.

McVeigh even had an idea for a new American flag, one that he felt would correctly reflect the aggressive government stance against gun owners. McVeigh's version of Old Glory would have the phrase "COMPLIANCE OR DEATH" diagonally scrawled in black letters across the stripes of red and white. Such wording, he thought, would tell the world that America's leaders felt that they had the right to interfere with the affairs of sovereign nations. McVeigh's words struck a chord with Moore. Moore had been a very successful businessman, but he, too, was concerned about the way the government was heading.

The Tulsa gun show ended on a Sunday, and as it was wrapping up McVeigh received an invitation. Moore and Anderson wanted to show him their ranch. He was among a select group of people. Only a handful had ever been invited to visit their Arkansas paradise. They could use a strong, young back to help catch up on the chores from winter. He could sleep on the living room couch. Short on cash, and with no particular place to go, McVeigh accepted the offer. He raked leaves, worked in the fields, and helped bag packets of ammunition. In his free time, he read their gun magazines and listened to his shortwave radio. Updated on the latest developments unfolding in Waco, McVeigh told Moore about his visit to the Texas city. He hadn't been able to see much during his trip. Federal agents had cordoned the area off for miles, and it bothered McVeigh that he couldn't get a good look at the actual site of the standoff.

Moore could see how deeply disturbed McVeigh was by the events in Waco. He told McVeigh about his own concerns for security on the ranch and invited his houseguest to offer suggestions on developing a security system. They walked the perimeter of the ten acres, but McVeigh was unable to offer any solutions. Moore was opening up to McVeigh. It was a mistake for which he would later pay dearly.

Bartering was common practice in the survivalist culture, and as Moore and McVeigh became better acquainted they began trading some of their wares. One day, Moore noticed the "WHITE POWER" T-shirt McVeigh had received for joining the Ku Klux Klan back in his Army days.

"Hey, Tim," Moore said, looking at the T-shirt. "I'll take that."

"Okay," McVeigh said, "you want that? Give me two fifty-foot lengths of fuse. And let's say you give me one of them newfangled high-concentration smoke grenades from Canada. And why don't you give me a couple of them flares?"

McVeigh's first visit to the ranch lasted ten days before he decided it was time to shove off. To Moore, their guest seemed antsy, restless. Maybe he and his girlfriend were too easygoing, Moore wondered. Maybe the pace of life on the ranch wasn't fast enough for McVeigh.

But McVeigh loved the place. He called his father and told him how much he enjoyed Moore's rural digs.

"Dad, I've found the best place in the world to live," he enthused. "It's here in Arkansas."

The reality was that Tim McVeigh was a long way from putting down roots, in Arkansas or anywhere else. He got back into his Spectrum and headed back north, toward Michigan.

In mid-April, McVeigh pulled his car into the driveway of the Nichols family farm, just in time for planting season. Terry Nichols was the third of Joyce and Robert Nichols's four children. There were two older brothers, Les and James, and a younger sister, Suzanne. Their parents had divorced in 1974, a year after Terry graduated from Lapeer West High School. Ranked in the upper half of his class, Nichols had dreamed of one day becoming a physician or dentist, but dropped out of Central Michigan University after one semester. His parents' marriage of twenty-five years had ended badly.

The Nichols family farm belonged to Nichols's mother, Joyce. A feisty woman of German and English extraction, Joyce Nichols was a woman given to excess. According to Lapeer police officer Bill Dougherty, she once went wild when he tried to arrest her after a hit-and-run accident in the early 1970s. According to Dougherty, Joyce began throwing beer bottles out the window of her car after he ordered her to pull over by a cornfield. When Dougherty tried to arrest her, she fought with him and refused to allow him to handcuff her. Then, when Dougherty ran to his patrol car to call for backup, Joyce reached into her backseat, came up with a chain saw, and went after the police officer with it.

"She tried to start it, but it had no gas in it," Dougherty recalled.

Joyce denied the allegations, but later pleaded guilty to driving while intoxicated. "I never touched that chain saw. It stayed in the backseat," Joyce later said. "I'm not a violent person."

After her marriage dissolved, Joyce purchased a 160-acre farm in Decker, Michigan, a town of about two hundred located in what's known as the state's geographic "thumb." Her son James moved out to the farm and took care of it. James Nichols believed in organic farming. He avoided using herbicides or pesticides on his crops of corn, navy beans, barley, wheat, and rye. A fiercely independent thinker, Nichols had little trust in the federal government; those who followed it blindly he called "sheeple," not people.

His younger brother, Terry, of course, held similar views. In 1981, after his marriage to Lana Padilla, a real estate agent and twice-divorced mother of two, Nichols took up residence on the farm to begin rearing a family. James Nichols followed his younger brother's romantic footsteps and married Lana's sister, Kelli; in time, each of the two sisters would give birth to sons. Yet the pleasant symmetry of this story soon ended in divorce for both couples. By the end of May 1988, Terry had decided to make what seemed like a last-ditch effort to get his life on track—enlisting in the Army, where he would meet Tim McVeigh.

After receiving his hardship discharge in May 1989, Terry Nichols returned to the farm. United by the common thread of personal failure, Terry and James Nichols took their anger at the system to new heights of defiance. They renounced their citizenship and rejected the law of the land. As far as they were concerned, government lacked the power to issue driver's licenses, mandate child-support payments, or take action on unpaid bank loans.

In one appearance in front of Judge Donald Teeple of the circuit court in nearby Sandusky, Terry Nichols instigated a shouting match when he refused to approach the bench. Nichols stood at the back of the courtroom, questioning the judge's authority. According to his brother, Terry was convinced that if he did not go past the bench, the judge had no jurisdiction over him.

Teeple read a legal statute informing Terry that, if he did not step forward and testify as required in this hearing, he would go to jail.

"I'll give you five minutes to think about it," the judge said.

Nichols agreed to cooperate, to a point. He lowered his voice and came around the rail, as requested.

Chase Manhattan Bank had sued Nichols for refusing to pay his credit card debts, and in 1992 the bank obtained a judgment against him for $18,365.52. Before returning dunning notices to the bank, Nichols had written the words "dishonored with due cause." He later tried to pay off his debt by creating a "Certificate of Credit" and sending that to the bank.

During a hearing on Nichols's dispute with the bank, Judge Teeple wore a look of confusion as he inspected the certificate Nichols had sent the bank.

"Where'd you get this?" Teeple asked.

"Why?" Nichols responded. "You want some?" He went on to explain to the judge that since the bank had given him credit, he had decided to return the favor with this certificate.

Later, in a letter to the bank's lawyers, Nichols posed a question: "How can anyone pay anything with no real true genuine money?"

Nichols described himself as a "non-resident alien, non-foreigner, stranger to the current state of the forum." He insisted that "no average individual can understand the laws, rules, codes and garbage language that all lawyers use." He despised lawyers and was certain that "if all the bloodsucking parasites [lawyers] disappeared, this whole world would be better off. Most lawyers don't even understand or know the law themselves. It boils down to who can throw the most garbage and see what sticks."

According to McVeigh, Terry Nichols intentionally ran up his credit card debt after embracing a common-law movement that believed that banks were fraudulent institutions. Believers in the common-law movement hung their hats on obscure court rulings to exonerate themselves from debt, despite a mountain of case law to the contrary.

Joyce Nichols didn't like hearing that Terry was ignoring his debts. Whatever faults she might have, she insisted that she reared her sons and daughter to pay their bills.

"You better pay up," she told Terry one day. "When you borrow ten dollars, you pay back eleven dollars."

James Nichols also took a turn before Judge Teeple, refusing to pay a hundred-dollar dental bill for his son, Chase, who lived with his ex-wife.

"You've been paying your child support for many years," Teeple said. "Why won't you pay it now?"

James said he didn't want to pay the bill because he didn't want his son to have "poisonous" silver mercury fillings put into his mouth. He also told Teeple that the judge had no jurisdiction over him. Teeple, relatively new on the bench, started poking through his court papers, trying to figure whether there was some legal technicality in the case that kept him from having jurisdiction. He couldn't find a thing.

"Why don't you think I have jurisdiction?" Teeple asked.

James launched into a discussion of what he considered to be his current situation. He fell back on the same language as his brother, declaring himself a non-resident alien, a non-foreigner, and a stranger to the current state of the forum. In other words he was no longer a United States citizen, and thus, in his view, not subject to the power of Teeple's rulings. The judge found his arguments interesting, but he was hardly persuaded. "If that's your position," Teeple said, "there's not much sense in me discussing it further." He sentenced James Nichols to thirty days in jail for contempt of court and refusal to pay child support. After three days in jail, James made a call to his brother, Terry. He hated to give up his battle with the court system, but he badly needed to get back to the farm; there was work to be done. He asked his brother to pay the dental bill so he could get out of jail. Terry handled it, and Teeple released him.

Like his brother, James Nichols contended that U.S. currency was worthless because it was no longer backed by the gold standard. According to his neighbors, James Nichols red-stamped his paper money with the phrase "discharged without prejudice."

McVeigh entered the disenfranchised world of the brothers Nichols with an earnest goal: to expand his survival skills. Hooking up with James and Terry, McVeigh thought, would help him learn how things were done on the farm, help him gain the skills he would need to live self-reliantly and self-sufficiently.

To his great pleasure, McVeigh soon discovered that James Nichols was a gifted mechanic. In his visits to the farm in Decker, McVeigh would make a point of working with James; it was a kind of education he wished his father had been able to offer.

McVeigh was fascinated by all aspects of farm life, from putting up bales of hay and straw to repairing tractors. Occasionally James Nichols would hand him ten dollars for his labor, but for the most part the free lodging and hands-on training were pay enough.

McVeigh's father would come to believe that the Nichols brothers helped put wild ideas into his son's head, but Tim McVeigh didn't need the Nicholses, or anyone else, to put him into a radical frame of mind. He found plenty of people in Michigan farm country who harbored suspicious feelings toward the government, but those people were preaching to the choir when they spoke to McVeigh. He had been to war and back; he was a voracious reader and follower of the news; he had done his homework. His mind was his own, and he did plenty of preaching himself.

McVeigh felt very much at home in the two-story, five-bedroom farmhouse. He thrived in the fresh, open air of Michigan agrarian life. And he admired the Nichols brothers for their resourcefulness. McVeigh gave Terry Nichols credit for going the extra mile—in this case, the extra eight thousand miles—to find a new mate after his divorce, rather than waiting lamely for fate to bring another woman into his life. Nichols had met the former Marife Torres in 1989, when she was barely out of high school; several months later he proposed, and in November 1990 the petite, seventeen-year-old Filipino girl married the Michigan man, almost twice her age.

Like many girls in the Far East, Marife allowed herself to be shopped as a mail-order bride because it could provide a ticket to the golden land of America. After the wedding Nichols returned to the United States for what he thought would be a short separation while he made arrangements for Marife to join him. Weeks turned into months, and Marife, still at her island city home of Cebu, became pregnant with another man's child. But Nichols was willing to overlook the infidelity, and he brought Marife to the United States in 1991. On September 21, 1991, Marife's son Jason was born.

Although she had been plucked from deprivation overseas, life in America wasn't quite what Marife Nichols had expected. She would complain that she felt more like a servant than a wife, waiting obediently on her husband, his brother, and their friend Tim McVeigh. Friendless in a foreign land, Marife would grow jealous of the ever-increasing time Terry spent with McVeigh. Feeding three men and caring for her toddler son was hard work. McVeigh helped out whenever he could, cleaning and sometimes assisting in the cooking.

Like Marife, McVeigh was an outsider in Decker. A child of an outer ring of suburbia in New York State's western corner, McVeigh was now in a much different part of the country, a land of flat, freshly plowed fields as far as the eye could see. There were no fast-food restaurants or strip malls to mar the countryside, just the occasional bar or general store. But McVeigh plunged into the backwater culture, striking up friendships with relative ease.

The Michigan farmers marveled at McVeigh's Gulf War experiences, and he couldn't resist a chance to exploit their gullibility. One day, as he sat with some neighbors around the Nichols kitchen table, McVeigh told them, "I have a computer butt chip in me—from the Gulf War."

Philip G. Morawski, a farmer who lived several miles down the road, took McVeigh at his word. He listened carefully as the ex-soldier explained that the government had injected his buttocks with the computer chip just before heading over to the Gulf. McVeigh complained that his rear end was in terrible pain after receiving the shot.

It was a tall tale that McVeigh had told. A few days before he flew over to the Middle East, McVeigh and other members of his company had indeed been injected in the buttocks with a shot, and it was painful. It hurt so much that a few soldiers passed out during their exercise workouts. Some soldiers began to circulate a rumor that the shot contained some kind of computer chip. McVeigh quickly checked it out with friends in a medical platoon. They told him that it was a massive immune system booster shot, not a microchip, that was causing his fellow soldiers so much pain. Relieved to hear the true story but still amused by the rumor, he joined in spreading it. In Decker, the farmers who heard him tell the story years later failed to pick up on McVeigh's dry sense of humor.

There may have been another reason some of his companions in Decker believed the story—the demon alcohol. Just as he had experimented with drugs in Arizona, McVeigh once again found himself looking to external stimulants for comfort: in the friendly company of local farmers, he began boozing heavily for the first time in his life. Never a beer drinker, he developed a taste for rum and Coke; for a healthier buzz he sometimes chose vodka and orange juice.

It was during this period, too, that McVeigh was first exposed to the practice of creating explosives. Some of the workers on the Nichols farm were experimenting with small homemade bombs. They would combine household chemicals in plastic jugs and try out different ways of detonating them, according to James Nichols. It was something they did more out of boredom and curiosity than anything else, and it would be some time before McVeigh himself would begin experimenting with similar materials. The thought of using a bomb in a terrorist act had not yet crossed his mind.

During his entire time in Decker, though, he was thinking about the standoff at Waco, which was still continuing. Shortly after arriving at the Michigan farm, he told Terry Nichols that he wanted to make another trip down to the site to see whether he could help somehow. Would Nichols join him? "Somebody needs to go down there and do something," McVeigh said. "Selling the bumper stickers didn't help, Terry."

McVeigh wasn't sure what he and Nichols would do if they went down to Waco, but he was overcome with the urge to make a second trip, and Nichols shared the feeling.

Though James Nichols intended to stay behind and tend the farm, he, too, was outraged at the conduct of government agents in the case. He felt that the best way to end the standoff was for Americans to show up en masse at Waco, march onto Mount Carmel, and get between the Davidians and the feds. "Ten thousand people should stand there shouting at the FBI, 'Go home! Go home! Go home!' " he said.

In preparation for the long ride to Texas the following day, McVeigh crawled under his car on the morning of April 19 to change the oil. He and Nichols had decided to take McVeigh's little car, rather than Nichols's pickup, for greater fuel efficiency. His Spectrum—the Road Warrior, he called it—and its turbocharged engine had always been faithful to McVeigh.

McVeigh recalls that he was in the middle of draining the oil, listening to a talk-radio host expounding on the standoff at Waco, when suddenly a voice hollered from the farmhouse. Someone came running outside, screaming, "Tim! Tim! Get in here! It's on fire!"

At first, McVeigh had no idea what the commotion was about. All he could tell from the voice was that something terrible was happening. He slid out from under his car and raced into the farmhouse. There it was, on the Nicholses' old color TV—the Branch Davidian complex, Mount Carmel, in a raging fire.

For ten minutes, McVeigh stood stock-still in the parlor with the Nichols brothers, transfixed by what he was seeing. He stared in silence, his heart racing.

No words would come.

Mount Carmel, the wooden complex where the Branch Davidians worshiped and lived under the rule of David Koresh, was engulfed in flames. Armored vehicles were ramming the walls. In the intense heat, the ropes that tethered the Davidians' Star of David flag to its pole burned away, and the flag drifted into the fire. McVeigh was struck by the symbolism: the Davidians had fallen. Tim McVeigh, who almost never cried, found that tears were streaming down his cheeks.

When federal agents later raised their own flag over the smoldering ruins, McVeigh's anger neared the point of exploding. *People died in that house,* he thought. *How crude and ruthless and coldblooded can these guys be?*

Finally, he snapped out of his stunned silence. "What is this?" he wondered aloud. "What has America become?"

He and the Nichols brothers stayed up late into the night discussing one of the bloodiest events in the history of American law enforcement.

James noticed the flag blowing in the wind and remarked that the feds must have picked a windy day on purpose so the building would catch fire quickly. "It was rigged," he said. "The government wanted it to burn because the government couldn't win. The public sentiment was changing." As they talked, McVeigh's emotions ranged from frustration and anxiety to searing rage. The blaze at the Waco compound, more than any other single event, was a turning point in his life. He no longer had any reason to go to Waco, but now he was beginning to think that something else would have to be done. *Something.*

McVeigh was sure from the beginning that the federal government would do everything in its power to cover up the atrocities committed at Waco. In the days that followed the deadly fire, crucial evidence—including a steel-reinforced front door to the complex—disappeared, while other evidence was moved or destroyed in the federal investigations. The disappearance of the door made it harder to determine the trajectory of bullets, obscuring who had fired first on February 28, the start of the standoff.

The government's use of CS gas, the tear gas McVeigh had been doused with as a soldier, enraged him. The memory of his own experience with the gas made the thought of using it on women and children unbearable to him. To McVeigh, Waco epitomized the arrogance of federal law-enforcement agents in dealing with the public—everything that was wrong with intrusive government. In his mind, it was the ultimate bully attack. And as days and weeks passed without a sufficient explanation for what happened, McVeigh grew more certain that the government—just as it had in Idaho at Randy Weaver's Ruby Ridge cabin—was engaged in a massive whitewash to exonerate the agents who had led the charge.

History, he thought, *certainly was written by the victors.*

It would take six years before the U.S. Justice Department, under pressure from Congress, reopened the Waco investigation. Attorney General Janet Reno would appoint former Senator John C. Danforth of Missouri to independently investigate, as Danforth put it, the "dark questions" of whether the government had been responsible for "bad acts" at Waco—including the deadly fire—and to determine, once and for all, whether there had been a cover-up. For Timothy McVeigh, and for the people of Oklahoma City, all that would come four years too late.

A month after the deaths at Waco, McVeigh was back with the Fortiers in Arizona. His friends noticed that McVeigh's hatred for the government had intensified, taking on a harsh new edge. He warned Mike and Lori that the time had come to take action against the government. McVeigh combed through newspapers and right-wing periodicals, scouring them for new examples of lawless behavior by government agents.

"How does the ATF justify no-knock search warrants?" McVeigh asked. "They think someone is going to flush a gun down the toilet? I read the newspaper diligently every day. At least once a week, you find out about federal agents breaking the law. A Customs agent or FBI agent selling drugs.

CIA selling drugs. Waco and Ruby Ridge were two of hundreds of incidents." To him, it was clear Ruby Ridge and Waco were not isolated cases, but part of a dangerous pattern.

For five months, McVeigh stayed in Kingman, a long stretch in one place for him. For a while, he tried to settle down. He rented a house trailer on the old Route 66, obtained a post office box at the Mail Room in Kingman, and took up his old trade as a security guard. He even considered buying a house and called his father asking for four thousand dollars to get the transaction rolling. Bill sent a money order. When the deal fell through, McVeigh phoned his father again and promised to repay the loan.

Gun shows provided McVeigh with extra income and, along with that, the camaraderie he enjoyed. He was now setting up shop at a gun show every week or two. He was quickly devolving from a disgruntled veteran with some questions about his government into a virulent antigovernment activist.

At one of the shows, a T-shirt caught his eye. On the front side it carried a picture of Abraham Lincoln with the words SIC SEMPER TYRANNIS—THUS EVER TO TYRANTS, and on the back the Liberty Tree, with droplets of blood falling from it. Superimposed over the tree were the words of Thomas Jefferson: THE TREE OF LIBERTY MUST BE REFRESHED FROM TIME TO TIME WITH THE BLOOD OF PATRIOTS AND TYRANTS. At fourteen dollars, the shirt was a bargain.

The Founding Fathers would surely sympathize with his anger for the government, he assured himself. Making the rounds along the gun-show circuit, he made other purchases: another T-shirt, this one bearing a picture of Waco and the words FBI—FEDERAL BUREAU OF INCINERATION; an ATF baseball cap, punctured with two bullet holes. Intrigued by the idea of giving federal agents a scare, McVeigh began selling the hats himself. He also distributed cards printed with the name and address of Lon Horiuchi, the FBI sharpshooter who had killed Vicki Weaver at Ruby Ridge, in the hope that somebody in the Patriot movement would assassinate the sharpshooter and others who took part in Waco and Ruby Ridge.

McVeigh's activism went further. He started selling flares and flare launchers, which he said could be used like rockets. To interested parties, he also passed out cards for Roger Moore of the American Assault Company, who had a replacement supply of special fuse-lit flares. In giving his sales pitch to sell the flares and launchers, which he had built up at the Nichols farm, McVeigh edged closer to openly discussing attacks on the government, even when he knew that one of his customers was an undercover detective.

"What could you use these for?" the undercover detective asked at a Phoenix-area gun show.

"Well, you know those helicopters," McVeigh said. "The ATF bastards . . . you know? These guys are civilian pilots, and they've never seen anything like this in front of them."

"Isn't that illegal?" the customer asked.

"Listen," McVeigh answered with an air of confidence. "Thirty-seven millimeters is legal, as long as there is only one and a quarter ounces of propellant and the barrel is not twisted." McVeigh felt sure he'd thrown the detective for a loop with his answer. He was sure there was nothing illegal about his vague suggestion of shooting flares at an ATF chopper. But he also knew he had given the cop something to think about.

That same spring McVeigh called Terry Nichols to ask him a favor. When he had moved from Pendleton back in February, he'd left many of his possessions at his father's home. Now he wanted Nichols to make the five-hour drive from Michigan to Pendleton to pick up McVeigh's TV set, baseball glove, some cooking utensils, and other items, including a load of empty sandbags that he figured would be a hot item among survivalists at gun shows.

Nichols obliged, heading to western New York with the now-pregnant Marife and her toddler son Jason in the truck beside him. Nichols arrived at Bill's house on a Sunday afternoon; as Marife and Jason stretched their legs in Bill's lush green yard, Bill brought out the boxes. He'd remembered Nichols was a farmer from Michigan; he'd thought they might trade notes on farming and gardening, but their talk was brief.

"I'm going to go golfing, but I'm afraid it's going to rain," Bill said.

"It won't rain. There's dew on the ground, and it never rains when there's dew," Nichols assured Bill.

For some reason, before leaving, Nichols felt compelled to tell Bill McVeigh that his son was in good hands. "Tim's out in Arizona," he said. "He's got Fortier out there."

Fortier? Bill wondered. It was the first time he'd ever heard the name.

The Nichols family piled back into the truck and pulled away, heading back to Michigan with McVeigh's possessions crammed into the back of the truck.

McVeigh showed up one day for a visit at the Fortier home wearing one of the ATF baseball caps with the bullet holes. Fortier had reacted almost as strongly to the bloodshed at Waco as McVeigh and Nichols; he believed that the FBI had started the fire and thus was guilty of manslaughter at the very least, while McVeigh called it outright murder. He had personally returned to Waco to inspect the ruins of Mount Carmel. This time there were no federal agents to chase him away, only a perimeter fence with signs designating the site a NO TRESPASSING, CONTAMINATED ZONE.

In the weeks that followed, McVeigh's hunger for information on the Waco story became all-consuming. He read stories that turned his stomach—assertions that human remains surfaced from time to time on the grounds. He listened to the 911 tape of the Davidians calling the local sheriff for assistance. Later, he watched portions of the videotape made by the Davidians inside their home during the siege; the children he saw in the video appeared to him to be happy and thriving—not abused, as the government had alleged. He heard allegations that Koresh picked young girls to become his wives, committing statutory rape with them; that he considered himself a messiah and gave sermons in front of his entire congregation graphically discussing sexual intercourse. But even if all that did happen, McVeigh fiercely believed that Koresh's followers should not be punished for the wrongs of their leader. And none of them, McVeigh believed—even Koresh at his worst—deserved to be burned, gassed, and killed.

McVeigh was haunted by thoughts of the agony the Davidians must have experienced in their final days. *That was psychological warfare,* he thought. *Bright lights, noise, music, the rumbling of armored vehicles circling like vultures, day and night.* He and Fortier watched a Patriot movement video called *Waco, the Big Lie,* which further convinced McVeigh that the government's sole intention was to destroy the Davidians. And McVeigh soon developed a kind of evangelical zeal to spread the message about Waco, lest the enormity of the government's actions diminish over time. His gun-show inventory expanded to include copies of Waco videos he spliced together detailing the government's actions, and whenever the chance presented itself he handed out pamphlets with titles like "U.S. Government Initiates Open Warfare Against American People," "What Do You Know About the Waco Inferno," and "Waco Shootout Evokes Memory of Warsaw '43." And he took his proselytizing beyond the gun-show context as well. One morning, at the end of his overnight shift as a guard for State Security, a private company, he asked his relief supervisor whether he could show him something.

"Sure," said Gary Steinberger, whose shift overlapped with McVeigh's by about thirty minutes.

McVeigh went out to his car and brought a television and VCR into the guard station.

Steinberger grew concerned. TV sets and anything else that might distract a guard from his duty were prohibited by State Security; the firm even went so far as to ban discussions on political and religious beliefs between employees at a work site. A week earlier, McVeigh had asked whether he could bring in a TV, and Steinberger had informed him of the policy. Now McVeigh was in direct violation.

"Watch this," McVeigh said.

"This time, and only this time," Steinberger said.

McVeigh slipped the tape into the VCR. Steinberger watched federal agents driving armored vehicles at the Branch Davidians' home in Waco. There was no mistaking that the tape, which lasted about twenty minutes, cast the government in a negative light.

When it was finished, McVeigh asked what Steinberger thought.

"It was an interesting tape," Steinberger said, "but it really didn't prove anything to me either way."

McVeigh asked Steinberger whether he could give him some printed material.

"Sure," the supervisor said.

He produced a three-ring binder and removed a pamphlet from it. The title of the material was "United States Government or Nazi Germany?" Highlighted portions of the pamphlet drew parallels between the American government and Hitler's dictatorship.

McVeigh used every avenue he could think of to publicize his views. He changed the greeting on his answering machine every couple of weeks, often quoting snippets from Patrick Henry: "I have but one lamp by which my feet are guided, and that is the lamp of history," callers heard McVeigh intone when he wasn't available to take a call. "There is no way of judging the future but by the past." "Give me liberty or give me death."

As the Fourth of July fireworks celebration approached in Kingman, McVeigh and Fortier discussed the possibility of forming a militia to prepare for battle against the New World Order, which they thought had been previewed at Waco. They would try to recruit militia members by leafleting during the fireworks display. *What better time than Independence Day to seek out a couple more comrades, people of the same philosophy,* McVeigh thought.

McVeigh drove to Las Vegas, rented a computer at a Kinko's, and went to work typing up eight pages of random quotes on subjects ranging from gun control to taxation. When he was done organizing them by subject, he printed up one hundred sets. McVeigh would give his future militia members something to think about.

Driving through the desert on his way back to Kingman, he noticed a family stranded in a car with a flat tire. McVeigh pulled over. He sized up the husband: he was a suburbanite, McVeigh could see, unaccustomed to rugged country. The man told McVeigh that he and his family lived in Las Vegas. Seeing the wife and two little children, a boy and a girl, broiling inside the car, McVeigh set out to fix the flat, but the spare in the trunk was flat, too. He considered putting his spare on the disabled car, but it wasn't the right size.

"I could take you and your family into Kingman," McVeigh suggested to the father. The family was headed to Phoenix, but the father thought that it was probably a good idea to turn around and head back home to Las Vegas, which was closer than Phoenix. Since McVeigh estimated Vegas was only eighty miles away, he volunteered to take the family home, an offer the family accepted gladly.

The family squeezed into McVeigh's little Road Warrior, and he wheeled across the highway's sandy median, even though there was no U-turn crossing. The mother, seated in the back with the children, gasped. McVeigh grinned to himself. *Typical suburbanite,* he thought. *Unaccustomed to doing anything out of the ordinary.*

McVeigh's good deed nearly soured as they reached the home stretch on a highway just north of Vegas, when a police officer pulled him over for driving 62 mph in a 55 zone.

As the officer walked up to his car, McVeigh discreetly slipped his handgun beneath his seat. The officer ordered McVeigh out of the car.

"What's going on?" the officer asked.

McVeigh explained how he had picked the family up in the desert and was giving them a ride home. The policeman was around his age, he noticed, and sported a military-style brush cut similar to his own. McVeigh tried to make a connection. "Listen, dude, let's be real," McVeigh said. "You pulled me over because I've got the New York license plates. That's no problem. I understand you have to check."

The officer gave McVeigh a look that McVeigh interpreted as a nod of agreement. Satisfied that McVeigh wasn't up to anything illegal, the officer sent him on his way without a ticket.

At the family's house in Las Vegas, the father offered McVeigh cash for ferrying them home.

"Listen, man, I did this as a courtesy," McVeigh said.

The man insisted that he wanted to compensate McVeigh for his kindness, and McVeigh finally consented. "I'm in a tight situation right now," he said, "so I can't say no to your money."

The father slipped a fifty-dollar bill into McVeigh's hand. McVeigh let out a little whoop of glee; he hadn't expected that much generosity.

There was another unexpected bonus. On the way to Vegas, McVeigh had told the man and the woman he had just been there, putting together leaflets describing how the government was taking away people's rights. As McVeigh was taking their flat spare tire from his trunk, the father asked for a copy of the literature. McVeigh gladly obliged: it was another chance to get his message across.

Back in Kingman, McVeigh never did get around to leafleting the Fourth of July fireworks show. He wound up handing out the leaflets at gun shows instead. And McVeigh's wanderlust would take him far beyond the show circuit in the next few months, as he continued his search for kindred spirits.

McVeigh drove to the wilds of southern Montana to look into a church near Yellowstone National Park that was gaining attention as a quasi-survivalist group. He was impressed with its efforts to stockpile food and munitions, and the people certainly seemed pleasant. But their New Age religious ways failed to trip his trigger.

In Kingman, McVeigh paid a visit to the local Seventh-Day Adventist Church, but he found that the service bored him as much as the Catholic Masses of his childhood. McVeigh had never been inclined to criticize people for their religious views, but he concluded that organized religion wasn't really for him. He believed that the universe was guided by natural law, energized by some universal higher power that showed each person right from wrong if they paid attention to what was going on inside them.

"Science," he would tell friends, "is my religion."

McVeigh stopped in at the *Soldier of Fortune* convention in Las Vegas about the third week of September. He ran into Roger Moore and Karen Anderson and agreed to help out at their sales table. Moore and Anderson had spent part of the summer visiting military bases, searching for evidence that foreign military equipment was being stockpiled in the United States for the New World Order. When they found nothing, their interest waned. Until soldiers of the New World Order were knocking at her door, Anderson said, she didn't want to make a big deal about it.

As they discussed the events at Waco, Moore recalled later, he noticed how pronounced McVeigh's anger on the subject had become. His blue eyes were "bright and flashing" when he discussed the deadly siege, according to Moore—who would feel it even more directly when he ran up against McVeigh's dark side on the convention floor soon thereafter.

Moore had explained that the *Soldier of Fortune* convention was a non-political gun show, and he strictly adhered to that policy. Even the word "patriot," while not banned from the convention floor or the sales tables, was a loaded term. Moore had just finished talking with a man who he noticed was wearing a police badge on his belt. The badge was partly obscured by his jacket, but Moore noticed it. As the man walked away, McVeigh followed him, grabbed him by the arm, and started talking about Waco. When he returned to Moore's table, McVeigh announced, "I'm going to leave for a while and go get lunch." Two hours later, he returned from an all-you-can-eat buffet at a nearby casino.

Moore exploded.

"You don't ever leave the table for two hours!" he bellowed. "You didn't tell me you were going to be gone for two hours."

McVeigh looked around. Feeling as if everyone was drawn to the commotion and staring at them, he focused back on Moore. *Who the fuck is this guy?* McVeigh thought. *I'm just visiting. I volunteered to give him a little help behind the table. I left at a slow time when he didn't need me. He's not paying me. I'm not his employee, and here he is screaming at me.*

As Moore laid into McVeigh, it became clear that it was McVeigh's provocation of the police officer that had really set him off. The show's organizers were strict about their nonpolitical ground rules, Moore was afraid that McVeigh would get him kicked out of the convention and barred from returning.

McVeigh did not take kindly to the admonishment. He got into Moore's face like an Army sergeant. As their squabble escalated, an official of the gun show came over and asked them to leave the booth. Moore and McVeigh walked to a refreshment stand. In time they cooled off, but that night, as they were preparing to return to the motel room, Moore informed McVeigh he was not welcome there. To McVeigh, the signs were clear: Moore was nothing but a profiteer who placed making money well ahead of the interests of the Patriot movement and its disciples.

McVeigh had once again pulled up stakes in Kingman, Arizona, to seek out the elusive state where a man could be truly free. He bounced from one gun show to the next, from one state to the next; paradise could not be found. The state of the country deeply troubled him. For most of his twenty-five years, McVeigh had seemed easygoing and confident to those who knew him. But on October 20, 1993, he revealed a dark and brooding side in a letter to his sister Jennifer. He desperately wanted someone in his family to understand the depth of his convictions, and the despair that accompanied them. He had tried to tell Bill McVeigh how he felt about Waco, but his straitlaced dad wasn't interested; "Tim, why are you always focusing on Waco?" was all he could think to say.

McVeigh bore no anger at his father; he recognized that his father was from a different generation—one that, in his opinion, blindly supported the American government. And even if he and his father were politically estranged, that was no reason not to remain on good terms.

But now, in this letter to Jennifer, McVeigh was compelled to reveal a struggling side of himself. He described his suicidal state of mind when he had gone to his grandfather's home shortly after his discharge from the Army.

"He never knew why, but one day, I showed up at his door, freezing outside, in only sweatpants and in total breakdown," McVeigh wrote. "Gramps, I'm sure, never told anyone about that day, and I respect him greatly for that, as I spent an hour upstairs 'losing it.' It was almost suicide at that point, but rage, but denial, but acceptance . . . all these feelings were battling for control."

He wrote that he needed to "tell it all" to Jennifer about his "lawless behavior and attitude." He had "an urgent need for someone in the family to understand me." He implored her to share the letter with no one, since it could "endanger my life." The letter rambled, but there could be no doubt the person writing the words was distraught and disillusioned—so much so that he would conjure up a fantastic scenario to justify his outrage. McVeigh wrote:

> Why would Tim (characteristically non-drinker), super successful in the Army (private to sergeant in 2 years) (Top Gun) (Bronze Star) (accepted into Special Forces), all of a sudden come home, party HARD, and, just like that, announce he was not only disillusioned by SF (special forces), but was, in fact, leaving the service?
>
> Now here's what led to my current life: It all revolves around my arrival at Ft. Bragg for Special Forces. We all took intelligence, psychological, adeptness, and a whole battery of other tests. (Out of a group of 400.) One day in formation, ten Social Security numbers were called out (no names) and told to leave formation. Mine was one.
>
> The 10 of us were told that out of the select group of 400, we had scored highest on certain tests. We had been selected because of our intelligence, physical make-up (165 lbs. 6 ft. being "ultimate warrior [sic]" type—I was only slightly off—160 lbs. 6' 1½, and physical abilities. We were to feel special, part of a hand-picked group).
>
> We were all asked to "volunteer" (talk about peer pressure!) to do some "work for the government on the domestic, as well as international, front." What I learned next, both from the briefings, and from the questions and private talks included:
>
> 1) We would be helping the CIA fly drugs into the U.S. to fund many covert operations.

2) Military "consultants" were to work hand-in-hand w/civilian police agencies to "quiet" anyone whom we deemed a "security risk." (We would be gov't-paid assassins!)

3) Many other details—to verify these last two, see the enclosed article, or watch, again the movie "Lethal Weapon."

It also gives you new insight on things like WACO, etc. they were murdered by hit men.

It was all a fairy tale, but the impressionable nineteen-year-old believed what her brother wrote. She was certain that something terrible had happened in the military to change her brother from a spit-and-polish soldier to the broken shell he described in his letter. "If anyone was career military, it was Tim," she said. "He loved it. He was top of this, top of that." Somehow, she figured, someone in the military had deceived her brother, and when he learned the truth it had changed him forever.

McVeigh has since explained that the letter was his way of introducing Jennifer to his mind-set at the time; he defends the fabricated story about Special Forces corruption as something that seemed well within the realm of possibility (though it's also clear that disappointment over McVeigh's own failure in trying out for Special Forces may have injected a certain zeal into his allegations). Based on news reports he had heard about federal corruption, he'd become convinced that the government was involved in drug-running, and the story helped illustrate for his sister the depth of his distrust.

One autumn Sunday afternoon not long thereafter, McVeigh arrived at his father's home while Bill was watching football. He still owed his father the four thousand dollars he had borrowed in his unsuccessful attempt to buy a house, and now he paid him back in hundred-dollar bills.

"Dad, I didn't feel safe sending this in the mail."

After an hour's visit McVeigh drove off, headed back to Michigan for another stay with Terry Nichols.

•   •   •

About a month after his melodramatic letter to his sister, McVeigh found himself confronting true tragedy in his own midst. He was staying with Terry and Marife Nichols on the morning of November 22, 1993, when he was awakened by a scream. A moment later, Marife burst into the nearby bedroom where McVeigh was sleeping. Her voice was so frantic that McVeigh leaped out of bed buck naked.

"What's wrong?" McVeigh asked.

"Jason! It's Jason!"

As McVeigh threw on a pair of pants, Marife raced into Jason's bedroom and carried her son's body to McVeigh's doorway. The toddler had suffocated with a plastic bag taken from inside a banana box. The box had been left in Jason's room, and the boy had apparently climbed out of his crib in the middle of the night and somehow gotten his head tangled inside the plastic bag.

Drawing immediately on his Emergency Medical Services training, McVeigh knelt down and placed a hand on Jason's neck to check for a pulse. Nothing. The boy's skin was cold and clammy. *He's been out too long; he's cold,* McVeigh thought. *A body maintains heat for a while, and he feels like room temperature.*

McVeigh tried to get a pulse on the wrist. Not a trace. He tilted the boy's head sideways and put his ear above Jason's mouth. Not even the faintest breath. He lifted up Jason's shirt, and that's when he knew for sure. He had hoped to see the rise and fall of his chest, but it was motionless. Jason must have been dead for several hours. McVeigh realized that it was futile to try and resuscitate the boy—even if he could, the boy could not have escaped without severe brain damage—but Marife's frantic look told him he had no choice.

McVeigh began one-man CPR. "Marife," he yelled. "Go get Terry and call 911."

Marife ran downstairs. An instant later Nichols was at McVeigh's side, and they began two-man CPR. After a couple of compressions, McVeigh said, "Terry, take over alone. I'm going to go get my car. This kid's got to go to the hospital."

McVeigh realized an ambulance would take fifteen minutes to get to the house and another fifteen to get to the hospital. He knew his little car could get to the hospital in ten minutes at most. He pulled up to the front door of the farmhouse. Nichols had carried Jason downstairs and placed the boy on the parlor floor—on almost the exact spot, it occurred to McVeigh later, where he had stood watching television the day of the deadly fire at Waco.

Nichols was trying to perform CPR with one hand and trying to hold the telephone in the other, while talking to the 911 operator. McVeigh took the phone.

"The ambulance is on the way," the operator told him. "Wait for the ambulance, wait for the ambulance."

McVeigh thought it was a mistake, but the operator had already persuaded Nichols. McVeigh told Nichols he could sit in the backseat of the car doing CPR while McVeigh drove, but Nichols wasn't budging, and eventually McVeigh relented; it wasn't his call to make.

Marife reached sheer hysteria.

"He's not breathing, Terry!" she screamed. "He's not breathing!"

In between breaths, Nichols looked up. "Marife," he said, "we're doing that for him." McVeigh started counting breaths out loud, but nothing would calm the bereaved mother. McVeigh set down the phone. He lifted Marife off the floor and carried her upstairs. "Marife," McVeigh said, "you stay in your room until you calm down, and you don't come down until then."

At last, the ambulance arrived. McVeigh offered Terry and Marife his car to follow it to the hospital, since it was already warmed up. "Take a few minutes. Get what you need, because you'll be at the hospital all day," he advised.

From the hospital, Nichols called the farmhouse and informed McVeigh that his car had died just short of the hospital, though he'd been able to coast into the parking lot. The little turbocharged car had still beaten the ambulance to the hospital.

As for Jason, there was no word on his condition.

McVeigh held down the fort at the farmhouse, fielding calls from relatives who had been alerted by neighbors. McVeigh was amazed at how quickly the community mobilized after hearing the ambulance call over the police scanner. A number of people arrived with food. The gesture left a lasting impression on McVeigh, who couldn't imagine such a thing happening in some of the snobbier suburbs back at home. *In this community the people are bringing their entire Crock-Pots and good ceramic dishes,* he thought. *These are good people.*

When James Nichols arrived home, McVeigh updated him and then headed off to the hospital, where he tried to comfort Marife. Marife seemed to listen for an instant before fading away. McVeigh sensed it was useless even to try, especially when the doctor entered the waiting room.

"I'm sorry," the physician said, "he's gone."

"What do you mean?" Marife cried out. "What do you mean? I want to see him!"

Irv Wilt, Nichols's stepfather, had arrived. After the emotional roller coaster they'd just been on with Marife, McVeigh found the older man's composure a relief. A Detroit cop for twenty years, Wilt was able to hold back his emotions and take control for the family, offering to handle the funeral arrangements in their stead.

At the wake, the coffin was open.

"Marife wants to bury him with a Barney doll," Nichols told McVeigh.

Nichols, whom McVeigh described as frugal, had never given in to Jason's pleas for a Barney doll in life, but now things had changed. Jason was buried with a brand-new Barney doll on one side of him, and on the other a toy truck.

Only four pallbearers were needed to carry the little casket. They were McVeigh, farmhand Kevin Nicholas, Nicholas's father, and Terry's other brother, Les. McVeigh was impressed by the gentle nature of Les Nichols, a man whose body had been badly scarred in a fiery accident in the early 1970s.

A few days after Jason was laid to rest, the Nichols family invited Marife's midwife over to the farmhouse. Nichols and McVeigh thought the midwife might be able to console Marife, who was racked with grief. The midwife had delivered Terry and Marife's daughter Nicole on August 1, 1993.

From another room McVeigh overheard the distraught Marife telling the midwife that she suspected McVeigh or Terry might have had a part in Jason's death. According to McVeigh, the midwife tried to calm Marife, dismissing her suspicions and counseling her to forget them.

A couple of days later, after speaking on the phone with her family in the Philippines, Marife said she wanted her son's body exhumed. A relative had told her that examination of the child's fingernails would determine if a person had been murdered or died naturally. McVeigh and Nichols told her the idea was absurd, and eventually Marife let go of the idea that either he or her husband had harmed Jason.

An investigation by local authorities eventually concluded that Jason Torres Nichols's death was accidental. But an investigator had taken a brief interest in McVeigh when he discovered that the guest at the Nicholses' farmhouse had used two different names. He had identified himself to authorities as Tim Tuttle, the alias he used at gun shows. But later, at the hospital, he called himself Tim McVeigh.

Who was he?

McVeigh, who cooperated with the investigation, explained that many people who sold items at gun shows used a different name for business. He had taken the Tuttle name from Tuttle Creek Dam, he said, a place he had visited during his Army days at Fort Riley. The explanation satisfied the investigator, but left an interesting question mark in an incident that otherwise reflected well on McVeigh.

After Jason's death, Terry and Marife Nichols went through with their plans to move west to Las Vegas for a fresh start. Lana Padilla, Nichols's first wife, was already living there with their son, Josh. McVeigh called Fortier and told him of Jason's death, and to let him know that Terry and Marife might be stopping in Kingman on their way to Las Vegas. Not long after that, they arrived in the Arizona town. During their visit Terry told Mike how he hoped to find employment as a carpenter in Las Vegas; Lori and Marife passed the hourlong visit discussing their infant daughters.

On Christmas Eve 1993, McVeigh again turned to his only confidant among his relatives. He told Jennifer that he had come to consider himself an outlaw, and that if she wanted a clear-eyed perspective on America she might have to reconsider her definitions of "good" and "bad." It was important, he said, for her to know that the government could no longer be thought of as the defender of virtue. "In the past, you would see the news and see a bank robbery and judge him a 'criminal,' " McVeigh told her. "The Federal Reserve and the banks are the real criminals, so where is the crime in getting even? I guess if I reflect, it's sort of a Robin Hood thing, and our government is the evil king."

Jennifer had come to accept her brother's secretive ways. She understood why his political views were becoming progressively more extreme. She could see how some of the things he would say could shock people. But she loved her brother.

. . .

By February 1994, McVeigh was ready for another move. He was no longer content spending time on the Nichols farm. He called Fortier at Kingman's True Value Hardware store, where he was the bookkeeper. Could Fortier find him a job there? Sure, Fortier said, he could work in the lumberyard behind the store. McVeigh accepted.

McVeigh stayed in his old room at Mike and Lori's for a week before renting a small house in Golden Valley, a few miles outside Kingman. The rough cut of the precast brick exterior gave the house a sturdy, secure look, while the beamed ceilings inside reminded McVeigh of a log cabin. He felt at home there—enough so that he felt comfortable inviting Mike and Lori over for dinner. But McVeigh wasn't cooking that night. Terry Nichols was.

With his wife and daughter temporarily back to the Philippines, where Marife was pursuing an education in physical therapy, Nichols decided to hang out with McVeigh. Nichols enjoyed cooking, especially baking wheat bread, and McVeigh was content to let him earn his keep by helping with KP duty, just as McVeigh had helped out back at the farm in Michigan. After two weeks, though, Nichols took off; Las Vegas hadn't worked out for him, and he was looking for yet another new start.

McVeigh and Fortier resumed their antigovernment dialogue, focusing more than ever on the New World Order. McVeigh had heard rumors of a big buildup of military hardware at the local National Guard armory. It sounded like something worth investigating. The friends sneaked into the armory one evening, but all they really came away with were a few pioneer tools—an ax, a pick, and a shovel—that they stole from the grounds. McVeigh covered up the theft by painting the green military tools a sandy brown. It was the latest in a series of petty thefts—failing to report overpayments in his Army paychecks, skipping out on credit card bills run up from gambling debts—that ran counter to McVeigh's usual code of conduct, suggesting that his recently declared "outlaw" status was becoming more than just a political position.

That spring of 1994, a more serious accusation of theft hit home for McVeigh. McVeigh had made an attempt to patch things up with Roger Moore, paying another visit to the Moore ranch in Arkansas, but the visit ended on a nasty note when Moore confronted McVeigh with an unexpected charge. "I'm really not happy about you stealing my flare launcher design," Moore complained. Karen Anderson, who was in the living room working on some ammunition, witnessed the confrontation, and she could see how angry McVeigh became. "He just never said anything. He set his jaw and sat down and picked up a magazine and started reading," she said. Later that same day McVeigh left, never to return.

Fortier was seeing some unpleasant changes in his friend. McVeigh's house in Golden Valley was increasingly taking on the air of a bunker. In each corner of the house were loaded rifles. In the backyard was what McVeigh described as a bullet berm, a pile of scrap lumber fifteen feet long and four feet high, which he'd taken from True Value. The wall of wood would provide a shield if the feds ever started shooting, McVeigh explained. Fortier realized that McVeigh believed the New World Order might actually target him personally.

Still a regular on the gun-show circuit, McVeigh had been picking up bad vibes. There were persistent rumors about a huge series of impending federal raids on the homes of gun owners. McVeigh was determined to protect himself. True, he also had a more practical reason for building the berm so close to his little Arizona house—it gave him easy access to firewood for his wood-burning stove. But Fortier knew his real reason: Tim McVeigh was resolved to be prepared for a Waco standoff at his doorstep.

It was during this period, too, that McVeigh first began making and exploding his own small bombs. Unlike the ones brewed with chemicals in a plastic jug at the Nichols farm, what he built was a small pipe bomb. Mike and Lori arrived one afternoon in May just as he was completing it. They headed to a mountain pass and hiked a couple miles into the hills before McVeigh tucked the bomb, packed with black powder, beneath a three-foot-round bolder. Mike and Lori ran hundreds of feet away for cover before shouting, "Okay, we're ready." Amused by their fear, McVeigh lit the fuse. The bomb belched a cloud of smoke and split the pipe down the middle; the rock survived with barely a scratch. For an otherwise bored and restless young man the experiment was just a cheap thrill, a way to pass the time. People did that kind of thing out in the desert.

.   .   .

McVeigh's time with his friends hit a snag when a telephone call from his father summoned him home. His grandfather had fallen ill; he had been taken to Lockport Memorial Hospital. Surgery to repair his stomach, damaged by years of taking insulin shots, had failed. "If you can come home, I'll pay your airfare," Bill offered. "You should really see your grandfather." McVeigh grabbed some of his videotapes and jumped in his Road Warrior. He raced to Las Vegas, where a round-trip airline ticket to Buffalo awaited him.

Ever since his breakdown at Ed McVeigh's house, Tim had wanted to find a way to put his grandfather at ease. Now, at last, the opportunity to explain his behavior seemed within his grasp.

The visit itself proved anticlimatic. McVeigh had been hoping for a long, deep discussion with his grandfather, but Ed had a roommate, which made for an awkward situation. There was no way McVeigh could open up with a stranger lying within earshot.

He tried to salvage the visit, producing a video from Desert Storm detailing the role his unit had played in the war. If he couldn't bare his soul to his beloved grandfather, he certainly could try to make him proud of his grandson. But there was no VCR in Ed's room, indeed none available to patients at all. Just seeing his grandfather would have to be satisfaction enough.

Back at Bill McVeigh's Campbell Boulevard home, McVeigh tried to show his father another video, this one about Waco. But Bill refused to watch. He wasn't interested.

Some time later, after returning to Kingman, McVeigh took measures to distance himself from another former confidant who wouldn't share his interests. For years, he had stayed in contact with Steve Hodge, his good friend from Meyer Road in Pendleton, but now they had hit a philosophical impasse over McVeigh's hatred of the federal government. McVeigh no longer had use for a friend like that, and in July 1994 he put all his rage down on paper, firing off a twenty-three-page farewell letter to his boyhood friend. McVeigh proclaimed his devotion to the Declaration of Independence, explaining in detail what each section meant to him. He also described his impressions of Waco, and of what he saw as the government's efforts to steal personal freedoms. "Those who betray or subvert the Constitution are guilty of sedition and/or treason, are domestic enemies and should and will be punished accordingly," McVeigh declared.

It also stands to reason that anyone who sympathizes with the enemy or gives aid or comfort to said enemy is likewise guilty. I have sworn to uphold and defend the Constitution against all enemies, foreign or domestic, and I will. And I will because not only did I swear to, but I believe in what it stands for in every bit of my heart, soul and being.

I know in my heart that I am right in my struggle, Steve. I have come to peace with myself, my God and my cause. Blood will flow in the streets, Steve. Good vs. Evil. Free Men vs. Socialist Wannabe Slaves. Pray it is not your blood, my friend.

Their friendship was over. Later, when Hodge's sister, Vicki, made an effort to patch up the friendship, McVeigh remained firm. He wanted nothing to do with Steve Hodge, he told her. He was traveling on a different road.

By now McVeigh felt no compunction about advertising his increasingly apocalyptic worldview on his chest, however incongruous the venue. A couple of weeks after breaking off his friendship with Hodge, he attended a birthday party for a three-year-old child who was the daughter of Lori Fortier's best friend, Norma Koalska. McVeigh wore his Liberty Tree T-shirt, with Jefferson's quote: THE TREE OF LIBERTY MUST BE REFRESHED FROM TIME TO TIME WITH THE BLOOD OF PATRIOTS AND TYRANTS. He saw nothing unusual about wearing it to a child's birthday party, he would later say; after all, everyone else was in T-shirts and jeans.

Mike and Lori were married on July 25, 1994, at the Treasure Island Hotel in Las Vegas, with McVeigh standing at Mike's side as his best man. The maid of honor was Norma Koalska. The newlyweds headed west to California for a week of honeymooning, while McVeigh returned to Kingman to watch their mobile home and two pet cats. It wasn't difficult for McVeigh to come up with a wedding present. With the help of Lori's mom, he set to work cleaning the house, figuring it hadn't had a thorough cleaning in years.

A few days after the newlyweds returned, McVeigh left to visit Terry Nichols, who had moved to central Kansas to work as a ranch hand at the Hayhook spread in the town of Durham.

On his way to Nichols's new digs, McVeigh made a couple of side trips; he thought nothing of taking a detour of five hundred miles or more to visit a site that interested him. And his first stop was at a place that had taken on legendary status in more than one fringe community in American culture: the mysterious Area 51 military installation in Roswell, New Mexico. McVeigh had heard the many rumors about the site—that the military tested exotic aircraft, possibly even UFOs, at the remote outpost; that a UFO had once crashed at the site, and alien life forms had been found inside, but the incident had been kept secret. But it was more than just curiosity that drove McVeigh there. He was ready to stir up a little trouble, too.

McVeigh was outraged by reports that the federal government had posted threatening signs at the site, warning that the use of deadly force had been authorized against people who crossed a certain boundary into the installation. McVeigh wanted to test that one. He wanted to exercise his right as an American to walk on public land—and he wanted to carry a gun there.

McVeigh was eager to stand up to the rent-a-cops he had heard patrolled Area 51; as a former rent-a-cop himself, he knew that they possessed no greater right to make an arrest than the average citizen. His plan was to drive in as far as he could, and then hike up a mountain to where he could see the military base and airfield. Armed with his Ruger Mini 30, semiautomatic rifle, he was prepared to confront anyone who tried to stop him. *I'm on public land, buddy,* McVeigh planned to say. *Back off.*

After parking his Road Warrior and beginning his hike, he noticed two security guards rumbling down the road toward him in a white, unmarked jeep. McVeigh had already passed the "deadly force" sign and a sign barring photographs—which further upset him, since he had brought a camera. *You can't tell me on public land I can't take a fuckin' picture,* he thought. *No rent-a-cop can tell me that.*

As the vehicle drew closer, he decided to toy with the guards. He ducked for cover behind some scrub brush in a little gully about two feet deep. The jeep rolled up beside McVeigh's car, and the two guards, remaining inside their vehicle, looked over at the empty car. To McVeigh, they were like sitting ducks.

McVeigh lay in the gully, motionless and undetected, following his military instincts. Suddenly, McVeigh stood up and walked several steps over to the driver's side of the jeep. His gun was pointed to the ground; he knew he could have raised the barrel and wasted the guards with a pull of the trigger.

In the end, though, just knowing he had the chance was good enough for him; these guys were just rent-a-cops like he used to be—not real government workers, not his true enemies.

Instead he surprised them by saying a friendly "Hi!" Spooked, the guards drove off.

McVeigh waited until nightfall before hiking up the mountain; from the mountaintop, he was able to see the lights of the airfield. Early the next morning, at false dawn, he made a second trip up the mountain, hurrying to get a jump on the hot desert sun. He was intent on taking photos of Area 51. Shirtless and saddled with his backpack, he hiked with rifle in hand.

Halfway up, he heard the rotors of a helicopter in the distance. There was no doubt in McVeigh's mind it was a government Black Hawk, with its distinctive *fooof, fooooooof, fooooooooof.*

McVeigh stopped, turned around, and looked at the chopper approaching in the distance. Unperturbed, he resumed his hike. The sound of the chopper blades told him that the craft was coming up close. Still, he advanced, refusing to be intimidated by the chopper as it passed overhead and swooped in low, hovering in the air thirty yards in front of him.

For an instant, he considered taking cover and shooting at the helicopter with his rifle. But he wasn't in a combat mode, not yet. He knew the whole point of sending out a chopper was to frighten him. Most people, he knew, would have been scared out of their wits by a chopper flying that close, but McVeigh merely raised his free hand and waved to the chopper's crew, taking a little slap at authority. The craft hovered a second longer, then pitched back and left. McVeigh hiked to the top of the hill and snapped his photographs.

Later, as he drove away from Area 51, the white jeep fell in behind his car. McVeigh was certain that the rent-a-cops were running a license-plate check on him. No matter; he had accomplished his mission, challenging the government's authority and satisfying his curiosity in one fell swoop. He found no evidence of UFOs, but his interest in unidentified flying objects never flagged. Years later, on death row, he would watch the movie *Contact* six times over a two-day period, fascinated by the scientist played by Jodie Foster, who makes contact with an outer-space alien in the image of her long-dead father.

Leaving Area 51 and its petty guardians, McVeigh found contentment in the Road Warrior's driver's seat—his own little corner of the universe. Behind the wheel he was always in complete control, basking in the combination of serenity and excitement he found only on the road. He especially loved driving through the desert, but not only for the peace and quiet he found there. It was also a place rich in stories. On desert excursions with Fortier and Lori's father, Les Hart, McVeigh listened intently as the grandfatherly man told of the good old days, when trapping and gold mining were a way of life. Tales of stalking mountain lions and hunting for rattlesnakes intrigued McVeigh, who felt he and Les spoke the same language. They bartered, swapping cannon fuse for blasting caps. Les still liked to mine, and preferred McVeigh's cannon fuse. It was easier to string and light, said McVeigh, who turned around and sold Les's blasting caps at gun shows. It was people like Les, McVeigh felt, who made his travels worthwhile.

Another stop McVeigh made en route to Kansas that summer was at Sturgis, South Dakota, for a famous annual motorcycle rally that brought tens of thousands of bikers to South Dakota. He admired bikers for their independent lifestyle, but it was the stories he'd heard about "wild biker babes" that really attracted him to Sturgis. Though he himself didn't get lucky there, he had a lot of fun talking to bikers, who got a kick out of a T-shirt McVeigh wore to the rally, which carried a drawing of a six-gun and the slogan WE BRING GOOD THINGS TO LIFE.

Then, to investigate a tip, McVeigh drove hundreds of miles southeast to Gulfport, Mississippi. He had read in a right-wing newspaper that the town was being used as a staging area for U.N. troops and equipment, so McVeigh decided to run his own reconnaissance mission to investigate. Arriving at the location mentioned in the article, he hopped over a fence and began his inspection. He said he did find former Soviet and East Bloc utility vehicles at the site, but McVeigh noticed that the vehicles lacked weapon mounts or armor. He noted the name of the company performing the work, which was the clue that later helped him get to the bottom of the matter: as he would later discover, the transports were there being reconfigured by a local businessman for use in U.N.-sponsored humanitarian aid efforts.

McVeigh felt it was important for someone such as himself, with military experience, to check on such rumors personally. As concerned as he was about the New World Order, he also saw a danger in the increasing spread of mystified paranoia in the Patriot community. There were enough legitimate threats to worry about.

Arriving at Nichols's home in Herington, Kansas, at last, McVeigh raised the possibility of the two friends starting a gun-show business. McVeigh's car was fast, but it was small, with limited cargo space; Nichols, on the other hand, owned a big blue 1984 GMC pickup. Together they could haul plenty of inventory and make more money.

McVeigh even had an idea for a new product that was sure to bring them business at the shows. They could purchase fifty-pound bags of ammonium nitrate fertilizer and divide the contents up into smaller bags. Survivalists would snatch up the ammonium nitrate, a staple in the manufacture of explosives. Rumors on the gun-show circuit had it that the government was preparing to ban the sale of ammonium nitrate, and McVeigh was sure the fertilizer would sell like crazy.

Late that summer, McVeigh and Nichols made their first bulk purchase of ammonium nitrate.

7

"Won't Be
Back Forever"

More ominous news hit the gun-show circuit on September 13, 1994, when a new assault-weapons ban became law. The manufacture of certain semi-automatic rifles and handguns with detachable magazines and a combination of two features such as flash suppressors, pistol grips, grenade launchers, and bayonet mounts was now illegal. To McVeigh, it all fit the pattern: the government was continuing its effort to rid gun owners of their rights, and he himself was being forced into a new class of criminals, created by the federal government. One of the bumper stickers he had been selling since before Waco—WHEN GUNS ARE OUTLAWED, I WILL BECOME AN OUTLAW—had, in his eyes, proven prophetic. McVeigh had worked as a "straw buyer" purchasing assault weapons at gun stores. He'd fill out government firearms transaction forms listing himself as the buyer, then sell the guns at a profit to individuals looking to avoid filling out the government paperwork.

"They didn't want to have their names on the books. Most people assume it's because they are criminals, but in the Patriot or militia community people are paranoid to have their names on government forms," McVeigh later explained. "The way I approached it—well, shit, I've already got a record anyway of buying guns. I got the pistol permit in New York and they've got my fingerprints. So, I'll buy the gun and for a fee of ten or twenty dollars, I'll sell it to you as a private sale."

Existing federal law prohibited purchasers from misrepresenting themselves to gun dealers by intentionally claiming weapons were for them when in fact the firearms were intended for someone else. As for the new law banning assault weapons, McVeigh scoffed at that as well. Any time the opportunity presented itself, he snapped up guns, whether or not they were banned, and sold them for profit. But it was more than just a matter of dollars. It was a chance to aid fellow gun lovers who resented government documents prying into their personal business—gun ownership.

"The important part is that I had made up my mind that I didn't care if they were making them illegal or not," McVeigh said, reflecting on Washington politicians and the assault-weapons ban. "What enactment of the law did in effect was make me a criminal, simply by someone signing a piece of paper two thousand miles away."

McVeigh had become convinced that his heritage, his income, and perhaps his very life were threatened. It was more than he could accept. A line in the sand had been trampled by the aggressive federal juggernaut. He could no longer remain purely defensive, as a survivalist would. McVeigh was coming to the conclusion that he must take proactive steps to prevent the loss of the things he held dear. At night, he worried about federal agents bursting into his room and seizing all his weapons. Paranoid? He didn't think so.

While never associated with any of the formal Patriot organizations, McVeigh was a vocal participant in discussions at gun shows. Having been less than discreet with his remarks around law-enforcement officers, such as the undercover detective at the Arizona gun show who asked about his flare launchers, McVeigh was convinced that he was exactly the type of person whom federal agents would target first in the effort to disarm American citizens.

Rumors of even more gun legislation further hyped the atmosphere of fear among those in the gun culture. The new legislation, it was said, would outlaw civilian ownership of surplus ammo cans and require licenses for ownership of more than one thousand rounds, which would constitute an arsenal. Most repulsive to McVeigh was a rumor that the ATF would require residential floor plans from people seeking licenses, and that applicants would face unannounced checks of their homes. One rumor had it that the government was planning a massive raid on gun owners and members of the Patriot community in the spring of 1995. To McVeigh, history was repeating itself. The federal government had become equated in his mind with the British government of pre-Revolutionary America. McVeigh could take no more. *That does it!* he thought. *Enough is enough.*

He had made a decision. *It could be a sniper attack,* he thought. *It could be a firebombing, a kidnapping, an assassination.* Whatever form it took, Timothy McVeigh was going to engage in a major act of violence against the government.

In the midst of all this turmoil, a potentially explosive situation was developing in the Nichols household, where McVeigh was once again living. McVeigh had always tried his best to avoid flirting with Marife Nichols, who had returned from the Philippines. He genuinely liked Marife; unlike some of her critics, McVeigh never saw her as a foreign gold digger cashing in on an American husband. To him, she was just a young person trying to find her way in life, rather like the way he was. And just because her relationship with Nichols seemed more like friendship than true love, McVeigh saw no reason to dislike her. He helped her around the house, even changing Nicole's dirty diapers without complaint. Nichols was still winding down his employment as a ranch hand, so McVeigh drove Marife on shopping runs, and the two sometimes stopped for something to eat. On one occasion, McVeigh recalls Marife asked him if he were gay.

Definitely not, McVeigh said with a grin.

Preparing to go out of town, he asked her for a hug goodbye. The hug, he remembers, "quickly turned into a goodbye kiss."

When he returned, Marife was pleased to see him—so pleased that they "ended up in bed while Terry was at work," according to McVeigh, who in stating this confirmed an allegation leaked to the *Dallas Morning News* regarding the relationship. Marife, when contacted years later to respond to the claim, said only: "I don't think so."

The sexual relations, McVeigh said, continued for about two weeks before Marife left for the Philippines to start the fall semester of physical therapy classes. "We hugged before she left, and I don't believe either of us felt used," McVeigh said.

In early September of 1994, McVeigh called home. "How's Grandpa?" he asked his father.

"He's doing okay," Bill McVeigh said cheerfully. "You want to talk to him?"

Talk to him? Wasn't Grandpa in the hospital fighting for his life?

Ed McVeigh had rallied enough strength to leave Lockport Memorial Hospital and move into his son's home in Pendleton, where he took over the couch on which his grandson had slept after returning from the service. A nurse visited every day to take care of his medical needs. Tim McVeigh and his grandfather laughed and talked for half an hour, discussing old times and Tim's latest adventures. Ed McVeigh was delighted to hear his grandson's voice.

A week later, the old man collapsed as Bill helped him from the couch. "You think I should maybe call for an ambulance?" his son gently asked.

"Yes, you better. I feel that bad," Ed answered. He was beginning his final journey to death.

Meanwhile, back at the Nichols home, McVeigh was gearing up for his still-unspecified action against the federal government. He wrote Fortier a letter informing him that he had decided to take offensive action, and asking whether Fortier would assist him and Nichols once they settled on a plan. Lori must not know anything about it, McVeigh cautioned, but Fortier read the letter to his wife anyway. He then wrote back expressing curiosity about what he was proposing, though he refused to keep Lori in the dark. Two weeks later, McVeigh drove in from Kansas. He had a plan.

McVeigh and Fortier spoke outside the mobile home, leaning against a fence in the Fortiers' front yard. McVeigh was going to blow up a federal building, and he extended the invitation for Fortier to join him.

"No," Fortier answered. "I would never do anything like that, unless there was a U.N. tank in my front yard."

But McVeigh wouldn't give up easily; he felt there was still a chance that, when push came to shove, Fortier might participate. McVeigh returned to Kansas without a commitment, but by the end of the month he was on the phone with Fortier, asking him to rent a storage unit on the outskirts of Kingman.

"Use an alias and pay with cash," McVeigh instructed.

Mike and Lori drove out to Golden Valley and other outlying areas, but came up empty-handed. In early October, when McVeigh returned to Kingman, Fortier apologized for his failure.

"Don't worry about it. We already got one," McVeigh said.

Using his real name, Tim McVeigh had signed a rental agreement on October 4, 1994, for a storage locker at Northern Storage on Northern Avenue in Kingman. The cost was thirty dollars a month. The unit would be available through mid-February 1995.

As soon as he arrived, Lori Fortier noticed a change in McVeigh. In the past he had always appeared so clean-cut; now his brush cut had grown out and whiskers were sprouting on his face. The next day, when he briefly stopped by the house dressed in a Harley-Davidson T-shirt and a bandanna covering his head, she hardly recognized him. McVeigh returned a night or two later, telling Fortier to throw on some shoes. He wanted to show him something. Stepping out of the house and into McVeigh's car, Fortier found Terry Nichols waiting for them outside in his pickup truck. McVeigh followed Nichols's truck to the six-by-fifteen-foot storage unit on Northern Avenue. McVeigh walked into it and pulled back a blanket covering a stack of boxes. From the entranceway, Fortier saw that the top box contained explosives.

McVeigh and Fortier returned to Mike's home, and, in the privacy of the bedroom where McVeigh often stayed, Fortier was given a closer look at a couple of small cylinders containing explosives for a blasting cap. One was cigar-shaped and filled with white powder. The other, which looked more like a tube of toothpaste, held a red liquid.

The explosives, McVeigh said, had come from a quarry near Nichols's home in Kansas. He and Nichols had paid a visit to the quarry in the middle of the night.

It had been drizzling when McVeigh and Nichols arrived at the Martin Marietta Aggregates quarry in Marion, Kansas. McVeigh walked around each of the lockers he had scoped out to make sure that there weren't any burglar-alarm wires; the only cables he noticed were ground wires. He drilled out the first padlock, and the door swung open. His flashlight shined in on crates of Tovex, a high-explosive blasting gelatin shaped like eighteen-inch-long sausages. McVeigh carefully examined each fifty-pound box, checking the expiration dates. The more recent the dates, the greater the potency. He grabbed seven of the fresher boxes. *Like shopping for milk,* he thought.

After drilling out the lock on the second storage magazine, McVeigh and Nichols had stolen more than five hundred electric blasting caps and more than eighty spools of shock tube—ignition cord capable of instantly transferring a spark from fuse to explosive. The blasting caps came equipped with special explosive ingredients—the cigar-shaped container of ammonium nitrate powder and the toothpaste tube of red liquid nitromethane. The electric caps were later dropped from the plan; the danger of static electricity accidentally setting the bomb off prematurely was too great a risk. The volatile Tovex would serve as a booster to help ignite the main charge.

McVeigh had also noticed a third storage facility on the grounds of the quarry—the trailer portion of a tractor-trailer. He drilled out the padlock, pulled the doors open, and climbed up inside. His flashlight shone on an enormous quantity of explosives—forty thousand pounds of ANFO neatly packaged in fifty-pound bags stacked four and five high and five or six across, from one end of the trailer to the other. There must have been eight hundred bags in all, he estimated. A mixture of ammonium nitrate and fuel oil, ANFO was a main-charge explosive, the primary weapon in the quarry blasters' arsenal.

Incredibly, McVeigh turned his back on the ANFO and hopped back out of the trailer. ANFO lacked the wallop he was looking for. The bomb he was planning would consist of more than 5,000 pounds of ammonium nitrate fertilizer mixed with about 1,200 pounds of liquid nitromethane, 350 pounds of Tovex, and the miscellaneous weight of sixteen fifty-five-gallon drums, for a combined weight of about 7,000 pounds.

Before leaving the quarry and driving out to Arizona, McVeigh made a halfhearted attempt to cover his tracks by kicking dirt over the metal shavings that had fallen to the ground from drilling out each of the locks. (A quarry worker would later testify that he noticed the shavings.) *It wasn't the perfect crime,* McVeigh reflected, *but we got away with it.* McVeigh and Nichols drove in separate vehicles to Kingman. If Kansas authorities made a big deal of the theft, McVeigh figured, they'd be much better off stashing the explosives a few states away in Arizona.

On September 30 and October 18, Terry Nichols purchased a combined total of four thousand pounds of ammonium nitrate using the alias Mike Havens. McVeigh purchased smaller amounts. Whenever the opportunity presented itself, he pulled into the local feed and seed store of a small town and loaded up his car with fifty-pound bags of ammonium nitrate. He thought nothing of tossing ten bags into the backseat of the Road Warrior; he would have filled the trunk, too, if he weren't concerned about the unequal distribution in weight.

Between McVeigh and Nichols, they made about eight purchases before they had the amount of ammonium nitrate they needed. Since the fertilizer was legally purchased, there was no need to hide it across the country; a rented storage locker in Herington served as its repository. In the days after the theft of the explosives, McVeigh was eager to conduct a small-scale test of the ingredients he planned to use in the bomb's main charge. He figured that if these potent chemicals—ammonium nitrate and nitromethane— worked in a tiny blasting cap, they would possess greater potential in greater proportions. *If it works in the micro,* he thought, *why wouldn't it work in the macro? Physical laws stay the same.* A fifty-five-gallon drum could blow up just as easily as a blasting cap the size of a pen cap—if the correct proportions were applied. But he needed to check his theory and see for himself.

The Kingman desert would make the perfect testing ground. McVeigh filled a plastic Gatorade jug with ammonium nitrate prills—tiny BB-like beads—and poured in liquid nitromethane. A piece of Tovex sausage and a blasting cap served as the bomb's ignition. Only one thing was missing; he wanted Fortier to witness the test on his prototype bomb.

McVeigh pulled the loaded jug from the front seat of Nichols's truck, which was parked outside Fortier's mobile home. To Fortier, the contents looked like rock salt mixed with some kind of liquid fuel. "This looks like a lot of trouble," Fortier said. He refused McVeigh's invitation to watch the detonation and walked back inside his home. McVeigh, on his own, successfully exploded the bomb out in the desert.

Making a miniature prototype proved easy, but McVeigh knew he would require helping hands to assemble the full-scale, seven-thousand-pound bomb he was planning. And he knew that the way to do that was to manipulate Nichols and the Fortiers. He wasn't entirely comfortable with the necessity of involving them in a plan of his own making, but he believed that, in this instance, the end would justify the means. He was out to accomplish what he saw as a greater good. If friendship lost was part of the price to be paid, then so be it. He was the mastermind of the entire scheme, and his scheme required pawns. "I did manipulate people," McVeigh later admitted. "I don't like the feeling of having manipulated people, but sometimes we know in life the end result outweighs the means."

Alone with the Fortiers one evening, McVeigh told them that he had figured out how to turn a truck into a bomb. He intended to place the bomb's main charge in fifty-five-gallon drums tucked in the truck's cargo bay. And the blast would tear into the target he had chosen: the Alfred P. Murrah Federal Building in Oklahoma City. The explosion would occur on the second anniversary of Waco: April 19, 1995. He planned to ignite his bomb at 11 A.M., when federal workers were preparing for lunch.

"What about all the people?" Fortier asked.

"Think about the people as if they were storm troopers in *Star Wars*," McVeigh answered. "They may be individually innocent, but they are guilty because they work for the Evil Empire."

In reaching his decision to bomb a federal building, McVeigh had been operating in a purely military state of mind. The bombing, to him, was an act of tactical aggression—nothing more, nothing less. The Army had been his teacher in the horrors of war. He had learned to cope with unthinkable cruelty, and now he would put the lessons the Army had taught him to practice on native soil. "You learn how to handle killing in the military," he explained. "I face the consequences, but you learn to accept it."

When it struck, an unexpected act of massive violence that made America seem suddenly defenseless, the Oklahoma City bombing would remind many of that other day of infamy, Pearl Harbor. Yet McVeigh saw in the terrorist act he was planning an analogue to the Hiroshima bombing that hastened the end of World War II. The atom bomb at Hiroshima killed or maimed more than two hundred thousand Japanese civilians, yet history would view it as an act that saved many more lives by ending the war sooner. McVeigh felt his bombing was a necessary act, an act of extremism in the service of liberty. His actions would wipe many innocent people off the face of the earth, but someday, McVeigh was convinced, historians would call him a martyr, maybe even a hero.

It was not lost on McVeigh that the bombing would take place on what was not only the anniversary of Waco, but the anniversary of the opening battle of the American Revolution. Yet McVeigh wasn't looking to spark a revolution, but to end what he saw as a pattern of government-propagated violence and aggression of which Ruby Ridge and Waco might be only the beginning. A sharp, forceful blow, he believed, might bring government to its senses. For more than two years McVeigh had waited for redress in the matters of Ruby Ridge and Waco, and still the federal juggernaut, as he called it, showed no signs of reforming. Congress, President Clinton, and Attorney General Janet Reno were all aware that there was discontent. Letters and petitions objecting to the government's actions had been mailed to Washington. When federal investigations, at least initially, ruled that federal law-enforcement agents had done nothing wrong, McVeigh was appalled. The government, he felt, was laughing at people in the Patriot and gun communities. Violence was the only tactic he thought would succeed in silencing the laughter of the bully the federal government had become.

Fortier has since claimed that he heard McVeigh say he had selected the building in Oklahoma City because it was where the orders against Waco had originated. But McVeigh had other reasons. He knew that it was Reno, back in Washington, D.C., who bore responsibility for the orders that brought about the fiery end at Waco. Government field offices had provided backup support in the operation, but it was the green light from Reno that had led to the deadly conclusion of the fifty-one-day siege.

In fact, McVeigh had chosen the Murrah Building only after meticulously developing a list of criteria for potential attack sites. His target building, brimming with federal workers, had to have at least two federal law-enforcement agencies under its roof. And not just any agencies. It had to be two from a short list of three: the Bureau of Alcohol, Tobacco and Firearms, the Federal Bureau of Investigation, and the Drug Enforcement Administration. If there were additional law-enforcement offices, such as Secret Service or U.S. Marshals Service, McVeigh considered that a bonus.

Before settling on Oklahoma City, his possible targets included federal buildings in Arkansas, Missouri, Arizona, and Texas. McVeigh now says Fortier "checked out buildings in Phoenix or Tucson," adding that Nichols scoped out federal buildings in Kansas City, Missouri. McVeigh had even thought of heading to the capital of American government, Washington, D.C., and blowing up the J. Edgar Hoover FBI Building, as Earl Turner's crew had done in *The Turner Diaries*. In the end, McVeigh decided on Oklahoma City, right in America's heartland. "If I was an out-of-control mad bomber, there would have been approximately a forty-thousand-pound bomb I would have ignited in front of the FBI Building in Washington, D.C.," McVeigh says.

The Murrah Building, which he found listed in the government pages of the telephone book, harbored regional offices for the ATF, DEA, and Secret Service. Reports that he was specifically targeting FBI Special Agent Bob Ricks, the bureau's chief spokesman at Waco, were erroneous. When McVeigh learned that Ricks was assigned to Oklahoma City, that, too, was chalked up as a bonus. It didn't matter much to McVeigh that Ricks and other FBI agents were situated in a different building in Oklahoma City. For McVeigh, the psychological effect of Ricks's link to Waco and the resulting publicity from that connection were reward enough.

McVeigh had considered targeting specific individuals, among them Lon Horiuchi, the FBI sharpshooter who had killed Randy Weaver's wife, Vicki, at Ruby Ridge. He considered going after a member of the sharpshooter's family, to inflict the same kind of pain the surviving Weavers had experienced. But ultimately he decided that he could make the loudest statement by bombing a federal building. By destroying people who compiled a complete cross-section of federal employees, McVeigh believed that he was showing federal agents how wrong they were to attack the entire Branch Davidian family. In McVeigh's opinion, every division of the federal government had, at one time or another, mistreated the public. Now, McVeigh decided, was the time to make them all pay.

His cold, calculating mind also considered the architectural designs of the buildings he was considering, and the materials used in their construction. The front of the Murrah Building was made of glass, which he knew would shatter under the force of the blast. Another factor in his analysis, he contends, was a genuine desire to keep the deaths of nongovernment employees to a minimum; he says he ruled out a forty-story building in Little Rock, Arkansas, after spotting a florist's shop on the ground floor. "I was in Little Rock and actually went to the building listed as ATF offices and saw a ground-floor display window of what appeared to be a floral shop," McVeigh recalled. "I messed up, because within blocks is the main Little Rock federal building, and from pictures I've seen, it would have been a better target then the Murrah Building." The Murrah Building, nevertheless, made a good target, McVeigh says, because of the existence of a big open parking lot across the street, which could absorb and dissipate part of the concussion from the blast, minimizing collateral damage—deaths and injuries to people in nearby, nonfederal buildings.

And yet another cold thought crept into his reasoning—the photo opportunities. He wanted a big federal building, with plenty of open space around it, to allow for the best possible news photos and television footage. He wanted to create a stark, horrifying image that would make everyone who saw it stop and take notice.

Finally, Timothy McVeigh wanted a body count—the higher the better. The federal government, he reasoned, had unlimited amounts of cash to replace buildings, but the lives of federal employees could not be replaced. He needed to deliver a quantity of casualties the federal government would never forget. It was the same tactic the American government used in armed international conflicts, when it wanted to send a message to tyrants and despots. It was the United States government that had ushered in this new anything-goes mentality, McVeigh believed, and he intended to show the world what it would be like to fight a war under these new rules, right in the federal government's own backyard.

Back at the Fortiers' home, McVeigh set to work designing his bomb. There was so much to visualize—arranging the fifty-five-gallon drums holding the main charge in the truck's cargo bay, placing the Tovex sausage primer boosters, stringing the fuse to the bomb. Most important to McVeigh was the challenge of correctly arranging the configuration of the main charge in order to have the greatest possible impact on the Murrah Building.

Drawing sketches on paper would not suffice. No, McVeigh needed to see possible arrangements in three dimensions. He walked over to the Fortiers' kitchen cupboard and pulled out fifteen cans of soup, placed them on the floor, and started experimenting with possible setups. Mike was working down at the hardware store that day, but Lori Fortier was home. She glanced over and noticed that McVeigh had arranged the cans into a triangle—one of many designs he contemplated, though not the one finally selected. "It has to be a shaped charge," he told Lori. McVeigh also pored over a book on explosives he had obtained, which included directions on mixture ratios for making a bomb. Terry Nichols would help mix the bomb, Lori recalled McVeigh telling her.

To meet the expenses for his bomb, McVeigh told Lori, he planned to get Terry to help him rob a man from Arkansas whom he called Bob. McVeigh said he was uncertain whether he wanted to go with Nichols to commit the robbery; Bob, he said, knew McVeigh from the gun-show circuit, and McVeigh wasn't sure he could pull off the robbery without being recognized by Bob—whose real name, of course, was Roger Moore.

The need for money wasn't the only reason for targeting Moore. McVeigh was bitter and angry about the way his fellow dealer had treated him in their last two encounters. He had a score to settle with Moore. He wanted to hurt him seriously—even kill him. "I was indifferent on whether Moore should survive the encounter," McVeigh says.

Still, McVeigh couldn't risk becoming a fugitive in a robbery—not with the bombing itself hanging in the balance. He had too many loose ends to tie up—calls to chemical companies, barrel manufacturers, and demolition contractors. McVeigh had to focus his energies on collecting the apparatus for the bomb. Nichols would have to handle "Bob."

In calling different companies across the country, McVeigh used a calling card to spare the Fortiers the expense of long-distance telephone calls. Nichols had ordered the card under the alias Daryl Bridges from an advertisement in the *Spotlight*, a right-wing newspaper. Phone records from the calling card could create a damaging paper trail of corroborating evidence, if it were ever linked to McVeigh and Nichols, but for all his usual caution McVeigh showed little concern over this possibility.

It didn't matter to McVeigh, who forged ahead with his plan. His long-distance phone records trace his search for anhydrous hydrazine, a potent rocket fuel that was his first choice for a fuel to mix with the ammonium nitrate fertilizer. Researching anhydrous hydrazine, McVeigh discovered that the colorless, oily liquid was also used to cleanse the interiors of boilers; contacting an Oklahoma City chemical supplier, he identified himself as a newly hired contractor who had landed a job "flushing out the boiler system of a school up here in Kansas."

The distributor told him he could supply him with anhydrous hydrazine, but only in one-pint measurements. "Well, I've got a bunch of old barrels that are marked anhydrous hydrazine," McVeigh said. "Obviously, the last contractor used this stuff, and that's what I'm going to need." McVeigh hung up and pressed on for a distributor willing to meet his needs. He required drums of the rocket fuel, not pints. When he finally found a distributor willing to sell him the quantity needed, though, the cost was so high that he was forced to switch to another, more reasonably priced fuel: nitromethane. Dressed in biker duds, McVeigh told Tim Chambers, the fuel salesman at a car-racing track south of Dallas, that he and some fellow bikers needed the nitromethane for racing. The seller bought the story and sold him the fuel.

McVeigh was on a fast track to accomplishing his goal. But a disturbing thought nagged at him: What would Ed McVeigh think?

Bill McVeigh was worried about his father, but for different reasons altogether. Bill had been planning a trip out to Las Vegas for a holiday, hoping to hook up with Tim for a day or two. But his father had been ailing, and he wasn't sure about leaving him behind.

On a visit with Ed at the Lockport hospital, though, Ed encouraged Bill to take the holiday; he didn't want people fussing over him. So Bill made arrangements to catch up with Tim at the Golden Nugget in Las Vegas.

Bill and Tim McVeigh did meet up in Las Vegas as planned during the second week in October; they shared a meal, and afterward Bill slipped a few dollars his son's way so they could gamble together playing video poker. A couple of hours later, McVeigh returned to Kingman.

At the Fortiers' home, McVeigh told Mike he was taking a trip to New Mexico. Terry Nichols had been due in from Vegas to accompany him, but Nichols was late in arriving, so McVeigh had to enlist Fortier's help. He gave Mike the key and combination to the locks on the Kingman storage unit where the explosives were stored. Tell Nichols to pick up the material from the storage locker, McVeigh said, and meet him in New Mexico. When Fortier asked what that meant, McVeigh assured him that Nichols would know. Twenty minutes after McVeigh drove off in his Road Warrior, Nichols arrived and Fortier passed on the message. McVeigh and Nichols were headed to Kansas, but they would never catch up with each other on the road during that journey east.

On Sunday, October 16, 1994, at 2:30 P.M., Tim McVeigh's grandfather Ed died. Bill McVeigh had rushed home from Las Vegas the Thursday before, after Jennifer called to tell him her grandfather's condition was deteriorating. Bill tried contacting his son through Michael Fortier to tell him the news, but Tim was already on the road.

"Would you let him know his grandpa died?" Bill asked.

Fortier agreed to get the news to McVeigh, but in truth he didn't know exactly where McVeigh was; he would have to wait for Tim to check in. Five days later, McVeigh called Fortier from a pay phone in Junction City, Kansas.

"Tim, man," Fortier said, "your dad keeps calling. I don't really know what to tell him; I don't even know where you're at." McVeigh had been specifically keeping his father out of the loop about his whereabouts, not to mention his plans.

"Why is he calling?" McVeigh asked. "It must be some kind of emergency."

"Yeah," Fortier said. "He told me to tell you your grandfather died."

McVeigh thanked Fortier. Later he would recall his gratitude at being told in such a straightforward manner; he saw no reason to have bad news sugarcoated.

McVeigh had missed his grandfather's funeral, but he still felt compelled to return to Pendleton immediately. He called his father.

"Do you want me to come home and help you?" McVeigh asked.

"It probably wouldn't hurt," said Bill, who had buried Ed two days earlier.

McVeigh arrived home in early November and took on the job of organizing Ed McVeigh's possessions for an estate sale that would be held the weekend before Thanksgiving—a job for which Bill insisted on paying his son one hundred dollars a week. McVeigh dug into the work, though on his first weekend home he did travel to Ohio to work at a gun show.

That same weekend Terry Nichols also hit the road, heading south to Arkansas for a surprise visit to Roger Moore's ranch. Moore awoke about 9 A.M. on Saturday, November 5. Alone in the house, he stayed in bed for a quarter hour or so before rising. Karen Anderson was working a gun show in Shreveport, Louisiana. In the kitchen, Moore poured himself a glass of orange juice and looked out the window. Not much of a morning person, he decided to let the animals out of the barn and feed the horses, and then come in and feed himself breakfast. He was walking out past the carport toward the barn when he suddenly heard a man's voice behind him.

"Lay on the ground."

Moore turned around, only to confront the business end of a pistol-grip shotgun, pointed at him from fifteen feet away. In place of a shoulder sling, Moore noted, the gun was sporting a steel string; it was the kind designed to be used as a garrote. With one quick move, he realized, the intruder could easily loop the wire over Moore's head and slit open his windpipe.

The stranger meant business. He was dressed in combat boots, camouflage pants and shirt (which may have been covering a flak jacket), military gloves, and a black ski mask tucked beneath the collar of the shirt. He weighed 165 to 185 pounds and stood about five feet eleven; later, when he had a chance to think about it, Moore would realize this was not the tall, gangly Timothy McVeigh.

"What?" asked Moore.

"Lay on the ground."

He obeyed. The intruder walked up to Moore and placed the gun on the back of his neck. Was anyone in the house?

"No."

Following orders, Moore crawled inside.

Was Moore expecting any company?

"Yes, folks are coming from Hot Springs for an early lunch," Moore lied, hoping the gunman would be quick about his business.

In the living room, he was ordered to lie flat on his stomach. Moore complied. At one point he caught a whiff of the gunman, who smelled "like a pig yard."

The gunman locked Moore's hands and ankles in the plastic handcuffs known as police ties. A strip of duct tape was placed over his eyes and a jacket thrown over his head. Moore knew he had no chance in this situation. He could hear the gunman's footsteps on the wooden floors, going from room to room.

"Where is the money?"

"It's right inside the bedroom on the computer desk."

The gunman moved fast, making repeated trips in and out of the house, loading Moore's possessions, one by one, into Moore's van.

"Where is the safe?"

Cautious thus far not to antagonize the gunman, Moore slipped. "The money wouldn't be laying on the desk if I had a safe."

The gunman continued clearing out valuables: gold, silver, and precious stones, as well as eighty to ninety pistols, shotguns, and rifles.

Moore complained that his hands and feet were being paralyzed by the plastic handcuffs; the gunman removed the ties and bound his captive in duct tape.

"Are you a fed?" Moore asked, gaining in confidence.

The intruder made no response.

Moore grew bolder. "Could you please leave the Hornet?" he pleaded, referring to a .22-caliber Winchester he'd received from his father as a gift. But the appeal fell on deaf ears. Terry Nichols took the heirloom gun.

Undaunted, Moore also asked the man to spare his customized van, offering a Ford LTD instead. But Nichols wasn't interested in accommodating Moore. The van was already loaded; it was time to go. "There's another guy out there with a shotgun," Nichols warned. "We're coming back for the rest of it."

Of course it was a bluff. He had already stolen almost everything that wasn't nailed down, even the fitted bedsheets and pillowcases from Moore's bed and a pillowcase and quilt from Karen Anderson's bed.

"You don't have to worry about your guns," Nichols taunted as he left the house. "They're going to the gangs."

Moore waited until the van was down the driveway before he struggled free from the duct tape and picked up the phone to call for help. The line was dead. He grabbed a stainless steel .45 stashed in a magazine box beside his easy chair and walked over to the neighbor's house, where he called the sheriff's office. Deputies recovered the abandoned van about six miles from the ranch a couple of hours later.

In preparing their report on the robbery, a detective asked Moore for a list of people who had visited his property. At the top of that list was Timothy McVeigh, who Moore suspected was behind the robbery. He and McVeigh had split on bad terms, and Moore recalled that he'd even given McVeigh a guided tour of the property. Later on Saturday, Moore reached Anderson at the Shreveport gun show. Anderson noticed that Moore's voice quavered.

"In the morning, don't open your table," Moore said. "Walk around the show and try to find a Mini 14 and a riot shotgun." Moore knew his aim with the .45-caliber handgun wasn't much good. He wanted some serious fire-power back under his roof.

When Anderson returned home Sunday, the house was locked up tight. She saw Moore sitting in the living room, but he made no effort to open the door; he seemed beside himself. After finding her key and opening the door, she walked through the house. It had been ransacked. They estimated that sixty thousand dollars in valuables, including eighty-seven hundred dollars in cash, had been stolen. Homeowners insurance would cover just fifty-nine hundred dollars of the loss, according to Moore, who initiated his own efforts to try to retrieve his property.

McVeigh contends now that Moore and Anderson inflated the inventory list they submitted for insurance purposes, but in his mind the satisfaction of revenge was solace enough. Moore should have thought twice before accusing him of stealing the design plans for the flare launcher. At the Nichols farm McVeigh had built a dozen launchers using Moore's design, but it was with only the best of intentions. He knew Moore was stuck with an inventory of faulty flares, and that he'd designed the flare launcher to help him sell those flares once they'd been doctored to work as fuse-lit rockets. McVeigh made a few dollars, but he argued that his real goal was arming the Patriot community with an antihelicopter device. Moreover, he contends, with each set of launcher and flares McVeigh sold he handed out a card listing the American Assault Company as the source for replacement flares. If Moore failed to see the beauty in this arrangement, that was his problem.

McVeigh had another motivation for the robbery: the confiscation of Moore's gun collection. To McVeigh, the firearms were useless sitting in the ammunition dealer's house. He wanted to get the guns into the hands of people who would use them in defense of their homes when the federal raids started going down. "Moore would surrender his guns meekly to any federal agents, and I knew it," McVeigh said angrily. "So they were doing no good in his possession." The fact that Moore had asked the masked robber if he was a "fed" was another thread of proof in a growing tapestry of fear that raids were imminent, the way McVeigh saw it.

Yet McVeigh denies that he planned the robbery of Moore to get cash for his bomb project. He took pride in the fact that the bomb, despite the massive destruction it would cause, was relatively inexpensive to create. Truck rental would cost him about $250, fertilizer less than $500. The nitromethane cost $2,780, and he would spend a few more bucks on a cheap junker to use as a getaway car. The whole project, he estimated, would cost no more than $5,000. "What's five grand? There was no need to raise money; this was done on a shoestring budget," McVeigh said, pressing the point that there was more to the robbery than just money—revenge.

For his part, Mike Fortier believed that McVeigh saw the Moore holdup as a way to help pay Terry Nichols back, to begin to redress the balance with his old Army pal. Like Fortier, Nichols had often put a roof over McVeigh's head—and according to Fortier, Nichols had once accused McVeigh of free-loading.

After getting word that the robbery had been a success, McVeigh called Fortier from Pendleton. "This is a red alert call," McVeigh said, using a code they'd worked out in advance. "Terry did Bob." Fortier jotted down the phone number McVeigh gave him and went to a pay phone to call him back. In that second call, McVeigh advised Fortier to be on his guard. "Bob" might send private investigators to Kingman looking for him. McVeigh also asked Fortier to alert him if he observed anything out of the ordinary. The robbery had gone well, he told his friend in Arizona, except for one thing: Nichols hadn't killed Bob.

Sorting through Ed W. McVeigh's belongings in his old farmhouse on Bear Ridge Road across from the Erie Canal, McVeigh found a history book dating from his grandfather's childhood in the 1920s. In a section on income tax, it was noted that the income tax at the time was about five percent; the author had added a footnote, where he editorialized that five percent was an "outrageous amount." McVeigh wondered what the Founding Fathers would think of the income-tax allocation of 33 percent or more automatically withdrawn from paychecks in modern times.

His grandfather's death, in a sense, freed Tim McVeigh. He no longer had to worry about the possibility of Ed McVeigh ever finding out about his involvement in the bombing. McVeigh knew that the crime he was planning would have emotionally destroyed his grandfather, if he should ever find out who was responsible. But now Ed's death had lifted that thin thread of restraint.

McVeigh had only his other family members to consider, and this was a different matter indeed. To Tim McVeigh, whose family he considered little more than "acquaintances," the question of what would happen to other McVeighs after the bombing was less than taxing. If McVeigh were caught, he figured his father would be in for a rough time, but he knew Bill McVeigh would survive, because he was a strong man with strong friendships throughout the community. Jennifer and the others might be subjected to psychological harassment, but so long as none of them wound up being thrown into prison by the government in revenge, McVeigh could live with the consequences.

The weeks McVeigh spent preparing for his grandfather's estate sale hadn't been a comfortable experience; he'd become a stranger in his own hometown. There once had been a time when he could walk into his cousin and godmother Linda Daigler's house and help himself to anything in the refrigerator, but now he learned just how much had changed. When McVeigh stopped by to visit Linda, her new husband, Jim Daigler, answered the door. Linda wasn't home, but McVeigh walked inside and headed for the refrigerator, in search of a soft drink.

"What are you looking for?" Daigler asked.

"A pop," McVeigh said casually.

"I'll get it for you," Daigler said, an edge of annoyance in his voice.

During the visit, McVeigh recalls, he shared with Daigler a puzzling message he had heard on his grandfather's telephone answering machine. A woman had left these words on the machine: "Edward, I'm Jesus Christ, and you're coming up to see me now." To McVeigh, the message was a mystery: was it the work of a grief-stricken family friend with good intentions, or someone's idea of a malicious prank?

McVeigh decided to ask Daigler. "Is it possible that Linda called and left a message on Grandpa's answering machine?" he said. "It was a female's voice, and I can't figure out who it is."

Daigler was upset by the question. "I don't know, Tim," he snapped. McVeigh dropped the subject.

The friction between the two men accelerated at the estate sale. When McVeigh told him the asking price for Ed's snowblower, Daigler exploded. "Seven hundred bucks? Are you fuckin' nuts?" he thundered. "You come in my house and think you can just grab a pop without asking me?"

McVeigh was stunned by the outburst. He and his father had discussed how much they would charge relatives for the little-used snowblower, but decided to stick with its actual value. Daigler was shocked not to be getting a break on the price, but it was clear he had other grievances on his mind. When McVeigh stood firm on the price, he shifted topics. "You know, Linda was real upset about you accusing her of leaving that message on the phone machine. You upset the hell out of her and I want an apology from you."

The snowblower between them, Daigler began jabbing his finger at McVeigh's chest. "You go get your dad. You tell him what you fuckin' said."

McVeigh had to restrain himself from charging at Daigler. *Where does this guy get off telling me, a twenty-six-year-old combat veteran, to run to Daddy?* Rather than risk a scene, though, he agreed to get his father.

A few moments later, Tim and Bill McVeigh returned to the snowblower. His finger stabbing the air between, Daigler repeated his charge. "You tell your dad what you said that made my wife so fuckin' upset."

"Jim, I didn't say it that way. I just wanted to know . . ." McVeigh tried to explain that he was only curious about the phone message, which he repeated for his father.

"Tim, did you ask him about that?" Bill asked.

"Dad," McVeigh said. "I didn't mean it that way."

But Daigler wouldn't let up. Finally, McVeigh's patience ran out. *Enough of the peacemaker routine,* he thought. *He's not biting. This guy's just another bully.* McVeigh's eyes filled with that same "bright and flashing" look Roger Moore had noticed when they were discussing Waco.

"Jim," McVeigh said. "Get that fuckin' finger out of my face."

The finger poked the air one last time. McVeigh slapped it down and lunged at Daigler; only his father's strong arms were able to hold him back.

"You're just a little boy," McVeigh remembers Daigler taunting. "I'll kick your ass."

Daigler later said he wished the incident had never happened; he had always liked his wife's godson. For Tim McVeigh, the confrontation was further proof of a feeling he'd had ever since leaving Pendleton: *There's nothing for me here anymore.*

It wasn't as if he hadn't tried. McVeigh had even taken a stab at romance, going out for drinks with his old confidante Andrea Peters, the receptionist from Burns Security. He took her to a place called Brennan's, and they talked all night and into the wee hours of the morning. McVeigh told her of his adventures, how he was seeing the country and living out of his car; eventually, he told her, he would settle down to a job and family. Yet the evening ended with them no more than good friends.

No, there was nothing for him here—except, perhaps, for Jennifer. His younger sister still thought the world of him. In her eyes he was bright, intellectual; he saw the world in a different way, and he loved sharing his insights with her.

In the living room of their Pendleton home, Tim and Jennifer watched the Waco video *Day 51*, which he had spliced with a second video showing interviews of Branch Davidian children. "This was the video that got smuggled out," he said.

The government, McVeigh told Jennifer, had intentionally gassed and burned the Branch Davidians. There was no mistaking the rage in her brother's eyes; it was clear to Jennifer that Tim really believed the government had committed a crime at Waco. "He thought the people were murdered."

And it was at this point that McVeigh signaled to his sister that he had reached a decision. Without giving any specifics of his plan, McVeigh informed her that he had moved on from the propaganda stage to the action stage of his antigovernment mission. While he was in Pendleton, he used the word processor in Jennifer's room to type up a letter he planned to send to an American Legion post—a letter his sister checked for grammatical errors. The strongly worded letter, which he entitled "Constitutional Defenders," denounced the federal government's handling of Waco in McVeigh's typically heated terms, describing federal law-enforcement agents as "power-hungry storm troopers" and "fascist tyrants." The letter also carried his strongest written warning to date: militia groups, he wrote, had the right to react with violence when agents drew first blood.

Later, McVeigh would bang out a second, much harsher letter, which he intended to be found someday by federal agents. He might likely be dead by the time they read it, he knew, but he was glad to think its anger might outlive his own demise. He even banged out "ATF Read" as the heading.

The letter, laced with expletives, accused federal agents of trampling over the rights of American citizens. The tone was even more direct than the hate-filled letter he had used to sever his friendship with Steve Hodge.

"ATF, all you tyrannical mother fuckers will swing in the wind one day," McVeigh wrote, "for your treasonous actions against the Constitution of the United States. Remember the Nuremberg War Trials. But . . . but . . . but . . . I only followed orders. . . . Die, you spineless cowardice [sic] bastards."

During this period, Bill McVeigh also noticed a renewed intensity in his son's hatred for the government. Whenever President Clinton appeared on television, his son would glare and mutter to himself, "Someone should kill the son of a bitch." Bill never suspected that the angry words might have signaled any real threat, nor did he consider the possibility that his son might have benefited from counseling. After all, Bill knew he had shouted things as bad as that when he was watching the Buffalo Bills on TV.

Bill McVeigh might not have shared his son's enthusiasm for the gun world, but he was pleased when Tim was able to sell off the five guns Ed had left behind—four shotguns and the old .22-caliber rifle. McVeigh called the organizers of a forthcoming gun show in Hamburg, about forty minutes from Pendleton, and reserved a table under the name of Tim Tuttle. Bill overheard the phone conversation from the living room couch.

"Where the hell does Tim Tuttle come from?" he asked later.

"Sometimes you don't use your real name at gun shows," Tim explained.

On the stormy evening of November 22, a surprising news bulletin flashed across the television screen in the McVeigh living room. A fire was consuming Salvatore's Italian Gardens in Lancaster, a popular local restaurant half an hour from Pendleton that was known to people all over western New York for its lavish decor.

McVeigh had an idea. He grabbed one of his handguns, holstered it, and hopped into his car to check the fire scene for himself. He thought there was a chance that agents from the ATF would be there, assisting local fire investigators. He had no specific plan, but he had his gun with him.

Maybe, he thought, *I'll get a chance to shoot a federal agent.*

The weather was so bad that he couldn't tell if any feds were there, but the incident got McVeigh thinking about the possibility of launching future sniper attacks. Not far away from the smoldering restaurant was Calspan, the plant where McVeigh had worked at as a guard before hitting the road. He decided to stop by and see if anyone he knew from Burns Security was on duty.

On duty that night was Carl E. Lebron, Jr.—the same guard who had decided to record McVeigh secretly a couple of years earlier after hearing him discuss the possibility of stealing weapons from a military installation. McVeigh would not have been Lebron's first choice for a visitor on this rainy night.

"Tim, why are you here?" Lebron asked.

"Targets of opportunity," McVeigh answered mysteriously. He did not elaborate.

The sight of McVeigh showing up like this made Lebron uncomfortable. He remembered an earlier visit, when McVeigh had told him that, somewhere in his travels, somebody had fired shots at him on a ridge. When Lebron seemed to doubt the story, McVeigh had gone out to his car and brought in a dirty baseball cap with a hole in it.

Now, Lebron worried that his old co-worker had shown up because he was angry that Lebron had stopped responding to letters McVeigh had sent him from Kingman. Lebron said he stopped writing back after McVeigh asked him to photocopy some secret documents about Operation North Star, the clandestine government operation at Calspan.

But all McVeigh seemed to want was to talk politics again. "All you're doing is stomping your feet and reading literature about conspiracies," he told Lebron, who had never matched McVeigh's antigovernment zeal. "You're not doing anything." The two debated for a while, deciding eventually to shake hands and part as friends.

As McVeigh got ready to leave, Lebron asked, "Where are you going?"

"If I told you," McVeigh joked, "I'd have to kill you."

If he had known Lebron had once taped him secretly, McVeigh might not have left the guard unscathed. He had never considered Lebron a close friend, though they had spent many hours discussing politics and the New World Order. McVeigh had hoped another guard would have been working that night—preferably one who had served in the armed forces. At least then they could have jawed awhile about the military, the high point of Tim McVeigh's young life. Now all he had left were memories, and the two close friends he had retained from those days: Nichols and Fortier.

Throughout November, as he worked at organizing his grandfather's estate sale, McVeigh had remained in telephone contact with Terry Nichols. But on this rainy, windy night of November 22, it was impossible to get in touch with his buddy. Nichols was in a plane above the Pacific Ocean, flying to the Philippines to see his wife and infant daughter.

Before beginning his journey, Nichols had made a detour to Las Vegas, to fulfill an overdue fatherly obligation to his son, twelve-year-old Josh. The visit followed an admonishment from his first wife, Lana Padilla, who was angry that Nichols was never around when the boy needed him. Feeling unwanted, Josh had threatened to run away. But when Padilla had first tried to reach Nichols to seek his help with Josh, he was nowhere to be found. After Marife returned to the Philippines for the fall semester of physical-therapy classes, Nichols had quit his latest job as a Kansas ranch hand; he had bragged to rancher Tim Donahue, who had hired him, that he had a chance to double his twenty-three-thousand-dollar ranch-hand salary by working the gun-show circuit with a friend. The only friend Donahue had ever heard Nichols mention was a Gulf War veteran named Tim; the name had come up in a bizarre story Nichols had shared with his employer, in which Nichols contended that the government had implanted a computer chip in his friend Tim's buttocks to monitor his whereabouts.

For Padilla, there was nothing amusing about Nichols's disappearance from the radar screen. Unable to reach him by telephone, Padilla wrote him a letter in late October and sent it off to a post office box in Marion, Kansas, hoping it would find him. On November 6, Nichols called Padilla, who tore into him, angry that the only way to reach him was through letters. Nichols spent more time worrying about Waco and civil insurrection, she railed, than about his own son. Having robbed Roger Moore the day before, Nichols was now predicting to his ex-wife that the civil unrest over incidents like Waco would cause people to kill each other off.

During the second week of November, Nichols finally returned to Las Vegas to see Josh. Knowing how stingy Nichols could be, Padilla and her new husband invited Nichols to stay in her home rather than let him sleep outside in his pickup truck. The visit lasted almost two weeks, until it was time for Nichols to head across the ocean to visit his other family in the Philippines.

Before leaving, Nichols gave Padilla a disconcerting assignment. He handed her a sealed grocery bag, his truck keys, and a list of instructions for Tim McVeigh, and warned her that she should open the sealed package only if he failed to return from abroad. At the airport, Josh scooted out of the car to give his father a hug before he left, then returned to the car and broke into tears, telling his mother he was convinced he would never see his father again.

His mother consoled him, but she was worried too. And the mysterious package Nichols had given her made her all the more concerned. The next morning, unable to control her curiosity, she took the bag to her real estate office and ripped it open. Inside she found Nichols's life-insurance policy, a letter to McVeigh's sister Jennifer (which contained a second letter to McVeigh), and the combination to a lock on a storage unit. And there was one more item: written directions on how to locate a plastic bag hidden in a secret compartment behind the utensil drawer in Padilla's home.

If for some reason his life-insurance policy didn't pay, Nichols's note requested that the contents of the plastic bag be sent to Marife. But if the policy paid in full, the bag's contents were to be equally split between Marife and Josh. Padilla waited until mid-December, when her home was empty to investigate further. With the help of her son from a previous marriage, Barry Osentoski, she removed the utensil drawer. Behind a wood panel at the rear of the drawer was the waiting package. Inside she found a letter from Nichols to Tim McVeigh. It was filled with cryptic lines: "Your [sic] on your own now; Go for it!! As far as heat—none that I know" and "This letter would be for the purpose of my death."

Padilla was convinced that her former husband was not coming home. Along with the note to McVeigh, she found twenty thousand dollars in twenty-dollar and hundred-dollar denominations stuffed inside the plastic bag. Then, following the directions in the sealed package Nichols had given her, Padilla and Barry went to her ex-husband's storage unit and found more treasure—gold, silver, and what appeared to be jade stones. She also found a dark wig, a black ski mask, makeup, and panty hose hidden there. Padilla suddenly found herself wondering whether the ex-husband she looked to for help in raising their child was moonlighting as a bank robber.

On November 30, seven days after Padilla found Nichols's letter in the package he had entrusted her with at the airport, another bizarre message was found under even stranger circumstances. A lineman for the Metropolitan Water District of Southern California found a mysterious letter taped to the leg of a transmission tower near the California-Arizona border. The letter, in a brown envelope, was addressed to "SC" and signed by "Tim T." It was a letter of recruitment for actions against the federal government.

The letter was intended for Steve Colbern, a customer of Roger Moore's American Assault Company. Some time before the November 5 robbery of Moore's Arkansas ranch, according to McVeigh, Karen Anderson had learned that Colbern enjoyed doing desert survival "maneuvers" and had suggested to Colbern and McVeigh that they hook up. To McVeigh, Colbern sounded like a true patriot, a good man to recruit for help with his plans. Yet he was cautious in setting up a rendezvous. McVeigh asked Fortier to cover his back, just in case it was some kind of a setup. They drove out to the appointed spot in the desert, but nobody was there.

McVeigh decided to leave a note for Colbern. He climbed up the tower, taped the letter to the leg, and then taped a chemical glow stick to the letter; if Colbern was running late and showed up at night, the glow stick would help him find the letter. McVeigh also gathered some rocks and shaped them into an arrow pointing to the transmission tower. In his car, McVeigh turned a few doughnuts on the dirt road leading up to the tower. If Colbern was any kind of survivalist, he would see the telltale signs all leading to the letter.

"I will try to keep this generic in case it is intercepted," McVeigh's letter read.

> First off, I cannot be 100 percent certain of your legitimacy. This is the same way Randy Weaver was initially arrested, so I planned a rendezvous with a sniper over watch. No sense in all that until you are screened to your intentions.
>
> I am not interested in anyone who has money/gain as an underlying motive—conscious or subconscious. This came out in another "patriot" as his knee-jerk reaction to the crime bill. "Shit, it passed. I better sell my guns before they take them!" Tell me what's wrong with that whole mind set. On the other hand, if you are sincere, then you could be a valued asset. A man with nothing left to lose is a very dangerous man and his energy/anger can be focused toward a common/righteous goal.
>
> What I'm asking you to do, then, is sit back and be honest with yourself. Do you have kids/wife? Would you back out at the last minute to care for the family? Are you interested in

keeping your firearms for their current/future monetary value, or would you drag that '06 through rock, swamp and cactus . . . to get off the needed shot? In short, I'm not looking for talkers, I'm looking for fighters. Keep in contact. Notify me of any change of address or situations and respond to my other concerns. . . .

If after your initial leap of faith, you remain committed, I would eventually reveal our location. But again, on your end that is a risky proposition. You have to decide what risk to take to achieve a given goal. (What is your goal?)

All, Tim T.

P.S. And if you are a fed, think twice. Think twice about the Constitution you are supposedly enforcing (isn't "enforcing freedom" an oxymoron?) and think twice about catching us with our guard down—you will lose just like Degan did—and your family will lose.

Deputy U.S. Marshal William F. Degan was killed in the August 21, 1992, shootout near Randy Weaver's cabin in Ruby Ridge. If Colbern were indeed a federal agent, McVeigh's warning would not be lost on him.

McVeigh had originally planned to stay on in Pendleton through Christmas of 1994, but pulled stakes immediately after attending the early December gun show in Hamburg, New York. A few days later, Bill McVeigh received an upsetting phone call from a man who had bought a pistol from his son at the show. The buyer demanded to speak with Tim Tuttle.

Bill explained that Tuttle wasn't available.

"If I don't get the paperwork for the registration of this gun," the buyer told Bill, "I'm going to call the FBI."

Distraught at the prospect of his son finding himself in trouble with the FBI, Bill telephoned the Fortiers. After two calls went unanswered, he finally reached the Fortier residence at 6 A.M., forgetting about the two-hour time difference.

Mike Fortier agreed to pass on the message, and McVeigh eventually called his father to reassure him the matter had been squared away. If the

FBI was going to come after him, McVeigh thought, it wouldn't be for something so trivial as the paperwork on a gun sale. McVeigh spared his father from such reflections; yet, in a letter to Andrea Peters postmarked December 13, 1994, McVeigh dropped some hints about explosives and violence while throwing in one last attempt at romance.

"Hey, Gorgeous," he wrote.

> Poof goes your head, I know. I can take a hint, but this is my address anyway. If you ever need anything, let me know. 1. someone killed, blown up, etc. 2. a shoulder. 3. refuge. 4. fertilization from good stock when the clock starts ticking. I'll always listen. Don't hesitate to drop me a line. People may change superficially, but not underneath. Remember that.
>
> Take care and merry Christmas, Tim.

McVeigh also contacted Fortier in the second week of December, to ask whether he was interested in making some money.

"How much?" Fortier asked.

"A Benji squared," McVeigh said. Fortier did the math. Ten thousand bucks sounded good to him.

A few days later, McVeigh called Fortier and told him to come by the Mohave Motel in Kingman. Fortier and Lori arrived with a laundry list of items McVeigh had requested: two boxes, Christmas wrapping paper, scissors, tape, and the wooden stock to a rifle Fortier owned. McVeigh opened the door to his motel room and let his guests inside. As soon as he saw the wooden stock he reached for it, but Fortier pulled back.

"Why do you need my stock?"

McVeigh brushed aside the question, holding up a powerful rifle that looked like an M-16. "Will this do in a trade?"

Yes, it would.

McVeigh turned his attention to dividing the contents of a large box of silver blasting caps into the two smaller boxes Mike and Lori had brought. When he was finished, he asked Lori to gift-wrap the boxes while he and Mike talked.

McVeigh motioned to the rifle he had just given Fortier in the swap. If Fortier wanted other expensive weapons like that to sell, McVeigh said, he could have them for free. All he had to do was accompany McVeigh back to Kansas, where Roger Moore's weapons were hidden. McVeigh wanted to put the guns into the hands of people who appreciated firearms and wouldn't be so quick to let the federal government take them away. Fortier could sell the weapons on the gun-show circuit. The money he made, he could keep.

How the tables had turned. Only a few months ago, Fortier had refused McVeigh's request to max out his credit cards on cash advances. Now McVeigh was offering Fortier a free ride on the gravy train, compliments of the Moore robbery.

McVeigh explained to Fortier that he wanted to use the gun stock to help change the appearance of one of the stolen weapons, and he advised Fortier to do the same with the weapons he took from the Moore stash. "When you get the guns back here," McVeigh advised, "change the configuration of the guns. Take scopes off, change stocks, make them as cosmetically different as you can."

The next morning, the two friends jumped into McVeigh's Road Warrior and headed east on Interstate 40 with two Christmas-wrapped boxes full of electric blasting caps. Driving across New Mexico, McVeigh pointed to a yellow Ryder rental truck that had just passed them on the interstate.

"That's the vehicle," he told Fortier—the kind of truck he intended to use in the bombing, only he wanted one slightly larger.

Fortier told McVeigh that his plan to bomb a federal building "sounded stupid." He'd be better off standing on street corners, distributing leaflets. But McVeigh said his days of passing out literature were over. He thought back to his visit to Waco, when he sat on the hood of his car and sold antigovernment books and bumper stickers. A lot of good that had done. Words alone had proven impotent, McVeigh said. He needed to back his rhetoric with firepower. If anyone tried to stop him when he drove the truck bomb up to the Murrah Building, he told Fortier, he would kill them.

After spending the night in Amarillo, Texas, McVeigh and Fortier drove further east to Oklahoma City, where they slowly cruised the streets surrounding the Murrah Building.

"This is the one," McVeigh said, gazing up at the nine-story building and its dark-tinted windows.

He had scoped out the building once before, driving past it after coming across a listing for it in the government blue pages of a public telephone directory. The protruding elevator shafts at the rear of the building would be difficult to take down, McVeigh figured; research he had done on structural engineering had convinced him that the angles of the shell of the shafts strengthened that portion of the building. Driving around to the front of the building, Fortier gazed with McVeigh at the huge wall of "black glass" and a set of stairs leading down to the front doors of the structure. An access road leading up to the entrance concerned McVeigh: Was it big enough to accommodate the truck he was planning to use? Fortier assured him that three trucks that size could fit.

McVeigh insists today that he and Fortier drove away from the building without getting out of the car—or catching a glimpse of the day-care center on the second floor. "I didn't know there was a day-care center," he has said directly. The dark reflective glass made it impossible to see into the building, he says, and the only other way he could have known about the day-care center would have been to tour the building. Despite persistent rumors that would later have McVeigh walking the halls of the Murrah Building, McVeigh never had any intention of crossing its threshold. "I've never been in the Murrah Building in my life," he says.

Indeed, McVeigh has expressed actual regret about the destruction of the day-care center—a convenient position in hindsight, of course. Yet McVeigh has never expressed remorse over the deaths of the many federal employees in the building, a fact that makes his statement about the children more difficult to discredit.

"Mike Fortier and I were in front of the Murrah Building and that glass was black, just a sheen. You couldn't see kids in there. I recognized beforehand that somebody might be walking down the road with their kid or bringing their kid to work. However, if it was known there was an entire day-care center, it might have given me pause to switch targets. That's a large amount of collateral damage," McVeigh reflected.

In a subsequent interview with *60 Minutes*, he refused to comment on the day-care center, except to say it was "terrible" children were in the building. McVeigh was holding back. He had long come to the conclusion he would have changed targets had he known about the day-care center.

Once he and Fortier had finished casing the Murrah Building, McVeigh steered his car into an alley beside the nearby YMCA building. He needed to find a suitable parking spot for a getaway car. The alley, he told Fortier, would provide the benefit of a shield from the blast, protecting the escape car. The question remained open whether to park the getaway car ahead of time or have Nichols waiting in it the morning of the blast. McVeigh and Nichols could plant the getaway car before returning to Kansas to mix the bomb, leaving McVeigh to drive back down alone, deliver the bomb, and escape in the getaway car. Or Nichols could drive the getaway car into the alley the morning of the bombing, waiting there for McVeigh while he parked the truck in front of the Murrah Building. It was a decision that would take more time to settle than the twenty minutes McVeigh and Fortier spent that December day in Oklahoma City.

Turning north to Kansas, McVeigh resumed his grooming of Fortier on the finer points of working the gun-show crowd. "Wear camouflage pants," he suggested. "It's a better selling technique. And use a fake name." Fortier could find out when and where the forthcoming shows would be held from a calendar McVeigh was expecting in the mail. McVeigh hammered home the importance of altering the appearance of the stolen guns; at one point, he even told Fortier to take out a piece of paper and write down a reminder to switch rifle stocks around and remove scopes whenever possible.

The final two hundred miles of their journey to central Kansas complete, McVeigh stopped briefly at a storage locker in Council Grove where the stolen guns from the Moore robbery had been stashed. After removing a box from the locker, McVeigh then drove on to the Herington storage unit, where he looked in on the bags of fertilizer he and Nichols had collected for the bomb. McVeigh and Fortier then headed eighteen miles north to Geary Lake State Park, one of the possible sites McVeigh had selected for mixing the bomb. He told Fortier he liked the location. It was off a major highway, and people often used it as a rest stop; a Ryder truck wouldn't seem out of place there. The close proximity to Fort Riley, where soldiers were coming and going all the time, made moving vans and trucks a common sight.

The two former soldiers finished their day driving seven miles farther north to Junction City, where they ate dinner and McVeigh rented them a motel room at the cheaper single rate. Before driving up to the motel office, he told Fortier to get out of the car.

"I'm just going to say I'm alone," McVeigh said. He knew he would still get a room with two beds.

Fortier slipped into the darkness.

After renting the room, McVeigh went out to move his car, but it wouldn't start. In a hurried hush, he called, "Hey, Mike, get back over here." Fortier gave the car a shove and McVeigh pop-started it.

In the motel room, McVeigh lavished Fortier with a gift of two pistols and some ammo and clips from the box he had taken earlier from the Council Grove storage shed. The next day Fortier hit the jackpot. McVeigh loaded the trunk of a Ford Crown Victoria Fortier had just rented with so many guns from the storage shed that Fortier feared that the weight might cause the rear bumper to drag. All McVeigh asked in return was that Fortier wipe the guns clean of his fingerprints.

Before parting ways, they drove to a Pizza Hut for lunch and then to a gas station. Still concerned about the weight from the guns, Fortier asked McVeigh to watch whether the rear bumper looked suspiciously low.

"Go ahead and drive. I'll follow you and look at it as if I'm a cop following you. I'll pull up next to you and tell you thumbs-up or thumbs-down," McVeigh said.

When the country road was empty of oncoming traffic, McVeigh rolled up beside Fortier and gave him a thumbs-up. The old Army buddies headed their separate ways.

Two days later, Fortier pulled into his driveway in Kingman. He waited until nightfall before he and Lori went out to the Crown Victoria and brought the stolen guns into their home, stashing them in a closet.

Lori had received a call a few hours earlier from McVeigh. He told her he had been in a car accident in Michigan. On his way to the Nichols's ranch hand Kevin Nicholas's home, where he had been staying on and off in December, McVeigh had turned in to a gas station off of the I-75 Bridgeport exit, south of Saginaw, and a man in a pickup truck had rammed him from behind. Luckily, the blasting caps had not ignited. McVeigh could count his blessings, happy to have walked away from the crash uninjured. His beloved Road Warrior was less fortunate. The crumpled metal of the body dug into the wheel wells of the car, making it almost impossible to drive; the little front-wheel-drive car barely made it into a lot behind the gas station.

McVeigh called Kevin Nicholas for help. He knew he could count on Nicholas, with whom he'd struck up a friendship on the Nichols farm; McVeigh had even chosen to spend this Christmas with them, finding he felt more comfortable with Nicholas and his family than with his own.

When Nicholas arrived at the accident scene, he began loading McVeigh's possessions into the back of his pickup truck to take him to his house, where he was welcome to stay.

At one point, he picked up one of the Christmas packages and prepared to toss it into the truck bed.

"Don't!" McVeigh shouted.

McVeigh suddenly found himself in a dilemma. He had no intention of telling his friend of his plans, but somehow he had to explain the reason for his reaction. Seldom at a loss for words, McVeigh looked at Nicholas, who asked what was in the package. "I can't tell you what's in those boxes." He needed to think. Traveling with four hundred electric blasting caps, the remaining number from the five hundred he'd stolen from the quarry, was heavy baggage.

When he stayed with Kevin and his fiancée, Sheila, McVeigh would sleep in the same room as her young daughter, Olivia, whom he affectionately called "Miss Nellie." Sometimes he awoke in the middle of the night to find the four-year-old nestled by his feet in the top bunk. McVeigh considered it an honor that Kevin and Sheila trusted him to share the same bedroom with Miss Nellie, and it worried him to think she might come anywhere near his dangerous cargo, which he was planning to sell. He took the two festively wrapped boxes and hid them out of reach in the garage, covering them up so Olivia wouldn't mistake them for real Christmas gifts.

"Kevin, I feel I have this obligation to tell you," McVeigh said. "In those boxes I have blasting caps."

To McVeigh's great relief, Nicholas trusted his judgment and asked no more questions. It was well-known, after all, that McVeigh worked the gun-show circuit and handled dangerous merchandise. McVeigh was glad he didn't have to get Nicholas any further involved. McVeigh had hoped to sell the blasting caps to David Paulsen, a military supplies dealer who lived near Chicago. After meeting Paulsen at a gun show in Kalamazoo, Michigan, the first weekend in December and following up with some thirty-four telephone calls, McVeigh thought he had struck a deal. But the younger Paulsen turned out to be a no-show when it came time to make the transaction, McVeigh reported with a note of disgust. He did not take kindly to the snub; Paulsen would pay dearly. That, however, was a score to settle on another day.

The harsh side of Tim McVeigh never showed itself in the Nicholas home.

Nicholas's fiancée, Sheila, had found McVeigh a thoughtful listener to the details of a painful divorce she had endured before moving in with Nicholas. McVeigh would sit for hours at her kitchen table, listening patiently, and she was grateful for his attention. McVeigh had also befriended Gwenda Strider, Sheila's aunt; he felt close enough to Strider that he would write her shortly before the bombing, in a letter that would offer an insight into his mind-set in early 1995.

Before returning to Kingman in January 1995, McVeigh made a final bid to save his Road Warrior from the junk heap, asking James Nichols if there was anything he could do to fix the car. In the past Nichols had done mechanical work on McVeigh's car free of charge, but this was a body-repair job, and that wasn't Nichols's specialty. "I work with steel, not tin," Nichols said.

So McVeigh finally gave up the Road Warrior, the trusted soldier that had shuttled him from gun show to gun show for years. And in doing so, McVeigh found he felt just a little more free to forge ahead with his plans for Oklahoma City. McVeigh bought a beat-up green 1983 Pontiac station wagon from Nichols and headed southwest.

On his way back to Kingman, McVeigh ran into a severe Midwestern snowstorm. Police were chasing motorists off the roads, which McVeigh predictably resented. He was from western New York; he'd lived through the Blizzard of '77. He could navigate any snowstorm Mother Nature could throw at him. At a gasoline station, he met several stranded motorists who were talking about spending the night in their cars.

"Well, if you're going to do that, point your tailpipe downwind so you don't asphyxiate yourselves," McVeigh suggested.

Some mentioned the possibility of setting up cots in the station's two repair bays, but McVeigh wanted none of it. "Do you have a local map?" he asked.

The attendant spread one out on the counter.

"Point out real quick where we're at," McVeigh said.

"You're right here."

McVeigh listened to a radio DJ in the background announcing what roads were closed. With that information, he charted an alternative route south on back roads that skirted past the storm. Several other motorists, he noticed, had gathered around the map.

"Okay, I'm leaving," he said, extending an invitation to those who cared to follow. Outside, he topped off his gas tank and plowed forward into the snow, which was as high as the chassis on his station wagon. A caravan of nine other vehicles followed him into the storm, and for what seemed an eternity Timothy McVeigh led them in a cautious charge on twisting, treacherous roads.

Back in the desert country of Kingman, McVeigh settled into his room at the Uptown Motel. When the Fortiers arrived for a visit, McVeigh was eager to know how the gun sales were progressing. Fortier confessed that he hadn't gotten around to it.

"What did we talk about for a twelve-hour drive?" McVeigh asked, shooting Fortier a look.

Either he's a complete scatterbrain or he's just zoned out from crystal meth, McVeigh thought. When Fortier's attempts at conversation were rebuffed by a visibly angry McVeigh, the evening ended abruptly.

But there was work to be done, and McVeigh couldn't afford the luxury of prolonged frustration with Fortier. The two got past the rough patch, and by February McVeigh had turned Fortier into an eager gun-show entrepreneur. Fortier liked the feel of cash in his hand. When he returned to the motel room after his first show in Reno, he waved a wad of it at McVeigh. There should have been jubilation, but McVeigh had some tough news: Terry Nichols had returned from the Philippines, and he was "pissed off" to hear that some of the guns he'd stolen had been given to Fortier.

McVeigh proposed an arrangement that he thought would make things right. He told Fortier to fork over two thousand dollars, which he would forward to Nichols as payment in full. Fortier handed over a thousand dollars and said he'd pay the rest later. McVeigh took a thousand dollars from his own pocket and told Fortier he would front him the cash. He put the two thousand dollars in an envelope and set it aside for Nichols. But a second gun show, in St. George, Utah, had proved a disappointment. Hardly any guns had sold. "Oh shit, how can I pay?" Fortier groused. But from McVeigh's perspective, Fortier had no legitimate gripe, considering the fact that he'd been given a gift of ten thousand dollars in guns. What was two thousand dollars? Once again, for McVeigh the overriding point of unloading the guns was to put the weapons in the hands of people who could appreciate and use them, not just to make a few bucks. To be sure, McVeigh watched his pennies, but money was not something to come between friends. "If one guy left his wallet at home and you were out driving and you wanted to stop at a store, the other guy would just buy something. It was no big deal," McVeigh says. "The whole money thing was back and forth. We never took advantage of each other." Fortier didn't quite see it that way.

Terry Nichols had more pressing worries. Upon returning to Las Vegas in mid-January, he found that the cash-filled plastic bag he'd secretly stashed in his ex-wife's kitchen was missing. Nichols accused Lana of betraying his trust. She said she'd figured he was dead, judging from the tone of the letters he had left behind. One had read like his "last will and testament," Padilla recalled. Nichols persisted. He wanted his money. Padilla explained that she had put the cash in her office safe.

The veins in Nichols's neck began to bulge. He was very much alive, and he wanted his money. At some point, a phone call from McVeigh interrupted the exchange; after hanging up, Nichols told his ex-wife that McVeigh was now asking to borrow money for the purchase of a vehicle. "Would you give it to him but not give it to Josh or me?" Padilla asked. Later that day Nichols showed up at Padilla's office; she gave him the bag of cash. He returned the next day after discovering he'd been shorted five thousand dollars. Padilla told him she was keeping the money for their son, but after more discussion she agreed to turn over another two thousand dollars to Nichols and place the remaining three thousand in a savings account for Josh. Nichols took the money and headed back to Kansas, where he purchased a small house in Herington priced in the mid-twenty-thousand-dollar range. He insisted that the real estate agent, Georgia Rucker, arrange the transaction through seller financing, thus, eliminating the need for a bank mortgage. By the time Rucker finished her dealings with Nichols, she was convinced he had renounced his U.S. citizenship, though he never came out and said it.

After the third gun show in Tucson, Arizona, Fortier squared up with McVeigh, paying him the remaining one thousand dollars; the friendship was back on track. Mike found customers not only at gun shows, but among his acquaintances. In one instance, he swapped a gun for a half-pound of marijuana and an eight-ball of crystal meth. Having quit his job at True Value because of a bulging disk in his spine, Fortier now had plenty of idle time for drugs; money from the gun sales, income-tax refunds, a small benefit from

Veterans Affairs, and the generosity of Ila and Les Hart, Lori's parents, enabled the Fortiers to pay their bills. Lori would later recall the early part of 1995 as easy street for the couple, who spent day after day four-wheeling in their jeep, renting movies, and visiting friends. When McVeigh wasn't out in the desert practicing survival skills, he often joined in on the fun.

But his thoughts, more than ever, were turning toward Oklahoma City and settling a score. From a lonely outpost in the desert on February 10, he wrote his Michigan friend Gwenda Strider, whose niece was engaged to Kevin Nicholas:

> As far as the main context of your letter, I really don't know what to tell you, except write your representatives in Congress—they represent the people and they listen to them. (Yea, right!) No, really, let me try to explain—I was in the educational/literature dissemination (desert wind wreaking havoc on my already scratchy writing) field for quite some time. I was preaching and "passing out" before anyone had ever heard the words "patriot" and "militia."
>
> I passed on that legacy about ½ year ago. I believe the "new blood" needs to start somewhere; and I have certain other "militant" talents that are in short supply and greatly demanded. So I gave all my informational paperwork to the "new guys" and no longer have any to give. What I can send you, is my own personal copies; ones that are just gathering dust, and a newsletter I recently received.
>
> If you are willing to write letters, I could pass your name on to someone; but let there be no doubt, with the letters I have in mind, the literature that would be forwarded to you for copying; etc., you would probably make a list. Currently, there are over 300,000 names on Cray Supercomputer in Brussels, Belgium; of "possible and suspected subversives and terrorists" in the U.S., all ranked in order of threat.

McVeigh's allusion to the New World Order and how its leaders supposedly tracked their enemies by computer was, he later explained, a way to keep Strider on her toes and stir her curiosity. His note continued:

Letters would be of an "on notice" nature, like the ones many people (myself included) wrote to Lon Horiuchi (the FBI sniper who blew Vicki Weaver's head off), saying, in effect: "What goes around comes around. . . ." Hey, that's just the truth, and if we're scared away from writing the truth because we're afraid of winding up on a list, then we've lost already.

Moving to the main point of the letter, McVeigh cited the bravery of the Founding Fathers who were willing to give up their lives in standing up to the English crown. He too would do the same:

Hell, you only live once and I KNOW you know it's better to burn out, then [sic] . . . . . . rot away in some nursing home. My philosophy is the same—in only a short 1–2 years, my body will slowly start giving away—first maybe knee pains, or back pains, or whatever, but I won't be "peaked" anymore. Might as well do some good while I can be 100% effective! Sorry I can't be of more help, but most of the people sent my way these days are of the direct-action type, and my whole mindset has shifted, from intellectual to . . . animal, (Rip the bastards heads off and shit down their necks!, and I'll show you how with a simple pocket knife . . . etc.)

McVeigh signed off: "Seeya, The Desert Rat."

McVeigh also continued to write his sister Jennifer. He wanted to prepare her somehow for his plan to "go afoul of the law in a big way." In one letter, he warned her "something big is going to happen in the month of the Bull"— the astrological month of Taurus the bull or, in other words, April. In another letter he asked if she had followed his instructions and destroyed a previous missive. "That [earlier letter] had a lot of sensitive material in it, so it's important to know whether it was intercepted by the G-men or Dad." (Jennifer had burned it in the garage of their father's Pendleton home.) In yet another letter, McVeigh wrote:

Of course you must realize, then, that I'm not living in Arizona. You know how hard it is to get into that deep of a lie with

Dad? It's painful, especially how you have to look so confident when telling stories (lies). Why am I running? I am trying to keep my path "cool," so in case someone is looking to "shut up someone who knows too much" I will not be easy to find. I have also been working and establishing a network of friends so that if someone does start looking for me, I will know ahead of time and be warned. If that tip ever comes (I have "ears" all over the country), that's when I disappear, or go completely underground. Believe me, if that necessity ever comes to pass, it will be very difficult for anyone to find me.

His network included Mike and Lori Fortier, people Jennifer was told she could trust "in case of alert." If Jennifer wanted to call him, she should be careful: "Don't be lazy—use the pay phone and take a roll of quarters." And he warned her that "private investigators" might be tailing her into bars. "They will be watching you." To make a point, he mailed her a picture of himself disguised as a biker.

In addition to his concerns about "G-men," McVeigh also realized that Roger Moore and Karen Anderson suspected him of planning the November 5 robbery. In a flurry of letters back and forth, they had tried to lure McVeigh to their ranch on the premise that he could help solve the crime. Once there, they intended to stare him down "and he would eventually blink," according to Moore, who dangled a carrot in one of the letters by informing McVeigh that three other people had been robbed in the region and that substantial rewards were being offered. "If you come back here and solve these [cases], you'd have a hundred thousand dollars," Moore wrote.

McVeigh wasn't biting.

In a response to a letter from Anderson giving details of the robbery, McVeigh was just as coy:

When I first read it, it sounded like simple robbery—but as I examined the details and thought about it—it was a pro job, and I'm more convinced by the minute that it was a government job.

[S]omeone had to watch you for days to set that up. Then, if they went through all that trouble, why didn't they just kill

you? My theory, they wanted you alive to scare others away
from the patriot cause by telling the story.

Anderson and Moore had indeed told their story. A four-page letter they
sent to a gun group called the ".50 Caliber Club," notifying the organization
of the robbery, ended with "P.S. Our main concern is to find the perpetrators
so that we can determine whether this had something to do with law enforcement or a patriot group . . . or a professional, possibly retired SEAL or
Special Forces person because we do not feel safe on our own property because this happened on our own turf and having to carry a sidearm or assault
rifle with you to the barn while either walking or riding is not what we had
planned for our later life."

To throw Anderson off the track, McVeigh wrote her a letter saying he
had been run off the road by a car with government agents. It was a wild fab-
rication, but at worst, he reasoned, it might cause her to think, *Boy, this kid's
really out there.* Anderson persisted, at one point asking McVeigh to come
and help them put up some fencing. McVeigh realized mind games might not
be enough to hold the two at bay forever; Moore was a wealthy man who
could hire a team of private investigators if he wanted serious help in solv-
ing the robbery.

In a bid to ensure that their curiosity would be stalled until after the
bombing, McVeigh eventually called their bluff and wrote to say he would
visit the ranch on May 1—a date he never intended to keep. Moore replied
with a feint of his own: a patronizing letter packed with buzzwords referring
to the New World Order and the United Nations conspiracy to take over the
world, designed to convince McVeigh that he was on the same wavelength.
He told of taking night-vision photographs of equipment at U.S. military
bases and sending the pictures to right-wing magazines. The letter was full
of paranoid warnings: "Watch out for the radiation, virus spray and all other
type of electron mind-altering devices," he warned, and secure "some space
blankets to keep out of satellites' eyes." (The blankets were supposedly made
of a material that made it impossible for spy satellites to tell there was a person sleeping underneath.) His letter ended with a request "to let May go"—
passing, in other words, on McVeigh's suggestion for a visit—and "if you
want, write when you move or have news. My best, Bob."

Moore was hoping to delay the early May visit because he knew there was a chance Anderson might be away at a gun show at around that time, and the prospect of being alone with McVeigh was unappealing. Moore even closed the letter with the word "Burn," co-opting the salute with which McVeigh ended his own letters to Moore. Moore had done his best to craft a letter that would enflame the paranoia of an antigovernment fanatic. The only trouble was, McVeigh wasn't quite as easily manipulated as Moore expected him to be.

In manipulating Mike and Lori Fortier to assist him in his plans, McVeigh claims they misconstrued his intentions when he asked Fortier to order him fake identification. It was not for the purpose of obtaining a credit card to take out cash advances to support himself. McVeigh needed a phony driver's license for the rental of the Ryder truck. His suggestion that Fortier max out his credit card, McVeigh explains, was merely a side suggestion in response to Lori ordering free CDs under fake names.

"Listen, if you're into scams like that," McVeigh had told Fortier, "max out your credit cards and don't worry about it. They usually don't bother with amounts under three thousand dollars." The only downside, McVeigh explained, was that they'd ruin their credit rating. "So get as many credit cards as you can and do it all at once."

Using a typewriter he borrowed from Lori, McVeigh typed information onto the blank license. When he was finished, he asked whether he could use Lori's iron to laminate the document; she refused, fearing that he would ruin the iron. She volunteered to iron the license, and when she did she noticed the name McVeigh had given himself: Robert D. Kling.

McVeigh had selected the alias because he had known a soldier by the name of Kling with whom he shared physical characteristics. He also liked the name because it reminded him of the Klingon warriors of *Star Trek;* even Lori had joked about the reference, and McVeigh knew it would make the name easy to remember. "It fit too perfect." Even the address he chose—428 Maple Drive, Redfield, South Dakota—had been carefully selected. He picked an ordinary name for the street, but went to a map to find just the right town. Redfield caught his eye, and when he remembered that Redfield was also the name of a type of gun scope, the matter was decided. The birthday McVeigh assigned Robert Kling—April 19, 1972—matched the month and day Waco went down in flames. Ironing the elements of the laminated license together, Lori sealed McVeigh's new identity, but did it poorly. McVeigh later used a hair dryer to reseal the edges.

At the beginning of March, two weeks after McVeigh had resumed living in his old bedroom at the Fortiers' home, Mike headed off to "back school" at a military hospital in Prescott, Arizona. He returned by the middle of the month with a new regimen of exercises, including a daily walk, to strengthen his ailing spine. McVeigh often joined him on those walks; they offered an opportunity to talk freely. On one particular evening stroll, McVeigh revealed that Terry Nichols was backing out of his commitment to help prepare the bomb. He was having marital problems. Marife was fed up with playing second fiddle to the friendship between McVeigh and her husband. Her jealousy, McVeigh later said, made it very difficult for him and Nichols to go on as friends.

"There was always that friction there. I think I first became aware of it when Jason died at home in Michigan," McVeigh says.

"What would you do? Would you kill him if he doesn't help you?" Fortier asked.

"No," McVeigh answered. "Terry will have to help because he's in it so far."

The truth was, McVeigh wanted a willing helper, not just a friend acting under pressure. He needed someone who shared his commitment to teaching government a lesson it would never forget. Forcing Nichols into helping him wasn't what he was after. Yet something in the tone of McVeigh's answer had left Fortier with the distinct impression that McVeigh actually had considered murdering Nichols before rejecting the idea. McVeigh was aware of how cold his response had sounded. He could have smiled and put Fortier at ease, but he chose instead to let the chill of the moment play out before turning to Fortier and issuing a challenge: "I need somebody."

The words hung heavy on the night air. McVeigh tried to sell Fortier on helping him out by taking a part in the mixing of the bomb's raw material. "You're like the person who sits on a bench in a basketball game. Somebody comes out of the game, and you come in."

"Tim," Fortier snapped, "you're always using metaphors. Why don't you just speak in English?"

McVeigh gave Fortier the benefit of the doubt. His friend was strung out from the pressures of marriage and fatherhood. "Okay, Mike, I will. I have been telling you most everything that's going on because I expected you to be there if I needed you."

"I thought you were just telling me," Fortier said. He refused to take part in the mixing.

McVeigh couldn't believe what he was hearing; he couldn't believe that Fortier never expected to play a larger role in McVeigh's plot. But McVeigh wasn't about to give up on Fortier. He was planning to drive the getaway car to the airport in Las Vegas and abandon it there to throw authorities off the trail; would Mike pick him up there and drive him out into the desert after the bombing? Again, Fortier refused.

McVeigh tried yet another tack. He suggested that Mike leave Lori, that they become a couple of "desperadoes," living outside the law of the land. Fortier again refused.

"You're domesticated," McVeigh complained, "pussy-whipped." It was another form of challenge: McVeigh knew Mike had always been his own man, and now he was doing his best to goad him. But Fortier refused to budge.

McVeigh's opinion of him began to slip. He remembered how Fortier had once told him that the only way he would participate in the bombing was if a U.N. tank had pulled into his front yard.

But it wouldn't be a U.N. tank rolling into his yard, McVeigh knew. There were already enough federal and local law-enforcement officers for a takeover under martial law. McVeigh wondered whether Fortier had learned the lesson from Waco: what kind of tanks had torn up the Branch Davidians' front yard?

"What if the tank was in your neighbor's yard? Wouldn't you go to your neighbor's aid? What if it was in the yard of David Koresh?" McVeigh asked.

It eventually became clear to McVeigh that Fortier was only interested in defending his own yard. For too long, McVeigh realized, he had been ignoring his friend's selfish nature. McVeigh, on the other hand, felt consumed by a drive to save his neighbors from the all-consuming federal juggernaut—a motivation which, in McVeigh's violently constructed vision of the battle of good and evil, drew him ever closer to the Murrah Building.

. . .

On the afternoon of the last day of March 1995, after Mike announced plans to start baby-sitting his niece and possibly two other children, McVeigh packed up and left the Fortiers for the last time.

"Man, Mike, I couldn't handle a house full of kids," McVeigh said. But that wasn't his real reason for leaving. The fact was, he needed to be on the move. Now, more than ever, he wanted a private place where he could get his thoughts together and prepare for the action ahead.

He moved into a room at the nearby Imperial Motel on Route 66 in Kingman. At the registration desk, dressed as usual in his surplus camouflage fatigues, he gave his address as Fort Riley, Kansas. He spent the next twelve days in lockdown mode, almost entirely alone, thinking and planning. At night, he entertained himself with skin flicks on the Spice Channel. He left the room a few times, hiding a cache of explosives and weapons that he planned to use to fight off police, if necessary, after the bombing.

McVeigh was still unsure of what he would do after the bombing. Would he plan other terrorist acts? Hide out somewhere, armed to the teeth, waiting for the feds to come after him? He wasn't sure yet. As a distraction, he left his room one night for an impromptu visit to the Fortiers. Mike and Lori were socializing with their neighbors, playing cards and smoking crystal meth. McVeigh wanted to trade an ammo can.

"Sure," Fortier said, anxious to get rid of McVeigh. The look of determined hatred in McVeigh's eyes had begun to spook him; he knew McVeigh wasn't pleased with his refusal to go along with the plan, and the sooner he was on his way, the better.

They headed to McVeigh's old bedroom and made the swap. McVeigh gave Fortier a hard-cover ammunition storage unit that contained explosives. He asked Fortier to hold onto the cache for safekeeping; one day, he said, he might come back for it.

On three other occasions, Fortier visited McVeigh at his motel room. By this point Fortier had grown afraid enough that he had begun carrying a weapon for his own protection. A thought haunted both of the Fortiers: would McVeigh kill them because they knew too much?

Yet McVeigh was unaware of the fear that his looks and demeanor had inspired in his two friends. Twice during this period, he passed on to Fortier books he'd stolen from the Mohave Community Library—an attempt, he says, to rekindle their waning friendship. McVeigh was upset that Fortier wouldn't help him with the final preparations for the bomb, but he also understood Fortier's devotion to his wife and young daughter. McVeigh noticed that Fortier was carrying a firearm, but never thought that it had anything to do with him. To McVeigh, after all, carrying a gun was normal behavior. He thought it was strange that some people *didn't* carry guns.

The last visit between McVeigh and the Fortiers took only a few minutes. Mike and Lori had stopped by just long enough to return one of McVeigh's books. After handing it to McVeigh, Fortier offered his hand in friendship. Moved by the gesture, McVeigh clasped his buddy's hand with both of his. In Fortier's eyes he thought he could read the pain of separation. In truth, what he saw was fear.

Mike and Lori Fortier turned and left the motel room. They never made any attempt to contact authorities and warn them in advance of the bombing. They have since contended that they believed McVeigh would abandon his plans to bomb the Murrah Building. With nobody willing to help him, Lori hoped, McVeigh would just drop the idea. Mike thought that Tim was headed up to Colorado to see another part of the American West.

They would not see McVeigh in person again until his 1997 bombing trial, where they would be the two star witnesses for the prosecution.

To his sister, McVeigh sent final instructions. Jennifer should extend her spring-break vacation in Pensacola so that she couldn't be linked with the event that was to come in the month of the Bull. There was an air of finality in those last letters to Jennifer: He mailed her some of his most treasured personal memorabilia—his military records, his Starpoint High School yearbook and school records—for safekeeping. It seemed strange to Jennifer that he would go to this trouble, but McVeigh rarely did anything without a reason.

He had, in fact, planted a seed to toy with the federal agents should they discover his school records. On the sleeve of an early grammar school report card, McVeigh had noticed a blank question, "What do you want to be when you grow up?" As a boy, he had left it unanswered, but now as a man, he had an answer. McVeigh wrote "gun shop owner," knowing that would drive some of the federal agents wild. He imagined them saying that even as a boy he had dangerous inclinations. Gun shop owner!

The day before leaving for Florida, Jennifer gathered up most of the antigovernment material he had given her, dating from 1992, and put it in a box, which she entrusted to her best friend, Rose Woods of Lockport.

In one of his last letters to Jennifer, McVeigh had written: "Won't be back forever."

8

Ready to Kill

In the final days before leaving the Imperial Motel in Kingman, McVeigh tried calling Richard Coffman, a representative of the National Alliance. If any group might be willing to suggest a place he might seek refuge after the bombing, McVeigh figured, the National Alliance—an organization chaired by the author of *The Turner Diaries*—would be it.

McVeigh left three messages on Coffman's answering machine. Identifying himself as Tim Tuttle, he said he would be leaving the Kingman area soon. McVeigh knew that he had to play it cautiously in asking for help, though; he didn't want to tip his hand. He'd tell the National Alliance that he was making a "serious request for a safe haven," but would remain vague about why, if he spoke with Coffman. But he never left a number where Coffman could reach him, and ultimately failed to connect with the group.

Elohim City, the Oklahoma enclave of racial separatists, also made McVeigh's shortlist of prospective hideouts. He phoned there in search of Andreas Strassmeir, a mysterious German national known as "Andy the German," whom McVeigh had met at a gun show.

A "polite older woman" answered the phone, McVeigh recalls, and told him Andy was out. It was another dead end, but McVeigh took it in stride. There was always the Arizona desert, where he knew he could find cover. But now it was time to leave and head east. On the morning of Wednesday, April 12, one week before his target date, McVeigh checked out of his twenty-dollar-a-night room at the Imperial and cut across the country one last time.

The journey, McVeigh confirms, included a side trip to Oklahoma City, to confirm that there'd been no new road construction since he'd last checked. It had been a couple of months; he needed to know whether any new obstacle was likely to stand in his way. *I have to make sure everything is open and clear,* he thought.

Everything was.

"You never know," McVeigh recalls. "There could have been detours from construction."

When he pulled up to the rented storage unit in Herington, Kansas, on Thursday night, McVeigh noticed wisps of smoke coming from under the hood of his old station wagon. He turned the car off and sat for a moment. He suspected the radiator was leaking, but a quick look under the hood revealed a more serious problem: he'd blown a head gasket. He took a chance, started the wagon, and drove north to Geary Lake, deciding he'd rather try that than risk running into the town cop who routinely patrolled the grounds around the storage lockers. Hemorrhaging steam, McVeigh made it to the lake in time to camp out for the night.

In the morning McVeigh refilled the radiator with water from the lake, crossed his fingers, and hoped his car would start again. The engine cranked over. McVeigh pulled into the Firestone service center in downtown Junction City. It was 9 A.M. on Friday, April 14. He told the attendant he was pretty certain the head gasket had blown. The last owner, James Nichols, had experienced the same problems.

"Yep, you're right," said a mechanic after taking a quick look at the engine.

"Didn't you use to be a customer here, drive a little white car?" asked Tom Manning, the Firestone manager.

"It was gray. You were close," McVeigh said, pulling back the hood of his sweat shirt to give Manning a better look. "I'm Tim McVeigh."

Manning remembered McVeigh from his days at Fort Riley, when he'd brought his old Road Warrior in for servicing several times.

Feeling comfortable with Manning, McVeigh said, "Tom, I got three hundred bucks. You tell me if it's cheaper to fix this old piece of shit or if I need to go buy a car at some junkyard." He needed a car that could get him back to Michigan, he said—figuring quickly that over the next several days he'd be driving roughly that distance across the country. Manning estimated that it would cost five hundred dollars to replace the head gasket, which was more than three times the value of the hundred-twenty-dollar SKS rifle and thirty dollars cash McVeigh had traded James Nichols for the car.

"Here, I'll call a car dealer I know and see what he's got for you," Manning said. He dialed D.E.L. Motors and handed the phone to McVeigh, who was put on hold. Suddenly, another option popped into Manning's head.

"Hey, I got a car for you, Tim," Manning said. McVeigh hung up the phone and the two went outside to inspect a yellow 1977 Mercury Grand Marquis. It had a few problems, the least of them a broken gas gauge; Manning played it safe, stopping at a gasoline station during their test drive and pumping in a few gallons. The Mercury's transmission slipped, the engine burned oil, and the tailpipe spewed raw gasoline; its odometer read ninety-seven thousand, but McVeigh suspected the eighteen-year-old car was probably making its second run at one hundred thousand miles.

Manning drove a hard bargain for a car that was missing on a couple cylinders. He told McVeigh he couldn't part with it for less than $300, never letting on that he'd purchased the clunker for only $150 a few days earlier. McVeigh would also have to sign the station wagon over to Manning, who intended to sell it for scrap.

"As long as this car can get me to Michigan," McVeigh said, drawing three hundred-dollar bills from his camouflage wallet. McVeigh threw Manning a curve at the last minute, complaining that he wouldn't have enough money left to reach Michigan. But Manning proved magnanimous, handing McVeigh back a fifty-dollar bill, which McVeigh thankfully tucked into his wallet. He had purchased the wallet only recently because it folded open with a middle section, where he could display an old badge from his days at Burns Security. If the getaway car broke down in Oklahoma City, McVeigh figured, he could commandeer a vehicle by flashing the badge at an unsuspecting motorist and passing himself off as a cop in pursuit of the bomber.

McVeigh told Manning to mail the paperwork from the transaction to the Nichols farm at 3616 N. Van Dyke Road in Decker, Michigan, adding a note of credibility to his story. Then, as Manning gave the car a final once-over, McVeigh took a walk over to the nearby bus depot. With the phone card he and Nichols shared, McVeigh used a pay phone to call the local rental agent for Ryder trucks, Elliott's Body Shop. Giving the name Robert Kling, he asked for a quote on renting a truck to drive to Omaha, Nebraska—roughly the same distance, McVeigh knew, as Oklahoma City. Once he got the quote, he told Elliott's to go ahead and start processing the paperwork. He'd stop by the next day. Before returning to Firestone, he also placed a call to Terry Nichols at the house he'd recently purchased in Herington. McVeigh could have used a couple of quarters to make the two phone calls, but he had grown used to the "Daryl Bridges" calling card—well aware that each time he used it he automatically generated a computerized billing trail that would one day come back to haunt him. "I could have just as easily purchased a nameless calling card at any truck stop," McVeigh contends.

Back at Firestone, he found it hadn't taken much to ready the car. A small leak in the transmission seal was shored up, and the rear right tire was replaced. Manning obliged McVeigh with a decent spare tire, and even threw in a couple extra quarts of transmission fluid. Then he watched as McVeigh loaded his possessions from the station wagon into the car: a green canvas duffel bag of clothes, a gallon jug of orange hand cleaner, jumper cables, a towrope, a couple quarts of oil. The only thing left was to transfer the Arizona license plate from the station wagon onto the back of the Marquis, which McVeigh handled himself. By 10:30 A.M. he was back on the road, driving down to Geary Lake to meet Terry Nichols.

The day did not unfold smoothly. McVeigh's new getaway car was acting up by the time he caught up with Terry at the lake, stopping and starting erratically. At first McVeigh thought it was a problem with the battery; Nichols gave him a jump-start, and he drove to Wal-Mart to pick up a new one. But before he had installed the new battery, the problem seemed to fix itself. McVeigh held onto the new battery overnight, then returned it on Saturday. The car trouble, which he chalked up to a lazy alternator, provided McVeigh with an inspiration. When he dropped off the getaway car in Oklahoma City, he decided, he would place a note on the windshield: NOT ABANDONED. PLEASE DO NOT TOW. WILL MOVE BY APRIL 23. (NEEDS BATTERY & CABLE)

At 4 P.M. that Friday, he registered at the Dreamland Motel in Junction City under his own name, giving the Nichols farm as his address. McVeigh informed Lea McGown, owner of the Dreamland, that he'd be staying for several days. The nightly room rate was twenty-four dollars, but McVeigh thought he might get her to do a little better. "Well, you know," he cajoled, "why don't you just cut it to twenty bucks?" McVeigh loved to bargain, but he admits that he was also flirting with McGown, whom he found to be an attractive older woman.

McGown agreed to the discount, and accepted McVeigh's cash payment of $88.95 for four nights. As she would reveal later, the hotelkeeper was also sizing up McVeigh, though not in a flirtatious way. A divorcée whose grown son and daughter lived with her, McGown sensed that something was different about McVeigh. He himself was neat and orderly, yet the car he drove was old and worn. The two just didn't match. When he asked her if he could park a truck in the motel lot during his stay, she agreed; with so many soldiers moving in and out of Fort Riley on a regular basis, moving vans were common. But as a precaution McGown assigned him to room 25, which was beside her office. That way she could keep an eye on him, and ask him to leave at the first sign of trouble.

About 9 A.M. Saturday, McVeigh walked into Elliott's Body Shop to finalize rental of the twenty-foot truck he had called about the day before. Vicki Beemer, secretary to Eldon Elliott, owner of the body shop, had quoted Robert D. Kling two hundred dollars for the one-way trip to Omaha. The fee included the fifteen-dollar charge for a hand-truck rental, and reflected a 10 percent military discount. Kling had said he would need the truck from Monday, April 17, until Friday, April 21, two days longer than the trip would take. Elliott's waived the charge on the additional days, but charged an eighty-dollar deposit, to be refunded when the truck was dropped off with the Ryder agent in Omaha.

"Can I just pay the whole thing today while I got the money and I won't spend it?" McVeigh asked, playing the part of so many soldiers he had known.

"Yes, you can," Eldon Elliott obliged.

Before finalizing the transaction, Elliott asked Kling about his decision to decline the customary offer of insurance on the truck. It made no difference to him whether Kling took out coverage, he explained, he felt obligated to warn him that the decision would leave him liable for any damage to the truck. McVeigh kept a straight face. "I won't need any," he answered. "I'm not going very far. I'm a good driver. I drive these deuce-and-a-halfs out at Fort Riley."

Not a problem. The truck, equipped with side and rear doors, would be ready and waiting at 4 P.M.

By 9:36 A.M. Saturday, McVeigh was back at his motel room. He called Nichols, but there was no answer. McVeigh went out for a walk. He hiked through an old quarry and into a wooded area, where he sat down to organize his thoughts. His mind always worked better, he felt, when he could get out into the solitude of nature.

He hadn't expected Nichols to be out, but it was no big deal; he knew Terry had his hands full over this Easter holiday, tending to both his toddler daughter, Nicole, and his son, Josh, who was in town visiting until Monday. With no television in the house to distract the children, and, of course, Marife's frequent refrain that her husband was spending too much time with McVeigh, it was no surprise to find Terry off entertaining his family.

Around five o'clock, after his hike in the woods, McVeigh grew hungry. He called the Hunan Palace Chinese Restaurant in Junction City and asked for an order of Moo Goo Gai Pan to be delivered to his room at the Dreamland. McVeigh gave Kling as his name, but he had to correct the restaurant worker, who heard the name as "Ling."

After waiting about an hour, McVeigh grew impatient and called the restaurant back. The woman explained that orders were backed up because of heavy rains.

"Listen, the bridge is out, so you have to come through Fort Riley, the main post, to get here," McVeigh explained, trying to hasten the delivery.

At last, Jeff Davis, a twenty-two-year-old deliveryman, arrived with the $9.65 order. McVeigh handed him eleven dollars and told him to keep the change. In a development that would lead to considerable speculation, Davis would later tell government investigators that he believed the man who accepted the delivery was someone other than Timothy McVeigh. The person who opened the door to McVeigh's room was a tall, blond-haired man, he said, but not McVeigh.

Yet McVeigh insists today that Davis was mistaken. McVeigh says that he was the one who opened his motel room door and accepted the delivery from Davis; his own hair may have been light enough to pass for blond, and no other hard evidence has ever surfaced to support Davis's contention.

McGown also said she heard different voices coming from McVeigh's room during her nightly patrol of the property; she remembered taking a moment to walk extra slowly as she passed his room a second time, trying to make them out. McVeigh figures that she might have been hearing the TV or his radio; it is even possible, he speculates, that he might have been talking to himself. But he remains adamant that he had no guests in his room at any time during the four days he spent at the Dreamland watching television and reviewing his plan.

While millions of Americans were celebrating Easter Sunday, Timothy McVeigh was preparing to drive to Oklahoma City and stash a getaway car there. McVeigh had arranged to meet Nichols early that afternoon at a pizza restaurant near Nichols's home. McVeigh then would drive the Mercury to downtown Oklahoma City, with Nichols following in his truck. The two would then ride back to Kansas together.

But there was a problem: Nichols failed to show. In the last few weeks McVeigh had begun to suspect that his friend's enthusiasm for the bombing was waning, that Nichols was getting cold feet. As he waited, his anger grew. *Fortier dropped out on me,* he thought in disgust. *Now Nichols?*

Infuriated, McVeigh punched Nichols's number into a pay phone. When Nichols picked up the phone McVeigh let loose, screaming so loud that Nichols's son, Josh, could hear his voice through the phone ten feet away. This action was "for keeps," McVeigh shouted, and it must move ahead. He cursed Nichols, threatened him; his voice rising, McVeigh extended the threat to Nichols's family. One anonymous phone tip, McVeigh promised, was all he needed to put the authorities on Nichols's trail.

"*Get in your fuckin' truck!*" McVeigh screamed. "*Now! This is for keeps!*"

Nichols finally gave in. "Okay," he said, "I'm on my way."

Before he could leave, Nichols had to explain to his family why he was leaving them for at least ten hours on Easter Sunday. He told them he had to drive to Oklahoma City to pick up McVeigh, who had brought a used TV all the way from Las Vegas that belonged to Nichols. That Nichols's family was willing to accept that as an excuse says as much as anything about the close relationship between the two Army buddies.

Before he could leave, though, Josh pleaded with his father to take him along. It was his last full day in Kansas before he had to fly out to return to his mother in Las Vegas; the long ride together would give them some time together.

But Nichols refused, saying it would be too uncomfortable with three people in the truck on the way back. He promised to spend some time with the boy on Monday, maybe even rent some videos to watch together on the TV he was bringing home.

When Nichols showed up at a pizza shop where McVeigh was waiting, McVeigh had little to say.

"Okay," barked the still-enraged McVeigh, "let's go."

They drove five hours to Oklahoma City, Nichols following McVeigh's old clunker. The ride gave McVeigh time to think about the partners he'd chosen. Nichols and Fortier had been in the Army, but they'd never been to war. They didn't understand that war means action. Hard choices. Life and death. McVeigh had wanted a willing partner to take up his crusade of violence, and he wasn't pleased that Nichols had gotten cold feet. Though he saw no alternative, McVeigh hated having to twist Nichols's arm in this final stage of the plan. For McVeigh, these closing days with Nichols would involve a kind of "poker game," and fear was the card he used in forcing Nichols to ante up. He knew that Nichols feared him, and he had used that to his advantage, making it clear to Nichols that his family could be in danger if he did not cooperate. The threats touched a nerve, as McVeigh knew they would: Nichols was trying to raise a second family after failing with his first, even going so far as to accept Jason, Marife's child out of wedlock, as his own when he brought his pregnant Filipino bride to the United States. Despite their age difference, Nichols and Marife had cemented their union with the birth of Nicole and a second child soon to follow, and he was devoting real effort to making the marriage work. And, as if that wasn't enough, Nichols also had his son Josh and his relatives back in Michigan to consider, all of whom would be easy targets if McVeigh decided to get nasty.

Like it or not, McVeigh's threats were simply too powerful for Nichols to bail out.

They arrived in Oklahoma City that evening. McVeigh had selected a parking space several blocks from the Murrah Building for the getaway car. Parked in an out-of-the-way location, beside a vacant house in a parking lot with overgrown shrubs, it wasn't likely to attract much attention. The beat-up old Marquis wouldn't be a very hot target for thieves, and anyone drawn to it would be put off by the handwritten note explaining that it needed a battery and cable. Before parking it, McVeigh removed the Arizona license plate from the back of the car; he then backed up close enough to some of the shrubs that no one would notice it was missing. Before walking away, McVeigh placed a gas-station tissue wipe over the gas cap. If the tissue was missing when he returned on Wednesday, he would know that someone had tampered with the vehicle.

Tucking the Arizona license plate down the small of his back—he would later hide it in the Herington storage unit—McVeigh emerged from the parking spot and settled into Nichols's truck for a long and uneasy ride home. Barely a few sentences were grunted between the two men on the entire haul back to Kansas. When Nichols returned home shortly before two o'clock in the morning, he found his son waiting up for him.

At 9:40 the next morning, McVeigh called Nichols's house from his motel room. The call lasted fifty-seven seconds. About 3 P.M., McVeigh left his motel room, dressed in jeans and a green flannel shirt. It was drizzling lightly as he walked over to the Grandview Plaza Stop & Shop to call for a cab. By the time David Ferris, a Junction City cabbie, dropped McVeigh off ten minutes later at a nearby McDonald's, the rain was falling so hard that it was nearly impossible to see out the window of the cab. At McDonald's, McVeigh ate a hot apple pie and sipped a juice. A video camera recorded his pit stop at the eatery, but McVeigh was unconcerned.

After five minutes or so the rain eased up, and McVeigh began walking toward Elliott's Body Shop, a little over a mile away. About three-quarters of the way there, a young man—possibly a college student, McVeigh reckoned—pulled over and called out, "Do you need a ride?"

"Sure." McVeigh accepted the hospitality, though reluctantly. Inside the car, he ran a hand through his brush cut, drying off his hair, and it occurred to him to wonder whether the driver's thoughtful act would one day come back to haunt him. A moment later, he hopped out of the car and stepped into Elliott's Body Shop.

Before McVeigh could drive off with the truck, Eldon Elliott tried one more time to sell McVeigh on the insurance. *Insurance?* McVeigh thought. *Are you kidding me, buddy, the way you're going to get this truck back?*

"Have a safe trip," Elliott said, adding that if McVeigh were ever back in town he should "come in and see us." McVeigh smirked to himself.

The time stamp on the computer-generated Ryder rental agreement, McVeigh noticed, was 4:19 P.M., the numbers of the month and day of the conflagration at Waco, and of his own upcoming target date. McVeigh has since dismissed the coincidence as an eerie fluke; there was no way, he said, that he could have planned his comings and goings right down to the minute. And yet, as he considered it, the numbers 4 and 19 seemed to take on all kinds of meanings. Adding them up gave you 23, which was the date of his birthday in April. He had given his alias, Robert Kling, a birth year of 1972, which, when subtracted from 1995, equaled 23. McVeigh was fascinated by the numerical coincidence.

By 6 P.M. Monday, with the Ryder truck parked outside, McVeigh had retired for the evening into his room at the Dreamland. Leaving nothing to the last minute, he laid out his clothes for the next day and packed before sacking out for the night. It was important that he start conserving his energy. He set his shortwave radio alarm clock for 4 A.M., but on Tuesday morning his eyes snapped open five minutes before the alarm sounded. His internal clock had always been that way.

He hopped out of bed and slipped into his clothes. At 4:30 A.M., McVeigh walked out to his truck, which was parked beneath the sign in the Dreamland parking lot. After looking the vehicle over, he climbed into the cab and started it.

From her office, Lea McGown watched as he prepared to leave. To her, it looked as if he was reading a map. McVeigh might have glanced at one, but he had long ago charted and memorized his route. He still prided himself on military precision; everything he needed to know was locked up safely inside his head. McVeigh had practiced his course in dry runs, preparing for all kinds of contingencies, from flat tires to run-ins with police. He was ready for anything.

Pulling out of the Dreamland's parking lot, McVeigh drove twenty-five miles south to the storage unit in Herington. Situated on a hilltop overlooking the town, the site was isolated, so damage would be easy enough to contain if a mishap should occur with the explosives. Nichols was supposed to meet him there, but once again, Nichols was a no-show.

Angrily, McVeigh began to calculate how difficult it would be for one man to load the truck and mix the bomb components. *The hardest thing to do alone*, he thought, *would be loading the three fifty-five-gallon drums of liquid nitromethane.* Each metal drum weighed more than four hundred pounds. It would be tough going, wrestling the drums one-by-one off the wooden pallet and onto the hand truck. It would be even tougher wheeling the drum up the truck's rear retractable ramp into the cargo bay.

But McVeigh saw a way around all this work. "I decided I would siphon the nitromethane into the thirteen other empty barrels I planned to use for the main charge. With each of those drums holding roughly one hundred pounds of fuel, I figured I could manage it," McVeigh recalled in explaining how he overcame the obstacle. But before taking that step, he busied himself loading the fifty-pound bags of ammonium nitrate fertilizer—108 of them—cradling each bag in his long, sinewy arms as he walked it up into the truck.

Just as he was finishing with the bags of fertilizer, Nichols arrived. The two men eyed each other.

"Why don't we get into my truck and talk about things?" Nichols suggested.

Not interested, McVeigh said. This was time to work, not talk. Nichols didn't press the issue. McVeigh's tirade of threats from Sunday was still fresh in both men's minds.

"Dude, the truck is already halfway loaded," McVeigh said.

And so Nichols joined McVeigh muscling the vats of nitromethane up the ramp—McVeigh pushing the hand truck, Nichols pulling it. The crates of highly explosive Tovex sausage soon followed, along with spools of shock tube and cannon fuse. Once the last of the load—the plastic fifty-five-gallon drums, several five-gallon buckets, and a bathroom scale—were inside the truck, McVeigh climbed into the cab and drove north on Highway 77 with Nichols following in his pickup. They were heading to Geary Lake, the site McVeigh had chosen for the mixing. (Another site, an obscure dirt road off of 77, south of Herington, had been McVeigh's first choice, but recent heavy rains had rendered it unusable.)

About 7:30 A.M., shortly after McVeigh and Nichols arrived at Geary Lake, they almost had a visitor. Robert Nelson, an employee of Elliott's Body Shop, was driving to work when he happened to catch sight of a Ryder truck near the lake. His curiosity stirred, Nelson drove a short distance up a gravel road in search of the vehicle, but was unable to catch sight of it. Trees and a hill, he said, blocked his view. Rather than go farther, he turned around and left.

Unaware of the near miss with Nelson, McVeigh and Nichols parked beside the lake and went to work. Following the directions he had gleaned from his research on high-explosive measures, McVeigh mixed nitromethane fluid with each of the fifty-pound bags of ammonium nitrate fertilizer. The fifty-five-gallon drums were each big enough to hold several bags of fertilizer and more than one hundred pounds of liquid fuel. Nichols poured the fuel into the five-gallon plastic buckets, weighing out measurements of twenty pounds on the bathroom scale. They soon speeded up the process by marking the wall of each drum at the appropriate level.

With daylight streaming in through the cargo bay's side door, which faced the deserted lake, the translucent walls of the drums allowed McVeigh to see when the fuel reached the line he'd marked on the drum walls. Time was of the essence. "The longer the truck was parked, the greater the chance of detection," McVeigh later remarked.

At about 9 A.M., McVeigh and Nichols hit high alert, when a man and boy unexpectedly launched a boat onto the lake's choppy waters and started fishing about twenty-five yards from shore. McVeigh closed the side door and cracked open the rear roll-up door of the truck, letting in just enough light for them to continue their work. Every few minutes, McVeigh peeked outside to make sure the fisherman and his young companion weren't beaching the boat and coming over to visit. People in this part of the country were friendly, and it occurred to McVeigh that they just might innocently stop by to say hello. He earnestly hoped the fisherman would figure that whoever was in the truck was preparing for a move to or from Fort Riley and didn't want to be disturbed.

In actuality, fisherman Richard Wahl had not made that assumption. The sight of a solitary Ryder truck in the middle of nowhere had seemed odd to him. Upon arriving, he momentarily stopped his car "to look and see if there was a place to turn around in case it got ugly," he recalls. While at the lake, Wahl and his son kept a wary distance from the Ryder and never saw anyone in it.

Lucky for him. McVeigh now admits he was prepared to murder the fisherman if he got too curious. If he noticed the fisherman approaching the truck, McVeigh intended to hop out and meet him halfway. He'd explain that he was a soldier "just resting up from a move." But if the fisherman made one wrong move, he had resolved to kill him. McVeigh recognized that such an act would mean the murder of a completely innocent person, but he would not risk the whole bombing mission over one nosy fisherman. Disposing of the body would be easy enough: He would put it back in the cargo area of the truck with seven thousand pounds of explosives.

The boy was a different story. A child couldn't represent the same kind of threat as an adult, and McVeigh decided that he would let him live. He would gag the boy's mouth and bind his hands and legs, McVeigh would either hide him in the dead man's car or leave him in a motel room. In either case, by the time the boy was discovered, McVeigh would be far away.

When Wahl and the boy finally left, more than an hour later, McVeigh and Nichols stood down from their high alert. Relieved, they went back to work. "He didn't come over, and thank God that didn't happen. This would be a person stumbling into something he shouldn't have," McVeigh recalls of the tension.

Work on the bomb progressed at a steady but tedious pace. Each barrel, when filled with both ammonium nitrate and nitromethane, weighed nearly five hundred pounds. Four black barrels, which had lift-off lids, were the easiest to fill. The other remaining barrels—one blue and eight white—all had to be filled through narrow holes at the top of the drums, using a funnel. The process took a while, but before long the bomb started taking shape in the configuration McVeigh had designed. The barrels roughly formed a letter T, with the top flush against the front of the cargo bay wall closest to the truck's cab. It wasn't the best configuration, McVeigh reflected; for pure destructive power, the optimum configuration would be to place all of the barrels on the side of the cargo bay closest to the Murrah Building. But seven thousand pounds of unequally distributed weight, he realized, would either break an axle or flip the truck over. Even if neither happened, the truck would list to one side, and the last thing that McVeigh wanted was to draw attention as he drove toward Oklahoma City.

At the base of the T, closest to the roll-up rear door, McVeigh created a curve with a few remaining barrels, forming the start of a backwards J. This would deliver the bomb's fury that much closer to the target. And to add even more power to the explosion, he added seventeen bags of ANFO—ammonium nitrate wetted down with fuel oil—to the back of the truck.

With the configuration of the main charge completed, McVeigh began work setting up the dual-fuse ignition system he had designed. He drilled two sets of holes through the back of the cab, behind the driver's seat, and matched them with similar holes drilled into the wall of the cargo box. He then ran plastic fish-tank tubing through the holes, creating a conduit for a two-minute fuse and a second, five-minute fuse, which would serve as a backup. The tubing would protect the fuses from "road chips" and other flying debris.

To strengthen the links, McVeigh went back inside the cargo bay and wrapped the ends of the tubes together with duct tape, anchoring them to the wall to make it more difficult to disable the fuses by yanking them from the outside. Only a precious little block of time was needed, McVeigh knew, for the fuses to burn beyond the tubes and into the cargo box. He had timed how long it took for cannon fuse to burn—thirty seconds per foot. Leaving nothing to chance, he had spray-painted the plastic tubing yellow to help it blend in with the Ryder truck.

When the time came to light the fuses, McVeigh would use a simple cigarette lighter. He had deliberately chosen this form of manual ignition over timers and remote-control devices. Setting the fuses by hand minimized the risk of an accidental or premature explosion. Of the bombers who mistakenly killed themselves in delivery of their wares, McVeigh had learned, most died because they depended on electric fuses and mercury switches, which were all too easily set off by an unintended jolt or static charge.

Inside the cargo box, McVeigh placed the ends of each fuse into the hulls of separate, non-electric blasting caps. The thin, silvery aluminum caps were easily bendable. Some people, he'd heard, crimped the fuses with their teeth in a gesture of bravado, sometimes blowing up their teeth in the process. McVeigh played it safe, using a pair of pliers. The blasting caps were also fastened to two lines of shock tube, which, when the caps exploded, would instantaneously transfer a spark to the Tovex. McVeigh had packed one of the five-gallon buckets full of the eighteen-inch lengths of Tovex sausage and strategically placed it at the intersection of the T. On one side of the T he placed one of the barrels to form a triangular shield around the bucket, which would act like an oversized blasting cap and detonate the main charge. He was proud of the ignition system he had constructed. *The perfect redundancy,* he thought. *Two fuses completely independent of each other and wired into completely independent caps.*

If for some unimaginable reason they failed, he created a third redundancy, which could cost him his life but ensure detonation of the bomb. Tucked in the front corner of the driver's side of the cargo bay he placed more explosives that could be ignited on impact. As a last resort, he would fire his pistol at close range to set them off. The blast thundering into the Oklahoma City morning would certainly devour him, but it didn't matter to McVeigh. To him life was a small price to pay for the lesson he intended to teach.

The building of the bomb nearly finished, McVeigh found he had more than enough explosive energy to spare. McVeigh realized that the three metal drums that had contained the nitromethane and the pliers he had used to crimp the blasting caps were excess evidence, and he figured the quickest and most efficient way to dispose of the objects was simply to leave them in the back of the truck—to be destroyed with the rest of the vehicle.

The job of mixing the bomb completed, McVeigh wiped down the inside of the truck's cab for fingerprints, lest any identifiable shred of the cab survive the blast. Then he washed up in the lake, changed into a fresh set of clothes, put on a pair of gloves, and climbed back into the cab. He placed his bomb-sullied clothes in a bag. He would dump them later in a trash receptacle on the way to Oklahoma. More than three hours had passed since he and Nichols had started construction of the bomb. Now they parted company; it was the last time they would see each other as free, unshackled men.

Leaving Geary Lake, McVeigh cracked open a ham dinner from his MRE provisions, devouring it as he drove south on Highway 77. Nichols also headed south, but turned off at Herington, eating lunch at home before going to an auction at Fort Riley. McVeigh continued farther south. Before crossing the Kansas state line into Oklahoma, he purchased forty dollars' worth of gas. He then drove into northern Oklahoma and headed south, stopping for the night in a small gravel lot near a roadside motel.

The following morning, he intended to drive up to the Alfred P. Murrah Federal Building at eleven o'clock. But when dawn arrived, McVeigh made a last-minute change of plans. Waiting any longer than necessary behind the motel, he realized, might prove dangerous. He could no longer risk an encounter with an inquisitive local. And so McVeigh made a "command decision," and advanced the bombing to nine o'clock in the morning. It was a decision he would later regret; he had failed to consider that a large number of nongovernment citizens would appear in the building first thing in the morning for various governmental services at the Murrah Building. But now, as dawn broke on Wednesday, April 19, those realities were far from his mind. McVeigh looked around the parking lot and set his sights southward.

In a matter of hours, he would shower hell on Oklahoma City.

III
BOMBER

9

Ground Zero

It was after 7 A.M. when Timothy McVeigh pulled out of the parking lot where he'd passed the night. By nine o'clock he would be closing in on his target in Oklahoma City.

On this day McVeigh would not drive with his usual abandon, sliding through turns with no regard for speed limits. He would take special care to keep the Ryder truck safely on the highway. Of course, the main reason was caution; with seven thousand pounds of explosives behind him, he could hardly afford a traffic accident.

But McVeigh had another reason—a tactical reason—for taking his time. He did not want to get there too early, before the Alfred P. Murrah Building filled up with people. He wanted his body count.

It was an issue to which McVeigh had devoted considerable thought. He knew that the vast majority of workers in the building—more than five hundred of them—worked during the day. He had considered setting off his bomb at 11 P.M., or even at 3 A.M., when the only fatalities would be a few security guards, maybe some cleaning people. With any luck, he thought, a federal agent or two might be lingering in the building, perhaps listening to a wiretap or filling out a report.

But that wouldn't accomplish what he wanted, McVeigh felt. The feds would just dip into their endless reserves of cash and put up another building. "The government could give a shit about a building," he concluded. "They've got bottomless pockets of cash to build a new one." The federal juggernaut would hardly lose a step. His entire purpose was to make a statement that could not be ignored; he had no interest in mounting an action that would be little more than a footnote in history.

To McVeigh, a serious loss of human life was the only way to put a sufficiently powerful exclamation point behind his message to the American government.

The American military had been using the same philosophy for years, he would argue. American bombing raids were designed to take lives, not just destroy buildings. The atom bombs that brought a bloody end to World War II—the bombs in whose image he saw his own—were designed to kill not just hundreds, but hundreds of thousands of people. He claimed to take no pleasure from killing. But in his mind, McVeigh had no trouble justifying what he was about to do.

At least two of the agencies he most despised—the ATF and the DEA—would be affected by the blast, as would the Secret Service. As for the other agencies in the building—such as the Social Security Administration, the Department of Housing and Urban Development, and the Department of Agriculture—they were all part of a government he regarded as evil and out of control.

Many of the people he planned to kill today had nothing to do with the law-enforcement agencies that were involved in the deaths at Waco and Ruby Ridge. And to justify this to himself, McVeigh summoned an image that had remained with him since his childhood: the destruction of the Death Star in the 1977 motion picture *Star Wars*.

McVeigh saw himself as a counterpart to Luke Skywalker, the heroic Jedi knight whose successful attack on the Death Star closes the film. As a kid, McVeigh had noticed that the *Star Wars* movies showed people sitting at consoles—Space-Age clerical workers—inside the Death Star. Those people weren't storm troopers. They weren't killing anyone. But they were vital to the operations of the Evil Empire, McVeigh deduced, and when Luke blew up the Death Star those people became inevitable casualties. When the Death Star exploded, the movie audiences cheered. The bad guys were beaten: that was all that really mattered. As an adult, McVeigh found himself able to dismiss the killings of secretaries, receptionists, and other personnel in the Murrah Building with equally cold-blooded calculation. They were all part of the Evil Empire.

"I didn't define the rules of engagement in this conflict," he said later. "The rules, if not written down, are defined by the aggressor. It was brutal, no holds barred. Women and kids were killed at Waco and Ruby Ridge. You put back in [the government's] faces exactly what they're giving out."

Aside from constructing the bomb itself, McVeigh had performed careful reconnaissance in preparing for every aspect of his plan. On one of his previous trips to Oklahoma City he had scouted the exact route he would take to get there, looking for speed traps, highway construction, possible road hazards, and, especially, underpasses too low for the truck. On the morning of the nineteenth, McVeigh was careful to stay at or below the speed limits, and to signal all his turns and lane changes. Even with his precautions, though, McVeigh eventually noticed that a marked police car had fallen in behind him. The cop stayed behind McVeigh for several miles, riding his tail as he neared the city.

Again and again McVeigh glanced at his rearview mirrors, trying his best to look unconcerned. The cop was still there.

"At this point, I'm thinking, *Why is he following me?*" McVeigh recalls. "*I know it's not my driving. Is there some problem with the truck?*"

Like a soldier, he began running scenarios through his head. What would he do if the cop tried to pull him over? If the stop was for some traffic infraction, would the cop ask to look into the cargo area?

He wasn't that far from Oklahoma City. McVeigh decided that if the cop tried to pull him over, he would ignore him and head straight for the Murrah Building. McVeigh resolved he "would run the cop off the road if I had to."

He was also prepared to use the black Model 21 semiautomatic .45-caliber Glock pistol he was wearing in his shoulder holster. The gun was loaded, and McVeigh was ready to draw the weapon and start firing if he needed to. In the chamber, the handgun had a Black Talon bullet, sometimes known as a cop-killer. Once it penetrates a human body, the Black Talon mushrooms, ripping apart the victim's internal organs. In the clip of the gun were thirteen more bullets, standard high-velocity rounds.

But the problem with the police car took care of itself. Just as McVeigh was thinking about how he would run him off the road, the officer veered off down another road.

McVeigh rolled on, focusing on the mission ahead.

The nubs of the two fuses he had installed the day before were sticking into the cab of the truck, just behind his left shoulder. McVeigh planned to light the two fuses, park the truck in the small parking area in front of the Murrah Building, and walk away. "If I needed to, I was ready to stay in the truck and protect it with gunfire until the bomb blew up," McVeigh says.

And although McVeigh considered his an essentially military mission, he had not neglected to carry with him the evidence of the apocalyptic political ideology that had first triggered his plan.

The date he chose for the bombing was significant in two ways. Not only was it the second anniversary of the Waco raid; just as important to McVeigh, April 19, 1995, was the 220th anniversary of the Battle of Lexington and Concord, the "shot heard 'round the world" that began the war between American patriots and their British oppressors. To McVeigh, this bombing was in the spirit of the patriots of the American Revolution, the stand of a modern radical patriot against an oppressive government.

As a token of his defiance, McVeigh was wearing his favorite Patriot T-shirt—the one with a drawing of Abraham Lincoln and the phrase SIC SEMPER TYRANNIS—"Thus ever to tyrants"—that was shouted by John Wilkes Booth after he shot Lincoln in the head in a Washington, D.C., theater in 1865. On the back of the shirt was the jolting image of a tree with droplets of red blood dripping off the branches, and superimposed on the tree, McVeigh's favored quote from Thomas Jefferson: THE TREE OF LIBERTY MUST BE REFRESHED FROM TIME TO TIME WITH THE BLOOD OF PATRIOTS AND TYRANTS.

McVeigh was expecting to be either captured or killed after the bombing, and he had packed a plain white envelope with articles he hoped would be found in the old Mercury. He was counting on police to leak details of the articles to the news media, and on the media to gobble up the leaks and pass his message on in turn to the public.

The collection of documents inside the envelope offered a varied and disturbing window into McVeigh's philosophy. There was a bumper sticker that read, WHEN THE GOVERNMENT FEARS THE PEOPLE, THERE IS LIBERTY. WHEN THE PEOPLE FEAR THE GOVERNMENT, THERE IS TYRANNY. Under the printed slogan—a quote from the Revolutionary War patriot Samuel Adams—McVeigh had scrawled, "Maybe now, there will be liberty!"

Also included was a pamphlet, "The American Response to Tyranny," equating the American militia movement with the colonists who rose up against the British 220 years earlier.

"At sunrise, on Wednesday, April 19, 1775," it read,

> 400 government troops arrived in Lexington, Massachusetts, to disarm the citizens, so as to destroy any potential resistance to the growing tyranny of government in that time. About 100 colonists, none of whom had any strictly personal reason for becoming involved in what was about to occur, gathered with their assault rifles on the green just above the bridge. No family members were in jail, neither had they been shot by the British. No economic gain motivated these men to stand against the British forces. No monetary value could have been placed on their risk to life that they feared. They stood, and fought, on principle for their rights and for liberty.

The pamphlet's author contended that most modern-day Americans lacked that kind of courage. But men who belonged to militia groups two centuries ago were different.

"The motto of many American militias was, 'Don't tread on me,' which was symbolized by a coiled rattlesnake—an animal which, when left to exist peaceably, threatens no one, but when trodden upon, strikes as viciously and with as deadly an effort as any creature on earth." McVeigh used a marker to highlight this section about the rattlesnake striking. He considered his bombing to be a strike for the greater good of the American people, rather than a crime motivated by greed.

The packet, more than a quarter-inch thick, also included articles criticizing the government's handling of the Waco siege. Some of the articles referred to federal agents as "Gestapo" or "Terrorist Goon Squads." One article made the same link between the Waco raid and Adolf Hitler's attacks on German Jews that militia groups had been making since the event itself.

And there were dozens of other items: quotes about liberty from Jefferson, Patrick Henry, Winston Churchill, and John Locke, whose writings about big government helped inspire the American Revolution. "I have no reason to suppose that he who would take away my liberty, would not, when he had me in his power, take away everything else," Locke wrote, in a famous passage McVeigh copied and stashed in his sampler. "Therefore, it is lawful for me to treat him as one who has put himself into a 'state of war' against me, and kill him if I can."

Another document quoted Samuel Adams's challenge that those who value wealth more than liberty should "crouch down and lick the hands which feed you."

There was even a copy of the Declaration of Independence; on the back, McVeigh had written: "Obey the Constitution of the United States, and we won't shoot you."

Perhaps most telling, though, was the inclusion of a quote from Earl Turner, the protagonist of *The Turner Diaries*, whose protest of gun laws and political correctness culminated in the bombing of the FBI headquarters and other government buildings.

"The real value of our attacks today lies in the psychological impact, not in the immediate casualties," Turner writes in his diary. "More important, though, is what we taught the politicians and the bureaucrats. They learned this afternoon that not one of them is beyond our reach. They can huddle behind barbed wire and tanks in the city, and they can hide behind the concrete walls of their country estates, but we can still find them and kill them."

McVeigh was fully expecting to be stopped in his tracks by the end of the day of the bombing—whether killed by the bomb, killed in a shootout with police, or arrested in his getaway car. Indeed, even the simple gesture of leaving the license plate off the Mercury, he knew, would make it easier for cops to apprehend him.

McVeigh was not suicidal, but he had developed an indifference to life, his own in particular. Like Earl Turner, McVeigh had decided his cause was more important than his life. And he knew that once he was stopped, the news media would swoop in and tell the public every detail of his arrest, his trial, his life story, and his politics.

About 8:50 A.M., McVeigh entered Oklahoma City, a proud community of 440,000 people. The weather was warm and sunny, the sky a brilliant blue. Most people in the downtown area were just settling into what promised to be an ordinary workday. McVeigh wore no expression as he sat at the wheel of the truck. He was devoting every ounce of energy to scanning his sur-roundings, running over in his head every contingency he might face in the next few minutes.

At the first stoplight he encountered in the downtown area, he reached into his pocket and pulled out a pair of green foam earplugs. Someone had given McVeigh the plugs a couple of years earlier, when he was working se-curity at a Monster Truck show back home. He crammed them into his ears.

Nobody in downtown Oklahoma City took much notice of the yellow rental truck as it rumbled up NW 5th Street a few minutes before 9 A.M. Ry-der trucks drove through the city all the time. It was one reason McVeigh picked the Ryder.

He was surprised how little traffic there was on NW 5th.

Keeping his eyes peeled for onlookers, McVeigh pulled the truck briefly over to the side of the road, just long enough to pull out a disposable lighter and ignite the five-minute fuse to his bomb. The sizzling fuse began to fill the truck cab with smoke and the acrid smell of burning gunpowder. As he con-tinued along NW 5th Street, McVeigh had to roll down both windows to let some of the smoke out.

Just past the Regency Towers apartment complex, a block from the target building, McVeigh had to stop for a traffic light. Now, he lit the shorter bomb fuse—the one he had measured at approximately two minutes.

For the longest thirty seconds of his life, McVeigh sat watching the red light, with both fuses burning. His fingers tight on the steering wheel, he glared up at the light, willing it to change.

The light turned green. McVeigh made sure to ease away from the inter-section. No stomping on the gas pedal. No frantic movements.

He approached the building carefully. As his eyes fell upon it, the enormity of what he was about to do hit Timothy McVeigh as if for the first time.

Just as quickly, he pushed the thought aside.

McVeigh finally spotted the location he had chosen for the bomb—a drop-off point, several car lengths long, cut into the sidewalk on the north side of the structure. Not one car was pulled up there when he arrived, and when he realized that fact, McVeigh breathed a sigh of relief. If the drop-off spots had been filled with cars, he'd decided, he would drive onto the sidewalk and crash his truck into the building. That would not be necessary now.

As calmly as any delivery-truck driver making a routine drop-off, McVeigh parked right below the tinted windows of the America's Kids Day Care Center on the second floor.

McVeigh looked over his creation one last time. The fuses were still burning, the shorter of the two nearly complete. The vehicle was parked exactly where he wanted it, its back end facing the building.

He grabbed his envelope full of antigovernment articles, locked up the truck, and walked away.

In the next half-minute, perhaps a dozen people saw McVeigh walking away from the Murrah Building. He was wearing a nondescript blue windbreaker over his Abe Lincoln T-shirt, with a black baseball cap, Army boots, and faded black jeans.

Looking straight ahead, McVeigh walked at deliberate speed toward the nearby YMCA building, across NW 5th at the intersection of Robinson Avenue.

He never looked back.

From his earlier visits to downtown Oklahoma City, McVeigh knew he could make it behind the YMCA building in plenty of time to avoid the blast, even walking at normal speed.

As he crossed NW 6th Street, a block from the Murrah Building, he noticed a police car parked on the side of the street. Looking out the corner of his eye, McVeigh couldn't tell if there was an officer inside the car, and he wasn't about to stop for a closer look. He wondered whether the cop would be looking right at him when the moment came.

He kept walking.

McVeigh counted off the seconds to himself as he walked north into an alley off NW 6th Street. He was now about 150 yards from ground zero, the spot where he had left his truck. Now, with the police car out of view, McVeigh broke into a jog for the first time.

That bomb should have blown by now, he thought. For an instant he wondered if something might have gone wrong.

Oh man, am I going to have to walk back there and shoot that damn truck?

Then he heard the roar.

And felt it.

The Murrah Building's explosion lifted McVeigh a full inch off the ground. Even muffled by earplugs, with the YMCA and other buildings forming a buffer, the sound was deafening. It was the equivalent of three tons of TNT. When he looked up, McVeigh could see buildings wobbling from side to side, plate glass showering down into the street around him. He felt the concussion buffeting his cheeks.

The brick facade tumbled down from one of the buildings. A live power line snapped and whipped toward McVeigh. Some falling bricks struck him in the leg, but he was able to hop out of the way of the power line. Smoke and dust billowed high into the air. Fires erupted.

Just like at Waco, McVeigh thought. *Reap what you sow.*

The blast had rocked hundreds of downtown buildings. Every one of the structures in a sixteen-block area surrounding the blast was damaged, some so badly they would have to be demolished.

Fragments of the Ryder truck had rocketed in every direction. A mangled piece of truck frame, four feet long, soared skyward and landed on the roof of a building nearly two blocks away. Another piece of the vehicle, its 250-pound rear axle, whirled like a boomerang the distance of two football fields before crashing down on the hood of a red Ford Festiva near the Regency Towers Apartments, narrowly missing a man named Richard Nichols, his wife, and their young nephew.

McVeigh refused to look behind him, never stopped to gaze at his handiwork. He kept walking, eyes straight ahead, toward his beat-up getaway car, still parked in a lot several blocks from the blast site, its PLEASE DO NOT TOW sign still in the windshield.

He almost bumped into a man rushing in the other direction, toward the rising smoke at the Murrah Building. The shaken man, dressed in a dark uniform, looked to McVeigh like he worked for some kind of delivery company.

For a few seconds they were just a couple of strangers, sharing their nervous observations after the horrific experience.

"Man," said the delivery worker. "I thought that was us blowing up!"

"Yeah," McVeigh said. "Me too."

Minutes later McVeigh was at his Mercury. He gave the car a quick look. The piece of tissue he'd left in the gas tank had not been disturbed; no one had messed with it.

But when he got behind the wheel, his eighteen-year-old getaway car wouldn't start.

He tried several times; the engine wouldn't turn over. McVeigh smelled gasoline.

He stomped the gas pedal to the floor. No luck.

He tried again, and again.

Finally, the old engine coughed to life. McVeigh put the pedal to the floor. His tires squealed as he hauled ass out of the parking area. *I do not want to get caught in Oklahoma City,* he thought.

The automatic transmission in the old car was slipping badly as McVeigh headed north. By 9:10 A.M., eight minutes after the bombing, he had regained his composure and was driving under the speed limit.

An observer watching the scene from a helicopter would have seen many of the people of Oklahoma City rushing toward their crippled federal office building. They would have seen drivers abandoning their cars on the road and running toward the blast scene to provide what help they could. They would have seen the flashing emergency lights on dozens of police cars, fire trucks, and ambulances, all heading toward the rising dust and smoke.

And if they looked closely, they would have noticed an old yellow sedan heading slowly in the other direction. After delivering his ghastly wake-up call to the American government, McVeigh was cruising out of town.

He did not go back and look at what his bomb had done to the Murrah Building. The sound of the explosion told him all he needed to know. *With a noise like that,* he figured, *the whole building must have gone down.*

He was certain that many had died, and he had no regrets. In fact, he could feel the anxiety leaving his body.

It's over, he thought.

10

Body Count

As McVeigh headed north, Oklahoma City was reeling from the worst disaster in the state since the Dust Bowl storms of the 1930s. That morning, not a single Oklahoman could have known or cared about the reasons behind the bombing, or about the life and obsessions of the as-yet-unknown bomber. They were dealing with a firestorm, a real-life nightmare so bloody and horrifying that thousands of people would be haunted by it the rest of their days.

McVeigh's bomb did not take down the entire nine-story building, as he hoped it would, but it punched a gaping horseshoe-shaped hole in the north side of the structure. As the northern face came crashing down, employees and visitors to the building tumbled down with it.

The blast killed 167 people; 163 of those killed were inside the building at the time of the blast. A 168th victim, a nurse who rushed to the scene trying to help the injured, died while assisting in the rescue efforts. One woman was killed across the street in the Athenian Building, which housed a Greek restaurant. A man and a woman died in the Oklahoma Water Resources

Building, also across the street. Another woman was killed as she walked through a nearby parking lot. And at least 509 people were injured, many of them seriously. McVeigh's bomb killed twenty more people than the 148 Americans killed in combat during the Gulf War.

Eight of the victims were federal law-enforcement agents, and five others were law-enforcement support personnel.

Many of the dead, as McVeigh knew to expect, were employees of other federal agencies—non-law-enforcement agencies such as the Social Security Administration, the Federal Highway Administration, the Agriculture Department, and the Department of Housing and Urban Development. Although McVeigh considered those agencies part of the federal juggernaut, he did not consider them his targets.

And some of the victims, such as the children in the day-care center and the civilians who were in the Murrah Building that morning to inquire about government services, were people McVeigh would regret killing. He would regard their deaths as "collateral damage."

Some were annihilated instantly. Some fell several floors to their deaths. Some were crushed beyond recognition, mangled, or decapitated. Some lost arms or legs. Some bled to death while rescuers tried to find them. Some were horribly burned or disfigured.

Ninety-nine of the dead worked for the federal government. The other sixty-nine did not.

The dead ranged in age from three months to seventy-three years.

The bomb killed nineteen children, ages five and younger. Four of the children were visitors to the building; the fifteen others were babies and young children from the day-care center. Their bodies were carried out of the building and laid on the pavement outside, covered with blankets; their playground behind the building was pressed into use as a temporary morgue.

Soon after, the medical examiner's office brought two refrigerated trucks to the blast scene to store the bodies until they could be taken to the morgue. One by one, technicians put the bodies through X-rays, fingerprinting, dental examinations, and blood tests, all for identification purposes.

Three unborn children were killed, including the unborn son of Carrie Ann Lenz, a Drug Enforcement Administration employee who, just before the blast, had been showing her co-workers an ultrasound videotape of her baby.

The bomb killed a cross section of Americans—one hundred twenty-five Caucasians, thirty-four African-Americans, five Hispanic-Americans, two Asian-Americans, one Native American, and one Pacific Islander. Five married couples, all of whom were nearing retirement age and had gone to the Murrah Building to get information about Social Security, were also among the victims.

McVeigh's former colleagues in the Army were hit hard. The Army had personnel working on the third and fourth floors of the Murrah Building, on the devastated north side. Seven employees of an Army recruiting office were killed.

Also killed there was three-year-old Kayla Marie Titsworth, who was visiting the fourth-floor Army office with her family. Her father, Sergeant William Titsworth, her mother, Chrissie Titsworth, and her sister, Katie, five, were all injured in the blast. The family had driven in from Fort Riley just that morning, and had parked their car outside the Murrah Building only minutes before McVeigh arrived with his bomb. Thirteen other Army employees were injured.

The fatalities included Secret Service agents Donald Ray Leonard, Alan G. Whicher, and Mickey B. Maroney, veteran agents who had faced danger all over the world protecting presidents, popes, and other dignitaries.

Three of the slain victims were close relatives of Oklahoma City resident Daina Bradley, who did not work for the government. Bradley had come to the Murrah Building to get a Social Security card for her baby boy, three-month-old Gabreon D. L. Bruce. Bradley and the baby were accompanied by her mother, Cheryl E. Hammon, her sister, Felicia Bradley, and her daughter, Peachlyn Bradley, three.

Bradley noticed a Ryder truck as it parked outside, and saw the driver get out of the vehicle. Soon after, she saw a flash of light come over a desk in the Social Security office. The next thing she knew, Bradley was lying in six inches of water. Her leg was buried under a huge mound of rubble. Her mother, son, and daughter were dead, her sister terribly burned. Bradley was trapped beneath the rubble for five hours. The rescuers who finally freed her had to cut off her right leg at the knee to do it.

Similar stories abounded, as the world would learn in the coming days and weeks. Patti Hall, a veteran employee of the Federal Employees Credit Union, was another who experienced a brush with death. Hall, fifty-eight, worked on the third floor. As McVeigh was driving up to the Murrah Building, she was stepping out of her office into a hallway with a can of air freshener in her hand. She had gone out with the air freshener because a man with terrible body odor had just passed through the hallway.

Just as Hall pressed down on the button of the air freshener, the Murrah Building blew up. For a fraction of a second, before she blacked out, she wondered in astonishment whether there was some kind of connection between the explosion and her spraying the air freshener.

Hall suffered cuts, bruises, and broken bones all over her body; she was in a coma for five weeks before recovering. But she was luckier than Robbin Ann Huff, thirty-seven, her co-worker in the credit union. When Hall walked out of her office, Huff sat down at Hall's desk to talk for a minute with another employee. Pregnant with her first child, Huff was killed.

Richard E. Williams, the assistant building manager for the General Services Administration, knew virtually every federal employee who was killed or injured in the blast. Williams, fifty, had worked in the building since it opened in 1977. Working his way up from maintenance mechanic, at one time or another he had been around to every single office in the building.

Williams was standing in his first-floor office, less than one hundred feet from McVeigh's ground zero, when the bomb hit. Hundreds of pieces of broken glass, stone, and metal pummeled the right side of his body as if they'd been shot from a cannon. He fell, nearly unconscious. Two of his closest friends in the office, Steve Curry and Mike Loudenslager, were killed.

As he lay in a haze, with his right hand broken and his right ear hanging on by a flap of skin, Williams heard a voice call out: "Hang on. I'll be right back." An Oklahoma City policeman, Terry Yeakey, had noticed Williams's arm rising from a pile of rubble. Yeakey, six-feet-four and built like a bull, carried the 225-pound Williams out of the building on his back.

Williams had served in the Air Force in Vietnam. The Oklahoma City bombing, he said, was a hundred times worse than anything he witnessed during the war. "In the war, you knew the enemy was coming after you. You were prepared. You could defend yourself," he said. "We had no warning for this."

Most of the dead would not be positively identified for several days. For some, it took weeks.

All Oklahoma—indeed, all of America—was in shock.

.   .   .

As he headed north in his Mercury, McVeigh says, he felt the satisfaction of a mission accomplished. In his mind, he had watered the tree of liberty— with the blood of Oklahoma City.

McVeigh maintains that he was not nervous as he drove away. He knew the toughest part of the job was behind him. And he didn't care whether he got caught.

Still, he was on high alert, scanning the highway intently.

He was an hour's drive north of Oklahoma City, heading toward the Kansas border, giving little thought to the implications of what he'd done. He wasn't following the news on the radio; the Mercury didn't even have a radio. He had access to a police scanner, but hadn't bothered to bring it. He just wanted to drive, to see what happened.

He did think back to how he had dealt with his first killing, back in the Gulf War. When he blew away the two Iraqis, he didn't dwell on it right away. "In a combat situation," he said, "you do your duty and set your feelings aside. It's like saving your emotions in a memory bank for later access."

He looked for helicopters and police cars, marked or unmarked. He drove at what he considered the normal speed for motorists, about two miles per hour above the speed limit. He signaled all his turns and obeyed all traffic signs and signals.

So far, the only complication had been a construction project that squeezed traffic into a single lane for a few miles. He'd been stuck behind a bus for a while. Otherwise, the drive was incident-free. After pulling off the bloodiest attack on American territory since Pearl Harbor, he was driving away a free man.

But McVeigh figured he might run into trouble soon enough. He'd left his future in the hands of fate by leaving the license plate off his car. And if he did get stopped, the envelope of clues on the seat beside him would help police tie him to the crime in Oklahoma City. Indeed, though McVeigh wasn't exactly eager to get caught, there was a part of him that was curious to see how things would play out if he did.

Ultimately, McVeigh figured, some officer would pull him over for the missing plate, but it would probably happen somewhere in Kansas. Cops in Oklahoma, he was sure, would be too busy dealing with the bombing.

And if no officer stopped him? McVeigh's rough plan was to head up to Kansas and clear out the storage shed in Herington. He might put the license plate back on the Mercury and camp out at Geary Lake for a day or two. After that, McVeigh imagined he might wind up in Arizona or the forests of the Northwest, and continue his war against the federal government.

He wasn't planning more bombings, but he would find other ways to be a thorn in the government's side. It occurred to him that he might select individual targets—federal agents, perhaps—and pick them off one by one. "If I was out in the woods with those jackboots," he would boast in a later interview, "I could take them out by the dozens. No exaggerating. Warfare in the woods is what I was trained for."

As McVeigh rolled through the Oklahoma countryside along Interstate 35, he noticed an oncoming vehicle, a nondescript red sedan. It was rocketing toward Oklahoma City. McVeigh figured it had to be doing 110 miles per hour.

That's a government car, McVeigh thought. *Federal agents. On their way to the Murrah Building.*

Sixty miles north of Oklahoma City, McVeigh noticed a marked Oklahoma Highway Patrol car by the side of the road. A trooper stood outside the patrol car, looking over a minivan. *Probably a speeding arrest,* McVeigh thought. He wondered why Oklahoma troopers would be bothering with speeders at a time like this.

About twenty minutes later, at 10:20 A.M., McVeigh saw what looked like the same state trooper in his rearview mirror, coming up fast, at a good ninety-five miles per hour. He was in the passing lane, roaring up alongside McVeigh.

McVeigh pretended not to notice, but his peripheral vision was locked in on the trooper.

The trooper's car was almost past him when McVeigh noticed the front end of the vehicle dip slightly. The police cruiser slowed down and fell in alongside McVeigh's car. The trooper at the wheel was Charles J. Hanger, a nineteen-year police veteran known for his ability to bird-dog traffic violators.

For Hanger, the morning had already been hectic. The first televised reports of the bombing had been noticed at his troop headquarters a few minutes after it happened. Hanger and other troopers were directed to hurry to Oklahoma City and report to the command post near the Murrah Building.

Hanger took off toward Oklahoma City at more than a hundred miles per hour. With his siren blaring and emergency lights flashing, he'd traveled about ten minutes toward the bombing site when his radio broadcast an order to return. They already had enough help at the command post.

Hanger was indeed the trooper McVeigh had seen by the side of the road near a minivan, but he wasn't stopping speeders. He'd been helping two women get assistance for their disabled vehicle. Right around the time McVeigh had driven by, one of the women had told Hanger that her husband was an Oklahoma City firefighter. She was worried that he might get hurt at the bombing scene.

"I'm sure he'll be okay," Hanger told her.

Now Hanger was heading back north when he happened to glance at an old Mercury with a big primer spot on the left rear quarter panel. It was McVeigh's junker getaway car, sans license plate.

As he drove wheel-to-wheel with the Mercury, Hanger glanced over and gave McVeigh a little nod. McVeigh nodded back. Now the trooper fell in behind McVeigh and turned on his emergency flasher, directing McVeigh to pull over.

McVeigh complied. He slowed down, pulled over, and parked on the shoulder of I-35, easing the right tires of his car onto the grass, a few inches off the pavement.

Hanger parked behind him. They were about twenty minutes out of Perry, a small town south of the Kansas border.

McVeigh sat in his vehicle. It was decision time.

For a moment, he considered the option of pulling out his Glock and killing the trooper.

As Hanger stepped out of his patrol car, McVeigh emerged from his. McVeigh sized up the trooper. He noticed that Hanger was alone, and had no bulletproof vest. McVeigh sized up his options. If he drew on the trooper, he figured the element of surprise—plus McVeigh's expertise—would put Hanger at a severe disadvantage.

If I want him, I can take him, McVeigh thought. But then he thought again: *No, not a state trooper. Stand down.*

If Hanger had been a federal agent, McVeigh would probably have started shooting. But McVeigh had a grudging respect for local and state cops and sheriffs, and their right to do their jobs. McVeigh felt no hatred for a state trooper stopping a car without a license plate. He would not draw his gun on this officer of the law.

Hanger was wondering what McVeigh was up to as he watched the younger man step out of the battered Mercury. Most people just sat in their cars, nervously waiting for the trooper to approach. By stepping out of his car, McVeigh put Hanger on edge.

This seemed like a fairly routine traffic stop, just a missing license plate. But during another seemingly routine traffic stop exactly two weeks earlier, twelve miles north of this spot, a motorist had pulled out a gun and fired at another Oklahoma trooper. That incident—which ended with the trooper firing back and wounding the motorist—had Hanger and other Oklahoma cops on guard.

Now, Hanger stood behind his open car door, watching McVeigh's hands closely as he approached his patrol car. Cautiously, Hanger began walking toward McVeigh.

Hanger looked at the Mercury, then back at McVeigh.

"You don't have a license plate," he said.

McVeigh glanced at the rear bumper of his car.

"Huh. No," McVeigh said.

Hanger began making notes in a book he was carrying, but the trooper kept a wary eye on McVeigh.

"Do you have insurance?" Hanger asked.

"No, I just bought the car."

"You have a registration? Do you have a bill of sale?"

"Not yet, but I have a license."

McVeigh reached back into his pants pocket and pulled out his camouflage wallet.

As McVeigh took out his Michigan state driver's license, Hanger noticed a bulge under McVeigh's windbreaker.

"What's that?" Hanger asked.

"I have a gun," McVeigh said.

McVeigh spoke calmly. He wanted to avoid showing any signs of aggression or inflaming the situation.

Hanger reached out toward McVeigh and felt for the Glock. Then he pulled out his own gun and pointed it at McVeigh.

"Move your hands away, slowly," Hanger instructed. "Get both hands up in the air."

Hanger pointed his gun at the back of McVeigh's head. He directed him to put his hands on the trunk of the Mercury, bend over, and spread his legs. The trooper was having a bit of trouble removing the Glock from McVeigh's shoulder holster.

"My gun is loaded," he warned the trooper, so there wouldn't be any accidents removing the gun.

"So is mine," Hanger said.

McVeigh told Hanger he would also find a clip of ammunition and a knife attached to his belt. Keeping his gun at the back of McVeigh's head, Hanger took away the Glock, the knife, and the ammo clip, tossing them onto the shoulder a few feet away. He then patted McVeigh down for any additional weapons and cuffed his hands behind his back.

Hanger asked McVeigh why he was carrying a weapon.

McVeigh answered that he felt it was his legal right to carry it.

"You know, when you carry a gun around like that, one wrong move could get you shot," Hanger told McVeigh.

"Possible," McVeigh said.

Hanger marched his handcuffed prisoner toward the police cruiser and put McVeigh in the front seat on the passenger side. He clicked McVeigh into a seat belt and went to retrieve the weapons and ammo he'd just seized.

Hanger unloaded the gun, briefly examining the deadly Black Talon bullet he took from the chamber. He put the knife and the ammo in the trunk of his patrol car, then got back into his cruiser and called his dispatcher on his cell phone. (Troopers had been asked to confine their use of the radio to emergencies and matters related to the bombing.)

Examining the Michigan driver's license McVeigh gave him, Hanger asked the dispatcher to run a computer check to find out whether McVeigh had a criminal history, or if there were any arrest warrants out for him. The dispatcher quickly reported back: no warrants, no record. Tim McVeigh had never been arrested in his life.

Hanger also wanted the dispatcher to run a computer check on the Glock, to see whether it had been stolen. He was turning the unloaded gun around in his hand, looking for the serial number, when McVeigh spoke up.

"The serial number is VM769," McVeigh said.

Just as McVeigh spoke, Hanger was finding the serial number for himself. "Well, you're close," he told McVeigh. "It's VW769."

"I knew it was an M or a W," McVeigh said.

That's unusual, Hanger remarked. He didn't know many people who memorized the serial numbers of their guns.

"Well, I do," McVeigh said.

The gun was not stolen, the dispatcher reported. Hanger read McVeigh his Miranda rights. McVeigh said he understood his rights and told the trooper that it would be okay to ask him some questions.

Hanger wanted to know why McVeigh was driving without a license plate.

McVeigh said he'd bought the car only a few days ago, from a Firestone dealer named Tom up in Junction City. McVeigh said he had an Arizona plate from his former car, but that he hadn't put it on the Mercury. He'd figured he'd be better off driving without a plate than using the old one.

Hanger asked for a second time why McVeigh was carrying a gun.

"For personal protection," McVeigh said. "I have a concealed-weapon permit for it in New York."

"That's not valid here," Hanger said.

"Yeah," McVeigh said, "I know."

He told Hanger he'd been in the military and had done some work as a security guard back in New York State. He had a security guard's badge in his wallet, which Hanger confiscated. McVeigh explained that he was in the middle of a move from Kansas to Arkansas, and was on his way to Kansas to pick up some of his belongings.

McVeigh gave Hanger permission to search the Mercury. Leaving the prisoner alone in the police car, Hanger examined the car.

Inside the car, on the front seat, he found McVeigh's baseball cap, his PLEASE DO NOT TOW sign, and the white legal-sized envelope. The envelope was sealed and had no writing on the outside. In the trunk, Hanger found a small toolbox with a few tools inside, some soiled rags, and a few leaves and twigs. Hanger locked up the Mercury, leaving all the items inside.

Back in the patrol car, McVeigh had an idea. The handcuffs, he found, weren't that tight. They allowed him some movement. He was able to reach into his back pocket and pull out a business card, which he left in the folds of the car seat.

The card was from Dave Paulsen, a young military supply dealer from the Chicago area, whom McVeigh had met at a gun show in late 1994. On the back of Paulsen's card, McVeigh had written "TNT $5/stick need more." Next to Paulsen's phone number, McVeigh had scrawled, "Call after 01 May, see if I can get some more."

Leaving the business card in Hanger's car was a dirty trick McVeigh was playing on Paulsen. McVeigh was upset that Paulsen had talked with him about the possibility of selling McVeigh some dynamite, strung him along for weeks, and had failed to go through with the deal. McVeigh had also tried to sell Paulsen some blasting caps.

McVeigh had made a special point to carry Paulsen's card with him on the day of the bombing. He knew Paulsen would face some hard questions if police found the card.

Dirty for dirty, McVeigh thought.

Sure enough, as it turned out, FBI agents did wind up going to Illinois, questioning Paulsen at length, and searching his residence. Paulsen later admitted to agents that he spoke to McVeigh about selling him some dynamite but was just "stringing him along."

As the trooper walked back to his patrol car, he noticed McVeigh squirming around in the front seat.

"Why were you fidgeting?" Hanger asked.

"The cuffs get kind of tight," McVeigh said.

"I wouldn't know," Hanger said. "I've never been in handcuffs."

They were ready to ride to Noble County Jail in Perry, where McVeigh would be booked. Hanger wanted to know if McVeigh was willing to pay to have his car towed to Perry, the county seat, or if he preferred to leave it locked up on the shoulder of the road until he could get bailed out and retrieve it.

Just leave it, McVeigh said.

Hanger wondered whether there might be something valuable to McVeigh in that sealed envelope on the front seat. He asked whether McVeigh wanted him to go and get it for him.

"No," McVeigh said. "Leave it there."

They chatted a bit on the way to Perry—a cop and his prisoner, making small talk. Always fascinated by firearms and fast cars, McVeigh asked Hanger what kind of gun he carried.

"A Sig Model two-two-eight," Hanger said.

"Oh," McVeigh said, "a nine-millimeter."

Noticing that Hanger's police cruiser was almost brand-new, McVeigh tried to coax the trooper into showing him how fast the car would go. Hanger declined.

The trooper told McVeigh that a lot of police officers from this part of the state were on their way to Oklahoma City because of a big explosion in the federal office building. He asked McVeigh whether he'd heard about the tragedy.

"No," McVeigh said, "I don't have a radio in my car."

It was nearly 11 A.M. when they pulled into the parking lot of the Noble County Jail in Perry. McVeigh took off his jacket, and Hanger got his first look at the odd and unsettling T-shirt his prisoner was wearing. Hanger didn't look too closely, but it registered in his mind that he'd never seen a shirt like this before, with its picture of Abe Lincoln on the front and illustration of a tree on the back. But Hanger didn't really read the slogans that captioned the drawings.

Hanger and Marsha Moritz, the jailer, booked McVeigh on four misdemeanor charges: transporting a loaded firearm in a motor vehicle, unlawfully carrying a weapon, failing to display a current license plate, and failing to maintain proof of insurance.

She had the prisoner empty out his pockets, which yielded two commemorative Revolutionary War coins, four .45-caliber bullets, a pair of Fit to Be Tried–brand earplugs, a small bottle of aspirin substitute, and $255 McVeigh was carrying in his wallet.

Moritz took the new prisoner's mug shot against a height-measurement poster; in his thick-soled combat boots, McVeigh was well over six feet two. His face betrayed no emotion as he stood and held a card in front of his chest, showing his prisoner number, 95–057, and the date, 04–19–95.

The prisoner-screening process went routinely until Moritz told McVeigh she needed to know his next of kin, in case he got sick or something happened to him in the jail.

McVeigh didn't answer at first. After an awkward silence, he gave the name of James Nichols. McVeigh's Michigan driver's license listed the James Nichols farm in Decker as his home address.

Other than that, McVeigh was surprisingly loose for a man being arrested for the first time. As Hanger prepared to fingerprint him, he asked McVeigh to wipe the perspiration off his hands.

"Most people I arrest are sweaty," Hanger said.

"No problem," McVeigh said. "My hands are dry."

McVeigh smiled and raised his eyebrows when he saw Moritz bring out a pair of rubber gloves.

"What are you going to do with those?" he wisecracked.

"You never know, do you?" McVeigh remembers her kidding back.

But the light mood didn't last long. There was a TV set in the office, and the continuing broadcast about the bombing cast a pall over everyone in the Noble County Sheriff's Department.

Moritz and Hanger exchanged a few words about the tragedy—how terrible it was that so many people had been killed and injured, how sad it was that it all happened in their backyard, just about sixty miles away.

McVeigh pretended to pay little attention to the television, but he was watching and listening to every word. This was his first opportunity to see what his bomb had done to the Murrah Building.

His initial reaction was disappointment. *Damn,* he thought, *the whole building didn't come down.*

But McVeigh says how that even that revelation had a silver lining for him: with part of the Murrah Building still standing, in its ruined state, the American public would be left with its carcass, standing as a symbol.

McVeigh then heard someone in the office mention how horrible it was that the blast had destroyed a day-care center in the building, killing a group of children.

This news hit McVeigh harder. He had never intended for children to be among his victims; though he had no feeling at all for the government workers he had slain, the presence of children among his victims did cause him a moment's regret. Yet even that sliver of humanity was matched with a more coldblooded reaction: within a moment he recognized that the deaths of innocent children would overshadow the political message of his bombing. In the court of public opinion, he figured, this would be a disaster for his cause. *The media's going to latch on to that,* McVeigh thought. *Everybody's going to say, "He's a baby killer."* "The day-care center," he would later say. "If I had known it was there, I probably would have shifted the target."

Everyone in the sheriff's office was listening closely as a TV reporter gave the first sketchy descriptions of a possible suspect: a white male, somewhere between five feet nine and six feet one.

A deputy who was listening to the report looked over and eyeballed McVeigh.

"Gee, you're a recent arrival," he remarked.

"That ain't me," McVeigh said, laughing off the suggestion. "I'm six-two. Listen to that description."

There was no further talk about the description. For the next two days, McVeigh would linger in the jail in this peaceful little town of fifty-three hundred people, awaiting his court appearance. As a first-time offender charged with a few misdemeanors, he stood a good chance of getting a quick release on low bail.

He had been stopped eighty miles north of the bombing, seventy-eight minutes after it occurred, carrying earplugs in his pocket and wearing a T-shirt celebrating the assassination of an American president. But so far, no one had any inkling that he might have anything to do with the bombing.

Marsha Moritz thought McVeigh was an unusually cooperative and polite prisoner. But she noticed one odd thing about him: the T-shirt. She mentioned it to Hanger after McVeigh had removed his personal clothes and put on an orange jailhouse jumpsuit to be taken to the cellblock. The T-shirt had already been stored in a paper bag with McVeigh's other personal effects.

"Wasn't that a strange T-shirt he had on?" Moritz said to Hanger.

"What do you mean?"

"Well, it had a strange saying on it."

"I didn't read it."

11

"Timmy's All
Over CNN"

During the two days McVeigh spent in the Noble County Jail, he stretched on a cot and tried to catch up on his rest. With four other inmates in the cell, he didn't really sleep much. He ate a few bad meals, watched, listened, and wondered what would happen next.

Everyone in the jail was talking about the bombing—everyone but McVeigh. He wasn't saying much of anything. Instead he pretended to snooze as the other prisoners and jail workers hung on every word of the twenty-four-hour media coverage of the bombing.

Despite his low profile, McVeigh was actually listening closely as those around him talked about the blast and the rising death toll.

Rescuers were still pulling bodies out of the building, and it looked as if the fatalities would exceed one hundred. Jailers and prisoners alike, they were almost all Oklahomans. Everyone was still in disbelief. *How did this happen? Who would do such a thing?* McVeigh concentrated, and maintained his poker face.

"You know, I can make a small bomb out of a bottle of Drano," McVeigh heard one prisoner boasting to a guard.

"I can, too," the guard said.

On occasion the others tried to draw McVeigh into the conversation, but he acted aloof, uninterested. He was considering his next move—wondering what effect the bombing would have on the government, wondering how long it would take the feds to tie him to the crime. He sure as hell didn't want to talk with these guys about it.

One of the main reasons McVeigh kept his military brush cut was that it made people think twice about messing with him. It intimidated people, made them wary. When McVeigh let it be known he didn't feel like talking about the bombing, his jailmates backed off.

There was some idle talk, though. One of the prisoners, a frequent guest at the jail, asked McVeigh what he was in for.

"Hanger arrested me for having no license plate and a concealed weapon," McVeigh said.

"That Hanger would ticket his own grandmother," the prisoner said, scowling.

At one point, McVeigh's jailmates asked him about his military haircut, and he revealed that he'd served in the Army during Desert Storm.

"Oh yeah?" a prisoner said. "I'll bet you saw some bombs over there." McVeigh changed the subject.

In the last few months, he knew, he'd set up a cat-and-mouse game for the authorities. Sometimes, as he made the elaborate arrangements for the bombing, he'd used fake identities. He was the gabby Daryl Bridges, making hundreds of phone calls, or the contentious Tim Tuttle, spouting off on politics at gun shows. Or he was Robert Kling, signing the paperwork to rent a Ryder truck.

But on other occasions, he left clear clues about his real identity. He'd given his real name at the Dreamland Motel, and parked the big yellow Ryder there for all to see. Before that he'd left angry antigovernment rhetoric on his sister's word processor, and his hatred for the government had been expressed in dozens of letters to friends, family, and even the press.

Leaving that license plate off his getaway car was, in a sense, his first move, almost an invitation to the authorities to apprehend him. Leaving the package of damning documents in the car was the second.

And yet McVeigh didn't want to make it too easy for them. He wanted to make the government's prosecutors and investigators work hard for any arrest or conviction.

And once they did arrest him, McVeigh decided, he would admit to nothing. He would make the federal government prove its case, and he would take every opportunity to inconvenience and embarrass them along the way.

McVeigh was glad of one thing: once the feds got hold of him, he would be kept in a federal prison. From what he'd heard, the federal prisons were cleaner and had better food than a local facility like the Noble County Jail, with its parade of bologna sandwiches and toast-and-oatmeal breakfasts.

Waking up in his cell on the morning of April 21, two days after the bombing, he wondered why federal agents hadn't come for him yet. *What's happening? Haven't they found that stuff in the Mercury?*

He would soon find out. While McVeigh was languishing in jail, hundreds of federal agents and police officers were chasing leads all across the United States, hoping for a break that would lead them to the Murrah Building bomber.

To many observers—from politicians to average citizens—the obvious assumption was that foreign terrorists, most likely Arab, were responsible. After all, the bombing of the World Trade Center in New York City had been masterminded by a group of Arab extremists operating out of New Jersey.

However, at the FBI's Behavioral Science Unit in Quantico, Virginia, Special Agent Clinton R. Van Zandt was offering a different opinion. Van Zandt had served as the lead FBI negotiator at Waco in the weeks before the tragedy in 1993. Asked by a supervisor to put together a psychological profile of the Oklahoma bomber, Van Zandt said immediately that the date—April 19, the anniversary of the deaths at Waco—was the key.

"You're going to have a white male, acting alone, or with one other person," Van Zandt said. "He'll be in his mid-twenties. He'll have military experience and be a fringe member of some militia group. He'll be angry at the government for what happened at Ruby Ridge and Waco."

"We think it's more of a Third World–type terrorist," the supervisor told Van Zandt.

But within two hours of the Oklahoma City blast, some clues would be pointing police in the directions of two Americans—and former soldiers, no less.

The first huge break was recovering the 250-pound rear axle from the Ryder truck, the one that hurtled through the air for a full city block before landing on a little Ford Festiva. Federal agents found a confidential vehicle identification number—AVA26077—stamped on the axle. Most people have no reason to care about the eight-digit confidential numbers, known as CVINs. But they are well-known to police and experienced car thieves as hidden identifiers used for tracking stolen vehicles when the seventeen-digit public vehicle identification number—the one displayed on top of the dashboard—is destroyed or removed.

Later, Oklahoma County sheriff's deputies digging through the rubble found the rear bumper from the same truck, its Florida license plate intact.

A series of computer checks showed that the axle and bumper came from a truck owned by Ryder Rental Inc. of Miami. The 1993 Ford truck, with a twenty-foot cargo box, had been rented two days earlier at Eldon Elliott's body shop in Junction City, Kansas. And the renter was a man named Robert Kling.

Eight hours after the bombing, agents were on their way to Junction City, near Fort Riley, to talk with Elliott and his employees. Using information from the body-shop workers who had seen Kling, an FBI artist quickly drew up composite sketches of Kling and another man who was in the shop when he rented the Ryder. The possible suspects were designated John Doe No. 1 and John Doe No. 2.

Agents spent the next day taking the sketches door-to-door through the Junction City area. On Thursday, April 20, the evening after the bombing, they hit paydirt at the Dreamland Motel. The manager, Lea McGown, recognized Doe No. 1 as a recent guest. But she didn't know him as Kling. She knew him as Timothy McVeigh. And, yes, she recalled, she saw him in a Ryder truck, one of those big yellow rentals. And he had an old yellow Mercury, too.

Finally, the authorities had a name—indeed, two—for their possible suspect. And soon they had another lead. When he registered for his room at the Dreamland, McVeigh had listed his residence as the Nichols family farm in Decker, Michigan. Before long, investigators would be looking in the direction of an old Army buddy of Timothy McVeigh's—a man named Terry Nichols.

McVeigh was now the subject of one of the most intensive manhunts in American history. A massive task force of investigators, working out of Oklahoma City, began making phone calls to police stations in Oklahoma. Maybe, they thought, this guy was already sitting in a jail somewhere. It was worth checking around.

Again, a computer came through with key information. A check with the National Crime Information Center at FBI Headquarters in Washington showed that, less than two hours after the bombing, an Oklahoma trooper named Hanger had run a computer check on one Timothy McVeigh near the town of Perry. On Friday morning, two days after the bombing, an ATF agent called the Noble County sheriff's office in Perry. Did the Sheriff's Department know anything about this McVeigh?

The sheriff, Jerry R. Cook, remembered the name. The Highway Patrol had locked him up on traffic charges not long after the bombing. Cook was not sure whether McVeigh had been released yet. He went to check his records and then came back to the phone.

"Yeah," the sheriff said. "We got him incarcerated."

"Yeah! Put a hold on him!" the ATF agent told Cook. "Don't let him go."

"We found him! We found him!" agents shouted out in the task-force office in Oklahoma City. Veteran FBI Special Agent Floyd M. Zimms was as excited as anyone. He'd been working nonstop on the case for two days, without so much as a nap. Finally, here was the break everyone had been chasing.

"All right!" Zimms told Agent Danny O. Coulson, one of the leaders of the task force. "We gotta go!"

"Let's do it," Coulson said.

Within minutes agents had bolted out the door, headed for a waiting helicopter. The chopper took them north along I-35 to an old Mercury parked along the road. At one point in the flight, agents looked behind them. A TV news helicopter was following.

Meanwhile, valuable help was coming from an unrelated source in New York State. The Buffalo office of the FBI, twenty-five miles from McVeigh's hometown, had received a tip from McVeigh's old co-worker, security guard Carl E. Lebron, Jr.

Lebron, the man so troubled by McVeigh's venomous talk about the government that he had used a hidden recorder to tape McVeigh, lived in a town just to the south of Pendleton called Amherst. On the night after the bombing, he was watching coverage of the investigation on TV. His eyes opened wide when he saw the police drawing of John Doe No. 1.

Could that be him? Lebron thought. *Tim McVeigh?*

He spent a restless night, tossing and turning in bed. First thing the next morning, he headed straight to the FBI office in Buffalo.

"I think I might know who the Oklahoma City bomber is," Lebron said.

The office receptionist gave him a funny look, but picked up the phone and called for an agent.

"What do you have?" Special Agent Eric Kruss asked when he came out to the lobby to see Lebron.

Lebron told the agent about McVeigh's extremist political views, and his rage over the deaths at Waco. He mentioned that McVeigh had visited Waco to protest. He also turned over a photo of McVeigh, a Waco videotape, and some antigovernment pamphlets McVeigh had given him—along with an address McVeigh had used in Kingman, Arizona.

Kruss listened politely to Lebron's tale, writing down the information.

"Thank you," Kruss said. "We'll look into it."

The meeting lasted only ten minutes, and as he drove home, Lebron began to wonder whether he had made a mistake.

The bombing had touched off a hysteria. There were thousands of tips like this—many of them well intentioned, but way off-base—flowing in to FBI offices all over the country. Lebron's information would be checked out, like the rest. There was no reason to get excited yet.

But that would change, very quickly. Not long after receiving Lebron's tip on the morning of April 21, the FBI office in Buffalo received word from Oklahoma that Timothy James McVeigh, born April 23, 1968, had been linked to the Ryder truck that carried the bomb. McVeigh, arrested by Hanger on traffic charges after the bombing, was from Pendleton, barely thirty minutes from downtown Buffalo. The young man's father, Bill McVeigh, was still living out there, on Campbell Boulevard.

The information came in almost simultaneously with Lebron's departure from the office. By the time he got home, Lebron had a call from an FBI supervisor. "We want to talk to you some more," the supervisor said.

This time, Kruss came out to Lebron's house and chauffeured him downtown.

Back in Oklahoma, the investigation was now moving very fast. In Oklahoma City, FBI agents were typing up arrest warrants for not only McVeigh but Terry Nichols and his older brother James as well. The McVeigh warrant included information about the Ryder truck axle, the traffic arrest near Perry, recollections of witnesses in Junction City, and Lebron's revelations about McVeigh's hatred for the federal government. Once U.S. Magistrate Judge Ronald Howland signed the warrant, federal agents were free to arrest McVeigh for the bombing and take him into federal custody.

McVeigh knew nothing of any of this that morning as a deputy led him down to the Noble County courtroom, in the same building as the jail. McVeigh was scheduled for an appearance on his misdemeanor charges before County Judge Danny G. Allen. Assistant District Attorney Mark Gibson would prosecute the case. The appearance was expected to be brief; more than likely, Allen would release him on minimal bail. The whole matter was about as routine as it gets.

Sheriff Jerry Cook realized, with some alarm, just how close McVeigh had come to being released a day after his arrest. Normally McVeigh would have been in court on Thursday, and as a first-time offender released shortly afterward with little or no bail. But Allen had a busy calendar, so McVeigh's appearance was bumped to Friday.

God didn't want him to get loose, the sheriff thought.

About 10:15 A.M., Gibson was standing in the courtroom, waiting for McVeigh's court session to begin. Sheriff Cook walked in and handed him a note.

"This guy, McVeigh, is the one the FBI has been looking for in the bombing case," the note said. "We need to keep him in custody."

Gibson looked at the sheriff. "You're yanking my chain," he said.

"No, I'm not," Cook said.

Gibson made a quick call to the U.S. attorney's office. Sure enough, it was true. The court appearance was delayed, and McVeigh—who had been waiting in an empty courtroom nearby—was taken back up to his cell on the fourth floor.

"The judge isn't ready for you just yet," Cook told McVeigh.

There was a prickly new vibration in the courthouse, and McVeigh picked up on it immediately. He saw a wide-eyed look on Cook's face as the sheriff escorted him on the elevator ride upstairs. He could sense a change in the demeanor of other jail employees, and prisoners, too. The people around him, he noticed, were giving him sideways glances.

It's happening, he told himself.

When he got back up to his cell, he could see that word was getting around fast. One by one, the four prisoners who shared the cellblock with him were taken away for a few minutes.

They're questioning these guys, asking them if I made any admissions about the bombing, McVeigh thought.

Looking out a window, McVeigh could see a police officer on the roof of a nearby building. Somebody thought he noticed a helicopter from one of the news agencies. A prisoner hollered to McVeigh, "Hey, dude, did you do it? Are you the bomber?" He didn't answer.

McVeigh tried to use one of the jail pay phones to call a lawyer, but the phone was out of service. The phone system had been shut off by the Sheriff's Department.

"McVeigh," a deputy said, "there are some government agents here. They want to talk with you."

McVeigh agreed to see the agents; he wanted to see what the government was up to. Two FBI men from the bombing task force—Special Agents Floyd Zimms and James Norman, Jr.—were waiting for him. They wanted to interview him in a room usually used by the Noble County Board of Elections.

As he walked in the room, wearing handcuffs, McVeigh looked around. He bent down to look under a table for recording devices. Finding none, he sat down at the table. He was in combat mind-set, but was working hard to control his emotions. These were federal agents: he was determined not to show any sign of weakness, not to give them any satisfaction.

"Do you have any idea why the FBI wants to talk to you?" Zimms asked.

"That thing in Oklahoma City, I guess," McVeigh said. He didn't think the remark could be taken as any kind of confession; with men posted on nearby buildings and a news helicopter overhead, anyone might have guessed that something was going on with the bombing case.

"That's exactly right," Zimms said. "Our investigation today has showed you may have information about the bombing. Before we ask you questions about it, I'm going to read you your rights."

McVeigh gave the agents his name, height, and weight—six feet two, 160 pounds.

"Your place of birth?" one agent asked.

McVeigh refused to answer. They could dig that up for themselves. "I'm just going to give you basic physical and descriptive information," the ex-soldier said. "I guess I shouldn't talk to you guys without talking to a lawyer first."

The agents turned up the pressure. According to McVeigh, Zimms opened a manila envelope, pulled out a series of glossy pictures of children killed and horribly maimed in the bombing, and slid them across the table to McVeigh. One of the agents then warned McVeigh that he could be facing the death penalty.

McVeigh's face was blank, expressionless. "I want an attorney," he repeated.

The agents—who later vehemently denied brandishing photos of dead children—ended the questioning. This was going nowhere.

"I just want to tell you a little of what's happening right now," Zimms said. "Federal charges are being filed against you this afternoon in connection with this bombing. Later today, you'll be officially charged and transported back to Oklahoma City."

As he looked at McVeigh's blank face, Zimms thought, *This guy has a tape loop running through his mind. The loop keeps repeating: "I'm a soldier. I accomplished my mission. I got caught, but I'm still a good soldier."*

As they prepared for the move to Oklahoma City, McVeigh was concerned about his safety. To the FBI agents, he mentioned the case of Lee Harvey Oswald and Jack Ruby. Oswald had been silenced before he could tell his story, and McVeigh didn't want that to happen to him. He had no doubt that there were people in Oklahoma who hated him every bit as much as Ruby hated Oswald—more, perhaps. An angry mob was already gathering outside the courthouse, and he felt there was a real chance that someone might take a shot at him.

"Can I have a bulletproof vest?" McVeigh asked.

No, a police official told him. None was available. Nor was he allowed to have a pair of shoes for the trip to Oklahoma City.

McVeigh tried one more request. "Can you take me out onto the roof and let me get onto the chopper?" he asked. Can't do that, an agent said. This building isn't set up for a chopper to land on it.

Coulson, Zimms, and Norman could see a crowd problem developing outside, but they were certain that McVeigh could be well protected. Highly qualified federal agents were already fanning out, checking the rooftops and perimeter. A number of law-enforcement officers—Zimms included—would be surrounding McVeigh as he left the building; if somebody fired at McVeigh, the cops stood a good chance of taking a bullet, too.

Coulson later said he was unaware, at the time, of McVeigh's request for a vest. When he learned of the request, he said, "Fuck him. If he was worried about it, he shouldn't have bombed the building." Coulson considered McVeigh "one of the most horrible, demented people in the history of the criminal justice system." But he still realized that it was his duty to protect McVeigh.

McVeigh made no more requests. *I'm not going to whine about it,* he decided.

He still had to appear briefly before Judge Allen on the charges from the Hanger arrest. While waiting to see the judge, McVeigh was put into a holding room. An attractive black woman prisoner, whom McVeigh had seen earlier in the day, was in an adjoining room. There were steel bars between them, but McVeigh and the woman were able to talk to each other.

McVeigh couldn't see out the courthouse window from where he was sitting, but the woman could. "Hey," McVeigh said. "You're my eyes and ears. Are there a bunch of suits up on that roof?"

The woman peered up out the window.

"Yeah," she said, "they're up there."

"Tell me if you see any choppers, other than the news chopper that's already up there," McVeigh said. "I'd like to see that chopper crash when it runs out of fuel."

The woman said something to McVeigh about the bombing.

He joked to her, "Now you can do the *Geraldo* show."

A guard came to take McVeigh to court. The woman wished him good luck, and he thanked her.

The court appearance was brief. It was handled routinely, except for the large number of deputies in the courtroom, and Gibson's request that

McVeigh be held on a five-thousand-dollar bond, extremely high bail for a first-time misdemeanor offender. Judge Allen authorized the bond request.

As part of the routine court proceeding, McVeigh was asked where he lived. "I don't really live anywhere," he said. Gibson, a Navy veteran, recognized McVeigh's military bearing, and in his eyes saw a cold, soulless look that would linger in his mind.

By 5 P.M.—fifty-six hours after the bombing—a team of eight agents from the FBI and ATF had arrived in Perry by helicopter, with orders to bring McVeigh back to Oklahoma City. Along the way they had made a brief stop to secure McVeigh's getaway car, which had been left along the highway, completely unattended, for more than two days.

A convoy of vehicles—including Sheriff Jerry Cook's family van, the only vehicle available that was large enough for McVeigh and all the federal agents with him—pulled up outside the courthouse to await his emergence.

The world was about to get its first look at the Oklahoma City bomber.

FBI officials would later deny that the Perry jail walkout was designed as a media event, or that anyone called the news agencies to give them the location of the photo opportunity. They would deny accusations that they delayed the prisoner move until all the top media outlets could get there. They would insist that escape prevention and the safety of McVeigh and others were their only priorities as they moved their prisoner on that afternoon. But there were plenty of cameras in place when McVeigh, still wearing the bright orange jail jumpsuit, left the courthouse for the flight to Oklahoma City.

The news photos and videos sent worldwide by satellite showed the prisoner, tall, wiry, and grim, his eyes cold and narrow as he left the building with his police escorts. As the cameras whirred around him, though, McVeigh was still preoccupied with the potential for a Jack Ruby–like strike on his life. Squinting into the bright afternoon sun, he scanned all the local buildings for snipers, moving his eyes slowly from left to right and then up and down in a Z pattern he had learned in the Army. A longtime student of sniper tactics, McVeigh was trying to see into windows. *If there's a sniper, he'll be standing back a bit,* McVeigh thought. *He won't be hanging the gun barrel out the window where everyone can see it.*

He heard the screams of the crowd as he made his way toward the waiting van, his shackled feet restricting his ability to move quickly. "Look over here, motherfucker," one man shouted. "Baby killer! Look me in the eye!"

McVeigh did not turn his head, nor hunch his shoulders. He walked erect, still scanning the area.

Coulson, a hostage rescue expert, was the FBI agent coordinating McVeigh's move out of Perry. As they were about to board the chopper, Coulson put his hand on McVeigh's shoulder and told him that he expected him to act like a gentleman.

"Yes, sir," McVeigh said, determined not to give the federal agents any reason to rough him up during the trip.

In his demented way, this guy is conducting himself like a soldier, Coulson thought.

Coulson, McVeigh, and a team of federal agents got into the chopper. They left Perry behind just as millions of Americans were tuning in to see McVeigh on the evening news.

Back in western New York, friends who had known a gentle, fun-loving Tim McVeigh were astonished. His boyhood friend Todd Carter learned the news after work on Friday, when his mother rang his cell phone while he was out at a bar after work. The bartender turned on the TV, and there was Tim McVeigh—the brother he never had, the kid from Hinman Road who always wanted to be the good guy in their childhood games—walking out of a courthouse in an orange jumpsuit. Carter could not believe how *stern* his old friend looked.

Mollie McDermott, another former next-door neighbor who had viewed McVeigh as a trusted big brother, had just spent a pleasant day at Walt Disney World in Orlando, Florida. When she returned to the home of a friend and turned on the TV, there was Tim. She went into counseling for six weeks, trying to come to grips with the news.

While his friends were learning what had happened, McVeigh was being taken on a stomach-churning helicopter flight to Oklahoma City. Concerned that unknown terrorists might try to blow the chopper out of the sky with a Stinger missile, Coulson sent a note up to the pilot, telling him to use evasive action on the trip back to the city. That he did, zigzagging above the Oklahoma countryside at high speed and low altitude, sometimes dipping below the tree line. As the agents grabbed onto straps to maintain their balance, McVeigh, held in place by a seat belt but unable to grasp at the straps himself, was jolted from side to side, the chains cutting into his skin. McVeigh was convinced that the pilot was merely hot-dogging at taxpayer expense, trying to scare his prisoner while giving himself and his buddies a rush. *These guys are adrenaline junkies,* he thought. *Just like I was in the Army.*

The federal courthouse in Oklahoma City, only a block to the south of the Murrah Building, had been temporarily shut down after being damaged by the bomb. So McVeigh's first federal court appearance was scheduled for a military courtroom at the Tinker Air Base in Oklahoma City.

He got off the helicopter, stepping onto the asphalt in his socks before being hustled into a waiting FBI van and rushed to the air base. Members of a SWAT team, outfitted in full military gear and carrying semiautomatic rifles, escorted him into a building on the base. Police officers and dogs guarded the entrance as McVeigh passed by. He frowned as he saw the small army awaiting his arrival. *Another waste of taxpayer money,* he thought. *All these guys carrying military rifles, escorting one unarmed prisoner chained at the hands and feet?*

Even with the chains on, he noticed, some of the guards were close enough that he could have reached out and grabbed one of their rifles. He could make some trouble with one of those, he thought.

Before his hearing, McVeigh had a brief opportunity to speak with John W. Coyle III and Susan Otto, who had been appointed by the court as his lawyers for the federal case. They met in a secretary's room at the air base, and there McVeigh dropped a thunderbolt on the two Oklahoma City lawyers.

"Are you really my attorneys?" McVeigh asked.

We are, if you want us, Otto and Coyle told him.

"Is this room secure?" McVeigh asked.

The attorneys said they believed it was.

"Okay, then," McVeigh said. "Yes, I did the bombing."

They spoke for half an hour, with McVeigh giving them as many details as he could about his actions.

U.S. Magistrate Judge Ronald Howland, wearing his judicial robe but sitting behind an ordinary desk in the small courtroom, called the proceedings to order at 8:30 P.M. on April 21, almost sixty hours after the bombing. Prosecutors introduced the FBI arrest warrant, accusing McVeigh of using an explosive device to "maliciously damage or destroy" the Murrah Building.

McVeigh, still guarded in the courtroom by a trio of armed FBI agents in military gear, sat ramrod straight, looking forward during most of the hearing—except for a moment when he became convinced that an ATF agent was trying to stare him down, and returned the glare.

The accused bomber told the judge that he understood the charges, and that he accepted the appointment of Coyle and Otto as his attorneys.

After the brief court appearance, the SWAT team took McVeigh to the nearest federal prison, a medium-security correctional facility in El Reno, Oklahoma. Given his own wing in the prison, McVeigh sat in his cell in silence—exhausted, even exhilarated.

Back east in Pendleton, the bombing was about to shatter the life of yet another victim: Bill McVeigh.

On Friday morning, after receiving Carl Lebron's tip and the information about the traffic arrest in Oklahoma, the FBI office in Buffalo was mobilizing for a visit to the McVeigh house. The SWAT team was called in. Joseph Wolfinger, the special agent in charge of the office, called in two of his veteran agents, Dean Naum and J. Gary DiLaura.

"You and Naum are going up to the house," Wolfinger told DiLaura.

After meeting up with the SWAT team a short distance from Bill McVeigh's house in Pendleton, DiLaura and Naum slipped on bulletproof vests and made their last preparations for the visit to the house. At 1:50 P.M., DiLaura punched McVeigh's phone number into a cell phone and waited for an answer.

Like almost everyone in America, Bill McVeigh had been shocked and upset by the bombing. He had learned about it around three in the afternoon on April 19, when he awoke after sleeping off an all-night shift and turned on the TV. That evening, he spoke with fellow volunteers about the bombing while serving as bingo captain at Good Shepherd Catholic Church.

Thursday passed for Bill without too much thought on the subject, but as his midnight shift was coming to a close about 5 A.M. Friday, he picked up a copy of the *Buffalo News*. The paper carried the FBI drawings of two possible suspects in the blast, "John Doe I" and "John Doe II," and the sketches caught Bill's eye. *Well, at least it isn't Tim,* he thought. He'd never really imagined Tim could do anything that horrific, but in the last couple of years his son's unrelenting fury over Waco had unsettled Bill. He was relieved to see that neither looked—to him, anyway—much like his son. Bill worked several hours of overtime that Friday, and made a stop at his credit union office to pick up some cash for a forthcoming bowling trip to Reno, Nevada. He didn't get to bed until early afternoon.

Not long after, a phone call ended his slumber.

"Hello," Bill yawned.

"Is this Bill McVeigh?" DiLaura asked.

"Yes, it is," Bill said.

"This is the FBI," DiLaura said. "We're down the road and we'd like to talk to you. Please come to the front door."

"Well, I don't usually use my front door," Bill said. "I'll come to the garage door and open it." It would take a few minutes, he explained. He had to get dressed.

"That's fine," the FBI agent said.

Bill threw on some clothes and looked out the front bay window of his modest yellow ranch home. A car was already parked in his driveway, with two men inside.

Pulling cautiously into the driveway, the two FBI agents had not known what to expect. They knew precious little about Tim McVeigh, and even less about his father. Naum noticed the American flag on the pole in the middle of the McVeigh lawn, and it occurred to him that this might be the home of a militia zealot. DiLaura, too, was wondering whether law enforcement had somehow failed to notice a militia presence in western New York.

As DiLaura stepped out of the car, the thought crossed his mind that he and Naum were both eligible for retirement. *What a thing it would be,* he thought, *if the two of us were mowed down dead in front of this house.*

Bill walked from his living room into the kitchen, where a door opened into the attached one-car garage. He moved through the garage, crowded with garden tools, and reached to open a door for the FBI agents. At that moment, a sinking feeling hit him. The Oklahoma City bombing, he realized, had brought the FBI to his door.

DiLaura walked toward Bill cautiously, asking whether he and Naum could come inside and speak with him.

"Fine," Bill answered.

As he and the agents headed inside, Bill noticed more police cars parked out front. "What are all those other cars?" he asked.

"We'll explain," DiLaura said. "Can we go inside?"

"Sure," Bill said.

They walked through the kitchen, which opened to a tiny dining room with a table looking out on the backyard. On the wall beside the windows were photos of Tim McVeigh from his high school graduation and his Army years. Before Bill sat down, DiLaura opened a folder containing a copy of one of the composites Bill had seen earlier in the *Buffalo News*.

"Is this your son?" DiLaura wanted to know. He explained that Tim McVeigh was being held in Oklahoma on traffic charges, but that now the possibility had been raised that he was guilty of something far more chilling. Bill went numb.

"Did you see this picture in the paper?" DiLaura asked him.

"Yes."

"Is this your son?"

"No."

"Well, could it be?"

"It probably could be," Bill answered. "I wouldn't be surprised."

"Why do you say that?"

"Because he's been so upset about Waco, it probably wouldn't surprise me if he was involved in this."

The words sputtered from Bill McVeigh's lips before he had a moment to consider their import. He did not ask for a lawyer. "When I saw the picture," he said, "I really didn't think it was Tim, because the face is too fat. The only thing that makes me think it is him is the brush cut. The brush cut is perfect. The rest of it is not close to Tim, as far as I'm concerned."

But there was no mistaking his son's rage against the government, Bill continued. Every time something about Waco or Bill Clinton came on the TV, Tim would stomp his feet in anger or throw something. "He was very upset every time someone mentioned Waco," Bill repeated.

A phone call interrupted the interrogation. It was his older daughter, Patty. There were already reports on the radio down in Florida that Tim was the prime suspect in the bombing, and that he was about to be charged with the crime.

"I know," Bill said. He told her that he'd have to call her later. FBI agents were already in his dining room.

"Look, Bill," Naum said. "We believe your son is involved."

One of the agents asked Bill whether he was aware that April 19 was the anniversary of the incident at Waco. "No," Bill said. "I have no idea when Waco happened."

Naum and DiLaura could tell that Bill had nothing to hide, that he was likely to cooperate in the investigation. Working through Bill, they figured, was their best chance of getting to Tim and finding out what they really needed to know: was there a cell of terrorists out there somewhere, ready to blow up another building?

Bill told the agents they could search his house, and that the agents waiting outside were free to come in and have a look around. Four or five more agents emerged from their cars, and the team began their search. He even told the agents that Tim sometimes slept in his basement since his sister Jennifer took over his room when he went into the service. *Why hide anything?* he thought. He also pointed them toward Jennifer's own room. "She gets letters from him all the time. I don't."

As agents headed into the basement, Bill happened to notice that one of them was wearing a bulletproof vest. For the first time during the visit, he became angry. Why would anyone feel the need to wear a bulletproof vest into his home?

"What the hell have you got this on for?" he inquired.

"Bill, we didn't know what to expect," DiLaura answered. "You could have come out shooting at us."

It took less than thirty minutes for the Buffalo media to learn that FBI agents were chasing a local lead in the Oklahoma bombing case. A TV reporter and camera crew from Buffalo's Channel 4 arrived at the McVeigh home. Naum went outside to chase away the news crew: the FBI called in the New York State Police, who agreed to help with traffic, media, and crowd control. State troopers would spend the day keeping reporters from walking up the McVeigh driveway.

From his bay window, Bill caught a glimpse of something he had never seen before: a traffic jam on Campbell Boulevard.

Five state police cars would remain parked outside his home for days, to bar the media and curiosity seekers and to protect the home from possible retribution for the bombing. FBI agents advised Bill not to talk to the media, and he was grateful for the advice; indeed, he would realize even through his shock how grateful he was for the respect they showed him.

There was another phone call from Florida. Mickey had just arrived home from her job as a school-bus aide to the news that her son was in custody. Tim's older sister, Patty, was crying her eyes out, Mickey told her ex-husband, and screaming, "Timmy's all over CNN!"

The FBI had more questions for Bill McVeigh. If it does turn out that Tim was involved in this bombing, Naum asked, who might be involved with him?

One name shot into Bill's brain. "If Tim was involved, Nichols was probably involved," he said. He described his son's friendship with Terry Nichols, going back to their Army days, and mentioned that Tim had visited Nichols in Michigan "many times."

Bill also brought up Tim's friendship with Michael Fortier: from the agents' reactions, he was sure it was the first time they'd heard the name. Bill mentioned that Tim had told him that he could always get into contact with him by calling the Fortier home out in Kingman, Arizona. At that, Naum paused in his questioning.

"I have to go outside and make a phone call," Naum said. Bill insisted that the agent use the phone in his bedroom rather than having to take it outside before a crowd of onlookers.

They talked a while longer, and Naum repaired several more times to the bedroom to use the phone. Finally, Naum announced that the FBI wanted to take Bill out to Oklahoma to see his son.

For the first time, Bill became uncooperative. "I'm not going," Bill said. "I have to work tonight. I told my boss I'll be at work tonight. And I have a bowling tournament I'm going to on Sunday in Reno."

Bill's commitment to work was nearly sacred, but the truth is that he probably wasn't really thinking clearly. He was trying to cling to the routine details of life, as if none of this would matter on Sunday in Reno.

The standoff finally broke with the arrival of the McVeighs' pastor and family friend, Monsignor Paul Belzer. The priest spoke with Bill in his bedroom, away from the agents. Bill told the priest his reasons for refusing to go to Oklahoma with the FBI.

"You should probably go see Tim," Father Belzer said.

Bill reluctantly agreed. But "if I know Tim," he told the agents, "he ain't telling me anything, anyway."

Campbell Boulevard was closed to traffic so the media couldn't tail Naum and DiLaura as they drove Bill to the bureau's downtown Buffalo office. Before heading downtown, Bill offered a key to his home to an FBI supervisor in case the agents needed to go back into his home later, but the supervisor said they wouldn't be needing it.

An intensely shy man, Bill McVeigh sat nervously inside the FBI car as it wheeled past the mob of media. The agents and Bill made a quick stop for a bite at the nearest Burger King—the one where Tim used to work—on their way to the downtown FBI office. From 6 P.M. until 8 P.M., Bill sat in the office, doing virtually nothing. Another agent was assigned to keep him company.

Bill figured that Naum and DiLaura were passing what he'd told them along to the national task force that was working on the bombing. *I guess I've given them some good leads,* he told himself. He called a co-worker, who agreed to explain things to Bill's boss and his bowling friends.

With that out of the way, Bill turned his attention to more serious matters. From Florida, word was filtering back that Jennifer McVeigh was taking an angry and uncooperative tone with the FBI agents who had approached her for an interview.

Jennifer had driven down to Pensacola to visit a longtime friend, Dennis Sadler, for Easter break. Like her father, she had been shocked to learn that authorities had linked her brother to the bombing. Unlike her father, she had known her brother was planning some kind of protest—"something big"—against the federal government. She didn't know when, where, or what it would be; she hadn't known that her brother was planning to blow up a building. But she had known enough—and looked up to her brother enough—that the idea of federal agents questioning her made Jennifer McVeigh very nervous.

On Friday afternoon, as agents were talking with Bill McVeigh, Jennifer and Sadler pulled into a Hooters restaurant for food and beers. A federal agent, who had been tailing them, followed them inside. Jennifer became extremely upset at the sight of the agent's holstered gun, and she and Sadler left the restaurant in a huff.

When they got to the parking lot, they found more agents searching Jennifer's pickup truck. To Jennifer, the search confirmed what her brother had taught her about government agents: that they had no respect for the Constitution.

The two drove back to Sadler's place, with the agents continuing to follow them. Jennifer hurried into the laundry room of her friend's house and managed to burn a stash of pages clipped from *The Turner Diaries* that her brother had sent her. Shortly after that, agents searched Sadler's house, and took her into custody for questioning. Jennifer's attitude was defiant, angry, and defensive.

Agents would later tell Bill they had learned that Jennifer had told people at a Christmas party months earlier that "something big is going to happen," and that her brother would be involved. They had no information linking Jennifer to the bombing itself, but it was clear to Bill that agents were looking at her as a possible suspect in a conspiracy leading up to the act. With his son already in jail, the last thing Bill wanted was his daughter in trouble, too. He agreed to call Jennifer in Florida and try to talk some sense into her. "Just answer what they ask you," he urged, but his daughter was nowhere near as cooperative as he was.

By 10:30 P.M., the FBI agents called it a night, taking Bill over to the Hyatt Regency, a downtown hotel a few blocks away. Two agents bunked in the room across the hall from Bill's. Before going to bed, one of the agents asked Bill whether he wanted something to eat.

"No," he said. "But I could use a beer."

A six-pack was brought to his room. Bill drank two of the beers as he lay on his bed, watching himself on the 11 P.M. news, listening to reporters describe his son as a murderer and a terrorist. He had a hard time getting to sleep.

Down in Fort Pierce, Florida, Mickey McVeigh was straining under the barrage of news reporters asking questions about her son. She scrawled a note on a piece of paper and had authorities distribute it to the media.

"I just want to say I feel deep sympathy for the victims and families involved in the Oklahoma City bombing," she wrote. "I have had only brief contact with my son the past 10 years, and only know details from what I have been watching on TV the past few days. That is all I wish to say at this time."

The note was signed, "Tim's Mom," with a postscript, "Please leave our family alone."

On Saturday, Tim McVeigh was put in a lineup of suspects at the county jail in Oklahoma City. McVeigh was directed to put on a pair of jeans and a T-shirt, the same outfit worn by the other men in the lineup room. As preparations were being made for the lineup, one of the other men glared at McVeigh with visible hatred. McVeigh thought for a moment that the man was going to attack him.

During the lineup, two witnesses identified McVeigh as the man with the brush cut they saw near the Murrah Building about the time of the bombing.

I was there, McVeigh thought, *but these witnesses are wrong. I had a hat on that morning. There's no way these people could know what kind of haircut I had.*

The feds were hoping to get a confession out of McVeigh, but they could see he wasn't going to be an easy suspect to crack. They were hoping for help from another source. The government was flying a nervous and confused Bill McVeigh out to Oklahoma on a C-130 military transport plane to talk to his son. The feds were hoping the elder McVeigh could persuade Tim to cooperate in the investigation. That would make things easier for everyone.

At 1:30 P.M., the plane arrived at a military base in Oklahoma. Bill and his FBI escorts, DiLaura and Special Agent Andrew Goralski, were taken off the plane and told to wait in a room on the base. Inside the room, DiLaura noticed four military men from the base watching the bombing coverage on TV. Looking at McVeigh's image on the screen, one of the men muttered, "How would you like to be the scumbag that gave birth to that piece of garbage?" DiLaura glanced over at Bill, then back at the soldiers. "Hey guys, cool it," DiLaura said. "This is Tim McVeigh's father. You're not doing anybody any good, so just cool it."

"Why don't you go into another fucking room?" one of the men said. As they sat down in a nearby room, Bill looked at DiLaura, and the agent could see the pain in his eyes. "Thanks," Bill said.

Bill McVeigh and the agents were eventually driven to the FBI office in Oklahoma City, where Bill was to meet with Coulson and another supervisor in the investigation, Special Agent Bob Ricks, before he would see Tim. Inside the FBI building, DiLaura and Goralski showed their credentials and boarded an elevator with Bill and two other agents. Unexpectedly, the two Oklahoma agents pushed Bill up against the elevator wall and began patting him down for weapons.

Bill was stunned. "Don't worry," DiLaura told him, trying to take the edge off the moment. "This is standard procedure."

Bill's meeting with Coulson and Ricks wasn't much better. Ricks had been one of the leaders and spokesmen for the FBI at the Waco standoff, and Bill was direct about his son's reaction to the incident. "If my son is involved in this, it's because of Waco," Bill told the two agents. "I knew Waco upset Timmy. Every time he saw it on TV, he'd go crazy." Bill sensed that Ricks, in particular, was extremely touchy about references to Waco. Ricks lectured Bill that David Koresh—not law enforcement—was responsible for the deaths at Waco. Bill had felt it important to be honest and forthcoming in describing Tim's anger about Waco, and Ricks's defensive response upset him.

For their part, Ricks and Coulson didn't understand why Bill thought that the meeting had gone badly. They both felt some compassion for the elder McVeigh, and they maintain that they worked to keep the meeting as non-confrontational as possible. With two grown sons of his own, Coulson in particular was pained to think of what Bill McVeigh must be going through.

Bill spent the night in a hotel on the outskirts of Oklahoma City. Before taking Bill to the hotel DiLaura offered to drive him past the site of the bombed-out Murrah Building, but Bill demurred. That was one thing he did not need to see.

Later, DiLaura went to see for himself; to his eyes, the ruined structure looked more like a war zone than a crime scene. The sight gave him a new understanding of how deeply wounded the city must be by the bombing, and he resolved to wear a bulletproof vest whenever he was with Bill McVeigh in Oklahoma.

On Sunday, April 23, the death toll at the Murrah Building was still rising. The exhausted rescuers, often working in driving rainstorms, dug through the rubble in hopes of finding more survivors. They kept finding more bodies.

Thirty miles away, behind the bars of his cell at El Reno, Tim McVeigh was observing his twenty-seventh birthday. The day would also mark his first visit with his father since the bombing.

Before entering the prison, the four FBI agents who accompanied him informed Bill that they had no legal right to tell him what questions to ask his son. They could not force him to tell them what was said during the meeting, but if Bill felt like sharing anything he learned with them afterward, they would be willing to listen. "Bill, you're not acting as an agent for us," DiLaura said. "I want you to go talk to your son. What happens after that is entirely up to you."

Bill got the picture.

When they arrived at the cell where Tim was being held, Tim was sitting in the middle of it, with close to twenty corrections officers standing shoulder to shoulder, surrounding him. Before Bill entered the area, DiLaura angrily insisted to a prison supervisor that the arrangements be changed, and the official finally relented; by the time Bill walked in to see his son, a single officer was seated in the cell with him.

"Is this your father?" the prison supervisor asked Tim.

The prisoner nodded yes. He was wearing an orange jail suit like the one Bill had seen on TV.

Bill sat down beside his son on a wooden bench. They shook hands.

"How you doing?" Bill asked.

"All right," Tim said.

An awkward silence followed. Bill decided to give his son the advice he thought was best.

"Tell the FBI whatever you can," Bill said. His son made no response.

"What went on?" Bill asked.

"Dad, I'm not supposed to say anything," Tim said, explaining the advice his attorneys had given him.

Bill tried to ask the same question several more times, to no avail. After six or seven minutes, Tim ended the meeting.

"Dad, I think it's time to say good-bye," Tim said. "I think we've talked enough."

"If that's the way you feel, fine," Bill said. "I'm not here to pressure you. I'm here because they asked me to come."

They shook hands again, and Bill watched, crestfallen, as the guards led his son out of the small room and down a corridor.

The next morning, as Bill prepared to fly back to Buffalo with his FBI escorts, an embarrassed agent had some news for him. Back in Pendleton, federal agents had obtained a search warrant and broken into his house, looking for more documents. In the process, they had broken down a door. DiLaura, who was present a couple of days earlier when Bill offered his house keys to a supervisor, felt terrible; he and his fellow agents later took up a collection to pay for repairs to the door. Still later, Bill would learn that during the search the agents had wired his home and his telephone with listening devices.

When Bill finally returned to his home on Monday, he noticed that the state police had lowered his flag to half-staff. He did not disagree with their decision.

While Timothy McVeigh was refusing to reveal even his place of birth to federal agents in Oklahoma, Terry Nichols was being considerably more helpful to FBI men in Herington, Kansas.

Nichols, once so coolheaded as a unit leader at Fort Benning, had been in a virtual panic in the two days after the bombing.

After not hearing a word from McVeigh on the day of the blast, he went out the next day, April 20, and bought three newspapers, reading every detail about the explosion and the investigation. He also emptied out the storage locker in Herington, where he and McVeigh had stored some of their bomb materials.

Then he began to fear that the FBI was going to come questioning him about the ammonium nitrate he was storing. So he went outside and began tossing the crystallized chemical on the little patch of lawn in front of his modest home. One Herington woman observed that Nichols put so much of the stuff on his lawn, it looked like snow had fallen.

Nichols was correct, though, in his assumption that investigators would be looking at him. When the FBI learned that McVeigh had listed the Nichols family farm in Michigan as his home address, they began looking into McVeigh's ties to Terry Nichols and his older brother James, who still lived at the Michigan farm.

While driving to a lumberyard on the morning of April 21, Nichols heard a radio news broadcast mentioning him, his brother, and McVeigh as possible suspects in the bombing. Rattled, Nichols drove home and asked his wife, Marife, whether she had heard the report.

She had not, she said, and she couldn't believe it.

No, Nichols said, I'm not kidding. He was coming unglued, afraid that armed federal agents might be ready to storm his home, and that, in his words, "another Waco" would take place.

Nichols put his wife and baby daughter, Nicole, into his pickup truck and drove to a local surplus store. As Nichols got out of the vehicle at the Surplus City he had an overwhelming feeling that he was being watched and followed, and his intuition was right. A team of FBI agents was on his tail, watching his every move from a squadron of unmarked government sedans.

Nichols quickly got back into the truck, drove his family to the Herington Police Station, and rushed inside, cradling his daughter in his arms. In an outer office, he pelted questions at the officials he found there, Police Chief Dale Kuhn and Assistant Chief Barry Thacker. The officers had just been watching coverage of the bombing on TV; now here was one of the alleged bombers walking into their police station. When Thacker first saw Nichols with a baby in his arms, he wondered whether Nichols might be using his tiny daughter as a human shield, until he saw the frantic look on Nichols's face.

"What can I do for you?" Thacker inquired.

"I've seen my name and face on TV," said Nichols, his voice rising. "I'd like to talk to someone."

He wanted to know everything the Herington police could tell him about the bombing investigation.

Nichols repeated the question at least three times. Trying to calm the situation, Kuhn invited Nichols and his family into his office. He couldn't give them much information about what was going on.

"I'm afraid of the FBI," Nichols told the police chief. Nervously, he took his jacket off and invited Kuhn to search him for weapons. Kuhn did; Nichols was unarmed.

FBI agents were standing outside, with fears of their own. They'd watched Nichols go storming into the police station, and now were wondering whether he was becoming violent, maybe even taking hostages. Only when a call to Kuhn's office confirmed that everything was okay did they feel comfortable standing down.

When the agents finally entered the station, they told Nichols they had some questions for him. "Good," Nichols replied, "because I have some questions for you." He followed the agents into a basement room that Herington police and firefighters usually used for training. There, over the next nine hours, Nichols gave Agents Stephen Smith and Scott Crabtree an earful: a rambling marathon of facts, lies, and obfuscations that did no favors for his friend Tim McVeigh. Nichols, who so feared and despised the government, would cough up enough information that day to raise federal eyebrows from Kansas to Washington, D.C.

Nichols denied any knowledge of or involvement in the bombing. He insisted that he was with his family in Herington when the bomb went off. He didn't know where McVeigh was, he said, or what he was doing the day of the blast.

Nichols admitted that he had driven five hours to downtown Oklahoma City on Easter Sunday, three days before the bombing, and that he brought McVeigh back to Kansas with him. The purpose of the trip, he said, was to pick up an old TV set McVeigh had borrowed from him.

Nichols said McVeigh told him to lie to Marife about the trip, telling her that he was going to Omaha. "Just keep this between the two of us," Nichols quoted McVeigh as saying. Why all the secrecy over an old TV set? agents asked. McVeigh was often secretive like that, Nichols told them. Sometimes, he said, McVeigh would tell him things "in code."

Nichols told the agents that he believed he'd driven past the Murrah Building a couple of times while looking around for McVeigh that evening. He said he picked up McVeigh in an alley, but couldn't remember the specific location. On the ride back home to Kansas, Nichols said, he and McVeigh talked about a lot of things, including the forthcoming second anniversary of the tragedy at Waco.

Nichols recalled that McVeigh told him that "something big" was going to happen in the near future, but that McVeigh never specified exactly what.

"What are you going to do?" Nichols said he asked McVeigh. "Rob a bank?"

"Oh, no," he quoted McVeigh as responding. "I got something in the works."

McVeigh was more "hyped" about the Waco controversy than he was, Nichols added.

Nichols told the FBI that he had dropped McVeigh off in Junction City early on the morning of April 17. Early the next morning, about six o'clock, McVeigh had called and asked to borrow Nichols's truck, he said, and he let McVeigh use the truck for several hours.

The Murrah Building was bombed the morning of April 19. Nichols said he didn't hear a word about the bombing until the next morning, when he happened to see a TV news report while signing up for service at a cable TV office.

Nichols said he was shocked to learn that McVeigh had been implicated in the bombing. "When I heard his name on TV, I figured out why my name was on the radio, because I was his friend," he said. "I must not have known him that well, for him to do that. . . . I would be shocked if he implicated me. Tim takes responsibility for his actions, and he lives up to his arrangements."

Nichols said he couldn't see any reason McVeigh would bomb a federal building, but he added that McVeigh "could be capable of doing it."

"I suspect it now," Nichols acknowledged.

At first, Nichols lied to agents about possessing ammonium nitrate, claiming he'd never had any. Later, he admitted that he did own some, but insisted he used it only as a fertilizer. When the agents asked him why he hadn't told the truth from the beginning, he replied, "I thought it would make me look guilty in front of a jury." He figured that after the bombing, anybody who had ammonium nitrate would be in trouble.

As two dozen FBI and ATF agents waited anxiously upstairs, the interrogators in the basement kept turning up the heat. At one point during the long interview, agents played Nichols a tape of his ex-wife, Lana Padilla, and his thirteen-year-old son, Josh, imploring him to cooperate in the bombing probe.

"Hi, Dad, I love you. Cooperate the best you can," said Josh Nichols, his voice close to a sob. "The FBI is doing a nice job of helping us, and protecting us from the media. . . . Grandma says she loves you and believes in you. . . . We love you, Dad."

"Josh is safe and very concerned about you," Padilla said. "It's really necessary that, sooner or later, everybody know your family had nothing to do with this."

Padilla had handed over the contents of the mysterious package Nichols had left for his wife before his trip to the Philippines, and now the agents confronted him about it. One question Nichols would not answer was what he meant by the words "Go for it!" in the letter he'd meant for McVeigh.

But Nichols cooperated in other ways, giving the FBI permission to search his truck and his home on South Second Street. The residence provided a treasure trove of evidence. There, agents found guns, ammunition, a quilt, and some keys taken during the robbery of Roger Moore in Arkansas. They found ammonium nitrate, which was used in the bomb, and Primadet explosive, which Nichols and McVeigh had stolen from the stone quarry in Kansas. They also found the electric drill that was used on padlocks in the quarry burglary.

In addition, they found the Daryl Bridges telephone card used by McVeigh for phone calls all over the U.S. in his quest to obtain bomb-making materials. They found antigovernment books and articles, including some of the exact articles McVeigh had left in the white envelope in his Mercury.

They found books on bomb-making and a copy of *Hunter*, William Pierce's follow-up to *The Turner Diaries*. In one of its chapters, *Hunter* provided a virtual how-to manual for making a truck bomb that could take down a government building.

They found a receipt—with both Nichols's and McVeigh's fingerprints on it—for the purchase of a ton of ammonium nitrate. They found plastic barrels, similar to the ones they used for the bomb.

And, crumpled in a trash can outside the house, investigators found what they alleged was a hand-drawn map of downtown Oklahoma City, including the Murrah Building and the spot where McVeigh hid the getaway car.

By the end of the interview, the agents were more than satisfied with the information they had. They believed Nichols when he told them he was at home in Kansas when the bomb went off in Oklahoma City, though not his claim that he had nothing to do with the crime.

As the interview came to a close past midnight, they arrested Nichols on a material witness warrant and took him into custody. More substantial charges would be filed later.

Up north in Decker, Michigan, another team of investigators was zeroing in on James Nichols.

When the agents first called the Sheriff's Department in rural Sanilac County for help, a detective already knew some things about the Nichols family. The region is a stronghold of militia organizations, and Detective

Sergeant David Hall had spent time the previous year investigating a complaint that Terry and James Nichols had been experimenting with pipe bombs and other explosives, using fertilizer and diesel fuel. James Nichols had vehemently denied having anything to do with explosives; without enough information to file charges or even obtain a search warrant, the case had fallen dormant.

Federal agents descended on Michigan's Thumb on April 21, scouring the countryside for information that might link James Nichols to the bombing. They conducted a raid on his farm, finding some bags of fertilizer containing ammonium nitrate, a fifty-five-gallon drum of fuel oil, and some potential bomb ingredients, including some fuse line and blasting caps.

Investigators talked with his associates, neighbors, and critics. One Decker man reported having seen the Nichols brothers experimenting with small bombs, made in plastic soft-drink bottles with fertilizer, bleach, and other chemicals. This witness recalled a man named Tim who lived at the farm for a time, carried a handgun, and often wore camouflage clothing. A second neighbor reported that men working on the Nichols farm had experimented with small bombs—an apparent reference to the experiments of employees on the Nichols farm long before McVeigh had appeared there.

James Nichols swore that he had nothing to do with any of the bomb experiments, and none of the information police had tied him to the bombing in Oklahoma. But agents stopped him at a roadblock near his farm and arrested him, charging him with conspiring with his brother and McVeigh to make unregistered destructive devices.

During his arrest, said federal prosecutors, James Nichols gave out a flurry of violent rhetoric: an FBI agent reported that Nichols warned that "cops, judges, and lawyers" were in danger of being killed by an antigovernment group. James Nichols would spend thirty-two days in jail before a federal judge released him on bail. Later, the charge against him was dropped for lack of evidence. James Nichols insisted that he and his brother had had nothing to do with the bombing.

Back in Oklahoma City, after representing him for several days, McVeigh's attorneys wanted out.

Susan Otto, a public defender employed by the federal court system, and

John Coyle, who was in private practice, were well respected in the criminal courts as smart and aggressive defenders of their clients' rights. They both knew that defending criminal clients could be a tough, high-pressure, often thankless job. They'd done it for years. They could handle the pressure of representing an unpopular defendant.

But this case was different. McVeigh was arguably the most notorious, despised criminal defendant in America since Lee Harvey Oswald. He had blown up an office building, killing 168 people of almost every age, race, and religion.

Otto and Coyle did much of their work in the federal courthouse next door to the Murrah Building. Windows and doors in the courthouse had been blown out, and a number of courthouse employees were injured. One of the judges, whose office faced the Murrah Building, might have been killed if not for the bulletproof glass in his windows. Members of a jury in deliberation were also injured by the blast. Otto, in her eleventh year as a federal defender, also had an office in a building next to the courthouse that was damaged by the bomb. The explosion shattered her office windows; she felt fortunate that she had not been sitting at her desk at the time.

Otto and Coyle both knew people, and family members of people, who were killed or maimed at the Murrah Building. In the federal courts of Oklahoma City, defense lawyers saw the same federal agents again and again. They served on different sides, but the atmosphere was cordial. Otto was on a first-name basis with several agents and other government employees who were killed; one of the men killed was an old golfing buddy of Coyle's.

Protected by security guards, Coyle held a news conference in his office to announce his intention to withdraw. He revealed that he had received death threats after accepting the assignment, and before the cameras rolled he turned a set of framed photographs of his wife and children away from TV cameras so their faces would not be broadcast to the nation. But Coyle said that concerns over safety were not his main reason for asking to withdraw. He said he and Otto felt too many emotional ties to the case. Both lawyers had gone to the Murrah Building minutes after the bombing. They had seen the carnage with their own eyes. Coyle said the case caused him so much emotional turmoil that he didn't think he could provide the kind of dispassionate legal advice McVeigh needed.

In Coyle's opinion, this case required lawyers without such a strong emotional attachment to the events of April 19, 1995. And in twenty-one years of lawyering, Coyle said, he had never met anyone who needed an attorney as much as Tim McVeigh.

Speaking later on the subject in federal court, Otto rattled off the names of people she knew who had been killed or affected in some horrendous way by the bombing. Under the law, she said, Howland should release her and Coyle from the case, assigning it to someone with less emotional attachment.

"This is a case of extraordinary proportions. . . . We have found no case in the history of this country that is of such magnitude [as] the one we are involved in right now," said Otto.

"This is not an instance where Mr. Coyle and I are saying we want to be released because we are upset. We believe it is constitutionally required. Right from the very beginning, Mr. McVeigh is entitled to have this case considered by someone other than the persons who lived through these events."

Coyle and Otto could have had another reason for withdrawing, which they never revealed in news conferences, interviews, or court appearances: their knowledge that McVeigh was guilty. Since that first meeting at the Tinker Air Base, an unashamed McVeigh had confirmed his responsibility for the bombing to the two. His secret confession was part of the strategy he would follow throughout the course of his case. While refusing to plead guilty to the charges against him, he was honest—brutally so—with the lawyers and investigators who were assigned to help him.

"I bombed the Murrah Building, and here's why," he would say, then continue by explaining his position. Technically, McVeigh admitted, he was guilty of the crime. But he felt that his actions were a justifiable response to the tyranny of the federal government. He did not want to stand up in any court and deny bombing the Murrah Building. What he wanted was for his lawyers to craft a "necessity defense" in his case, admitting his actions but explaining why McVeigh considered the bombing absolutely necessary.

McVeigh was convinced that at least some jurors would be sympathetic to him after hearing all the details about Waco, Ruby Ridge, and the other government excesses that had motivated his actions. If the evidence was presented in a compelling way, he believed, some jurors would understand what drove him to become a killer.

Beyond any prediction about the outcome, though, McVeigh favored that defense strategy for another reason—a reason that was central to what he saw as the ultimate success or failure of his mission. He knew that his trial would be covered by news media all over the country, and he wanted to seize the opportunity to make his case about the federal juggernaut. Without an adequate forum to explain his action, his message would never get through to the public.

In meetings with his lawyers, McVeigh put all his cards on the table. He wanted them to have all the information about what he did—and to understand why. McVeigh realized that his candor put some of his defenders in a moral quandary: some defense lawyers don't care whether a client is guilty, but others find it difficult to represent defendants they know are guilty—especially of violent crimes. It is this very hesitation that compels some defense lawyers to ask their clients not to tell them whether they are guilty or innocent.

McVeigh understood the problem, and he addressed it up front when he spoke with his attorneys. "If this bothers you, knowing, in fact, that the person you're defending is guilty, just let me know," McVeigh told his attorneys. "I'm not going to hold it against you. You should move on."

McVeigh had great respect for both Coyle and Otto, who represented him for the first few weeks after his arrest. He could see the emotional toll the case was taking on the two lawyers, and he was impressed that they never betrayed him. Despite their friendships with fellow Oklahomans whose lives were ravaged by the bombing, they kept their knowledge to themselves and aggressively represented McVeigh in pretrial proceedings. When they finally opted out, it was hard for him to blame them.

Eight days after the bombing—before Coyle and Otto withdrew—a second hearing was held. This time, a visiting room in the El Reno prison was turned into a makeshift courtroom. It was an odd scene for a hearing of such magnitude: the room was equipped with vending machines for snacks and soft drinks, and drawings of Minnie Mouse and other cartoon characters decorated one of its walls, posted there to cheer young children visiting their fathers. Once again presiding from a wooden desk, Howland asked attorneys to speak loudly; they were competing with a nestful of chirping birds just outside the window.

Despite the informal setting, security at the hearing was extremely tight. Over Coyle's objections, McVeigh was kept in handcuffs for the hearing, a departure from normal federal court procedures.

The hearing, offering the first glimpse at evidence in the case, lasted more than four hours. There were two witnesses: Trooper Hanger, recounting the details of his now-famous traffic arrest, and FBI Special Agent Jon Hersley, who revealed that several eyewitnesses reported seeing a man who matched McVeigh's description near the Murrah Building the morning of the bombing.

The hearing grew heated when Coyle attacked Hersley for describing the Black Talon bullet in McVeigh's gun as a "cop-killer bullet." Coyle pointed out that it was McVeigh himself who had willingly told Hanger about the gun he was carrying. In that light, Coyle suggested, the "cop-killer" tag was out of line.

But Coyle's questions led him into troubled waters. "Is there any evidence that Mr. McVeigh killed a cop on that day?" he asked.

"Yes," Hersley shot back.

"He is a cop killer?" Coyle demanded.

"Yes," Hersley said. "The evidence points toward the fact that he blew up several federal law-enforcement officers in the federal building that morning."

"With this Glock forty-five?" Coyle asked.

"No," Hersley said, "with a massive bomb."

Hersley also testified that McVeigh's Abraham Lincoln T-shirt bore traces of an explosive substance known as penta erythrite tetral nitrate, or PETN, an allegation the FBI offered as proof that McVeigh was in or around the Ryder truck when it was loaded with explosives.

Bullshit, McVeigh thought. He had carefully changed all his clothes and wiped down the interior of the truck after mixing the bomb. Any trace of explosive material would have had to come from his gun, not from the bomb, he maintained.

Ultimately Howland ruled that the evidence presented by federal prosecutors appeared to be "very credible," and pointed to an "indelible trail of evidence that starts in Junction City and ends up at the front door of the Murrah Building." He ordered that McVeigh be held without bail.

.   .   .

McVeigh returned to El Reno, where he found that prison officials were increasingly on edge about having him. This was, after all, the state of Oklahoma; the death toll was now officially more than one hundred and rising. He heard that one of the women killed in the bombing was a close relative of a corrections officer at El Reno. Before long a special team of officers with fewer emotional ties to the bombing was brought in from Texas to guard McVeigh.

McVeigh had an entire wing of the prison to himself. And at all times when he was in his cell, a corrections officer would sit just outside, watching his every move.

In his rare and brief interactions with other prisoners, McVeigh was surprised to find that not every inmate greeted him with hatred. Some treated him with what he judged to be respect, though it may just as likely have been fear. Later, some would even approach him for autographs.

One day, while McVeigh was working out by himself in an exercise cage, he noticed something. A prisoner was holding a piece of paper to the tiny window of his cell.

McVeigh saw that a big letter *G* was written on the paper. The prisoner removed that piece of paper, and replaced it with another. This one bore the bold letter *O*.

One by one, the prisoner took a letter out of the window and replaced it with another. He was spelling out a message for McVeigh:

"G-O-O-D B-O-M-B."

McVeigh took it as a show of political support.

12

Indicted

McVeigh had no radio or TV in his cell, where he was confined most days for twenty-three hours. He passed the time reading, writing letters, and bouncing a racquetball off a wall. He would read more than one hundred books in the two years preceding his trial, from Colin Powell's autobiography to a book on abolitionist John Brown to classics like *Doctor Zhivago* and *Atlas Shrugged.*

Several weeks after his arrest, a federal judge allowed Coyle and Otto to withdraw from the bombing case. McVeigh tried to get Gerry Spence, the flamboyant Wyoming lawyer who had represented Randy Weaver after Ruby Ridge; Spence was just the type of fighter McVeigh wanted to represent him.

Court officials told McVeigh they'd passed his request on to Spence, but he never heard back; Spence later explained that he had declined the case because of family considerations.

Enter Stephen Jones, a politically active attorney from Enid, Oklahoma, ninety-eight miles northwest of Oklahoma City.

After a nationwide search for someone to represent McVeigh, U.S. District Judge David L. Russell reached out to Jones, who said he was both flattered and unnerved by the request.

Stephen Jones was fond of describing himself as a "small-town, county-seat lawyer," but Jones was no stranger to the spotlight. In the mid-1960s Jones had worked in New York City as a personal research assistant to Richard M. Nixon before he became president; years later, after the Watergate scandal turned Nixon into a national pariah, Jones wrote an article entitled "Was President Nixon Guilty?: A Case for the Defense" for an Oklahoma Bar Association journal. A vocal and energetic member of the Republican Party in Oklahoma, Jones had run unsuccessfully for the U.S. Senate, Congress, and state attorney general. But he had also served as general counsel to the Oklahoma chapter of the American Civil Liberties Union in the early 1970s, once representing the radical leader Abbie Hoffman when Oklahoma State University refused to allow Hoffman to speak on campus. During the Vietnam War, Jones also represented Keith Green, a student protester who was arrested for carrying a Vietcong flag during an antiwar demonstration at the University of Oklahoma. "I got fired from my law firm for representing Keith Green," Jones recalled.

Jones had handled more than fifteen death-penalty cases, including some particularly heinous murder cases involving some of Oklahoma's most feared and hated criminals. When Russell approached him to represent McVeigh, Jones was working on the federal appeals for Roger Dale Stafford, a serial killer whose bloody murder spree—he killed an entire family on one occasion, and six restaurant employees on another—had outraged the state.

After his appointment as McVeigh's lead counsel on May 8, 1995, Jones held a news conference.

Jones told reporters from the *Oklahoman* and other area news media that he would work hard to prevent the McVeigh case from taking on a circus atmosphere. He promised to avoid the pitfalls of "self-promotion" and "self-aggrandizement."

"My role is as old as the Constitution," Jones said. "Whether I perform professionally will be determined by how I conduct myself, and whether my client is satisfied, rather than the amount of column inches of publicity or the number of talk-show interviews."

Jones told reporters he hoped to bring out the truth about the bombing.

He said he did not want the Murrah Building blast to become one of the "running sores" of American history, like the prolonged controversies over the assassinations of John F. Kennedy and Martin Luther King.

"Whatever the result here, the public wants to know what happened or what didn't happen, who did it or who didn't do it," Jones asserted. "And they want it in a way that is consistent with our values as a nation."

For his part, McVeigh had mixed emotions after his first meeting with Jones. He was impressed by what he had heard about Jones's credentials. One expert told McVeigh that Jones was the best defense lawyer in Oklahoma, bar none.

At least this guy is not afraid to represent someone Americans hate, thought McVeigh, who also thought there was a chance Jones would even present his "necessity defense." But soon McVeigh began to suspect that Jones, despite his denials, craved the nationwide publicity the case had brought him.

Almost immediately after Jones took over, leaks began to spring in the McVeigh defense team, and in the most public of forums.

Eight days after Jones entered the case, the *New York Times* carried a story reporting that McVeigh had made a jailhouse confession to the bombing. Attributing its information to sources who had spoken with McVeigh in jail, the *Times* reported that McVeigh took responsibility for the bombing but denied knowing there was a day-care center in the Murrah Building.

Indeed, such discussions had taken place between McVeigh and his defense team.

At first, McVeigh was hopeful that the media leak of a confession meant that Jones was seriously considering using the "necessity defense." But as the leaks continued, he began to grow concerned. A month later, the *Oklahoman* published its own report on a leaked confession, reporting that McVeigh was contending he acted alone when he rented the truck and drove it to Oklahoma City. Again, the story—headlined MCVEIGH SOLO ROLE RE-PORTED IN BLAST—was an accurate leak of what McVeigh had told the defense team.

Like the *Times*, the Oklahoma newspaper cited unnamed sources, and in both cases Jones forcefully denied knowing where the information came from. He registered a complaint directly with the newspaper in an interview that was subsequently published in late June of 1995. "What you're doing is poisoning the atmosphere for a fair trial by reporting, ad nauseam, these leaks," he told the *Oklahoman*. "I would think that before you accuse my client of single-handedly committing mass murder, that you could at least get your source to go on the record." The leaks weren't coming from him, Jones insisted. He pointed out that forty people or more, mostly attorneys, had had access to McVeigh since his arrest.

The news leaks astonished and angered McVeigh. But he continued to show unusual frankness about the bombing with any and all members of the defense team, from attorneys to investigators to legal aides. And the content of his consultations with Jones and his staff was shared with a lot of people. McVeigh's defenders, who were being paid by the government McVeigh so hated, now numbered in the dozens. Many of the people on the team were Oklahomans; some of them—Jones included—knew people who had lost family members in the bombing.

McVeigh blamed the leaks squarely on Jones, regardless of who actually gave the information to the newspapers. Jones was lead counsel, the boss of the defense, and an important part of his job was to protect the sanctity of attorney-client discussions.

After the *New York Times* leak, McVeigh claims that he learned Jones had had a lengthy meeting with a *Times* reporter a few days before the first story ran.

"S.J. gave that to 'em—my own attorney!" McVeigh would rant years later. "I don't get this. I tell my attorneys something, and it goes into the newspaper?"

McVeigh said he was still hanging on to the hope that news leaks of confessional material would force Jones to use McVeigh's "necessity defense" when the case went to trial.

Jones admitted to McVeigh that he was giving information to the news media—though not, he said, attorney-client secrets—in hopes of getting reporters and editors on their side. McVeigh was getting hammered by the news media, all over the world, and Jones claimed he was just trying to help people hear his client's side of the story. "Tim always faced two trials, one in the court of public opinion and one in the court of law," Jones later wrote in his book about the bombing. "From the very beginning of the case, I set out consciously to cultivate members of the media and to let myself be cultivated in return. This wasn't a role I took to naturally."

Jones said he was also hoping the media, in its investigations into the bombing, would come up with information that would help the defense.

The defense lawyer encouraged McVeigh to take part in off-the-record prison meetings with reporters, including celebrity journalist Barbara Walters, one of the first reporters to visit him at El Reno.

McVeigh said he did not quite know what to expect as he sat down and looked into one of the most famous television faces in America.

"Do you have a girlfriend?" Walters asked, according to McVeigh.

McVeigh turned beet red.

"Oh, I shouldn't have asked that now," Walters said. "I should have waited to ask you that on camera, to get that reaction."

McVeigh wondered about Jones's motivations for pushing him into these meetings. He said he could detect a note of childlike wonder in Jones's voice when the attorney spoke about meeting Walters, and going out to dinner with other famous TV figures.

"I told Barbara some things about your case that she found very interesting," McVeigh said Jones told him after the Walters visit. He was increasingly convinced that Jones was "bantering" with his media friends about confidential attorney-client material.

At the same time, McVeigh sometimes agreed to visit with journalists without complaint—especially if they were attractive women. "You bring in good-looking chicks, I'll meet with them," he told Jones.

But the honeymoon between McVeigh and his new lawyer, if there ever was one, was already over. McVeigh quickly concluded that Jones wasn't taking him seriously.

Jones placated his client by listening to his suggestion of a "necessity defense"; according to McVeigh, the attorney even had one of his assistants investigate the chances of mounting such an argument successfully. In the end, Jones concluded it wouldn't fly, because McVeigh would have to prove he was in "imminent" danger from the federal government when he set off his bomb.

"But 'imminent' does not mean 'immediate,'" McVeigh argued. "If a comet is hurtling toward the earth, and it's out past the orbit of Pluto, it's not an immediate threat to Earth, but it is an imminent threat." And if the U.S. government was allowed to get away with what happened at Waco and Ruby Ridge, there was an imminent threat to the lives of gun owners, McVeigh said. "I would have no problem standing up at trial and admitting [the bombing], saying, 'This was a necessity,' " McVeigh said.

But Jones wouldn't bite. His responsibility was to give McVeigh the best possible defense, not a forum for his political views. He told McVeigh they would have to fight the charge, to force the government to prove McVeigh had bombed the building, and poke what holes they could in the evidence.

Furthermore, Jones simply did not believe McVeigh's contention that he acted alone on April 19, 1995. Jones was convinced there was a much bigger conspiracy—one he imagined might well have involved international connections. He did not believe that one former Army sergeant, with limited experience in explosives, could have pulled off everything McVeigh claimed, with only minimal assistance. McVeigh never wavered from his story: he alone drove the truck bomb to Oklahoma City, parked it in front of the building, and lit the fuses. And he alone made the decision to bomb the building during daylight hours, when it was full of people. Yet Jones seemed to think that McVeigh was sacrificing himself to protect others.

"There was no big conspiracy," McVeigh said. "It was mostly me. The few friends who helped me were acting under duress, and none of them had any control over when I was going to blow up the Murrah Building."

Nevertheless, at various times Jones tried to link the bombing to associates of Terry Nichols in the Philippines; to Osama bin Laden and other Arab terrorists; to a German descendent of a Nazi Party leader; to neo-Nazis in Great Britain; to Ramzi Yousef, mastermind of the World Trade Center bombing; and to associates of a white separatist group in the Oklahoma compound Elohim City.

All nonsense, McVeigh said. But Jones was convinced that the FBI had never really investigated the bombing thoroughly, and he was determined to crack open a conspiracy. The lawyer traveled to the Philippines, trying to prove that Nichols had met with terrorists there. He flew to Israel to learn about Arab terrorists, and to Great Britain to discuss the Oklahoma City bombing with experts on the Irish Republican Army. Jones hired a Harvard professor, an expert on Arab terrorists, to work with the defense team.

Jones said he had good reasons for these explorations. He was taking on a team of federal prosecutors and agents with unlimited resources, and his job was to represent McVeigh. In his book, Jones said he was convinced the FBI had not gone far enough to determine who besides McVeigh might have been involved in the bombing. After all, Jones noted, even the U.S. Justice Department had suggested in its charges against McVeigh and Nichols that they were assisted by "others unknown."

"It strains belief to suppose that this appalling crime was the work of two men—any two men," Jones wrote. "I had to consider the possibility that the Oklahoma City bombing could have been a very clever, well-executed conspiracy. Could it have been designed to protect and shelter everyone involved? Everyone, that is, except my client—who may or may not have been involved." And if McVeigh was involved, Jones added, would his role have been "the designated patsy"?

According to McVeigh, Jones began acting as though he was convinced his client was "delusional." Again and again Jones would send different members of the defense team to El Reno to hear McVeigh recount every detail of the story, only to hear McVeigh give the same version of events each time. Jones even hired an Oklahoma City psychiatrist, Dr. John R. Smith, to evaluate McVeigh and help determine whether McVeigh was delusional or competent to stand trial.

Smith, sixty-three at the time, had examined nearly one hundred accused killers as a court-appointed psychiatrist. But he'd never met anyone accused of killing 168 people. Nor had he ever been assigned to a case that hit so close to home. His own home, about a mile from the Murrah Building, had had a front window blown out by the blast. A piece of debris from the bomb had come crashing through a window in an office where Smith's daughter worked, fortunately injuring no one. He was already treating several of the bomb victims, who were traumatized by their experiences. Smith himself had driven past the Murrah Building less than half an hour before the explosion. When Jones's team approached him, they told Smith that they wanted him to judge the mind of "a man who drove off the interstate, set fire to a five-minute fuse, and then set fire to a two-minute fuse."

Smith talked with McVeigh for twenty-five hours, mostly over a five-week period in the spring and summer of 1995. Five years later, McVeigh gave Smith a written release to discuss their interviews with the authors of this book.

Smith found McVeigh very intelligent, with a 126 IQ, and very open to discussing his crime with a psychiatrist. By the second visit, Smith said, McVeigh was openly discussing the bombing, step by step, in chilling detail.

The psychiatrist saw no signs of remorse as McVeigh calmly explained how he designed, built, and delivered his bomb. *He talks about this crime like it's some kind of successful science project,* Smith thought angrily after one session.

And yet even in this confessed mass murderer Smith found things he liked, and reasons for sympathy. While others saw McVeigh as outgoing and happy-go-lucky, Smith found McVeigh deeply troubled by his parents' divorce and his war experiences. He pictured McVeigh in adolescence, trying to lose himself in the fantasy world of comic books late at night while his parents argued so furiously in the next room that McVeigh actually feared they might kill each other.

Others saw McVeigh as tremendously proud of his accomplishments in the military, but Smith saw a young man who was horrified by the killing of Arab soldiers. He listened closely to McVeigh's nightmarish descriptions of the killing he had done. To Smith, it was tragic that McVeigh never received counseling when he returned to the United States after the war. McVeigh told him he had looked into the possibility of getting treatment at a Veterans Administration hospital in Florida, but backed out when he was told he could not be treated under an assumed name. McVeigh was worried that receiving such counseling would be held against him when he applied for jobs.

McVeigh told Smith he had briefly experimented with methamphetamines after leaving the Army, but Smith saw no indications that McVeigh had ever been a heavy user of drugs.

While McVeigh proudly called himself a warrior, Smith could only picture McVeigh killing others from afar—while peering through the sights of a Bradley, or delivering a bomb and leaving the scene, but never face-to-face.

Smith had met many murderers who seemed to enjoy killing. McVeigh was different. His outlook on the bombing was cold and calculating, but Smith could see that McVeigh took no pleasure from the killings at the Murrah Building. McVeigh viewed the bombing as a mission that it was his duty to carry out, and he was convinced the bombing would change government in America.

"I expect to be convicted for the bombing, and I expect to receive the death penalty," McVeigh told the psychiatrist.

McVeigh also told Smith that, in scouting locations for his bombing, he had looked for a target he could bring down without killing a lot of people in surrounding, nongovernment buildings.

Smith concluded that McVeigh's life had been thrown into turmoil by a series of disturbing events: his parents' breakup, the killing he had done in the war, even the tragic death of Terry Nichols's stepson. But the Waco incident, Smith believed, was the flash point for McVeigh's anger.

As a boy, Smith said, McVeigh had been so upset by his parents' breakup that he created a fantasy world for himself. "He created this superhero role for himself," Smith said. "He fantasized all these monsters, which he fought."

As an adult, McVeigh came to see the U.S. government as the ultimate monster—especially after the Waco incident.

"Waco was not the sole reason for the bombing," Smith said. "But if there had been no Waco, I don't believe Tim would have bombed the Murrah Building."

Smith once tried to confront McVeigh about the pain his bomb had caused others. Smith had noted how much McVeigh seemed to enjoy talking to people, and now he tried to use this quality to provoke a reaction from him. "Instead of the death penalty, Tim, they should put you in a tiny little cell," Smith said. "You wouldn't be allowed to talk to anyone, ever again."

McVeigh looked surprised. He stood straight up from his chair. "You'd put me in a little cell like that?" he said.

"Tim, that's what you did to your victims and their families," Smith said. "They'll never be able to communicate with each other again."

The two quickly moved on to other topics. "Tim, have you ever loved any-one?" Smith asked.

"My father and my grandfather," McVeigh quickly answered.

"I noticed you didn't mention your mother or your sisters," Smith re-marked.

"Yes," McVeigh said. "I was just noticing that myself."

Smith could see that McVeigh was awkward with women, but he knew that McVeigh had cared deeply about a couple of women in his life. McVeigh once asked Smith if he could take some of his sperm out of the prison and give it to a woman, so she could become pregnant. Smith agreed to look into the legal requirements for such a venture.

Smith said McVeigh also told him of the brief affair he allegedly had with Marife Nichols, the wife of Terry Nichols.

Though he was horrified by McVeigh's crime and his cold attitude, Smith did not see him as an evil man. Clinically, he saw him as an essentially decent person who had allowed rage to build up inside him to the point that he had lashed out in one terrible, violent act. "I've seen it many times," Smith maintains. "Nice people do really terrible things."

The psychiatrist reported back to Jones that his client was not delusional—that he knew exactly what he did, and exactly what he was doing now.

As for McVeigh, he considered himself as sane as anyone. In the months after his arrest, he continued his voracious reading of all things antigovernment, and he enjoyed watching TV shows that questioned the government's actions. One night on cable, McVeigh enjoyed a viewing of *Brazil*, Terry Gilliam's surreal 1985 film about a futuristic society where citizens are dehumanized. One of the characters in the film is Harry Tuttle, a terrorist bomber played by Robert DeNiro. Some people later theorized that McVeigh had chosen the alias Tim Tuttle in honor of DeNiro's character, but the first time he saw the film was inside prison walls.

McVeigh was receiving interview requests from news media all over the world. He met with a number of journalists, but never spoke on the record.

In June 1995, he received a letter that interested him. It was from David H. Hackworth, the highly decorated former Army colonel whose book *About Face* offered a gripping chronicle of his experiences in the Korean and Vietnam Wars. Hackworth wanted to interview McVeigh for *Newsweek* magazine.

McVeigh admired Hackworth, and was impressed with his "soldier-to-soldier" request for an interview. McVeigh told Jones he wanted to speak with Hackworth, and Jones agreed, as long as he could be present to monitor questions and answers—and as long as the story would run on the cover.

Arranging the interview at El Reno, where prison officials were hypersensitive to any kind of publicity, was tricky. According to McVeigh, Hackworth, another *Newsweek* writer, and a photographer were falsely identified as defense investigators in order to secure permission for them to visit the prisoner.

The June 24 interview lasted a little over an hour, and the questioning was limited to issues outside the bombing evidence. McVeigh spoke with pride about his Army record, denied speculation that his parents' divorce had ruined his life, and also denied allegations that he had belonged to a militia group in Michigan.

Despite all the restrictions on the interview, Hackworth did manage to become the first journalist to ask McVeigh, point-blank and on-record, whether he bombed the Murrah Building.

"This is the question that everyone wants to know: did you do it?" Hackworth asked.

"The only way we can really answer that is we are going to plead not guilty," McVeigh said.

Hackworth pressed the issue.

"But you've got a chance right now to say, 'Hell, no!' " he said.

"We can't do that," McVeigh said.

"And if he says, 'Hell, no!' " Jones interjected, "the government isn't going to just say, 'Well, okay, that settles that.' "

It turned McVeigh's stomach to dodge Hackworth's question. It was just another missed opportunity to tell his story, to get his message out. But McVeigh kept his silence, much to his frustration.

After the *Newsweek* cover story appeared, Hackworth's visit became a subject of controversy at the prison. Prison officials accused Jones of misconduct, bringing Hackworth and his associates into El Reno under false pretenses. Jones denied any wrongdoing; he claimed it was his understanding that the warden put no restrictions on journalists visiting McVeigh, as long as the defense lawyers vouched for the visitors. According to McVeigh, the uproar was strong enough that Judge Russell personally traveled to the El Reno prison and told McVeigh, in a private meeting, that he could have a new lawyer brought in if he wanted. But McVeigh decided to stick with Jones. After losing Coyle and Otto, and bringing Jones up to speed, he simply didn't feel like going through the whole process again.

That summer, Jones asked for a private meeting to discuss defense expenses with U.S. District Judge Richard P. Matsch, a Denver judge assigned to try the case. At the meeting, also attended by a court clerk, Jones told Matsch about his efforts to uncover a conspiracy behind the bombing. In order to defend McVeigh properly, Jones said, he would have to hire bomb-tracing analysts, pathologists, anthropologists, and terrorism experts. He would also need authorization for secure communications equipment and photography equipment. And he would need to do some more traveling.

"I must have talked for a good hour, developing the theory that the bombing had to have been an operation far beyond the capacities of my client and Terry Nichols," Jones recalled in his book. According to Jones, the judge assured him that he had proved his case for authorizing such expenses. Jones said he also spent time explaining to the judge how he had developed relationships with some members of the news media, and that he had been exchanging information with some reporters. The defense team, Jones said, simply did not have the resources of the prosecution and the FBI, and had to get help wherever it could.

While warning the defense lawyer not to try the case in the news media, Jones said Matsch told him he understood his need for some bartering of information with news reporters. "As I said, quite candidly, the media, in the quid pro quo of things, had to be 'fed,' " Jones explained.

It was not the last such meeting between Jones and the judge. McVeigh, who was not always invited to be present, soon began to worry about the discussions, which he called the "Star Chamber" meetings. McVeigh suspected that Jones and Matsch were discussing the various McVeigh confessions that had been reported in the news media. He wondered how these reports were weighing on the mind of the judge.

On August 10, 1995, almost four months after the bombing, a federal grand jury handed up a fifteen-page indictment against Timothy McVeigh and Terry Nichols. They were accused of using a weapon of mass destruction—a truck bomb—"to kill and injure innocent persons, and to damage the property of the United States." The indictment accurately laid out many of the steps McVeigh and Nichols took to acquire and store bomb-making materials. It also accused them of financing the bombing with the proceeds from the Roger Moore robbery in Arkansas.

The indictment listed all 168 people killed by the bomb, ranging from little Gabreon Bruce, just three months old, to the senior victim, a seventy-three-year-old dentist named Charles E. Hurlburt.

Eight counts of the indictment addressed the killings of on-duty federal law enforcement officers: Mickey B. Maroney, Donald R. Leonard, and Alan G. Whicher of the Secret Service; Kenneth Glenn McCullough and Cynthia L. Brown of the DEA; Paul D. Ice and Claude Arthur Medearis of the Customs Service; and Paul Gregory Beatty Broxterman of the HUD inspector general's office.

Government prosecutors, as promised by Attorney General Janet Reno shortly after the bombing, would be seeking the death penalty.

Mike Fortier, McVeigh's Army pal in Arizona, was also charged, but on counts much less serious than those faced by McVeigh and Nichols. The reason: Fortier, when told by federal agents that he too could be facing the death penalty, had taken a plea deal. He would be the government's star witness.

Fortier admitted that he had helped McVeigh and Nichols transport and traffic in stolen firearms—the guns taken from Moore. He also admitted he had lied to FBI agents two days after the bombing, when they first came to ask him if he knew anything about it. And Fortier admitted that, in the months before the explosion, he failed to alert authorities about the bombing plot.

Fortier's wife, Lori, would also testify, describing how McVeigh had arranged a number of soup cans in her mobile home to demonstrate possible configurations for his barrels of explosives.

The government gave Lori Fortier immunity from prosecution, allowing her to stay home in Kingman, raising the couple's young daughter, and McVeigh understood why she and her husband had made deals. "Mike has a family," McVeigh said. "I don't blame him for doing what he had to do. I still consider Mike a friend."

Back in western New York, Bill McVeigh was growing increasingly worried about his daughter Jennifer. Jennifer was a headstrong young woman, whose own disdain for authority suggested that she took after her brother rather than her father. A chain-smoker, she had worked as a waitress in a country-music bar, where she sometimes took part in Jell-O wrestling contests before screaming patrons. Known as a bright, independent-minded student to classmates at Niagara County Community College, she took a confrontational attitude toward the Buffalo FBI agents who tried to question her.

The FBI had Jennifer in a tough spot. Agents had found many of the letters her brother had sent her; they also had learned that, a couple of years earlier, Jennifer had packaged and mailed to her brother a large quantity of bullets. She had no idea that shipping live ammunition through the mail was a federal crime until she learned that she would be forced to testify against her brother or face criminal prosecution for sending the ammo.

Jennifer had little use for the FBI agents who tried to win her trust. According to Jennifer, when the friendly approach didn't work, the agents used rough, intimidating tactics, showing her photos of dead babies from the bombing, telling her that Tim was "going to fry," and threatening that she, too, could face the death penalty. "They're trying to make me look like a bad person," she would complain after the interview. "They try to put words in my mouth."

Agents Naum and Caryl Cid spent endless hours interrogating Jennifer over a period of two weeks after the bombing. On some days they questioned her for twelve to fifteen hours, going over the letters her brother had sent line by line. Cid, a tough, experienced agent, tried to find ways to reach her. Bill McVeigh tried to persuade his daughter to cooperate. Even Mickey flew up from Florida to help the effort.

Naum and Cid worked with the FBI's psychological profile unit to find a strategy to open up Jennifer. The pressure was on; Attorney General Reno and FBI Director Louis Freeh were checking in with Buffalo every couple of days to find out how things were going. But nothing was working. The outspoken young college student was a hard case. To Naum, she seemed so angry and strident in defending her brother that she almost appeared to approve of the bombing itself, and she expressed little compassion for the victims. Her hard-edged responses made Naum suspect that she might somehow be involved in the conspiracy.

When Naum showed Jennifer a set of photos of babies who had been mutilated and killed by the bomb, Jennifer contends, the photos upset her deeply. Afterward, she went home and cried. But all Naum saw was a cold, unfeeling, defensive response. Naum followed up with a poster the FBI had made up, listing the charges and penalties she could face if she were tied into this crime with her brother.

"This is not TV. This is reality," Naum warned. "You're going to find your-self right in the middle. We believe you are directly involved. Show us you are not."

Some agents, Naum included, felt she should be indicted. Others dis-agreed. The issue was hotly debated among law-enforcement officials in western New York.

Naum then called Bill McVeigh. "Jennifer could probably use a lawyer, Bill," Naum said.

Within days after Bill hired Joel L. Daniels, a top Buffalo defense attor-ney, to represent Jennifer, Daniels had crafted his client an immunity deal. Daniels deftly walked Jennifer through a legal minefield. She would have to testify against her brother—mostly about his letters and his political be-liefs—but she would not be charged. Nothing she told the FBI could be used against her in a federal or state prosecution. It was a difficult decision for Jennifer, who loved and idolized her brother. Weeks after the bombing, when a man approached her in a bar and called her brother a baby killer, she punched him in the face.

The feds hadn't come up with any evidence of a wide-ranging conspiracy, but that did not stop the lawyer McVeigh sarcastically called "Sherlock Jones" from searching for one.

Jones was convinced that federal agents hadn't done enough to explore Elohim City, the white separatist group whose members lived in trailers in northern Oklahoma. Jones learned that Carol Howe, a former undercover in-formant for the ATF, told the feds that two men who frequented Elohim City had talked about bombing a federal building.

Jones alleged the two men—Dennis Mahon, a former KKK leader, from Tulsa, and Andreas Strassmeir, a German citizen whose grandfather helped form the original Nazi party—had had something to do with the bombing. But McVeigh denied the story. Yes, he admitted, he had met Strassmeir at a gun show in Tulsa; he had traded him a pair of military long underwear for a dagger. They had even discussed some political issues. But Strassmeir had no role in the bombing, and neither did Mahon, whom McVeigh said he'd never met.

Jones and the defense team maintained their skepticism about McVeigh's claims, especially after they gave McVeigh a polygraph test to examine the truthfulness of his statements about the crime. The polygraph examiner found that McVeigh was being truthful when he described his own participation in the explosion. But the test showed signs of evasion by McVeigh when he said no others, aside from those already charged, were involved in the bombing.

McVeigh offered an explanation, contending that the polygraph was thrown off by his own anxieties over being asked the same questions again and again. He said he was especially upset when the polygraph operator asked him if his sister Jennifer was involved in the bomb conspiracy. In the months before the bombing, McVeigh had used his sister as a sounding board for some of his most intense outbursts about the government. He had tried to prepare her for what was coming by telling her something major was going to happen.

But McVeigh had told his lawyers and investigators, over and over again, that Jennifer played no part in the bombing, and now they were raising the same question again. "My first reaction to that question, after two months of interrogation by my own defense, is rage," McVeigh recalled later. "It's anger that they were trying to get my sister in trouble by asking that question. It's anger that they are not believing me." He insists today that the questions about his sister and others riled him sufficiently to cause spikes in his metabolism and blood pressure.

Predictably, information about the polygraph test was leaked to the news media. In a March 1997 story, *Newsweek* reported that McVeigh failed the test when asked whether all his co-conspirators were known to authorities. "McVeigh confirmed his role in blowing up the Murrah Building," the story read, but the polygraph results created "fresh confusion" over the possible involvement of other people who were not charged in the case.

Once again, McVeigh was angry over the leak. He was also growing more frustrated with Jones's globe-trotting conspiracy investigations, which McVeigh considered a waste of time, defense resources, and taxpayer money. (Jones maintained that he was receiving one hundred and twenty-five dollars an hour for his work on the trial, fifty dollars below his normal fee.)

McVeigh felt that by doubting his abilities to build the bomb alone Jones was calling him a liar. McVeigh also felt Jones was insulting his intelligence by doubting that McVeigh had the intellect and technical ability to pull off

the crime. And every time Jones returned from overseas, brandishing snapshots taken on his travels, McVeigh felt like he was listening to an overex-
cited tourist talking about a vacation. "He was investigating me, not
defending me," McVeigh complained.

Jones and his defense team did have some success at pretrial motions for
McVeigh. At Jones's request, court officials agreed to move the case out of
Oklahoma. In another victory for the defense, Matsch agreed that McVeigh
and Nichols should have separate trials.

As co-defendants, the two bombing suspects were being isolated from
each other by prison and court officials. On the few occasions they wound up
sitting near each other in courtrooms, Nichols made one thing clear: he
didn't want to talk with McVeigh. During one court appearance, McVeigh
tried to whisper something to his old Army buddy. Nichols refused to even
look McVeigh's way, and asked a court official to have McVeigh seated farther
away.

Nichols was clearly trying to distance himself from McVeigh in every way.
He had told authorities that—if anything—he'd only unwittingly helped
McVeigh pull off the bombing. His lawyer, a crafty and outspoken Texan
named Michael E. Tigar, would defend his client by portraying Nichols as a
victim of circumstances, and trying to press the case that McVeigh was the
sole driving force behind the bombing.

McVeigh felt Nichols had "hosed" him with his nine-hour statement to
the FBI. But McVeigh never said a word against Nichols, either to the news
media or law enforcement. He had no desire to see Nichols or Fortier punished.

Nichols and McVeigh were moved from El Reno to a federal prison in Englewood, Colorado, in March 1996. The two high-profile prisoners were
rousted out of bed in the middle of the night, taken from their isolation cells,
flown to an airport near Denver in a military jet, and then hustled into a waiting helicopter for the move to the prison. This time, for whatever reason, authorities allowed McVeigh to wear a bulletproof vest during the transfer.

As the accused killer of 168 men, women, and children, McVeigh ran into
hostility each time he was moved to a new facility. After he and Nichols arrived in Colorado, McVeigh claims, an officer punched him hard in the chest.

"Welcome to Denver," the officer said. When he was being booked and fingerprinted after his arrival at Englewood, McVeigh stepped forward to allow a guard to pass behind him. The guard reacted as if McVeigh were trying to make a prison break. "Don't you fuckin' move!" the guard screamed.

Prison officials had reason to worry about McVeigh's safety. In a Wisconsin prison in 1994, a prisoner had used a mop handle in the fatal beating of serial killer Jeffrey Dahmer. McVeigh and Nichols were accused of killing nearly ten times as many people as Dahmer. Authorities worried that some inmate might try to make a name for himself by dispatching one of the alleged Oklahoma bombers.

McVeigh himself is struck by the fact that, in all his time in prisons, he has never encountered one prisoner who attacked him for the bombing, either physically or verbally. But if he had ever been moved from the federal prison to a state facility in Oklahoma, McVeigh is certain that someone would have tried to kill him.

Pretrial proceedings were moving ahead. At one point, McVeigh and Nichols were moved to Denver for three weeks of court proceedings. They were kept in a cellblock maintained by the U.S. Marshals Service.

Since he was not yet a convicted felon, McVeigh retained his legal right to vote in elections. From prison, he wrote back home to New York State and obtained an absentee ballot from the Niagara County Board of Elections. He used the opportunity to vote against President Clinton, casting his vote for the Libertarian candidate.

Fame came to him in ways big and small. No less an authority than *Time* magazine had named McVeigh one of its runners-up for 1995 Man of the Year, a distinction the magazine uses to designate the person who's had the biggest impact in the news—for good or bad. Newt Gingrich, then Speaker of the House, was the winner. The other runners-up included Microsoft billionaire Bill Gates and defense lawyer Johnnie L. Cochran, Jr., who helped defend O. J. Simpson in his murder trial.

"Was it Waco that set him off on a path through Arizona and on to Kansas, where he allegedly rented the Ryder truck that carried the bomb, and then to Oklahoma City?" the *Time* article mused. "Will his trial . . . exonerate him? And if not, will it somehow make comprehensible the mind behind that blank, ordinary face; a mind that led a man to slaughter strangers?"

One day, an attractive young woman came to see McVeigh with her

The Murrah Building before and after the bombing. *(top: Laurence K. Donahoe; bottom: Bob Lester Larue/Corbis Sygma)*

McVeigh's abandoned getaway car. Police returned to the scene of his arrest on April 21, two days after the bombing, once he became a suspect in the case. *(AP)*

The back of the T-shirt McVeigh was wearing when he was apprehended driving north from Oklahoma City after the bombing. *(AP/Justice Dept.)*

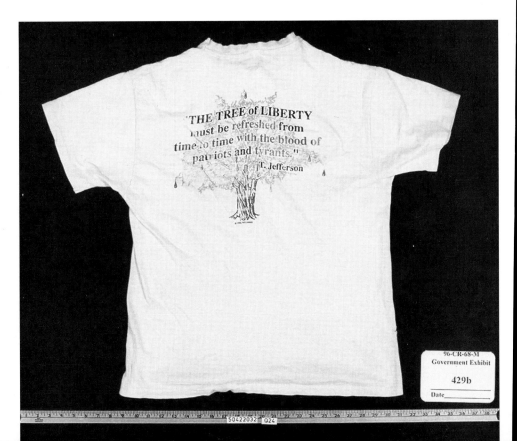

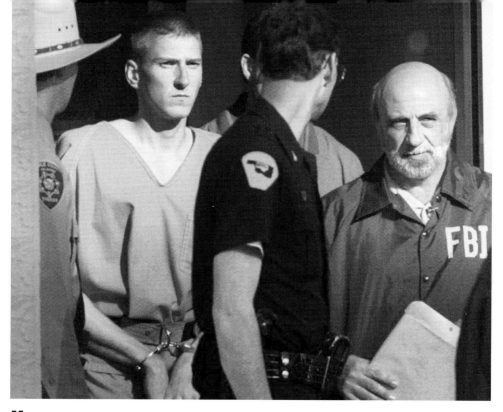

McVeigh leaves the Noble County Courthouse in Perry, Oklahoma, on Friday, April 21, 1995, after being identified as a suspect in the bombing. *(AP)*

Consulting with defense attorneys Stephen Jones *(right)* and Robert Nigh in June 1995 at the federal prison in El Reno, Oklahoma. *(AP)*

Terry Nichols in custody; he was later convicted of conspiracy. McVeigh contends Nichols was acting under duress. (AP)

Terry Nichols's wife, Marife, with whom McVeigh claims to have had an affair. (AP)

Jennifer McVeigh after testifying before a federal grand jury in August 1995. (AP)

Bill and Mickey McVeigh arriving at the Denver courtroom to hear the jury issue its decision on McVeigh's fate: Friday, June 13, 1997. (AP)

McVeigh on federal death row, Terre Haute, Indiana. (*Lou Michel*)

Looking through the witness viewing windows into the execution chamber, Terre Haute. (*Courtesy of the Federal Bureau of Prisons*)

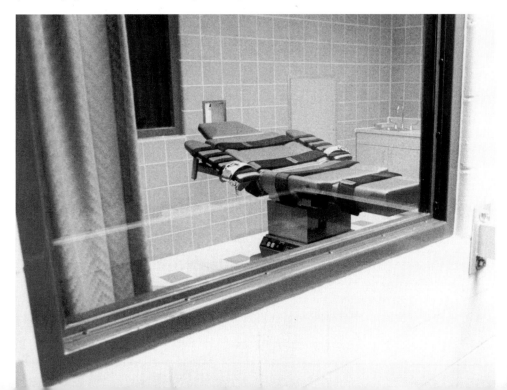

Jack, Mollie, and Liz McDermott, McVeigh's former neighbors, with the peach tree McVeigh planted near his home. *(Joe Mombrea)*

The Survivor Tree at the Oklahoma City National Memorial. *(Authors' collection)*

The memorial's East Gate, at left, commemorates the last moment before the bombing. At right is the Field of Empty Chairs. *(Merryweatherphoto.com)*

friend, an investigator for the defense team. When McVeigh asked the woman if he could take a sip from her can of soda, she seemed thrilled. "I'm keeping this can!" the young woman gushed.

McVeigh had begun getting mail, too, sometimes as many as twenty-five pieces a day. Much of it was hate mail, but more than a few letters came from people who said they agreed with McVeigh's disdain for government.

The letters ranged from shocking to touching to bizarre. One letter arrived from Oklahoma City, addressed to "Timothy McVeigh, Bombing Perpetrator & Asshole." The return address identified the sender as "Voices of Oklahoma." "LISTEN, YOU BASTARD," the author wrote. "Do you really know how much pain you caused our city and community? Your hatred of our government not only affected the victims and their families, but their friends and co-workers. Why didn't you and your scumbag friends go to Washington and protest like others do? If you're so unhappy with the government, why didn't you simply kill yourself? You reap what you sow, Asshole!!!"

Another anonymous writer claimed to be the mother of one of the children killed in the bombing. "Children have done nothing to you!" she wrote. "They have as much right to live as you! My first-born will never come back. I will spend the rest of my days wanting and missing him."

One bizarre request came from a woman in Denton, Texas, who sent some of her poems and asked McVeigh if he could use his influence to get her work published. Another woman, from Ireland, said the priest in her hometown was offering a Mass for McVeigh. Some women sent nude pictures of themselves. A young woman from Germany sent perfumed letters with lipstick kiss marks and erotic, extremely detailed stories of her sexual fantasies about McVeigh.

From a woman in Ann Arbor, Michigan, came the first of several marriage proposals McVeigh would receive in prison. She offered to move to Oklahoma to be closer to him.

And a woman in Baltimore sent a one-hundred-dollar check, telling McVeigh, "Don't give up, fight back."

But those who believed in McVeigh received a jolt on March 1, 1997. In a blockbuster story based on conversations between McVeigh and a member of the defense team, the *Dallas Morning News* reported another McVeigh confession.

This story was far more damning than the previous reports of jailhouse confessions by McVeigh. In talks with his defense team, McVeigh not only admitted his guilt, but also confirmed that he bombed the building during the day to increase the "body count," reporter Pete Slover wrote. "Some anti-government activists condemned the attack because of its high death toll, and one militia leader said Mr. McVeigh would have been a hero had he bombed the building at night to minimize casualties."

Slover quoted McVeigh's response to the defense staffer when he was asked in July 1995 why he had not bombed the building at night.

"Mr. McVeigh looked directly in my eyes and told me, 'That would not have gotten the point across to the government. We needed a body count to make our point.'"

The story added that McVeigh discounted conspiracy theories about the bombing, and that he insisted there was no John Doe No. 2 with him the day of the bombing. McVeigh said he alone delivered the explosive to the Murrah Building.

Slover reported that McVeigh made "several references" to Terry Nichols's participation in the bombing preparations, including the purchase of chemicals, and the robbery of Roger Moore. But McVeigh said he was unaware of James Nichols having any foreknowledge of the bombing, the report said.

Slover said his story was based on statements McVeigh made to his defense team between July and December 1995. He noted that, although McVeigh pleaded not guilty to the bombing, he never publicly denied the act.

Essentially an accurate report of McVeigh's talks with a defense investigator, the story caused a sensation. And although the story received wide criticism, details of the confession were picked up by most of the major media outlets in the United States.

For such a damning internal document to leak out to the public just one month before the scheduled start of a trial was devastating to Jones's defense plans. In the days after the report appeared, Jones expressed his anger and disgust at the Dallas newspaper for its "irresponsible" and "sensational" reporting.

How did it happen? reporters asked him. Where did the Dallas paper come up with something like that?

Jones seemed befuddled by it all. He offered several different scenarios.

"I think it's a hoax," he told the Associated Press.

He told the *Washington Post* that officials at the Dallas newspaper had revealed to him the identity of their confidential source for the material—a source, Jones said, who disliked the Dallas publication and was "setting up" the paper by leaking bogus information. "They just bought the Brooklyn Bridge," Jones said. "It's not anything I'm familiar with. If McVeigh said anything like that to the defense team, I think I would be aware of it."

And at a press conference in the Denver office he was using to prepare the defense, Jones offered: "I tell you . . . it is not a legitimate defense memorandum. It is not a confession by Tim McVeigh."

But McVeigh believes the statement was most certainly a legitimate defense document.

According to McVeigh, the defense team gave the *Dallas Morning News* a computer disk filled with internal FBI reports—known as 302 reports— without being aware that the notes of McVeigh's confessional remarks were included on the same disk.

If McVeigh, already one of the most hated men in America, had any chance of getting a fair trial before, he was convinced that it vanished on the day the Dallas newspaper ran its story. The words "body count" were burned into the memory of anyone who read or heard about the story.

Later, in his book, Jones offered yet another explanation for the leak to the Dallas paper. He said the McVeigh statement was a fake, put together by an investigator for the defense team. Jones said the investigator planned to show the fake confession to another person whom the defense believed was one of the conspirators in the bombing.

Jones said the defense hoped that the alleged conspirator might start talking if he believed McVeigh had already made a confession.

Jones blamed the leak on a defense-team member whom he referred to only as "X." He said that X reluctantly admitted to him that Slover had downloaded the information from X's laptop computer. According to Jones, X had received some helpful information from Slover in the past, and X was trying to reciprocate by giving Slover access to a few FBI reports. Instead, he mistakenly allowed Slover to download more than one hundred thousand documents.

After the incident, Jones said, he kicked X off the case. Jones said the incident was particularly painful because X was a trusted longtime friend. "He had betrayed the defense, he had betrayed our client, and he had betrayed our friendship," Jones wrote. "There just simply weren't words to express the sad frustration I felt."

McVeigh was livid. Jones could complain about being betrayed, but it was McVeigh who would bear the consequences.

He fully expected government prosecutors and the FBI to leak negative information about him, but most of the leaks seemed to be coming from his defense team—a group that now included nearly three dozen people, including fourteen lawyers, investigators, legal aides, and clerical workers. "It was a cluster-fuck," McVeigh said. "Give me two lawyers who know the case."

It was a strange contradiction: McVeigh knew he was guilty of the bombing, and was willing to be executed for it. Yet he wanted—demanded—a fair trial. He was determined to force the government to prove its case in court.

The Dallas story was not the end of the parade of confessions. Several other media outlets, including NBC News, ABC News, *Newsweek,* and *Playboy,* all said they had obtained information about McVeigh's secret discussions with his defense team.

Stating that its article was based on lawfully obtained documents created by McVeigh's attorneys, *Playboy* charted McVeigh's actions from the time he left Geary Lake on April 18, 1995, through the bombing itself, until the arrest by Trooper Hanger near Perry. The magazine said that McVeigh had admitted the bombing, and told his attorneys that the force of the blast smashed him into the side of a building as he made his getaway.

The McVeigh confession stories prompted Jones to ask Matsch to delay the trial. The judge refused, saying he did not believe the articles had as much exposure or acceptance in the public as defense lawyers believed.

But McVeigh was worried that the confession reports were having an effect—not only on potential jurors, but on Matsch himself.

Before the *Dallas Morning News* confession, McVeigh felt every one of Matsch's pretrial rulings on evidence had been fair—not always in McVeigh's favor, but fairly reasoned and based on the law. After the Dallas story, McVeigh felt Matsch had become certain of his guilt. "It finally convinced him I was guilty," McVeigh said. "It was like the straw that broke the camel's back." He felt the judge had decided that "this defendant is guilty, and I can't let him win this trial."

Another factor was the continuing national firestorm over the October 1995 acquittal of O. J. Simpson in one of the century's most publicized murder trials. Despite what many Americans considered overwhelming evidence that Simpson killed his ex-wife and her male friend in a posh Los Angeles neighborhood, jurors found Simpson not guilty. Simpson's trial had turned into a garish media circus, and polls showed that the Simpson case had caused many people to lose confidence in the criminal-justice system.

Under the circumstances, could Matsch ever allow a jury to find another celebrated defendant not guilty? McVeigh wondered.

Meanwhile, the tension between him and Jones continued to mount as the trial grew closer. Aside from all their other disagreements, Jones and McVeigh came from two different generations. Though he was more than willing to attack the FBI, Jones had grown up in an era when J. Edgar Hoover's agency was widely viewed as infallible—a basic predisposition that clashed with McVeigh's fanatical distrust of the feds. More and more, McVeigh felt Jones was humoring him, talking down to him, when McVeigh would offer suggestions on how the defense could attack the case.

McVeigh thought Jones gave far too much credit and respect to the FBI and its investigation techniques. The two men locked horns over the FBI laboratory's report on the bombing. McVeigh maintained that the report was incorrect in many of its basic conclusions about the blast. The FBI claimed the bomb was four thousand pounds, while McVeigh insisted it was more than a ton bigger than that—a point he hoped would cast doubt on the accuracy of the government's investigation. He presented Jones with a tricky challenge. "You can't say it comes from me, that this is way off," McVeigh said. "But you have to find some way to prove it."

Jones took off his glasses and looked at his younger client.

According to McVeigh, Jones asked, "Do you really expect me to believe that the FBI is that far off? You're telling me the FBI is wrong?"

"This is way wrong," McVeigh said. "Even some very fundamental observations in this report are wrong."

Frustrated by such disagreements, McVeigh claims he called a clerk at the Denver courthouse, asking if he could switch attorneys. He was told to direct his complaint to his attorney.

●　　●　　●

As the trial date approached, McVeigh passed the time reading a novel that, in many ways, mirrored his own story: *Unintended Consequences,* a vehemently antigovernment novel by John Ross, a gun-rights advocate from St. Louis.

Ross's 861-page book tells the story of Henry Bowman, a hunter and target shooter who becomes a terrorist after witnessing one government atrocity after another against members of the American gun culture. Instead of destroying a government building, Bowman assembles a team of assassins who murder government officials and agents one by one, in some cases dismembering their bodies and feeding them to pigs. The bloody story mixed fiction with real-life events, including the assault on Randy Weaver's family at Ruby Ridge; its cover featured a photo of the U.S. Constitution on fire and a black-clad government agent, helmeted and jackbooted, pointing his assault rifle at the throat of a defenseless, blindfolded (and bare-chested) woman.

Ross's book was not published until 1996, after the Oklahoma City bombing. If it had come out a couple of years sooner, it might have changed history. McVeigh considered *Unintended Consequences* a much more compelling story than *The Turner Diaries.* If he'd read Ross's book earlier, McVeigh says, he would have given serious consideration to a "war of attrition" against the government, mounting a sniper campaign picking off individual agents and elected officials, rather than blowing up an office building and taking the lives of innocent people, like the children in the day-care center.

"If people say *The Turner Diaries* was my Bible," McVeigh said recently, "*Unintended Consequences* would be my New Testament. I think *Unintended Consequences* is a better book. It might have changed my whole plan of operation if I'd read that one first."

On March 19, 1997, more than 350 Denver-area residents arrived at a building at the Jefferson County Fairgrounds for the first step in the jury screening process.

Potential jurors were required to fill out a forty-page questionnaire, which included questions about their exposure to publicity about the McVeigh case and their views on the death penalty and other issues.

For better or worse, McVeigh was about to get his day in court.

IV

INFAMY

13

"Oh, My God, He Did It"

He never had a doubt about the outcome.

From the first day of jury selection, McVeigh was convinced he was going to be found guilty and sentenced to die.

He came to think of the entire process as a charade. All of it—from the stern and solemn pronouncements of Judge Matsch to the extreme court-house security precautions, from the prosecutors' impassioned speeches to his own defense team's dead-end searches for the ultimate conspiracy theory—seemed to McVeigh like an extravagant and expensive exercise designed to make Americans feel better about sending the Oklahoma City bomber to death row.

He seldom showed much emotion as he sat in the courtroom and watched it all play out. But anger often raged inside him during the nearly five months from the start of jury selection to sentencing. "There were times when I felt like jumping to my feet and screaming, *Knock it off! Everyone here knows I'm guilty! Let's get on with it!*" McVeigh recalls.

Despite his cynicism about the process, McVeigh saw a propaganda value in this trial. He knew the news media would be there in full force to cover the man *Time* had called "The Face of Terror." But he hoped that the media coverage, through the testimony of various witnesses, could be turned to his advantage, helping the public to understand events like Ruby Ridge and Waco the way he did, as watershed moments in the emergence of a new American tyranny. Even McVeigh's preferred strategy, the "necessity defense"—admitting that he'd bombed the Murrah Building but explaining that without such drastic action America itself was in imminent danger—was motivated by the desire to express his opinion. McVeigh seemed unconcerned about whether most Americans could accept any justification for mass murder. Somehow, he retained the illusion that he could convince America that his actions were righteous.

When Jones finally persuaded McVeigh to drop the necessity defense—even McVeigh recognized it would be extremely difficult to meet the standard of proof for imminent danger—McVeigh reluctantly agreed to go along with Jones's strategy of attacking the government's evidence. Yet he clung to the notion that the trial proceedings could somehow be used to get his message across.

Jury selection was the first challenge. The task of finding an unbiased jury in a case involving perhaps the worst crime in American history, a terrorist act that killed more than one hundred innocent men, women, and children, was daunting—especially when the defendant's coldhearted confessions had been reported on several different occasions in the media. Yet Judge Matsch told McVeigh he was committed to doing so.

In a private meeting with the judge, the defense team asked Matsch if they could hire two jury consultants—professionals who specialize in observing jury selection and determining which citizens would make the most favorable jurors.

Matsch frowned. The judge said he wasn't a huge fan of jury consultants, and silently McVeigh agreed. He already felt smothered by his huge team of lawyers and defense experts. They already had enough trouble agreeing on things and staying out of each other's way. Why add more opinions to the mix and more people to the payroll? Why couldn't all those lawyers put their heads together and do their own jury evaluations?

But Jones pointed out that the prosecution had used jury consultants, and argued that depriving the defense team of the same right would leave them at a disadvantage. Matsch relented. Jones hired two consultants, a man and a woman, to assist in the selection process.

At one pretrial meeting in the judge's chambers, Matsch said he wanted to make sure McVeigh understood it was his legal right to testify in his own defense. McVeigh answered that he could not, especially because prosecutors in Oklahoma were considering the possibility of prosecuting him on state murder charges after the federal trial, and anything McVeigh testified to in the federal trial could be used against him in the state court. He admits now that there was another reason: "I just wasn't ready to tell my story."

It took a little more than three weeks to select a jury of twelve, plus six alternates. Meeting in the federal courthouse in downtown Denver, a total of ninety-nine Colorado residents took the witness stand, answering questions about their backgrounds, their jobs, their families, their knowledge of the bombing case, and their opinions on the death penalty and other legal issues.

Much of the process was routine, but there were several surprising and emotional moments during the selection interviews, as people from almost every walk of life—from teachers and homemakers to retired soldiers—were examined for jury service.

One potential juror was dismissed after revealing he was a retired employee of the Federal Highway Administration, and that he'd known one of the employees killed in the blast. He, too, might have been killed if he'd been in Oklahoma City that day, he told the room. Another woman was dismissed after telling the judge that she and her husband were tax protesters who hadn't paid income taxes in years. The woman said she strongly opposed many of the policies of the U.S. government, and could not, under any circumstances, vote for the death penalty. Opposition to the death penalty cost a number of candidates a chance to serve; others were dismissed because their answers indicated their minds were already made up about McVeigh's participation in the crime.

As he watched the proceedings, McVeigh grew increasingly frustrated with the defense team, whose approach to questioning potential jurors seemed haphazard and disorganized. Every day, it seemed to McVeigh, a different defense lawyer was handling the questioning, and McVeigh came to suspect that Jones was using jury selection as an opportunity to give some of the lawyers on the case a little "face time"—an opportunity to perform in the public spotlight in one of the most high-profile trials ever.

Seeing some of the defense lawyers in action in a courtroom for the first time made McVeigh less confident than ever about Jones and his team. To him some of the lawyers seemed "airheaded," others rude and confrontational—just what the defense didn't need at this point. Some of the defense lawyers even failed to ask obvious questions necessary to understand how potential jurors felt about the death penalty.

One potential juror did catch the attention of McVeigh and many others in the room. The man ran a cattle ranch in the wilds of Colorado, but in questioning he revealed that he had a second, more shadowy career doing secret work for the federal government. He said he flew jets for the government, but refused to say what agency he worked for, only that it was not part of the military. The man revealed that he had once been shot and wounded by a man trying to steal a plane he was using. He said he had flown for the U.S. government during the Vietnam War era, but instead of a uniform, wore jeans. He also revealed that he had once worked as a consultant to FBI agents investigating an incident that killed four people aboard a Learjet.

The man never said so, but many court observers, McVeigh included, had him pegged as a CIA operative.

With observers hanging on every word, the jury candidate also revealed an extensive knowledge of guns and explosives, and offered technical opinions on the makeup of the Oklahoma City bomb.

"What's the largest ammonium nitrate fuel oil explosion that you've ever seen?" Prosecutor Patrick Ryan asked the man.

"That I've personally put together?" the mystery man answered. "That I've personally detonated?"

"Yeah," said Ryan, surprised. "That you're familiar with."

"Six hundred pounds of ANFO," the man said.

"What is the velocity of detonation of ANFO?" Ryan asked.

The rancher had an answer on the tip of his tongue.

"It will vary between eight and eleven thousand feet per second," he said.

Have you ever killed anyone in this government work of yours? Ryan inquired.

The man hesitated. "I don't know," he said.

McVeigh, who had been bored to tears with most of the other prospects, was impressed. The rustic cut of this man appealed to him. And McVeigh knew what it was like to feel uncomfortable about killing for the American government, as this man seemed to be. "I want this guy on the jury," McVeigh said. "He's perfect. Talk about a jury of my peers!" Much to his dismay, Matsch dismissed the man from the jury pool; none of the lawyers on either side seemed to know what kind of juror he would make.

Most of the prospective jurors had some familiarity with the Oklahoma City bombing, and many acknowledged that they had seen tapes and still photos of McVeigh leaving Noble County Courthouse in his orange jumpsuit. Some recalled reading or hearing news reports that McVeigh had confessed to the crime, but few of the prospects gave the reports much credence. "It sounded like some kind of scam," one of the candidates said of the confession reports.

McVeigh found it hard to believe that jurors could completely put the confession reports out of their minds; bad enough that they'd even heard of them.

But after all of the potential jurors had been questioned, Matsch had his jury, seven men and five women in all. They were:

- A grandmother from Loveland, Colorado, whom some court observers came to nickname "Aunt Bea." She remembered crying and praying for the victims on the day of the bombing.
- A Denver woman in her fifties who taught disabled children. Of McVeigh, she said, "He looks like a nice kid. It's overwhelming to me that this person could do such a thing."
- A landscaper who said he was Catholic but was not aware that the Catholic Church was against the death penalty. He said he had no particular feelings on the death penalty, but added that he was distressed that children were killed in the bombing.
- A retired retail employee from a Denver suburb who said she had once served as a jury forewoman. A New Jersey native, she said she favored the death penalty in some cases.
- A Navy veteran from the Vietnam War who had worked in appliance stores and as a real estate salesman. When asked in a jury screening questionnaire if he had followed coverage of

the O. J. Simpson trial, he wrote the word "NO" and underlined it five times.

- A computer technician who recalled that he and other employees of his company had donated food and clothes to victims of the bombing. He remarked under questioning that he believed McVeigh was "a likely suspect" for the bombing, but added he had made no judgments on whether McVeigh was guilty. He had initially supposed that the bombing was the work of foreign terrorists.

- A part-time nurse and mother of three whose daughter had collected pennies with other students at her elementary school to aid the bomb victims. She said she had heard the bombing was linked to white supremacists, but said that that would not affect her judgment.

- A married maintenance man who said his brother had once been a witness in a murder-for-hire case in Denver. The man said he read the Bible once a week and had little knowledge of the bombing case.

- A music-loving juror who came to be nicknamed "Deadhead" by court observers. He was another Navy veteran, a father of three who managed a subsidized housing project and had suffered some hearing loss after years of Grateful Dead rock concerts.

- A young restaurant waitress who said she could conceivably impose the death penalty, but had spent several sleepless nights worrying about the responsibility of such a decision.

- The jury foreman, a native of the Netherlands who described himself as extremely open-minded. An engineer by trade, he said he would carefully evaluate the evidence before voting on a verdict because "there's been enough victims in this situation, and we don't need another victim."

- An Air Force veteran who worked with computer software. Married, with two daughters, the man said he occasionally listened to talk-radio shows, including Rush Limbaugh's, and called the death penalty a "viable" punishment for some crimes.

Three of the seated jurors acknowledged that they had heard, in some form, about McVeigh's confessions, but all three insisted that the reports would have no influence on their judgment.

While each juror held his or her own opinions on the death penalty, only those whom the court considered "death-qualified"—willing at least to consider the possibility of a death sentence—were allowed on the panel. As is standard practice in federal death-penalty cases, those who were avowedly against the death penalty, regardless of the crime, were eliminated automatically.

Many defense experts feel the "death-qualified" restriction gives an instant advantage to the prosecution, by keeping the strongest opponents of the death penalty off the jury and thus weeding out a large group of people who, potentially at least, might be sympathetic to the defense. McVeigh thought the policy was unfair. "But I can see the reasoning behind it," he said. "I guess it wouldn't make sense to have someone [who is] totally against the [death penalty] on the jury." In broader terms, though, McVeigh saw the policy as another example of how the court system tilts in favor of the prosecution, despite the pretense that criminal defendants are presumed innocent.

McVeigh wasn't encouraged by the final panel of the jurors. He had been hoping for a jury of freethinking blue-collar types, preferably younger people with a spirit of independence. What he got instead, he felt, was a staid, conservative group with whom he failed to identify in any way. And in the end he laid the blame with the jury consultants—and especially with Sandy Marks, a nationally respected consultant from Miami whose every comment and opinion seemed to rub McVeigh the wrong way.

"He picked a jury of his peers," McVeigh said. "Not mine."

The trial of *United States* v. *Timothy J. McVeigh* began on April 24, 1997. It was a unique federal trial in American history.

In deference to bombing victims and their families, two special acts were passed by Congress and signed into law by President Clinton. One of the acts permitted bomb victims who appeared as witnesses to watch the trial from the spectators' area on days when they were not testifying. The federal courts do not normally permit witnesses to watch trials, out of concern that something they see or hear could influence their testimony, but in this case that principle was overturned out of concern for the people of Oklahoma City.

The other act allowed victims and their families in Oklahoma to monitor the proceedings in an Oklahoma City auditorium via closed-circuit television, making McVeigh's trial the first in federal court history to be shown in that manner.

It was an unusual situation: the biggest mass-murder trial in American history, with more victims to accommodate than any previous trial.

Unique arrangements were also made for McVeigh's living quarters during the trial. Rather than boarding him in a local jail or prison, Judge Matsch had federal marshals build him a cell—ironically, in the federal office building next door to the courthouse. The purpose of the special room was not so much to provide comfort for McVeigh as to avoid the massive security problem of moving him through Denver from a jail to the courthouse each day. Yet McVeigh's quarters had many of the perks of a hotel room: a comfortable bed, a cable TV, a mini-refrigerator, and a bathroom with a shower. It had no windows, but it was equipped with motion sensors and surveillance cameras, including an infrared camera to monitor the prisoner at night. McVeigh was glad for the amenities, though the lack of privacy unsettled him; there was even a camera trained on his doorless shower stall. One morning McVeigh realized he'd had a wet dream the night before that may well have been caught on the infrared monitor.

Every morning, marshals would pick McVeigh up at 7 A.M. After being handcuffed and shackled, he was taken down to the basement parking ramp of the federal office building, put into a police car, and driven about one hundred feet to the elevator of the adjoining court building. Marshals were generally posted every thirty feet or so along the route, but on one occasion, McVeigh says, fifty marshals or more were lined up, forming a kind of gauntlet along the short path from one federal building to the other. McVeigh couldn't understand why the marshals had to put him in a car for a one-hundred-foot ride through a parking garage in the first place. "Can't we just walk over to the courthouse?" he asked.

"No," one of the deputy marshals said. "We do it this way."

Security preparations for the trial were extraordinary. The federal government raised the security level at the Byron C. Rogers Federal Building and Courthouse to Level 4 status—only one level below that of the Pentagon and CIA headquarters—for the duration of the trial. Officials were concerned about attacks from all quarters: the potential for an assassination attempt was never far from their minds, but neither was the fear that some antigovernment group might attempt to rescue McVeigh from custody—or even try to bomb the Rogers Building itself.

Officers from the Federal Protection Service patrolled outside the courthouse and other nearby federal buildings throughout the trial; additional metal-detector checkpoints were set up to screen all those who entered the courthouse, and mounted police routinely stopped nearby pedestrians to question them about their business. A Denver Police SWAT team with special training was on alert in the event of a terrorist attack. The perceived threat was strong enough that Denver's largest blood bank even issued a public plea for more donations, anxious to increase their stock of blood in case of a terrorist attack. Judge Matsch, who usually rode the bus to work from his farm near Boulder, began riding to work in a car driven by federal law-enforcement officers.

Unique as it was, the McVeigh trial was hardly the first controversial proceeding for Matsch. Since his appointment to the bench during the Nixon administration, he'd presided over some high-profile cases, including the 1987 trial of four right-wing fanatics for the assassination of an outspoken Denver talk-show host, Alan Berg.

A short, stern man with a handlebar mustache, sixty-seven years old at the start of the trial, Matsch ran a no-nonsense courtroom. One of his pretrial orders put a strict gag order on lawyers on both sides of the McVeigh case, holding that no one involved in the trial could make "any comments or statements outside the courtroom, concerning any of the evidence, court rulings, and opinions regarding the trial proceedings." Since the trial was an open proceeding, the judge reasoned, there were plenty of news reporters in attendance to tell the public what was going on.

Though technically it applied to both sides, in effect Matsch's order hurt McVeigh more than the prosecution in the court of public opinion. Everyone directly involved with the case was muzzled, but no such restrictions were placed on trial spectators, and in the end it was the traumatized Oklahoma City residents whose sound bites appeared most often on the evening news.

A series of crucial pretrial evidence rulings also came down in favor of the prosecution. The defense team wanted to put Carol Howe, a former paid ATF informant on Oklahoma's right-wing groups, on the witness stand. An attractive young woman from a wealthy family in Tulsa, Howe had become the linchpin of Jones's conspiracy theory—the scenario that, despite McVeigh's protests, had preoccupied him for months.

Howe claimed that, several months before the bombing, she had heard a group of right-wing extremists discussing plans to blow up a federal building. She linked the talk to Dennis Mahon, the white supremacist from Tulsa, and Andreas Strassmeir, the mysterious German army veteran who served as security director at Elohim City, the white-separatist compound in eastern Oklahoma.

In court papers, Jones described the defense hypothesis:

> A foreign power, probably Iraq, but not excluding the possibility of another foreign state, planned a terrorist attack(s) in the United States, and that one of these targets was the Alfred P. Murrah Building in Oklahoma City. The Murrah Building was chosen either because of a lack of security (i.e., it was a "soft target"), or because of available resources such as Iraqi POWs who had been admitted into the United States [and] were located in Oklahoma City, or possibly because the building was important to American neo-Nazis such as those individuals who supported Richard Snell, who was executed in Arkansas on April 19, 1995.

Snell, a white supremacist who also had links to Elohim City, had once been accused of plotting with others to destroy the Murrah Building in the early 1980s. He had later been convicted of two murders in Arkansas. By coincidence, he had been executed about twelve hours after McVeigh bombed the Murrah Building.

The defense team theorized that Arab terrorists, using the Philippines as a base, had enlisted the support and assistance of American neo-Nazis to blow up the Murrah Building. "The evidence collected by the defense team suggests that the desired ideology was found by the state-sponsored terrorists in Elohim City," Jones and his team wrote. "The defense for Mr.

McVeigh is not engaged in a fishing expedition," their brief added, rather defensively.

Prosecutors maintained the defense strategy was just that: a far-fetched fishing expedition. They came to call it "the Perry Mason defense," a nod to the TV lawyer's signature strategy of defending his clients by hunting down the real criminals.

McVeigh insisted that the entire Elohim City conspiracy theory was a red herring, a waste of his team's time and money. He swore that he had never met Snell or Howe; he admitted that he'd met Strassmeir once, at a gun show, and that he'd attempted to call Strassmeir at Elohim two weeks before the bombing, in search of a potential post-bombing hideout. He never wavered from his contention that neither Strassmeir nor anyone else at Elohim had anything to do with the bombing.

McVeigh never stopped Jones from pursuing his theories, calculating that they might help confuse the prosecution. But in the end Judge Matsch did the job for him, refusing to allow the defense team to present the conspiracy theories in the trial. The argument, he found, was simply too thin to be persuasive.

Along with blocking the conspiracy testimony, Matsch also decided to give prosecutors plenty of freedom to present testimony from victims of the bombing. The defense team argued that airing the horrifying recollections of the bomb victims would only upset the jury, while shedding no new light on whether McVeigh was the bomber. But Matsch allowed the victims' testimony. And the judge's ruling on the conspiracy theories and victim testimony were matched with a final pretrial blow to the defense—on a matter of particular pride to McVeigh himself.

Shortly before the start of the trial, the U.S. Justice Department's inspector general had issued a report blasting the FBI crime laboratory, and one of the agency's explosives experts, for reaching unscientific and biased conclusions about the Oklahoma City bombing.

The report criticized the FBI bomb expert, David Williams, for his estimates of the force, size, and makeup of the bomb, contending that Williams lacked the "objectivity, judgment and scientific knowledge" required for such an analysis. Rather than basing his determinations on forensic evidence, the report said, Williams had worked backward in the investigation.

For example, because the FBI learned that Terry Nichols had purchased four thousand pounds of fertilizer, Williams concluded that a four-thousand-pound bomb caused the blast. And because large white plastic barrels, and some blue-and-white barrels, were found at the Nichols home, Williams concluded that barrels of those colors were used in the bomb—a determination that would be difficult, if not impossible, to justify based on the few fragments found at the blast scene.

The defense team—and McVeigh especially—were enthusiastic about the Justice Department's finding, which concluded that Williams had "failed to present an objective, unbiased and competent report." It was the key weapon in their effort to discredit the government investigation.

Matsch, though, had other ideas. He would allow the defense to call an expert witness—Frederic Whitehurst, an FBI scientist who'd blown the whistle on shoddy practices at the lab. But Matsch would not allow the full Justice Department report to be presented to the jury, allowing only 6 of its 517 pages into evidence. It was the last in a series of rulings that further convinced McVeigh that Matsch—subconsciously, at least—had found him guilty.

Jones was worried about the judge's restrictions on the evidence he could present. But there were other concerns weighing on his mind. One of them, technically, had nothing to do with the McVeigh case: the O. J. Simpson verdict, which after eighteen months was still fresh in the minds of most Americans. The not-guilty verdict pronounced in the case of *California* v. *Simpson,* following one of the most publicized trials in history, had made many Americans suspicious of the courts. Jones knew the American public would not take kindly to an acquittal for McVeigh—a factor that would add to the already powerful pressure on the jury to convict.

And the defense faced another obstacle: a bulldog prosecution team, led by Joseph Hartzler, a feisty tactician from Illinois. Hartzler suffered from multiple sclerosis, and he used an electric scooter to maneuver around the courtroom, but his ailment did not handicap his ability to put criminals behind bars.

Hartzler volunteered to join the bombing prosecution team shortly after hearing the first reports of the tragedy on his car radio. He knew this kind of work: a decade before the Oklahoma blast, he had won convictions against members of a terrorist group who attempted to blow up a building in Chicago.

As he addressed jurors in a dramatic opening statement, Hartzler wasted no time appealing to their emotions.

He began with the story of one of the youngest bombing victims—Tevin Garrett, a toddler well short of his second birthday, who spent his days in the day-care center at the Murrah Building. Hartzler described how the boy had awakened early one beautiful spring day and playfully tugged on the cord of his mother's curling iron as she got ready for work. He painted the picture of a happy little boy, squirming, giggling, and wrestling on his bed with his mother as she got him dressed and ready for day care.

"She remembers this morning," Hartzler said of the boy's mother, Helena Garrett, "because it was the last morning of his life."

Hartzler told jurors how Tevin had cried when his mother dropped him off at the day-care center that morning, clinging to her as long as he could. Only after several other children began to comfort him and play with him would Tevin allow his mother to leave him behind.

"As Helena Garrett left the Murrah Federal Building to go to work across the street, she could look back up at the building, and there was a wall of plate-glass windows on the second floor," Hartzler said. "You can look through those windows and see into the day-care center, and the children would run up to those windows, and press their hands and faces to those windows to say goodbye to their parents. And standing on the sidewalk, it was almost as though you [could] reach up and touch the children there on the second floor. But none of the parents of any of the children I just mentioned ever touched those children again, while they were still alive."

McVeigh sat stone-faced as Hartzler painted verbal portraits of several other children, but he was raging inside. *I couldn't see any kids through those windows, and this bastard knows it,* he remembers thinking. Hartzler would later admit he had no idea if McVeigh was aware of the day-care center or not.

At 9:02 A.M. on April 19, 1995, Hartzler said, "a catastrophic explosion ripped the air in downtown Oklahoma City. . . .

"All the children I mentioned, all of them died, and more; dozens and dozens of other men, women, children, cousins, loved ones, grandparents, grandchildren, ordinary Americans going about their business. And the only reason they died . . . is they were in a building owned by a government that Timothy McVeigh so hated. . . .

"The man who committed this act is sitting in this courtroom behind me," Hartzler said. "After he did so, he fled the scene; and he avoided even damaging his eardrums, because he had earplugs with him."

He went on to describe McVeigh's arrest that morning, the T-shirt he was wearing, and the angry antigovernment materials—Hartzler called them McVeigh's manifesto—found in his car. He then went on to lay out the steps McVeigh and Nichols took to assemble their bomb, including hundreds of phone calls, purchases of bomb-making materials, and the robbery of the Arkansas ammunition dealer, Roger Moore.

As prosecutors would do again and again in the trial, Hartzler portrayed McVeigh as a phony and a coward. He assailed McVeigh for trying to hide behind the words of the Founding Fathers in justifying his act:

> You will hear evidence in this case that McVeigh liked to consider himself a patriot, someone who could start the second American Revolution. The literature in his car quoted statements from the Founding Fathers and other people who played a part in the American Revolution, people like Patrick Henry and Samuel Adams. McVeigh isolated and took these statements out of context, and he did that to justify his antigovernment violence.
>
> Well, ladies and gentlemen, the statements of our forefathers can never . . . justify warfare against innocent children. Our forefathers didn't fight British women and children. They fought other soldiers. They fought them face to face, hand to hand.
>
> They didn't plant bombs, and run away wearing earplugs.

McVeigh sat silently beside Jones at the defense table, his impassive expression masking a growing fury. McVeigh hated the way Hartzler talked about him; hated having his stash of documents referred to as a "manifesto." Most of all, he hated being called a coward.

If I was a coward, McVeigh thought, *I never would have done this. I would have just complained and whined about the government, and done nothing—like millions of other people.*

Jones began his opening statement by offering jurors another possible explanation for what happened in Oklahoma City that morning.

The defense lawyer recalled the story of Daina Bradley, the bombing victim who lost her mother and two children and had her leg hacked off by an emergency doctor while she lay in the rubble, trapped under tons of wreckage.

As Bradley stood in a lobby outside the Social Security office just after 9 A.M., Jones said, she looked out a window and saw a Ryder truck pull up and park outside the building.

"She didn't give it any particular attention until the door opened on the passenger side, and she saw a man get out," Jones said. "Approximately three weeks later, she described the man to the FBI agents, as indeed she did to us and to others, as short, stocky, olive-complected, wearing a puffy jacket, with black hair—a description that does not match my client. She did not see anyone else."

McVeigh could only sit in wonder at his lawyer's bluff. He alone, among everyone in the courtroom, knew there had been no stocky, olive-skinned man—or any other man—emerging from the passenger side of the Ryder truck. He alone knew there was no John Doe No. 2.

In a solemn, respectful tone, the defense lawyer went on to do something the prosecutor had not done. He read into the record the names of all 168 people who died as a result of the bombing. The process took Jones six full minutes.

In reading off the list of names, Jones's intention had been to demonstrate the defense team's respect for the victims and their families, but his action enraged some of the victims' family members. H. Tom Kight, a tall, distinguished man who was stepfather to bombing victim Frankie Ann Merrell, sat in the rear of the spectators' section with a look of utter disgust on his face. To his mind, Jones, the defender of Tim McVeigh, was the wrong person to introduce the names of the dead. "I thought to myself, *This Jones is a showboat,*" Kight said.

"For those of us from Oklahoma, the bombing of the Alfred P. Murrah

Building is the event by which we measure time," Jones said. "It is to my generation in Oklahoma what Pearl Harbor was to my mother and father's generation."

Jones took aim at federal prosecutors and agents. He charged that they spent a mere two weeks actually investigating the bombing, and then another two years building a case to nail McVeigh for the crime.

He was especially critical of the plea deal the government made with Mike Fortier, whom he portrayed as a conniving, self-serving dope dealer who gave McVeigh up to save his own skin. Fortier, he noted, had sworn to friends that McVeigh was innocent until FBI agents appeared on his doorstep and convinced him he could face fifty years behind bars—or even the death penalty—if he refused to turn on his Army buddy. At first, Jones pointed out, Fortier had called the FBI investigation a "witch hunt"; he told agents seven separate times that he and McVeigh had nothing to do with the bombing. Only after the FBI's threats got to him, Jones claimed, did he change his tune. Questioning Fortier's actions was another strategy that didn't sit well with McVeigh; he thought that if Jones went easier on Mike, Fortier might be inclined to return the favor. But as the trial moved ahead, Jones would attack Fortier more savagely than any other witness in the case.

As he continued his opening statement, Jones asked jurors to keep an open mind about the facts of the case. He asked the jury to accept that every incident—McVeigh being caught with earplugs after the bombing, for example—could have more than one explanation. "Tim McVeigh had earplugs," said Jones. "He was a hunter and a shooter, and he carried a gun with him, just like many hunters and shooters do. He had nitrates on him because that's found on guns and ammunition." He asked them to observe closely the evidence he would produce "both by direct and cross-examination, by exhibits, photographs, transcripts of telephone conversations, transcripts of conversations inside houses, [and] videotapes." And he made one further point that shocked McVeigh: going beyond claiming that the evidence would establish reasonable doubt about McVeigh's participation in the bombing, Jones contended that the evidence would establish that McVeigh was innocent.

"I have waited two years for this moment to outline the evidence to you," Jones told the jury. "[It] will establish not a reasonable doubt, but that my client is innocent of the crime that Mr. Hartzler has outlined to you."

It was a promise that Jones would not be able to keep, as 141 prosecution witnesses and 27 for the defense stepped forward to tell their stories.

Although their testimony shed no light on whether McVeigh was the bomber, the blast victims and their family members who testified provided many of the most dramatic and memorable moments of the trial.

Helena Garrett, twenty-eight, the mother of little Tevin, was one of the first persons called to the stand by the prosecution. Her appearance, brief in comparison to those of many of the other witnesses, reduced many in the courtroom—jurors included—to tears.

"You have two children?" Prosecutor Ryan asked Garrett.

"Yes, I do," she said.

"What are their names?" Ryan asked.

"Sharonda Garrett and Tevin Garrett." Sharonda is seven years old, she told the jury.

"How old is Tevin?" Ryan asked.

"He's . . ." Garrett began to answer, before correcting herself. "He was sixteen months."

Garrett recalled her son's playful nature, and described what it was like in the day-care center before the bombing, its infants' room full of cribs and rocking chairs, a changing table, and a refrigerator where the staff stored bottles of formula.

Garrett worked for the Oklahoma regents board, in a building near the Murrah Building. On the morning of April 19, 1995, Garrett was just getting ready to walk over and look in on Tevin when she heard a noise that sounded like thunder.

"It shook me," she said. "I screamed."

Garrett ran out onto the street and looked in horror at the Murrah Building. The explosion had blasted a huge, gaping, monstrous hole into the building, wiping away the day-care center along with much of the rest of the building.

"I tried to go over there, and there was a policeman," Garrett recalled. "He said, 'You can't go over there.'

"I said, 'My baby's in there!' He said, 'You can't go over there.' "

She then watched in horror as rescuers brought out the bodies of babies, one by one, and laid them in a row on the pavement.

Tevin Garrett's body was not positively identified until several days later.

Police used fingerprints to identify the boy, who suffered a head injury so severe that the funeral director would not allow Garrett to view his upper body.

McVeigh sat quietly during testimony such as Garrett's, weighing the emotional impact of the stories, and realizing he was powerless to do anything about it. Though he says he felt bad about the children's deaths, he refused to allow himself any show of emotion. At times, McVeigh would angrily scribble out notes for his attorneys. "Object! Object!" McVeigh would urge, but his suggestions were usually ignored. At one point, during a particularly emotional piece of testimony, Jones was surprised to find McVeigh putting his hand on Jones's knee. Jones thought McVeigh was showing some decency, that his client was making a gesture of shared sympathy. In truth, McVeigh was trying to signal his lawyer to object to what the prosecution witness was saying.

Throughout the trial, people in the courtroom—from reporters to those who lost family members in the bombing—studied McVeigh intently, watching his face for every reaction, particularly during the victim testimony. McVeigh knew how closely he was being scrutinized; he also knew he had a tendency to upset the victims' family members during pretrial hearings by joking with his attorneys or breaking into a grin when something said in the courtroom caught him in a funny way. From time to time, he even felt no compunction about flirting in public, trying to make eye contact with some of the attractive female news reporters. Some of the trial observers suggested that McVeigh looked like one of the celebrity guests from a TV talk show as he entered the courtroom each morning—smiling, joking with his attorneys, scanning the spectators' section for pretty women. Asked later to explain his refusal to offer even a pretense of respect for the victims and their families, he responded with a defense that was chilling in its calculated detachment:

> The victims are looking for some show of remorse. I understand and empathize with the victims' losses, but at the same time, I'm a realist. Death and loss are an integral part of life everywhere. We have to accept it and move on. To these people in Oklahoma who lost a loved one, I'm sorry, but it happens every day. You're not the first mother to lose a kid, or the first grandparent to lose a grandson or granddaughter. It happens every day, somewhere in the world. I'm not going to go

into that courtroom, curl into a fetal ball, and cry just because the victims want me to do that.

The trial moved along more quickly than expected. Prosecutors skillfully alternated dry, technical testimony with the riveting appearances of bombing victims. As it developed, some of the most damaging testimony would come from the prosecution witnesses who were closest to McVeigh: Mike and Lori Fortier, and McVeigh's own sister Jennifer.

McVeigh barely recognized Lori Fortier when she walked up to the witness stand in the first week of the trial. Gone was the trashy-looking, pot-smoking young woman who left her mobile home in such a mess that McVeigh felt compelled to clean it for her. In her place was a sharp-looking young woman in a black business suit. Her hair was dark and neatly coiffed, no longer the straggly-looking strawberry blonde that McVeigh remembered. She looked ready to address a corporate board meeting. The first witness who had any actual role in the bombing plot, Mike Fortier's wife made a credible appearance. She admitted her own shortcomings: she was a drug user; she had helped McVeigh laminate his Robert Kling driver's license; she had helped McVeigh and her husband traffic in stolen guns; and she had originally lied to authorities about the bombing. She had even wrapped blasting caps in Christmas paper, she admitted, so that McVeigh could transport them in the trunk of his car.

Lori Fortier was one of the three people, other than McVeigh, who had known ahead of time that McVeigh was planning to blow up a federal building. As she had for investigators before the trial, she recalled how McVeigh had sat on the floor of her trailer and used about fifteen soup cans to illustrate how he might arrange the barrels of explosives for his truck bomb.

When she saw the first news reports on the day of the bombing, Fortier recalled, she had no doubts. "I knew right away," she said, "it was Tim."

Jones's questioning of the government witness got off to a rocky start, with an oddly worded question. "Mrs. Fortier," the defense lawyer proposed, "would you agree with me that you either made false statements to agents of the Federal Bureau of Investigation; your parents, your mother and father; and your mother- and father-in-law and your best friends in April and May of 1995; or you're making false statements to this jury of strangers, yesterday?"

Hartzler objected to the confusing question, and Matsch made Jones rephrase it—twice.

Later, Jones hammered away at Fortier, raising questions about her failure to warn anyone of the impending tragedy.

"If your testimony is accurate," Jones said, "all you had to do to prevent the deaths of these one hundred and sixty-eight people was pick up the telephone?"

"Yes," Fortier said.

"And you did not do that, did you?" Jones demanded.

"No," Fortier said in a whisper.

Fortier had received full immunity from prosecution from the government, Jones pointed out, in exchange for testimony from her and her husband. Thanks to that deal Fortier would be able to go home after the trial to her young son and daughter.

One particular question Jones asked Fortier was inconsequential in the larger context of the trial, but it annoyed McVeigh tremendously: with a note of amazement in his voice, Jones asked Fortier why she would have fifteen cans of soup in their house.

Tim gave them to us, Fortier replied. McVeigh would sometimes give her soup and other foodstuffs, she said, especially when he was going on the road for a while.

McVeigh, the ardent survivalist, frowned at his lawyer, who couldn't seem to understand why anyone would want to stockpile food. To McVeigh, it was further proof that he and Jones came from two entirely different worlds. "I don't see what is so strange about somebody stockpiling a few weeks' worth of food, or even enough food for a whole year," McVeigh said. "Jones looks down his nose at somebody who thinks that way."

More substantively, McVeigh wondered where Jones's rambling interrogation of the Fortiers was going. Jones had had Robert Nigh and other defense-team members slaving away for days on a list of questions for the Fortiers. They would ultimately compile 118 pages of questions and more than 150 exhibits in preparing for their testimony, but it seemed to McVeigh that Jones largely ignored their advice, improvising a long and pointless examination of Lori.

The defendant became angry again during the testimony of Tim Chambers, the Texas racing-fuel salesman who had sold McVeigh the three fifty-five-gallon drums of nitromethane he had used to create the bomb. McVeigh had bought the barrels of highly explosive fuel, along with a siphon pump, from Chambers for $2,780 cash back in October 1994, telling Chambers he planned to use the fuel to race Harley-Davidson motorcycles with friends. Chambers recalled the purchase as unusual. He seldom received that much cash for a sale, and he'd never seen a motorcycle racer buy that much nitro at one time.

Chambers was not able to give a positive identification of McVeigh, but he did give a description of the fuel buyer that was not particularly flattering to McVeigh. Chambers struggled for the right words to describe the unusual customer, recalling him as a white male with sandy-colored hair and a medium build. But something else about the man's face stuck out in Chambers' mind. "His eyes were close together," Chambers said. "It looked like kind of like a possum face. The eyes are close together, and the nose isn't sticking out, and big and round. It's sticking down. It's longer than most."

Jurors looked over at McVeigh, who just leaned back in his chair and stared sourly at Chambers. McVeigh knew the feds had originally thought the bomb was manufactured with ANFO, which would have been far less powerful than the nitromethane formula he had actually used. The prosecution had located Chambers, he was convinced, only after his own defense team had leaked to *Playboy* that McVeigh had bought three barrels of nitromethane for the bomb at a Texas racetrack. And now, he mused, he had to listen to the witness call him a possum.

He would mull over matters like this each night when the marshals returned him to his little government-financed apartment in the basement of the federal building. Compared with his digs at the prison, this was the lap of luxury: his fourteen-dollar daily food allowance was supplemented by a collection taken up by his defense team, and most nights McVeigh would enjoy bacon double cheeseburgers from Burger King, Pizza Hut pizza, or soft tacos supreme from Taco Bell. Every so often, he even treated himself to a medium-rare "Cowboy Steak" from a Denver restaurant called the Rocky Mountain Diner. He felt no guilt about eating so heartily at taxpayer expense. "I enjoy every meal like it's going to be my last," he said.

McVeigh had a little exercise area on the roof of the building, surrounded by chain-link fencing. From there he could gaze out at the mountains and the blue Colorado sky, along with Coors Field, where the Colorado Rockies played baseball. Sometimes at night visitors from the defense team would stop by and help McVeigh pass the time; one young law student, Scott Anderson, frequently offered a listening ear while McVeigh would vent about the latest developments in the trial. They both assumed that every word of their conversations was being monitored by hidden listening devices, courtesy of McVeigh's government landlords.

In early May, the forty-eighth prosecution witness took the stand. If anyone had been a true admirer and shoulder for McVeigh to lean on in the years leading up to the bombing, it was this slender, attractive young woman. Yet, ironically, it was Jennifer McVeigh who would provide some of the most damning testimony of the entire trial.

It wasn't so much the information she provided—Jennifer had not one piece of specific evidence about the bombing itself—but the tone of her testimony that hurt her brother. It was obvious to anyone in the courtroom that she was a reluctant witness for the prosecution, that describing the content and tone of her brother's many letters and intimations of coming trouble was the last thing she wanted to be doing. Yet her reluctance made her all the more believable to the jury.

Wearing a navy blue pants suit, eyeglasses, and a conservative cream-colored sweater—a far more subdued outfit than she was used to—Jennifer received a grin from her brother as she entered the courtroom. McVeigh knew how painful the appearance would be for her. The courtroom was packed with people from Oklahoma City—including at least twenty-four relatives of bombing victims. He knew the Oklahomans would be hanging on his sister's every word, looking for some sign that she had foreknowledge of the bombing or was somehow involved in it. He also knew that Jennifer had been grilled for days, and threatened with indictment, by FBI agents. He wasn't looking for her to lie for him. He wanted self-preservation to guide his sister's testimony.

Because of Jennifer's protective attitude toward her brother, prosecutor Beth Wilkinson was obliged to take a hard line during much of the questioning. She pressed Jennifer for details about McVeigh's mind-set and his hatred of the government as if she were cross-examining a defense witness, rather than one of her own.

Walking Jennifer through a series of conversations with her brother, and letters he had sent her before the bombing, Wilkinson used his sister's testimony to paint a picture of McVeigh as a man ready to erupt into violence. In the months leading up to the bombing, Jennifer revealed, McVeigh had sent his sister many of his personal belongings, including his Army records, some photographs, and his high school yearbook. She recalled his telling her he was no longer interested in mere propaganda, in handing out literature with little hope of effecting any real change.

Now, McVeigh had told her, he was in the "action stage."

She recalled her brother's prediction in one letter that "something big" was going to happen during the astrological month of the Bull—a period of time that coincided roughly with the month of April.

"Did he ever tell you what that 'something big' was?" Wilkinson asked.

"No," Jennifer said.

"And you never asked him about it, did you?" Wilkinson asked.

"No," Jennifer said. She had burned the "something big" letter, she admitted, on her brother's instructions.

Jennifer also recalled how, in early 1995, she had come across a hate-filled, antigovernment document her brother had written and saved on her personal computer—the "ATF Read" letter. After finding the information on one of her disks, she said, she had asked her brother if he wanted her to erase it.

"Just leave it there," McVeigh told her. He wanted the government to find it one day.

In one of his letters to her, Jennifer recalled, McVeigh told her about the time he nearly got into an accident while carrying a half-ton of explosives in the trunk of his car.

"Did you ask him why he was carrying explosives?" Wilkinson asked.

"No," Jennifer said.

"Why not?" Wilkinson persisted.

"I don't think I wanted to know," Jennifer said. She also revealed that McVeigh had warned her to be careful because she might be followed by private investigators or "G-men," and warned her to use pay phones for her phone calls.

When she learned he was a suspect a few days after the bombing, Jennifer admitted, she had gone into a friend's house and burned some *Turner Diaries* clippings McVeigh had sent her.

"Why did you burn them?" Wilkinson asked.

"I was scared," Jennifer said. She said she knew that federal agents would eventually be coming to question her. And she recalled the chilling words at the end of one of her brother's last letters: "Won't be back forever."

It was powerful courtroom drama, and devastating to her brother's case. Defense lawyer Rob Nigh tried to soften the damage; he was convinced federal agents had created a lasting false and harsh image of McVeigh by staging his "perpetrator walk" from the Noble County Courthouse in the bright orange jumpsuit.

"Ms. McVeigh, you were not involved at all in the Oklahoma City bombing, were you?" Nigh asked. "Did you have any knowledge about your brother being involved in it, in any way, shape, or form?"

"No," Jennifer said.

Since Wilkinson had brought up the military records McVeigh had sent his sister, Nigh had an opening to lead the witness, one by one, through all the honors the Army had given her brother—an attempt to remind jurors of McVeigh's combat-veteran status.

Nigh then asked Jennifer about the hardball tactics of the FBI agents, who had questioned her for nine straight days, often eight or nine hours a day, sometimes longer.

For the first time, Jennifer began to cry. "They had big posters on the walls, all over the room," she said, including a big photo of her brother, along with FBI time lines describing the alleged movements of both Tim and Jennifer in the months before the bombing. The agents had even posted a large photo of Jennifer, an enlargement of a high school graduation picture they had taken from the dining room wall of the McVeigh home. Beneath the picture was a list of charges that potentially could be lodged against Jennifer if she was found to have taken part in the bombing.

Under one of the charges, an agent had written "Penalty Equals Death" and underlined it, Jennifer said.

"They told me [Tim] was guilty and he was going to fry," Jennifer told Nigh.

But if any of this was making jurors feel sorry for the tearful young woman on the witness stand, Wilkinson made sure they also understood why the FBI applied so much pressure.

"When the FBI showed you these charges, which you've clearly told us were upsetting to you, did they make you want to lie?" Wilkinson asked. "Or did they make you want to tell the truth?"

"I think they were intended to just get me to talk to them, by scaring me," Jennifer said.

"Did you understand them to be intended to make you tell the truth, or to lie?" Wilkinson demanded.

"To tell the truth," Jennifer said.

"And did you do that?" Wilkinson said.

"Yes," Jennifer answered.

McVeigh later expressed sympathy for his sister after she was grilled on the witness stand, but never enough to make him regret the bombing.

"In any kind of military action," he would say later, "you try to keep collateral damage to a minimum. But a certain amount of collateral damage is inevitable."

Jurors would learn much more about McVeigh's mind-set from the one trial witness who had the most direct information about the crime: Mike Fortier. His beard, scraggly long hair, earring, and sleeveless T-shirts replaced with a clean-cut new look, Fortier took the stand the morning of May 12, 1997, and swiftly proved himself the most powerful witness in the case.

Prosecutors had hit the jackpot when they persuaded Fortier to testify. Here was a witness who knew a great deal about McVeigh and the bombing—who could describe his plans, his motivations, his reasons for choosing the Murrah Building, even the calculating attitude he had taken toward the crime. McVeigh had confided in Fortier, traveling with him to Oklahoma City to case the building, telling him about the burglary of explosives from the quarry in Kansas; he had even taken him out to look at the storage locker where McVeigh and Nichols were keeping their bomb-making materials.

In Fortier, the prosecution also had a firsthand witness to McVeigh's behavior in the days immediately following the siege at Waco in 1993. McVeigh had turned up at Fortier's home in Kingman a few days after the incident, and unloaded all his feelings of outrage on his old Army friend. After moving to the Kingman area himself the following year, McVeigh seemed to become "more defensive," Fortier recalled, keeping guns behind the doors in his cinder-block house and stacking piles of wood outside to create a protective berm in case of a government attack.

McVeigh—with Fortier's encouragement and assistance—had even looked into the possibility of starting a militia group in the Kingman area, Fortier recalled. The group never got off the ground, but McVeigh and Fortier had visited with a militiaman in nearby Preston, Arizona, to find out how his organization was run. "He thought the U.S. government had declared war on the American people, and they were taking our rights away," Fortier said of McVeigh.

In 1994, Fortier said, he had received a letter from McVeigh declaring that he and Terry Nichols had decided to take "some kind of positive offensive action" against the government—and that McVeigh had asked Fortier to keep this letter from his wife. When McVeigh arrived in person about a week later, Fortier told the jury, McVeigh informed him that he and Nichols were thinking about bombing a government building. Fortier had upset McVeigh by turning down his invitation to join them, but by late October 1994 McVeigh had cooled off enough that he decided to spill all kinds of details about the plot he and Nichols were formulating.

As they sat in Fortier's living room, McVeigh had told him that he and Nichols were going to bomb "a federal building in Oklahoma City." It was during this meeting that McVeigh explained he had learned how to turn a truck into a bomb, arranging fifty-five-gallon barrels of explosives into a "shaped charge." McVeigh had even drawn a rough diagram for Fortier, illustrating the triangular design and placement of the fuses. McVeigh also told Fortier he wanted to blow up the building on the anniversary of Waco, around 11 A.M., when building employees were getting ready to have lunch.

Fortier revealed that McVeigh had told him he might turn the bombing into a suicide mission, staying inside the truck with his gun to protect the vehicle from anyone who might try to prevent the bomb from going off.

Why Oklahoma City? Fortier had asked. Fortier said that McVeigh believed the orders for federal agents to attack the compound in Waco had come from Oklahoma City, although this was later proven wrong.

If there was one moment in the trial that highlighted McVeigh's eerily childlike detachment from the reality of what he was planning, it came when Fortier described asking McVeigh about the potential victims of such a bombing. "He explained to me that he considered all those people to be as if they were the storm troopers in the movie *Star Wars,*" Fortier testified. "They may be individually innocent, but because they are part of the—the Evil Empire, they were guilty by association."

Fortier said that McVeigh had also given him further details about the break-in at the Kansas quarry, the theft of guns from Roger Moore, and about McVeigh and Nichols using "fake names" to buy some of their materials. Fortier described how McVeigh hired him to go to gun shows and sell some of the weapons stolen from Moore.

On the morning of the bombing, Fortier said, he had been up all night playing video games with a neighbor. When they turned on the TV, they saw pictures of the devastation from Oklahoma City. Immediately, Fortier thought of Tim McVeigh. "Oh my God," he remembered saying. "He did it."

And yet somehow Fortier was also compelled to tell the jury, "If you don't consider what happened in Oklahoma, Tim is a good person."

In his cross-examination, Stephen Jones hammered away at Fortier's credibility, pointing out that Fortier had negotiated a favorable plea deal that would give him a much lighter sentence—twelve years, as it turned out— than the possible death penalties faced by McVeigh and Nichols.

The defense lawyer also ripped Fortier for a series of contemptuous statements he had made to friends in telephone calls taped by the FBI shortly after the bombing.

"Did you make the following statement," Jones asked, "concerning if you were called as a witness in this case? 'I'd sit there and pick my nose and flick it at the camera'?

"And did you say, 'Flick it and then, like, kind of wipe it on the judge's desk'?

"Did you make the following statement: 'I've been thinking of trying to do those talk-show circuits for a long time, coming up with some asinine story and getting my friends to go in with it?' "

And hadn't Fortier also bragged that he would make "a cool mil" selling book and movie rights to his story, and coming up with a tale that would be "something that's worth the *Enquirer?*"

Jones also reminded Fortier that, shortly after the bombing, he'd been quoted as saying of McVeigh, "People cannot make their judgment on his guilt by what they read in the paper, and by what I see on TV. People are call-ing for his blood, to hang him in the street and whatnot, and in America, we believe that people are innocent until proven guilty."

Did you make all those statements? Jones demanded.

"Yes, sir," Fortier said.

Jones also blasted Fortier for initially telling the FBI that McVeigh had nothing to do with the bombing.

The point Jones was making—again and again—was that, if Fortier had willingly lied to friends, FBI agents, and the press about McVeigh after the bombing, he might just as likely be lying now. By then, though, the damage was done. Jones succeeded in exposing Fortier's character weaknesses, but for nearly everyone in the courtroom his testimony had the cold, clear ring of truth.

McVeigh knew that Fortier's testimony had given a substantially accurate account of their experiences together. If Fortier's recall of the details seemed erratic, it was hard not to chalk it up to his heavy drug use. But McVeigh was frustrated that no one ever asked Fortier one key question: when Fortier and McVeigh went to look at the Murrah Building months before the bombing, had they seen the day-care center? The prosecution never raised the issue with Fortier, McVeigh figured, because the feds knew Fortier would confirm that he and McVeigh never knew about the center—an answer that would hurt the government's effort to demonize McVeigh. But why didn't defense lawyers raise the question? One theory was that doing so would only have reinforced the image of McVeigh and Fortier casing the Murrah Building. But there were also fears that, if Fortier was really trying to "sing for his sup-per," giving the best possible answers to help prosecutors win their case in exchange for leniency, he might have felt pressured to embellish his testi-mony and claim McVeigh had known about the center all along. McVeigh thought Fortier would have told the truth, but it was a risk the defense wouldn't take. Years later, in a December 2000 interview, Fortier's lawyer, Michael McGuire, would confirm that Fortier never saw the day-care center. Hartzler later confirmed that Fortier told him the same thing.

As the trial progressed, McVeigh's frustration with his defense team only grew. There were just too many lawyers crowding all over themselves and getting in each other's way. As a soldier, McVeigh had spent hours upon hours in the cramped, stuffy turret of a Bradley military vehicle without a moment's claustrophobia; now, trapped at a defense table with six or seven suits crowded around him, McVeigh felt like he could barely breathe.

Indeed, at times the defense team's performance seemed like a disorganized mess. A prosecution witness would take the stand, and defense lawyers would start scrambling around for paperwork. *Whose witness is this?* McVeigh heard the defense team asking at times. Chances for timely objections and chances to make the government witnesses look bad sometimes flew by while defense lawyers were rummaging through their paperwork. And McVeigh also felt his team depended far too much on FBI reports in preparing their questions, instead of turning to him. For instance, he wanted his lawyers to bring a telephone and a calling card into court, to illustrate that anyone who knew the right code numbers—not just him and Nichols—could have used the Daryl Bridges calling card.

"All these calls the government is talking about," he protested, "they don't have my voice on tape for any of them."

McVeigh felt Jones's interrogations of prosecution witnesses were often badly disjointed and off the mark. "As an average man off the street," he has said, "I could have done better with my eyes closed. If I had to go through this again, I would defend myself, with one or two good lawyers to help me with paperwork."

And the picture certainly didn't get any better with the relative handful of defense witnesses presented by Jones. The "star" defense witness, bomb victim Daina Bradley, turned out to be a disaster.

In his very first words to the jury at the start of the trial, Jones had focused on Bradley and her recollections of the bombing. He told the jury that Bradley—the woman who became trapped in the rubble and had to have her leg sawed off by an emergency doctor—had seen a man who looked nothing like McVeigh get out of the truck that pulled up outside the Murrah Building as she and her family stood inside the Social Security office.

Called as a defense witness, Bradley said she thought she saw a man with an olive complexion emerge from the truck. But now, she could not describe such a man with any certainty. She also admitted that she had spent years in mental institutions, and that she suffered from severe lapses in memory— about all kinds of things, and especially about the bombing.

"I don't recall much," she testified. "You can tell me one thing one week, and I would forget the next week."

McVeigh was getting more agitated by the minute as the defense case stumbled forward. At one point, during a witness's testimony, jury consultant Sandy Marks, sitting behind McVeigh, had a nasty bout of loud coughing. McVeigh said he turned and glared at Marks, but Marks couldn't stop. Finally, an angry McVeigh asked Marks to leave the courtroom.

Just as angrily, according to McVeigh, Marks told him to shut up. (Marks said later he had no recollection of the incident.)

One effective defense witness was Dr. Frederic Whitehurst, the chemist for the FBI who had blown the whistle on irregularities in evidence-gathering practices at the FBI Crime Laboratory in Washington. Whitehurst, a Vietnam War combat veteran, had gone public with his allegations after becoming outraged at what he considered a lack of professionalism in the world-famous lab. His allegations touched off a Justice Department probe and received plenty of attention in the national media.

Although Matsch had severely limited the use of the Justice Department's inspection report finding deficiencies in the lab, he did allow Whitehurst to raise questions about sloppy record-keeping and possible contamination of evidence, including items recovered in the McVeigh investigation. Whitehurst's testimony specifically attacked the credibility of FBI Agent David Williams, the supervisor of evidence-gathering at the bombing site.

At times, Whitehurst said, contamination had been found in the "trace analysis" section of the lab where technicians conducted the tests that found traces of explosives on McVeigh's clothing, knife, and ear plugs. He criticized the lab for having carpeting that could be contaminated by the shoes of visitors, or agents coming back from a firearms range.

Questions were also raised about the handling of the clothes McVeigh was wearing when he was arrested by Trooper Charles Hanger north of Oklahoma City. The clothing had been stored in an ordinary shopping bag at the Noble County Jail; later, after being sent to the FBI lab in Washington, it was held in a box that, at some point, was left on the floor.

"I think it could lead to a contamination issue with the evidence," Whitehurst testified.

"Was there a policy or procedure for regular monitoring of each individual office for contamination in April and May of 1995?" Christopher Tritico, one of the defense lawyers McVeigh respected, asked Whitehurst.

"Not that I'm aware of," Whitehurst said.

But Beth Wilkinson of the prosecution team was able to blunt the effect of Whitehurst's testimony with one basic question.

"Do you have any knowledge of any actual contamination of the evidence in this case?" she asked.

He did not, Whitehurst conceded.

But McVeigh's defense team had spent less time investigating evidence contamination than he had hoped they would, lavishing time and money instead on the expeditions to Great Britain and the Philippines. Among other things, McVeigh found himself wondering how the FBI could have found traces of explosives on his clothing when he had never entered the Ryder truck's cargo hold the day of the bombing—unless, of course, someone had planted evidence, which McVeigh believed the FBI was fully capable of doing.

Because no witness could swear they saw McVeigh bomb the building—indeed, not one government witness could place him in the state of Oklahoma at the time of the blast—the government's case against him was circumstantial. This made the minute traces of explosives on his clothing and possessions especially important. But without clearance to use the Justice Department report to back them, the time the defense team did spend on evidence issues looked like so much grasping at straws.

In the end, for all the millions of taxpayer dollars—an estimated $20 million in all—spent on the defense, the case Jones and his team presented was notably weak. Taking less than four days to present its arguments, the team seemed disjointed and disorganized; some fifty different people had worked on the case, and at times it seemed like they were heading in fifty different directions. Jones himself took the dominant role in the examination of key witnesses; attorneys McVeigh considered more talented—Nigh and Tritico in particular—were relegated to the roles of bit players. Even their props looked chintzy: where the government presented an impressive scale model of the Murrah Building and other downtown sites in Oklahoma City, complete with a removable section representing the part that had been blown away by the bomb, all the defense team could muster was a balsa-wood replica of the Dreamland Motel, where he'd stayed before the bombing. The model looked like a "piece of junk" to McVeigh; "It cost, like, five thousand bucks for that stupid thing," he complained.

As the trial dragged on, McVeigh took to referring to his defense team as "a bunch of Keystone Kops." But at the same time McVeigh was asking his defenders to pull off a miracle. Despite their occasional use of fake names, he and Nichols had left clues all over the United States. Perry Mason himself would have had a hard time explaining away the things he had told the Fortiers, or McVeigh's prediction to his sister that "something big" was about to happen, or his and Nichols's purchases of bomb-making materials in the months before the blast. Worst of all, the defense team could not present any alibi witnesses. They could not tell the jury where McVeigh was or what he was doing the morning of April 19, 1995. The reason was obvious: they knew exactly where McVeigh was—parking a truck outside the Murrah Building.

In his closing statement, Jones tried appealing to the jury's sense of fair play. He asked them not to allow their sympathy for the victims to override their willingness to fairly evaluate all the evidence. He also asked them not to be influenced by the fact McVeigh had been convicted by the media "in the court of public opinion" long before the first witness took the stand.

The prosecution case had big holes in it, Jones said. The FBI had done sloppy work gathering fingerprint evidence and evidence about the makeup of the bomb. McVeigh's prints had not been found on some vital pieces of evidence—including the Ryder truck ignition key found near the truck bomb and the rental agreement for the truck. The witnesses who testified that McVeigh was the "Robert Kling" who rented the Ryder truck had foggy recollections, Jones said, and had been prodded by the FBI into pointing their fingers at McVeigh.

And the two key prosecution witnesses, Michael and Lori Fortier, were pointing their fingers purely in order to protect themselves. Jones tore into the Arizona couple, portraying them as conniving dope fiends looking to parlay the McVeigh case into a million dollars on the talk-show circuit. Jones claimed Michael Fortier was walking away with one of the most "extravagant" plea deals in the history of the criminal court system.

As Jones had pointed out earlier in the trial, if the Fortiers were telling the truth, either of them could have prevented the bombing with a single phone call to law enforcement.

> Why let Lori Fortier walk away with nothing, and Michael make the deal that he did? Because, without them, what we have is a series of isolated incidents. Michael and Lori Fortier served the function of Tarzan and Jane in the old Tarzan movies, where you've got a clump of trees here and a clump of trees there, and a clump of trees over there, and Tarzan and Jane had to swing from one clump of trees to the next. It's only by their swinging and maneuvering that the trees are connected. This is their significance.

Jones took time to point out that it would be unfair to convict McVeigh of the bombing just because he had read *The Turner Diaries* and carried antigovernment literature in his car. "I submit to you, ladies and gentlemen, that in the context of this case, this political literature and the word 'motive' mean nothing."

On the prosecution side, government attorney Larry D. Mackey touched on the heartaches caused by the blast. He also told jurors that prosecutors had provided them with exactly the kind of evidence that Hartzler had promised in his opening statement:

> When you retire to the jury room, evaluate what promises were made by Joe Hartzler against the evidence and see if we haven't kept our word. We promised and we've proven, in more ways than one, a number of important factual propositions.
>
> Number one, Timothy McVeigh, motivated by hatred of the government and in a rage over the events at Waco, deliberately and with premeditation planned the bombing of the Murrah Building.
>
> Number two, that he educated himself on how to build bombs.
>
> Number three, that he enlisted at least one co-conspirator

and attempted to recruit yet another, Michael Fortier, to help him in that criminal act; and that he and Terry Nichols acquired and attempted to acquire all the necessary components to build a massive bomb; that Timothy McVeigh carefully, very deliberately selected his target, the Murrah Building; he surveyed it; and that in April of 1995, he rented the truck, built the bomb and detonated it against the Murrah Building. That's the government's case. Promises made, promises kept.

Mackey reminded jurors of the emotional toll the bombing had taken on people in Oklahoma City. He reminded them of Helena Garrett and her little son, Tevin, who sobbed and tried to cling to her that morning when she dropped him off at day care. He reminded them of the horrifying testimony of Florence Rogers, a supervisor with the U.S. Department of Housing and Urban Development. Rogers had been sitting at her desk, with seven of her employees sitting in front of her, when the bomb exploded. The seven employees disappeared before her eyes, falling to their deaths as the nine stories of the Murrah Building quaked and pancaked into a heap. He reminded them of the story of Donna Weaver, who worked a short distance from the Murrah Building, where her husband, Mike, was employed as a government lawyer. When she heard the bomb blast, Donna Weaver ran out of her building to the Murrah Building, praying that her husband was all right.

"She described being shot from her chair, running down the street, following the sounds and the smoke and the sirens and the people," Mackey recalled. "She came around the corner, and she saw what you saw, a building that was gone. And in her words, she said, 'I saw Mike's office, and it was gone. And I knew he was gone, too.'"

The prosecutor lashed out at McVeigh for the T-shirt he wore on the day of the bombing, and its slogan celebrating the spilling of patriots' and tyrants' blood. The 168 people who were killed were not tyrants, Mackey said. Nor should they be characterized as storm troopers in some kind of *Star Wars* space melodrama. The bombing victims never knew what hit them—no more than Abraham Lincoln had when John Wilkes Booth fired a shot into the back of his head.

McVeigh had a right to protest the events at Ruby Ridge and Waco, Mackey allowed, but he had no right to turn his political agenda into an assault on innocent people. "In America," he said, "everybody has a right to their beliefs, a right to think and say what they do. This is not a prosecution of Tim McVeigh for his political beliefs. This is a prosecution of Tim McVeigh because of what he did. He committed murder. This is a murder case."

The prosecutor also noted that, unlike the perpetrators of crimes of passion, McVeigh had plenty of time to consider the consequences of his actions. "He told people of his intent to kill long before he killed. . . . Tim McVeigh had six solid months to abandon that intent, six solid months to think about it, think about it again, and walk away. And instead, he drove to Oklahoma City with the truck bomb."

And Mackey suggested that Stephen Jones had fallen short in his promise, made at the outset of the trial, that he would prove McVeigh was "innocent" of the bombing. "It was a bold promise," Mackey said. "He has failed to keep it. The evidence does not support it."

Mackey asked jurors to take one more thought with them to the deliberation room. "Who are the patriots?" he asked. "And who is the traitor?"

It took them twenty-three and a half hours of deliberations over four days, but jurors agreed with the prosecutor. On June 2, they reached their verdict: McVeigh was found guilty on all eleven counts filed against him. The jury found him guilty of conspiracy to use a weapon of mass destruction, use of such a weapon, destruction of government property with explosives, and eight counts of first-degree murder—one for each of the eight federal law-enforcement agents killed in the blast.

As he had throughout the trial, McVeigh remained expressionless as the verdict was read. He sat with his hands clasped tightly together, looking at Matsch. As federal marshals escorted him from the courtroom, he shook hands with Jones and Tritico.

In the spectators' area, about twenty-five bombing victims and family members sobbed and hugged each other. One man in the group triumphantly punched his fist high into the air. Back in downtown Oklahoma City, hundreds of people stood near the site of the Murrah Building, cheering as they heard the verdict announced on TVs that had been set up on the sidewalks.

When McVeigh got back to his room the marshals demanded that he give up his shoelaces and wristwatch, out of concern that he might be a suicide risk. McVeigh, who took pride in making himself a trouble-free prisoner before and during the trial, responded that the request was a blow to his dignity.

"If you do that, I go on a hunger strike," McVeigh said. "I've done nothing to make you distrust me. It's like punishing me for good behavior."

"Well, it's within my discretion," the district marshal, Tina Lewis Rowe, told McVeigh.

"Could you please use some better discretion?" McVeigh asked.

Rowe finally relented, a gesture McVeigh appreciated. "But just remember," she told McVeigh, "we're in charge here, not you."

For the McVeigh family, the hardest part of the trial—the penalty phase—was to come. Now, the same jury would decide whether Tim McVeigh should die for his crime. Prosecutors, pressing hard for the death penalty, would present testimony from more of the bombing victims and their families, highlighting the personal toll the crime had taken. McVeigh's lawyers, meanwhile, were left to try to convince the jury that McVeigh had a decent side, and that he had family members and friends who didn't want him to die.

Patrick Ryan, the federal prosecutor from Oklahoma City, pointed out that McVeigh's goal of killing law-enforcement agents had led to the deaths of 160 other people. Fewer than 5 percent of those killed were federal law-enforcement agents.

One of the agents' widows, Sonja Diane Leonard, was called to describe the effects McVeigh's bomb had on her and her family. Her husband was Donald Leonard, a twenty-four-year veteran of the Secret Service. Leonard, who was born just a few blocks from the site of the Murrah Building, had been a devoted father to his three sons from a previous marriage. He was also devoted to his job, traveling all over the globe protecting presidents, vice presidents, and dignitaries.

"I think he's been to almost every country in the world," Mrs. Leonard testified. "He always said there was no place that even compared to the United States of America."

On the morning of the bombing, Mrs. Leonard walked into a store in Tulsa, and was asked by a woman working there if she had heard about the bombing in Oklahoma City. Mrs. Leonard was unaware of it.

"Did you know anybody who worked downtown?" the store worker asked.

"Well, my husband does," Mrs. Leonard answered. "Where was it?"

"It was in the federal building," the employee said.

Mrs. Leonard called the Oklahoma City Secret Service office; no one answered the phone. She then called the agency's office in Tulsa and learned that six employees from Oklahoma City were missing. Her husband's death was not confirmed until two days later, when four government men in suits walked up her driveway and informed her.

A couple of days after that, her middle stepson, Jason Leonard, came to her at three in the morning, crying. "I want my dad back," he told her. "I want him to see me graduate from college. I want him to meet my wife and be at my wedding. I want him to see my first child."

Later, when Jason Leonard was married, a rose was left on the seat where his father would have been sitting.

"There is nothing in my life that is the same," Mrs. Leonard said.

Some of the stories told by rescuers and medical personnel were almost unbearably painful. Dr. Andy Sullivan, an orthopedic surgeon, described crawling through the debris to saw off the leg of the trapped and suffering Daina Bradley. While Sullivan performed the emergency amputation, he was being told by firefighters that a section of the building looked like it might collapse on him at any minute.

Unable to administer an anesthetic to Bradley, whose collapsed lung made it difficult for her to breathe, Sullivan was forced to perform the operation while Bradley shrieked and struggled beneath the blade. Sullivan, who was right-handed, was forced by the angle at which Bradley was trapped to operate with his left hand.

"I prayed," Sullivan said. "I prayed that she wouldn't die as a result of my treatment, and that if I died, my family would remember me."

A medical examiner, Dr. Fred Jordan, told how he used a refrigerated truck as a makeshift morgue as the body count continued to rise. Sue Malonee of the Oklahoma State Health Department described—in excruciating detail—a study she had conducted on the thousands of injuries suffered in the bombing.

A number of the police officers and firefighters who took part in the rescue efforts at the Murrah Building also testified for the prosecution. Some said the bombing had left them with awful nightmares. Oklahoma City Police Officer Jerry Flowers remembered discovering one of the dead babies in the rubble of the day-care center.

"There were toys laying around—wagons, baby clothes and stuff," Flowers recalled.

> I went to an area and started uncovering stuff, started digging, like everyone was doing. I uncovered a little baby's foot with a pink sock on it. I screamed out, "I found another one!"
>
> It was a little girl. She was a little baby girl, six months to a year old. Best I remember, a little pink dress on. And just as we got her uncovered, she was dead. One of the officers that was standing beside me grabbed the child and pulled her to his chest, and took her out of the building.

Emotions were running high as the witnesses told their stories. Jurors, again and again, burst into tears. One of the police officers, after completing his testimony, just sat in the witness chair, glaring at McVeigh. Judge Matsch excused him, but the officer just sat there, his eyes locked on McVeigh. McVeigh, his own eyes burning with hate, glared back.

Matsch told the officer a second time to step down from the witness stand, and the officer finally did so, still glaring at the convicted bomber.

Through most of the trial McVeigh had kept his emotions in check, but his mind was always running a mile a minute. He always kept an eye trained on the spectators from Oklahoma City, especially during testimony from bombing victims and rescuers. He always half expected to see some enraged spectator come bounding over the rail, going for his throat—a show of anger McVeigh claims he would have understood and respected.

The defense team tried to soften McVeigh's image, soliciting testimonials from the bomber's family members, longtime friends, and old Army buddies.

Jaws dropped in the courtroom when Jones admitted in his closing statement that, indeed, McVeigh had bombed the Murrah Building. After spending more than a month trying to convince jurors that McVeigh was innocent of the bombing, it was an outlandish reversal, and one that drove home just how hollow McVeigh's defense had been.

The defense lawyers tried to convince the jury that McVeigh's actions were not motivated by evil or hatred for individual victims. It was not a sadistic crime, like the bloody murder sprees of Charles Manson or John Wayne Gacy. It was not motivated by greed, like John Graham's 1955 bombing of a commercial airliner in Denver, where forty-four people were killed so Graham could collect on a thirty-six-thousand-dollar insurance policy he had taken out on his mother.

Rather, Jones said, McVeigh's crime had been motivated by his deep concern for his country and the direction its government was heading. Agree with it or not, he said, this was a political crime, a crime of ideology.

"Ms. Wilkinson told you, and I don't dispute it, that Mr. McVeigh killed more people in Oklahoma City than all of the American dead in the Persian Gulf War," Jones said. "I am not here to dispute your verdict."

Defense lawyers wanted a sentence of life imprisonment for McVeigh. They asked jurors to consider a number of "mitigating factors," including McVeigh's political beliefs, his service in the armed forces, his lack of a previous criminal record, and some of his past good deeds.

McVeigh "is not a demon," Jones said, "although his act was surely demonic." Instead, he put forward the notion that McVeigh was more like an "everyman" or "the boy next door." His crime had not arisen from a vacuum, he said; the bombing wasn't something McVeigh had decided on impulsively, but rather a misplaced attempt to elicit redress for the citizens the government itself had killed or hurt at Waco and Ruby Ridge.

Jones told the jury:

> Millions of Americans—millions, you know that—share Mr. McVeigh's views. They're as old as the struggle that led to the ratification of the Constitution. Mr. McVeigh acted on them. He acted on them because he understood what had happened, but more importantly, what had not happened. And so, he made it happen. They hurt, so you hurt. They died, so you die. They were innocent, you are innocent. What a terrible price to pay for a failure to account, for a failure to instruct, as a government must. This tragedy at Ruby Ridge, this tragedy at

Waco, could have been avoided. This tragedy at Oklahoma City could have been avoided.

Family members and old friends were brought in to tell flattering stories on Tim McVeigh's behalf. Experts on right-wing philosophy were brought in to explain why Ruby Ridge and Waco had become such flash points to people like McVeigh. Soldiers who served with him explained why McVeigh was so trusted and admired by his battle buddies. Their testimony was vivid, though at some point along the way, McVeigh learned that many of the defense witnesses had been greeted at the airport by FBI agents eager to escort them to their hotels and be helpful in any way they could. Their message was clear: we know you're here to help your friend McVeigh, but please don't forget your accommodating friends in the federal government.

At one point, Sheila Nicholas, the wife of James Nichols's farmhand, appeared before the court as a character witness for McVeigh. She described him as a warm, decent, friendly person—"just someone that you are kind of drawn to." She knew McVeigh loved guns and that he'd been angry at the federal government, but she considered him so harmless and trustworthy that she gave him the run of the Nicholas house and felt comfortable having McVeigh around her young daughter.

"It's your testimony that he was open and honest with you in his dealings with you?" Mackey asked.

"Yes," Nicholas answered.

"Did he tell you that he stored explosives in your garage?" Mackey followed up.

"No, he did not," Nicholas said.

McVeigh's parents had chosen not to attend the criminal portion of the trial, but they did fly to Denver for the last part of the penalty phase. Tired, nervous, and anxiety-ridden after two years in the spotlight, Bill McVeigh and his ex-wife, Mickey Hill, came to beg the jury to spare their son's life.

Bill, as usual, was able to keep his emotions under wraps during most of the visit to Denver. But Mickey, her nerves frayed even more than usual, couldn't handle all the attention. One day, as she and Bill were leaving the courthouse, she angrily turned and fired a middle-finger salute at a TV cameraman who was trying to get some video. The gesture rankled Bill, who was there to help his son, not make enemies for him. "Mickey," he scolded. "If you do anything like that again, I'm not going to be seen with you anymore."

Mickey also got a chance to visit with her son, and it was a painful encounter for McVeigh. Newspaper stories had reported that McVeigh had told friends his mother was a "bitch" and a "slut," and during one visit, Mickey confronted her son. "Tim, is that story true, that you called me a slut?" were the first words out of her mouth. McVeigh tried his best to change the subject and calm the waters. He didn't want to lie to his mother, but he didn't want to add to her pain, either. He told her he had come up with a way for her to deal with his imprisonment: "Think of it this way," he told her. "When I was in the Army, you didn't see me for years. Think of me that way now, like I'm away in the Army again, on an assignment for the military." His words seemed to calm Mickey down; the next day she told her ex-husband that it made it easier for her to cope, thinking of Tim that way.

On June 11 Bill and Mickey testified, the last two witnesses in a long and highly emotional trial. Their appearances were brief. Mickey, once such a beauty, looked tortured and beaten down on her arrival, whispering hello to her son as she approached the witness stand.

Mickey confirmed that she and Bill had divorced in 1986. She was now living in Fort Pierce, Florida, working as a school-bus aide, helping disabled children. Her nerves evident, she produced a piece of paper and tearfully read off a 201-word statement that had taken her three hours to compose the night before. Like most of the public comments Mickey had made since the bombing, the statement mixed an awkward note of self-pity with concern for the blast victims:

> I cannot even imagine the pain and suffering the people from Oklahoma City have endured since April nineteenth of 1995. This tragedy has affected many people around the world, including myself. I also understand the anger many people feel. I cannot tell you about Tim McVeigh, the son I love, any better than it has already been told the last three and a half days. He has—he was a loving son and a happy child as he grew up. He was a child any mother could be proud of. I still to this day cannot believe he could have caused this devastation. There

are too many unanswered questions and loose ends. He has seen human loss in the past, and it has torn him apart. He is not the monster he has been portrayed as. He is also a mother and father's son, a brother to two sisters, a cousin to many, and a friend to many more. Yes, I am pleading for my son's life. He is a human being, just as we all are. You must make this very difficult decision on my son's life or death, and I hope and pray God helps you make the right one.

Bill McVeigh followed. Never a comfortable public speaker, he took only a few minutes to describe himself as a lifelong western New Yorker who served in the Army from 1963 to 1965. He then showed a fifteen-minute videotape he had helped the defense team make, showing the happier times his son had enjoyed at various stages of his life in Pendleton. The tape compiled still photos and home movies from the McVeigh family collection, featuring childhood scenes of a young Tim McVeigh playing with his favorite toy train, riding on a tractor, and visiting with a plump Santa Claus.

Jennifer McVeigh wiped away a tear as defense lawyer Richard Burr asked her father about a photo of Tim and Bill, mugging together for the camera in their kitchen a few years before the bombing. McVeigh was raging inside. He had resented the defense team's suggestion that his parents take the stand, but he had reluctantly gone along with the idea. Now he felt it was a horrible mistake. He hated seeing his confused, devastated mother crying on the stand. Watching his shy dad grappling for words in front of a courtroom of lawyers, news reporters, and people from Oklahoma City was even worse.

"Can you identify that photograph?" Burr asked.

"It's myself and my son," Bill answered. "Somewhere between December of '89 and '92."

"Does it bring back memories?" Burr asked.

"Well, it's—to me, it's a happy Tim," Bill answered. "It's a Tim I remember most of my life. Oh, he's always good-natured, fun to be with, always in a pretty good mood."

"Do you love Tim?" Burr asked.

"Yes," Bill said. "I love Tim." He added that it wasn't just the Tim in the photograph he loved, but the Tim who was sitting in the courtroom with them that day.

"Do you want him to stay alive?" Burr asked.

"Yes, I do," Bill said.

Burr was trying to show McVeigh's humanity, hoping to strike a note of forgiveness in the jury. There was some sympathy in the courtroom, but not for Tim McVeigh.

H. Tom Kight, the businessman who lost his beloved stepdaughter, Frankie Merrell, in the bombing, sat in the spectator section. It tore him up to watch Bill McVeigh on the stand. Like many of the bombing survivors and family members of victims, Kight had no great affection for McVeigh's mother or sister. But his heart ached for the bomber's dejected father.

Mr. McVeigh, nobody blames you, he felt like saying. *We understand.*

Jurors deliberated McVeigh's fate for two days. While the jury was out, one of the deputy marshals tried to strike up a conversation with McVeigh about the government's actions at Waco. The marshal, like McVeigh, was an ex–military man, and during the trial he and McVeigh had spoken once or twice about their Army experiences.

The two got along well, but when the man brought up Waco, McVeigh just froze. His mind immediately cast back to his old security-guard friend, Carl Lebron, secretly taping their conversations as they ate Arby's roast beef sandwiches and talked about the government.

I can't do this, McVeigh thought. *This guy seems like a friend, but first and foremost he's a marshal.* Afraid of another setup, McVeigh cut the conversation short.

On deliberation days, McVeigh had to appear with the lawyers and the jurors before Matsch in the morning. McVeigh, who didn't like getting dressed up, had refused to wear suits or sport coats for the occasion. He had agreed to wear sport shirts with buttons on the front during the trial, but now he was showing up for the morning session in a sweatshirt. McVeigh said he wore it because it was chilly in the courthouse holding cell where he had to spend much of his day while the jury was deliberating.

"Tim," another marshal asked him. "If they call a verdict, where's your court shirt?"

"If I'm going to be sentenced to death," McVeigh said, "I might as well be comfortable."

. . .

On a Friday, June the 13th, jurors filed into the courtroom and solemnly gave Judge Matsch their decision: death for Tim McVeigh.

Bill McVeigh slumped down in his seat. Jennifer burst into tears. The verdict was no surprise, but hearing the words broke their hearts. McVeigh himself showed no reaction. But on the inside he remained convinced that the sentence would help drive home his point—that the American government was heartless and cruel.

In voting for the death sentence, the jurors decided that none of the mitigating factors raised by defense lawyers were strong enough to warrant sparing McVeigh's life. All twelve agreed that McVeigh intentionally used explosives to kill 168 people at the Murrah Building, and that the crime required extensive planning and premeditation. All twelve agreed that McVeigh truly believed federal agents were responsible for the deaths at Ruby Ridge and Waco, and that McVeigh felt federal law-enforcement officials failed to take responsibility for the killings. They all agreed that McVeigh believed federal law enforcement was using military tactics to turn the U.S. into a police state.

Ten of the twelve jurors agreed that McVeigh served "honorably and with great distinction" in the Army.

But none of the jurors agreed that McVeigh "believed deeply in the ideals upon which the United States was founded." None agreed with the defense team's contention that he was a "good and loyal friend" to those who knew him. Only four agreed that he had done good deeds for people over his lifetime, and only one agreed with the defense suggestion that he "deals honestly with others in interpersonal relationships."

As the judge surveyed each juror individually to confirm that all concurred with the death verdict, most looked away from the condemned man. But one juror made a point of locking eyes with McVeigh, not only while the judge was examining him, but through the quizzing of the next two jurors. Once again, McVeigh glared back for a while, then looked away.

McVeigh was not surprised or disappointed by the sentence. As he left the courtroom, he looked at the still-seated jurors and flashed them a peace sign.

His real disgust was aimed at his defense team, the judge, and, as always, the law-enforcement people who prosecuted him. The end result of *U.S.* v. *McVeigh*, he would eventually admit, was the conviction of a guilty man. But McVeigh felt cheated, convinced he had not received a fair trial. The story he hoped this trial would tell America had not been told.

Soon after the verdict, McVeigh boxed up a plaid flannel button-down shirt he had worn in the courtroom. He knew he would have no use for the shirt in prison, so he mailed it to Andrea Peters, his would-be flame. Tucked in with the shirt was a note, which read: "If you're cold or lonely, put this shirt on and think of me."

Judge Matsch did not formally pronounce the sentence until two months later. McVeigh had declined to testify at the trial, but he decided he would make a brief statement at the formal sentencing.

Not surprisingly, he had no intention of apologizing for his crime or offering any words of condolence to his victims. Instead he wanted to make a statement that would provoke Americans to think about their government. And he had an incentive to keep his statement extremely short: If he made a long speech, he figured, the media would quote only the one or two phrases that would make him sound most like a nut case. If, on the other hand, he kept his remarks to the length of a sound bite, they would stand a better chance of being broadcast in their entirety.

After a long search for just the right words, McVeigh finally settled on a statement that U.S. Supreme Court Justice Louis D. Brandeis, a hero to advocates of individual rights, had made in a 1928 bootlegging case. The issue in the case was the use of phone wiretaps to convict a group of men charged with running a liquor-smuggling operation in Seattle. In a 5–4 vote that helped make wiretaps an accepted practice in American police work, the Supreme Court ruled that police had not violated the Constitution when they bugged eight telephones to gather evidence on the gang of bootleggers. But Brandeis, a fierce proponent of the right to privacy, wrote a dissenting opinion—one McVeigh found appropriate to his own situation seven decades later.

Wearing khaki prison clothes and slip-on shoes, McVeigh stepped up to the podium in Matsch's courtroom. "I wish to use the words of Justice Brandeis," McVeigh said. "He wrote, 'Our government is the potent, the omnipresent teacher. For good or ill, it teaches the whole people by its example.'"

"That's all I have."

McVeigh had chosen only a small section of one paragraph, but there was much more in Brandeis's statement that resonated with his own beliefs. Brandeis considered wiretapping a lawless act, even if used by government agents for law enforcement. He warned that allowing police to wiretap the phones of citizens could be a dangerous step toward "tyranny and oppression" in America.

"Men born to freedom are naturally alert to repel invasion of their liberty by evil-minded rulers," the justice had written. "Decency, security, and liberty alike demand that government officials shall be subjected to the same rules of conduct that are commands to the citizen. . . . Crime is contagious. If the government becomes a lawbreaker, it breeds contempt for law; it invites every man to become a law unto himself; it invites anarchy."

By using only a snippet of the judge's words, McVeigh hoped he would inspire listeners to seek out the entire Brandeis opinion and devote attention to its message. In the wake of his statement, a number of newspapers and network news programs did just that.

The icy relations between McVeigh and Stephen Jones were now on public display. McVeigh had blasted Jones in an interview with his hometown newspaper, the *Buffalo News,* and Jones had responded by calling McVeigh an ingrate. Throughout the trial, McVeigh had started each morning in the courtroom by shaking Jones's hand and chatting with the Oklahoma lawyer about the latest developments in the case; now, McVeigh admitted that he'd felt like a hypocrite shaking Jones's hand, and had done so only to keep the news media and court observers from detecting trouble between them.

But now all pretense of friendship was gone. McVeigh refused to acknowledge Jones in the courtroom, conferring instead with his appeals attorneys, Nigh and Burr. Jones and McVeigh stood side by side in front of Matsch, but the two never exchanged a word.

Matsch made no speech condemning McVeigh's actions as he formally sentenced the bomber. He simply pronounced the jury's findings under the law: eleven death sentences for McVeigh.

> Pursuant to the Federal Death Penalty Act of 1994 . . . and the
> special findings of the jury, and the jury's unanimous vote rec-

ommending that the defendant shall be sentenced to death, it is the judgment of the Court that the defendant, Timothy James McVeigh, is sentenced to death on each of the eleven counts of the indictment.

McVeigh expressed no objection to the sentence; he was willing to die for his act. And yet he retained the belief that he had been "railroaded" by the "cumulative prejudice" caused by those aligned against him: the judge, Jones and the defense team, the prosecution, the FBI, the jury, the media, biased witnesses, and the public. "Please understand," he said after the trial. "I take full responsibility for my actions. When I complain, it is to raise awareness, not to get myself set free."

McVeigh was not the first client who blamed his conviction on his attorneys, Jones said in his own defense. In making his complaints, he pointed out, McVeigh had ignored the successes of the defense team: getting the trial moved out of Oklahoma; obtaining a separate trial from Nichols; suppressing incriminating evidence, including the testimony of robbery victim Roger Moore; and creating enough doubt in the minds of jurors that it took them more than four days to reach their verdict.

Jones later insisted he and his team had done their best, at considerable risk to themselves and their families, in taking on McVeigh's extremely unpopular and challenging case. In a statement issued after one of McVeigh's critical blasts, he said:

> It was the largest murder case in American history. We read 30,000 witness statements, listened to 400 hours of audio tape, watched 500 hours of video tape and examined 150,000 photographs, 7,000 pounds of debris, over 15,000 pages of lab reports and the medical examiner's files of 168 deceased persons, about a million hotel registrations and 136 million telephone records. There is no need for us to apologize for the cost of nearly $20 million, some of which was a direct result of the government's foot-dragging on discovery. The government has acknowledged spending over $82 million in the investigation and prosecution. I owed Mr. McVeigh the duty of loyalty, and I discharged that duty.

Ultimately, McVeigh concluded, the trial only served to prove his basic point: that the American government is corrupt, so far beyond repair that it cannot be fixed from within.

The sentencing complete, McVeigh was once again escorted from the courtroom by federal marshals. Their destination was a federal prison in Florence, Colorado, known as the "Supermax."

McVeigh had spent many a night awaiting news of his fate. From this point on, he would be waiting to die.

14

Murderers' Row

Any way the wind blows, doesn't really matter to me.

—Queen, "Bohemian Rhapsody"

Another government helicopter was waiting to carry McVeigh on his next step in the journey to death row.

This would be a far different helicopter ride from that of two years earlier, when McVeigh had been led down the steps of the Noble County Courthouse jail in Perry, Oklahoma, into the cries of an angry mob. Since then, much of the public outrage had quieted. The U.S. government had fought in court and won a conviction. There seemed to be consensus among the public that the McVeigh trial, so carefully controlled by Judge Matsch, had restored a measure of respect to a criminal-justice system that had been tainted by the O. J. Simpson trial. Timothy McVeigh was headed for execution, and few Americans seemed inclined to argue with the result.

After Matsch pronounced the death sentence, the marshals got McVeigh one last nonprison meal—two tacos and a soda—before preparing him for the trip to federal prison. McVeigh downed the tacos. Then, as he finished his drink, he scratched off a game tag from the paper cup. He laughed ruefully: he may have been sentenced to death, but he'd also won a free order of nachos and cheese. He handed the winning game tag to one of the marshals. "Have some nachos on Tim McVeigh," he said.

As they rode in a van to the helicopter pad, McVeigh talked with Chief Deputy Larry Homenick about his experiences with the news media. One of the top network news anchors, he recalled, had tried to get an exclusive interview by telling McVeigh that he shared McVeigh's love for the outdoors, especially Montana fly-fishing. "Here I am, facing the death penalty," McVeigh said. "And he's saying he likes fly-fishing. He thinks I'm going to tell him something I might not ordinarily say because he's a fly fisherman."

They arrived at the airfield. Wearing a bulletproof vest and shackles, McVeigh prepared to board the helicopter. At one point, Homenick and another supervisory deputy, Ken Deal, were lifting McVeigh into the chopper when Homenick lost his balance and fell backward into the chopper. McVeigh tumbled on top of Homenick. They both quickly regained their footing, though McVeigh's leg irons and handcuffs had cut him painfully during the fall.

Yet with no FBI agents, his sworn enemies, to eyeball him on the short flight—only Homenick, Deal, and their boss, Denver's U.S. Marshal Tina Lewis Rowe—McVeigh remained in good spirits. Once they were high over the rugged Colorado countryside, he turned to the others. "Hey," McVeigh said. "Could you put the chopper down and just give me a one-hour head start?" No such luck. Soon after, McVeigh spotted a small herd of elk moving below, and pointed the animals out to Homenick.

Later, McVeigh turned to Homenick. "You and the marshal and the Marshals Service have always treated me with respect, and I've appreciated that," he said. "I haven't always felt the same about the Bureau of Prisons. I want to tell you ahead of time, when we get close to the prison, I'm going to put on my BOP game face. I won't be the same person."

Sure enough, shortly after the prison came into view, Homenick saw McVeigh squint into the horizon at his new home, and he watched as the prisoner's face went blank, expressionless. It was a sight Homenick wouldn't soon forget.

The chopper touched down on a pad within the grounds of the nation's most secure prison, U.S. Penitentiary Administrative Maximum—the facility known as "Supermax," or, as the news media had dubbed it, "the Alcatraz of the Southwest." The sixty-million-dollar, 480-unit prison had been opened in 1995 as a home for the nation's most dangerous federal inmates.

The trip into the prison itself was a rude awakening for McVeigh.

Two towering correctional officers formed the welcoming party. They each took McVeigh by an arm and rushed him over to an armored vehicle. The marshals stepped into another vehicle and the convoy started a short drive on a road cutting through the arid grounds of the prison complex. McVeigh knew that he would be in for a rough ride when one of the two officers jammed his head down on the pretext of protecting him from bumping it as they climbed into the back of the vehicle.

"Keep your fucking head down," an officer shouted after the door to the armored vehicle shut, and they were seated on the two lengthwise benches. McVeigh wondered whether they were trying to keep him from scanning his surroundings, or to keep others from getting a look at him. The bigger of the two officers threw himself against McVeigh, sprawling atop the prisoner to keep him down. Each time the vehicle shifted gears or hit a speed bump, the officer's Kevlar helmet rapped against McVeigh's forehead. On the bench seat across from him, the other officer sat quietly, flexing his biceps.

"Oh, we've been waiting a long time for you, boy," chided the officer restraining McVeigh. "There's some men here that have been waiting a long time." His weight made it difficult for McVeigh to breathe. McVeigh took a measure of comfort in knowing that he was a high-profile prisoner; if the officer tried to kill him, McVeigh knew, there would be an inquiry.

The indoctrination continued. "You'll answer everything with 'Yes, sir,' 'No, sir,' or 'I don't understand.' You understand, motherfucker?" the bigger officer asked.

This guy's a drill sergeant, McVeigh thought. This, at least, was a game he knew how to play. "Yes, sir," he said.

Suddenly, a tiny smirk crossed McVeigh's lips, and the officer sitting across from him noticed.

"Are you laughing at us, motherfucker?" he demanded.

"No, sir," McVeigh said.

The officer lying on top rolled off McVeigh and sat upright. The game was over just as quickly as it had started.

"You can pull your head up now," Warden John Hurley told McVeigh when he arrived inside the prison. "Okay," McVeigh replied, as if the roughing-up had never happened.

Rowe and Homenick rejoined McVeigh while he was being processed. Then they escorted him to a special disciplinary unit of four prison cells, isolated from the general population, and left him to begin life on death row.

"Good luck, Mr. McVeigh," Rowe said.

McVeigh gave her a thumbs-up. "Marshal Rowe," he said. "Thanks for the tour."

For a man entering a super-secure prison to await the death penalty, McVeigh seemed markedly, almost willfully, unconcerned. *Any way the wind blows, doesn't really matter to me,* he thought, recalling the line from Queen's "Bohemian Rhapsody." On a personal level, McVeigh would welcome death; it would be his crowning achievement. The government, he reflected, would be doing him a favor, ending a long march that had turned hollow in the final years. His execution would be a relief.

As he sat contemplating his fate within the walls of the Supermax, it occurred to McVeigh that he could be considered the poster child for Generation X. Look up the dictionary definition of the Gen-X slogan "No Fear," McVeigh quipped, and you'd find his picture beside it. He sometimes found himself wishing the final moment would come sooner, rather than later. "I'll be glad to leave this fucked-up world," he said. "Truth is, I determined mostly through my travels that this world just doesn't hold anything for me." But as the weeks rolled by, the isolated hours he spent in the four-cell special disciplinary unit at Supermax provided time for self-examination, and he would come to realize that he was not immediately suicidal. "I figure, why not take a few years in retirement. Sit in my cell; write letters, make peace with everyone. What does that make the death penalty, if that's what it is?" In McVeigh's opinion, it was nothing more than state-assisted suicide. "I knew I wanted this before it happened. I knew my objective was a state-assisted suicide and when it happens, it's in your face, motherfuckers. You just did something you're trying to say should be illegal for medical personnel."

McVeigh also contended that the experience of prison, while it lasted, wasn't that difficult to bear. "These guys do my laundry. I lay in bed all day and watch cable television. I don't even pay the electric or cable bills. Is that torture?" McVeigh even found himself reminded of his old dream of becom-

ing a survivalist. Looking at the concrete and steel-reinforced walls of the ul-
tramodern Supermax, McVeigh thought, *I've always wanted to live in a
bunker, and now here I am.*

In truth, though, during his first few months there McVeigh hated life in
the Supermax. The lights in his cell never turned off, and at night, he found
it next to impossible to sleep. To make matters worse, the prison staff delivered breakfast at 4:30 A.M.—*to fuck with you,* McVeigh was convinced.

Suffering from sleep deprivation, he experienced increased paranoia and
aggression. In those first few months, when he would go to an outside cage
for recreation, McVeigh claims he would return to find his cell had been ransacked in searches conducted by the correctional officers. He believed that
the officers were making him pay a price for taking his recreation.

Worst of all, there was virtually no opportunity to talk with any other inmates. Each cell had a double set of doors to prevent voices from carrying.
Yelling or knocking on walls to communicate was impractical. Each of the
cells was separated by an empty room, which absorbed and deadened
sounds.

McVeigh tolerated the conditions for several months before blowing his
top one day at the warden and another prison official who were inspecting
the disciplinary unit. He spared no energy in telling Warden Hurley and the
other official exactly how he felt. Screaming and cursing, McVeigh told the
warden that he was playing by the institution's rules. In return, he wanted to
be treated like a human being.

"I make my bed, and do everything you ask me to do!" McVeigh hollered,
following up with a barrage of profanity.

"Tim, it does you no good to call my workers motherfuckers," Hurley said
calmly.

McVeigh noticed a man standing next to Hurley. "Who's that?" he asked.

"This man is my regional supervisor," Hurley answered.

McVeigh expressed immediate remorse for causing a scene. He hadn't
lost his military respect for chain of command.

McVeigh shared the disciplinary unit with extraordinary company. The
three other cells were occupied by three of the few men alive whose record
rivaled his own: Theodore Kaczynski, Ramzi Ahmed Yousef, and Luis Felipe.

Kaczynski, better known as the Unabomber, had been the last of the four
to arrive at the Colorado prison. He was serving four consecutive life sen-

tences in connection with sixteen mail bombings and attempted bombings he had perpetrated in seven states between 1978 and 1995. The bombings injured ten people and killed three—a computer-store owner, a public-relations executive, and an official of the California Forestry Association. He pleaded guilty to bombing and murder charges in January 1998, and was sent to the Supermax the following May.

Kaczynski, who graduated from high school early and entered Harvard at age sixteen, was mainly protesting the advancement of technology, but he also shared some of McVeigh's concerns about the loss of personal freedoms in America. Many of his bombs bore the initials FC, which stood for "Freedom Club." Kaczynski even embodied the survivalist principles McVeigh so ardently admired, having spent years alone in a secluded ten-by-twelve-foot Montana cabin before being captured by federal agents.

Ramzi Yousef was serving a 240-year sentence for his conviction as the mastermind of the 1993 World Trade Center bombing. In addition to the bombing, which killed six people, injured a thousand, and caused hundreds of millions of dollars in damage, Yousef was also convicted of plotting to bomb eleven airliners as they crossed the Pacific Ocean with American passengers. He belonged to a terrorist group whose members were suspected of planning an attack on Pope John Paul II, and he was suspected of plotting to kidnap and kill U.S. diplomats in Pakistan. In sending him to prison, a federal judge in New York City had called him an "apostle of evil."

At his sentencing, Yousef had made a long and angry speech denouncing the American government and its overseas policies. Like McVeigh, Yousef considered leaders of the American government the world's ultimate terrorists; his words might have come from McVeigh's lips. "You killed civilians and innocent people—not soldiers—innocent people [in] every single war. . . . You went to more wars than any country in this century, and then you have the nerve to talk about killing innocent people.

"Yes, I am a terrorist, and I am proud of it. And I support terrorism so long as it was against the United States Government and against Israel. . . . You are butchers, liars and hypocrites."

Luis Felipe was a native of Cuba who had been in and out of prison since age nine. The founder of the New York City chapter of the ultraviolent Latin Kings street gang, he had led a life that could not have been more different from McVeigh's. Known by the nickname "King Blood," Felipe had brought his own form of terror to the prison system. While serving time for various crimes of violence in New York State prisons, Felipe had used coded letters to continue managing his gang. Using code terms like "T.O.S.," for "terminate on sight," Felipe from his prison cell had ordered the beatings and murders of several people on the outside—including one beheading. In October 1997 Felipe was sentenced to life in prison, plus forty-five years; federal officials had relegated him to the Supermax to enforce his isolation from society.

With McVeigh added to the mix, the four constituted one of the most fearsome groups of prisoners ever housed in one facility at one time, let alone one disciplinary wing. One day McVeigh received a newspaper clipping in the mail that featured color photographs of him, Kaczynski, Yousef, and Felipe. The letter writer asked McVeigh to autograph the article. McVeigh happily obliged, signing it "The A-Team! T.J.M."

Some at the prison called the disciplinary wing "Celebrity Row"; to others it was "Bomber Row." When the four were first assembled at the Supermax, they were completely isolated from the rest of the prison population—and from each other. Confined to their cells at least twenty-three hours a day, their only relief was one hour of caged outdoor exercise twice a week—alone. When prison officials eased some of the restrictions on the four men some months later, they were finally allowed to take their outdoor exercise at the same time. And, through the walls of cages placed about ten feet apart, the four terrorists would exchange conversation.

With Felipe, McVeigh found he shared an appetite for women, and the two began trading pornography—"smut books," as they called them. With Yousef, McVeigh found himself involved in deep political discussions; Yousef even made frequent, unsuccessful attempts to convert him to the Muslim faith. With Kaczynski, McVeigh shared his fondness for the outdoors and wilderness.

Of all the inmates McVeigh came to know at the Supermax, he found he had the most in common with the fifty-seven-year-old Kaczynski. Initially, Kaczynski had refused to speak with McVeigh. "He fell for the propaganda against me," McVeigh believed. In truth, Kaczynski had some misgivings about the way McVeigh had executed the Oklahoma City bombing. Kaczynski's bombings had targeted carefully selected individuals, people he blamed for the ills of America. Kaczynski felt the Oklahoma City blast, killing scores of low-level government employees, was a "bad action" because it was unnecessarily inhumane. In time, though, Kaczynski came to believe that his fellow bomber had, like him, been demonized by false media reports. There was more than just a mutual appreciation for the outdoors between them; their political views often coincided.

One important link between the two men was their mutual disdain for federal agents and prosecutorial misconduct. McVeigh once gave Kaczynski a copy of *Tainting Evidence: Inside the Scandals at the FBI Crime Lab,* by John F. Kelly and Phillip K. Wearne, a book about the alleged manufacture of evidence by federal agents. The book struck a nerve in Kaczynski, who genuinely came to like McVeigh.

"You were in the Persian Gulf War?" Kaczynski asked one day.

"Yes, sir," McVeigh answered. "Ironic, isn't it? In Desert Storm I got medals for killing people."

Like McVeigh, Kaczynski preferred the idea of execution to life in prison. But when Kaczynski made his preference public, McVeigh thought his fellow prisoner had made a big mistake—particularly since Kaczynski was seeking a retrial. "Ted messed up," he said. "They're not going to want to seek death now because they know he's being tortured with life. . . . They won't give the opportunity for the death penalty again, either with a federal retrial or state trial. If one is serious about it, you never show your hand."

Kaczynski laid out his feelings about McVeigh and the bombing at Oklahoma City in an eleven-page letter to the authors of this book.

"On a personal level I like McVeigh and I imagine that most people would like him," Kaczynski wrote.

> He was easily the most outgoing of all the inmates in our range of cells and had excellent social skills. He was considerate of others and knew how to deal with people effectively. He communicated somehow even with the inmates on the range of cells above ours, and, because he talked with more people, he always knew more about what was going on than anyone else on our range. . . . Here at the ADX [prison] my senses and my mind are turned inward most of the time, so it struck me as remarkable that even in prison McVeigh remained alert and consistently took an interest in his surroundings.

Kaczynski said it was his impression that McVeigh was "very intelligent": "He thinks seriously about the problems of our society, especially as they relate to the issue of individual freedom, and to the extent that he expressed his ideas to me they seemed rational and sensible."

Like others who had known McVeigh throughout his adult life, Kaczynski noticed that even in his thirties McVeigh still seemed affected by his experience in the Gulf War. "I do recall his mentioning that prior to the Gulf War, he and other soldiers were subjected to propaganda designed to make them hate the people they were going to fight, but when he arrived in the Persian Gulf area, he discovered that the 'enemies' he was supposed to kill were human beings just like himself, and he learned to respect their culture."

Kaczynski said the two spoke about firearms, and McVeigh once told him that he liked a particular type of gun because it could be used with armor-piercing ammunition.

> I said, "So what would I need armor-piercing ammunition for?" In reply, McVeigh indicated that I might some day want to shoot at a tank. . . . I think McVeigh knew well that there was little likelihood that I would ever need to shoot at a tank— or that he would either, unless he rejoined the Army. My speculative interpretation is that McVeigh resembles many people on the right who are attracted to powerful weapons for their own sake and independently of any likelihood that they will ever have a practical use for them. Such people tend to invent excuses, often far-fetched ones, for acquiring weapons for which they have no real need.
>
> But McVeigh did not fit the stereotype of the extreme right-wingers. I've already indicated that he spoke of respect for other people's cultures, and in doing so he sounded like a liberal. He certainly was not a mean or hostile person, and I wasn't aware of any indication that he was super patriotic. I suspect that he is an adventurer by nature, and America since the closing of the frontier has had little room for adventurers.

Kaczynski said he never asked McVeigh if he was guilty of the bombing in Oklahoma City, and McVeigh never told him. But Kaczynski's critique of the Oklahoma City bombing offered a surprisingly humanistic perspective, though one that still accepted the notion of strategic domestic terrorism:

> [A]ssuming that the Oklahoma City bombing was intended as a protest against the U.S. government in general and against the government's actions at Waco in particular, I will say that I think the bombing was a bad action because it was unnecessarily inhumane.
>
> A more effective protest could have been made with far less harm to innocent people. Most of the people who died at Oklahoma City were, I imagine, lower-level government employees—office help and the like—who were not even remotely responsible for objectionable government policies or for the events at Waco. If violence were to be used to express protest, it could have been used far more humanely, and at the same time more effectively, by being directed at the relatively small number of people who were personally responsible for the policies or actions to which the protesters objected. Such protest would have attracted just as much national attention as the Oklahoma City bombing and would have involved relatively little risk to innocent people.
>
> Moreover, the protest would have earned far more sympathy than the Oklahoma City bombing did, because it is safe to assume that many antigovernment people who might have accepted violence that was more limited and carefully directed were repelled by the large loss of innocent life at Oklahoma City.

Soon after Kaczynski's arrival, he, McVeigh, Yousef, and Felipe were moved to an eight-cell range, where greater freedom and more communication were permitted. McVeigh and the others were now given control over the lights in their cells, which included showers, and were able to communicate by shouting through a single steel door. At mealtime, when the doors swung open and food trays were passed through slots in the steel bars, the inmates were able to have real, if brief, discussions. But their main occasion for contact remained the one-hour recreation periods. The only restriction was that those who were co-defendants in a particular case could not go out-side at the same time. Other tenants on the less restrictive range included Eyad Ismoil, Yousef's partner in the World Trade Center blast; Tony Jones, a Baltimore gang leader; a quiet and mysterious convicted killer named An-thony George Battle; and Terry Nichols, who joined McVeigh at the Super-max in 1998 following his federal court conviction and life sentence. McVeigh had little trouble establishing friendships with those around him, with a couple of exceptions: Battle, who had killed his wife and then used a hammer to kill a corrections officer in prison, spoke to no one—and Terry Nichols refused to acknowledge McVeigh's existence.

Nichols had fared better than McVeigh when his case went to trial—at least, if one considers a lifetime in prison a better punishment than execu-tion.

On December 23, 1997, another Denver jury convicted Nichols of one count of conspiracy in the bombing and eight counts of involuntary manslaughter. He was acquitted of first-degree murder charges, and of using a weapon of mass destruction. The message from jurors: they believed Nichols played a part in the bombing, but were not convinced that he inten-tionally took part in the killings and injuries at the Murrah Building.

Defense lawyer Michael Tigar pointed out repeatedly that Nichols was at his Kansas home, more than two hundred miles from Oklahoma City, when the bomb was detonated. In contrast to the stoic McVeigh, Nichols sobbed at several points of his trial, particularly when his own family was mentioned.

While awaiting sentencing in March 1998, Nichols sent Judge Matsch a sixteen-page letter, asking for leniency and offering an apology of sorts for the role he played in the crime. The letter made clear that Nichols felt the blame rested squarely on McVeigh.

"If I did anything to contribute to the cause of the Oklahoma City bomb-ing I am sorry, I'm truly sorry," Nichols wrote.

> I never never wanted to kill or harm anyone or to damage or destroy any buildings or property anywhere at anytime. This may sound hollow and superficial to some but I am sincere when I say that I would give my life if it would bring back all those that died in the bombing, especially the children.
>
> Perhaps I should have listened closer to what McVeigh was

saying. Perhaps I should have questioned McVeigh more about certain things . . . I never in my wildest dreams ever thought that I would know someone that would do a horrible terrorist act as what happened in OKC. I never thought that an American would carry out such a terrorist act in his own country . . . I'm sorry that I am too naive and too trusting of people.

On June 4, 1998, Matsch sentenced Nichols to life in prison without parole. He called Nichols "an enemy of the Constitution." As an additional, largely symbolic punishment, Nichols was ordered to pay $14.5 million to his victims. If he should ever come into money, in effect, Nichols would not be allowed to keep it.

Six months later, in December, FBI Special Agent Danny Defenbaugh, who led the investigation, told the *Oklahoman* and the *Tulsa World* that the government's $82.5 million investigation into the bombing had determined that there was no wider conspiracy than McVeigh and Nichols.

Defenbaugh said that none of the many conspiracy theories that had been suggested—including allegations that some foreign government or militia organization had been behind the bombing—had ever panned out. He said federal agents had checked 43,500 leads and eliminated 7,156 people as possible accomplices in the bombing.

Now, at the Supermax, McVeigh tried hard to draw Nichols out. He attempted to get a reaction from his former partner by joking about the conspiracy theory Stephen Jones had put forth in his book about the case. Jones contended that Nichols had gone by the code name "The Farmer" during his trips to the Philippines; now, every once in a while, McVeigh would break the silence and yell "Hey Farmer!" down toward Nichols's cell. He never got a response. "Nichols might be pissed at me," McVeigh concluded.

One day, another extraordinary opportunity presented itself. Looking through the narrow window at the back of his cell, McVeigh noticed Mike Fortier standing in an open portion of the recreation yard. Fortier had been sentenced to twelve years in 1998, and had also recently been transferred to the facility.

By yelling at the top of his lungs McVeigh knew he could catch Fortier's attention. His screams, he realized, would be heard by others, but McVeigh decided that he could not let the chance pass him by. It might never come again.

Fortier heard McVeigh and stepped over to the window. McVeigh made small talk for a while, he says, asking how Lori was doing and whether Fortier had sold his mobile home. Fortier said they had; Lori was living with her parents, and the family was doing about as well as it could be, considering the circumstances.

How was Fortier's father-in-law, Les Hart, holding up? McVeigh had enjoyed the company of the older man, who had shared stories of the Old West with him. McVeigh had read in an FBI report that Les had gone out into the desert and dumped all of his blasting caps when he found out that McVeigh had been charged in the bombing. "He was afraid to get caught with them," he said later. "He thought I had used his blasting caps to kill all those people. Les eventually admitted this to the FBI, and the FBI went out to the field and recovered the caps." Eager to put Les's mind at ease, McVeigh had sent him a short letter from prison after the bombing trial. "Don't worry, those were sold at a gun show," wrote McVeigh, referring to the blasting caps. Now McVeigh wanted to know whether the letter had gotten through. "Did Les get my letter?"

"No," Fortier answered. But then it became clear that Fortier thought he was talking about a letter sent in the last few weeks.

"No, Mike," McVeigh said. "I mean a letter I sent, like, seven months ago."

"Oh, yeah, yeah," Fortier answered. "He got that one."

McVeigh wanted to find a way to tell Fortier that he wasn't upset at him for testifying. He figured that Fortier might be blaming himself for McVeigh's receiving the death penalty, and he wanted to tell him that it was his own doing. But in the end McVeigh couldn't bring himself to speak so openly about his carefully calculated plan to have the government execute him. He feared that by making it known he had sought "a deluxe suicide-by-cop package" it might somehow hurt his chances of realizing it. McVeigh could only hope that his easygoing manner would let Fortier know he did not hate him.

But McVeigh says there was one final item he did manage to raise with Fortier.

"Mike," McVeigh said. "You were in front of the Murrah Building, right?"

Fortier looked around. "Yeah."

"Well, did you see a day-care center?"

"No."

"Well, I didn't, either."

"I told the prosecutors that I didn't think you did. I told them that."

"I tried to have my attorney ask."

In a veiled way, McVeigh had already tried to tell the world that he'd had no knowledge of the presence of a day-care center before the bombing. In an essay he wrote for the June 1998 edition of *Media Bypass*, an alternative-media publication that championed many of the causes of the militia movement, McVeigh compared the bombing in Oklahoma City to American military actions. "Hypocrisy when it comes to death of children?" he wrote.

> In Oklahoma City, it was family convenience that explained the presence of a day-care center placed between street level and the law-enforcement agencies which occupied the upper floors of the building. Yet when discussion shifts to Iraq, any day-care center in a government building instantly becomes "a shield." Think about that.
>
> (Actually, there is a difference here. The administration has admitted to knowledge of the presence of children in or near Iraqi government buildings, yet they still proceed with their plans to bomb—saying that they cannot be held responsible if children die. There is no such proof, however, that knowledge of the presence of children existed in relation to the Oklahoma City bombing.)
>
> When considering morality and "mens rea" (criminal intent) in light of these facts, I ask: Who are the true barbarians?

Though he maintains his position that he has no real regrets over his actions, McVeigh has confessed that he feels sorry for what happened to Nichols and Fortier. For all his planning and attention to detail, McVeigh had underestimated the power and breadth of federal conspiracy laws. He had acted under the naive assumption that as long as he delivered and detonated the bomb himself, no one else could be charged. The illegal act, he figured, was purely his own. McVeigh simply hadn't reckoned with the law.

"I did not calculate or know enough about conspiracy law to know that my actions could be held against them," he says now. "Because, in a conspiracy, you're all in it as one. Other people's crimes can be held against you." He remains outraged that Fortier and Nichols could face such serious punishment when they had no idea when the bombing was to occur. Perhaps most significant is his claim that the two men had no way of knowing that McVeigh would bomb the building when it was full of people. Nichols never had control of the truck, or knew the time that the blast would occur. "I could have delivered it anytime," McVeigh says. "It was my choice, and my control, to hit that building when it was full, as opposed to eleven P.M. or three A.M., when it would have been empty, except for possibly a security guard or cleaning crew." McVeigh acknowledges Nichols's involvement in the preparation of the bomb, if only to help dispel the lingering conspiracy theories that surround the case. But he maintains that Nichols's assistance in the mixing of the bomb components came under duress, only after McVeigh had threatened him and his family.

Despite his willingness to clarify Nichols's role publicly, he believes that the State of Oklahoma will succeed in its trial to condemn Nichols to death. But by the time the punishment is finally carried out, McVeigh believes, Nichols will be old enough that the penalty will be meaningless. "I don't think the execution of a man that is old is a punishment, but rather euthanasia," he says. "Whether he is guilty or not, he's going to get the death penalty because that's the nature of the prejudice. There is no way he'd get a fair trial in Oklahoma. And even if they give him the death penalty, state appeals take ten to fifteen years. Nichols will be close to sixty or seventy by the time they execute him. To me, that is not punishment, it is euthanasia. They're wasting their money killing an old man."

Fortier received a twelve-year prison sentence for failing to warn authorities of the bombing. A two-hundred-thousand-dollar fine imposed on him was later reduced to seventy-five thousand dollars. His wife never served a day in jail. Of all the roles played by his former friends during the trial, the only one that bothered McVeigh was the arrangement Lori Fortier worked out—one that, McVeigh believed, gave special treatment to Lori because she

is a woman. "I have a little bitterness in me toward Lori," he says. "Our society is reluctant to prosecute women. Look at the prison population, what is
it—one to ten, one to twenty, men to women in prison? Of the three people
who got caught up in it, Mike, Lori, and Terry, all probably should receive
approximately the same amount of jail time. Ten years or so. It all got heaped
on Terry." Appropriating Jack Nicholson's line from *A Few Good Men*—a film
he saw on cable while in prison—McVeigh fired back at those who refused
to believe that he alone could have been responsible for the bombing: "You
can't handle the truth—because the truth is, it was just me."

In late 1998, when it appeared that authorities were preparing to transfer
McVeigh to Oklahoma City to face a state trial on multiple charges of murder,
McVeigh undertook a preemptive strategy for self-protection. For most of his
life he'd been tall and gaunt, but the sedentary prison life had slowly caught
up with him; by the time he arrived at the Supermax he weighed 180 pounds,
a layer of flab swelling his nearly six-foot-two frame. Now, with the prospect
of going to Oklahoma, McVeigh began to bulk up even more. Starchy meals
he once picked at, he now devoured, aiming to tip the scales at two hundred
pounds. He had no intention of resisting the transfer, but he felt certain someone in Oklahoma might try to murder him before the trial even started, and
despite his death wish he wanted to be strong enough to go down fighting. (In
the end, his efforts were moot: Oklahoma declined to bring McVeigh to trial,
so long as the federal government carried out the execution.)

Prison life was wearing McVeigh down, both physically and emotionally. It
occurred to him from time to time that there had to be a better way to handle inmates than simply warehousing them so they could slowly die of heart
disease or old age. Of all the things he missed about life outside prison, one
of the greatest was the feeling of freedom, of the adventure that came with
being out alone in the elements. He fantasized about taking part in a secret
military mission like the convicts in the movie *The Dirty Dozen*, or becoming part of a traveling labor force put to work helping survivors of natural di-
sasters.

But as McVeigh thought more seriously about death, he found that what truly gnawed at him was missing the opportunity to have a family. McVeigh had always been frustrated in his attempts to connect with women; his only sustaining relief from his unsatisfied sex drive was his even stronger desire to die. As he grew older, the realization that he would be leaving this world without having brought children into it became a preoccupation. It was one of the few things he had failed to fully anticipate when deciding to end his life. Ever since his arrest, McVeigh had received a steady stream of letters from women who expressed romantic interest in him. From time to time he revisited the idea he had mentioned to Dr. Smith, the defense-team psychiatrist—the notion of smuggling his sperm out of prison for an artificial insemination.

But McVeigh tried to rein in his biological urge to father a son or daughter. If he ever managed to do so, he decided, he would have to do so anonymously. The life that any child of Timothy McVeigh's would have in American society, he was certain, "would be hell."

By the summer of 1999, McVeigh had come to accept his life in the Colorado Supermax prison. But he was about to experience a change of scenery.

On July 13, he was suddenly moved to the nation's only federal death-row facility at the federal penitentiary in Terre Haute, Indiana. The morning of the transfer, correctional officers told McVeigh that he was being taken from his cell for a medical checkup. The next thing he knew he was handcuffed and chained. Then, along with four other prisoners—including Anthony Battle and another convicted killer, David Hammer—he was put on a bus headed for the small airport in Pueblo, Colorado.

Heavily armed federal marshals accompanied the group on the jetliner flight to Little Rock, where they picked up four more prisoners. They then flew north to Terre Haute.

A total of twenty prisoners were transferred to the facility from federal penitentiaries all over the United States. The reason for the group transfer—dubbed "Operation Golden Eagle"—was explained in a news release issued by the U.S. Bureau of Prisons:

> On July 13, the United States Penitentiary (USP) Terre Haute,
> Indiana, opened a Special Confinement Unit to provide hu-

mane, safe and secure confinement of male offenders who have been sentenced to death by the Federal courts. As a result of this action, this week, inmates with Federal death sentences have been transferred from other Federal and State facilities to USP Terre Haute.

The physical design of this two-story renovated housing unit includes 50 single-cells, upper tier and lower tier corridors, an industrial workshop, indoor and outdoor recreation areas, a property room, a food preparation area, attorney and family visiting rooms, and a video-teleconferencing area that is used to facilitate inmate access to the courts and their attorneys.

The press release made no mention of the small brick building near the new unit, surrounded by chain-link fencing and razor wire, where authorities kept the padded cot—at first glance resembling a surgical table—on which McVeigh and others would one day be strapped and given their lethal injections.

McVeigh's unmarked white prison bus rumbled toward the federal penitentiary's rear entrance on a muggy, sweltering afternoon, right at the start of a summer heat spell. Each prisoner sat with an empty seat beside him; standing next to each prisoner was a member of an elite Bureau of Prisons reaction team. Each member of the team wore full military gear, including a helmet, and carried a billy club.

The tone for the trip was set quickly. "Okay," yelled out a corrections supervisor, "who are the troublemakers on this bus?" Someone pointed at inmates David Hammer and Anthony Battle, seated at the front of the bus like incorrigible kids from school. By the crude definitions of prison life, these were the troublemakers. Everyone on this bus was a killer, but these two had continued to kill inside the walls of prison. Hammer, already serving twelve hundred years for murder, had increased his penalty to death by strangling a cellmate. Battle, while serving a life sentence in Atlanta for killing his wife, had qualified for the death penalty after beating a corrections officer to death. They were both troublemakers.

But one prisoner in the group truly stood out. Only one of them had gone through life with a squeaky-clean record—without so much as a single shoplifting conviction—before the crime that put him on this bus. And only one had killed 168 people.

"McVeigh," shouted one of the prisoners, "all these guns—they're all because of you."

A local TV crew was waiting on a street corner near the prison to videotape the bus as it rolled by. Then, as it reached the rear gate to the prison, there was a complication. A federal marshal had been driving, but regulations held that once they entered prison property, a prison employee had to take over. The only problem was, it took thirty minutes to get a prison driver out to the bus. It was an edgy time.

As they waited, the prisoners gazed out at the old, red-brick facility, a pre–World War II relic that was about to become their last home. At the entrance was black ornamental ironwork. From rising angular towers, armed guards peered down at the prison yards. Greeting all visitors was a tall pole with an oversized American flag lazily draped from it. McVeigh hated the place from the start. *What a dump!* he thought. *Maybe there's a newer part we can't see from here.*

Finally, someone arrived to drive the bus inside the prison. After a short ride, the vehicle came to a stop. McVeigh, still in handcuffs and chains, was yanked from his seat by a corrections officer. He nearly fell on his face as his chain-connected feet stumbled down the steps. As the first prisoner off the bus, McVeigh realized that he was about to be used to set an example.

The officer slammed McVeigh against the bus and began a rough patdown to check for weapons. When he reached his crotch, McVeigh said later, the officer grabbed him "right in the balls." McVeigh stubbornly refused to acknowledge the pain, though he resolved to report the incident to his lawyers at the first opportunity.

The federal death-row facility had been constructed in 1995 at a cost of about $475,000, but it did not become operational until 1999, when the government decided it had enough death-row inmates—twenty was the magic number—to make it cost-effective.

There had been no federal executions since March 15, 1963, when Victor Feguer, a convicted kidnapper and murderer, had been hanged in Iowa. The federal death penalty was found unconstitutional in 1972; in 1988 it was reinstated, but only to be used against drug kingpins who murdered. But in 1994, several months before the Oklahoma City bombing, the roster of crimes that could carry the penalty was expanded to include about sixty more crimes, including terrorist bombings, hiring a hit man, killing during a car-jacking, and killing during a sex attack. And a new federal law passed in 1996, known as the Anti-Terrorism and Effective Death Penalty Act, was intended to limit stays of execution and speed up the appeals process for death-penalty cases—which before its passage often lasted eight years, and sometimes fifteen to twenty.

"For too long and in too many cases, endless death-row appeals have stood in the way of justice being served," President Clinton said in signing the law, five days after the first anniversary of the Oklahoma City bombing.

McVeigh was the fourteenth man to be sentenced to execution since the federal death penalty was reenacted, and he was convinced that the federal government was doing everything it could to put him on a fast track to the death chamber. The U.S. Supreme Court had refused to review his case the previous March, allowing his death sentence to stand. Then, in 2000, the federal courts denied his request that his conviction be overturned because of allegedly poor legal work by Stephen Jones. By the end of that year, McVeigh would give up his appeals altogether, sending Judge Matsch a letter saying he no longer wished to pursue the issue.

In mid-January of 2001, the Bureau of Prisons set May 16 as his execution date. McVeigh said he had no intention of asking clemency from the new president, George W. Bush. McVeigh called Bush "The Reaper" because of the high frequency of executions in Bush's home state of Texas. "I would not beg any man to spare my life," McVeigh said.

If his execution goes ahead as scheduled in May, he will be the first American put to death by the federal government since Feguer in 1963.

Death row is his home.

It took McVeigh months to become accustomed to his new life. In the dull, dehumanizing facility, he felt himself wasting away day by day. The first of the three daily feedings is offered at 5:30 A.M., but McVeigh almost always refused it, choosing to stay in bed each morning when the food attendant arrived.

McVeigh is allowed up to five one-hour sessions of exercise each week, in a small outdoor cage. At 7:15 each morning, a guard appears to ask McVeigh whether he wants a recreation period that day. But, again, McVeigh almost always refuses. If he can't feel the sun pouring down on him, he says, it doesn't feel like being outside. Yet McVeigh has expressed some anger that his once-fit body is no longer in "100 percent shape." Even his sharply sculpted military brush cut has lost its edge; the prison barber seems to take forever, he says, and even then, by McVeigh's standards, the cut is inferior.

McVeigh was offered an opportunity to take part in a painting class a few times each week, but again, he refused. "I can't paint worth a damn," he says. Instead he sleeps as long as he can, putting off the start of each day for as long as possible before rising at nine or so. He turns on *CNN Headline News,* one of the few things he still enjoys in prison. Lunch arrives at 10:30. He and his fellow inmates eat all their meals in their cells, rarely leaving for recreation, showers, or time speaking with visitors through a quarter-inch-thick wall of Plexiglas. It's at mealtimes that McVeigh feels most acutely his loss of humanity; he is reminded of the days he spent working the zoo back in Buffalo, where every day the same animals would receive the same allotment of food from the same zoo staffers at the same time. Like them, he spends hours pacing his cage until his next feeding.

After an afternoon nap comes dinner, often as early as 3 or 4 P.M., followed by a stand-up count of all inmates. In between, McVeigh reads and writes letters or watches programs on his TV, a thirteen-inch black-and-white set with cable to which he has twenty-four-hour access.

McVeigh was fascinated one night by an episode of the series *The West Wing,* featuring Martin Sheen as a fictional American president. In one episode concerning the death penalty, a convicted murderer was about to be executed, and lawyers for the convict were trying to persuade the president to issue a stay of execution. The president agonized over his decision. Finally, late in the night, he met with a dear old friend, a priest. The priest convinced him to issue the stay, but it was too late. The prisoner had already been put to death. The show ends with the crestfallen president asking the priest to hear his confession.

"I really liked that," McVeigh said. "That was thought-provoking."

Under George W. Bush, McVeigh predicted, the "federal juggernaut" will pursue more death penalty cases in the years to come, creating the need for death-row facilities on the east and west coasts, and new federal prisons in every state.

McVeigh's mail continues to be fascinating, whether hate-filled or supportive. It often includes long political dissertations, usually from people who agree with McVeigh's antigovernment views, as well as marriage proposals and offers of sex. His young female correspondent from Germany continued to write McVeigh sexually charged letters, sometimes printing each word carefully in a different color ink. McVeigh also hears from friends and family, including his father and his deeply troubled mother.

Time magazine, which once featured McVeigh on its cover, now wants him as a subscriber. A form letter from the publisher, sent to his post office box at the prison, offered him a "free mystery gift" if he would agree to sign up.

"As a publisher, I believe a magazine is only as good as the readers it attracts," the letter read. "Therefore, it is important to me that we obtain the readership of leading professionals such as yourself."

"It's about time someone gave me the proper respect," McVeigh said.

He often feels his isolated life has robbed him of his ability to communicate with others. Instead he spends many hours sitting and thinking, about his crime and his trial. He thinks about his former attorney, whom he despises. He mulls over "the strategy" for his forthcoming execution. He wonders about his relationships with other prisoners and prison staff members, and how he might improve them. He likes to "run scenarios" through his head, thinking about the past, present, or future events of his life.

McVeigh blames no one but himself for his place in the world. He has few regrets and no apologies. During a recreation period one day, a prisoner in an adjoining cage poured his heart out to McVeigh, telling him how his life had gone wrong.

When he finished, the inmate looked at McVeigh and asked, "Tim, where did you go wrong?"

"I didn't go wrong," McVeigh said.

To McVeigh, Terre Haute's renovated 1940s facilities pale in comparison to the Supermax. When he looks around his new cell, he spots a dozen things a prisoner could use to craft dangerous tools or weapons, from his metal-frame bed, TV shelf, desk, and stool to the glass TV screen and the ceramic toilet and sink, which could be broken into shards. At the Supermax, he noticed, almost everything was made of concrete or steel and bolted in place.

Even the mirrors in the cells at the Supermax were made from a highly polished steel. McVeigh also speculates that the overall design of the Terre Haute prison would make it difficult to repel an attack from the outside. "I don't have dedicated outside support," he says, "but I'm telling you, this place could not stop a properly planned liberation effort launched from the outside. They may learn this lesson the hard way if they start bringing in some international figures, Colombian drug lords, bin Laden people, et cetera. But trust me, if I was out there and had as few as five good men, I could launch a successful assault on this place."

In conversations with his fellow prisoners, McVeigh reports that he perceives a fear of death among some of the condemned. More than once, hearing an inmate declare "I'm going to win the appeal," or "I'm not here to die, I'm here to live," he has been convinced that many of his fellow inmates are whistling past the graveyard.

Yet others, McVeigh found, have accepted their fate and talk openly about it. Sometimes their discussions turn to the issue of whether autopsies should be conducted after they are executed. McVeigh's opinions on the subject are characteristically strong: he insists that prisoner autopsies after executions are invasive and unnecessary. What is the point of an autopsy when the cause of death is already known? He doesn't want scientists or criminologists dissecting his brain, looking for clues about what made him tick. He doesn't want them measuring his brain to find out whether it is different. To prevent the indignity, he intends to demand that his body be cremated immediately after the execution.

Despite his desire for cremation, McVeigh was angered when Congress, after his conviction, revoked his privilege to be buried in a military cemetery. He had toyed with the authorities on this subject by making remarks about it during phone calls he made from the prison at El Reno—calls he believed were monitored by federal agents. "Man, I plan on being buried in a veterans' cemetery, and they're going to have to pay for my burial, too, them motherfuckers," McVeigh recalls saying over the prison phone. Whether or not anyone was listening, the issue soon came to the attention of Capitol Hill, and lawmakers passed special legislation to bar the decorated veteran from being buried in any military cemetery. It was an honor McVeigh had never intended to seek; if he were buried in any cemetery, military or private, he knew the site would become an irresistible target for desecration. McVeigh wanted to spare his family the repeated trauma of dealing with shattered headstones or even the exhumation and mutilation of his remains. No conspiracy theorist a hundred years from now could start digging up his corpse to perform DNA testing to determine whether the real Timothy McVeigh had been executed after all.

Many Americans, McVeigh believes, will want to see him executed with their own eyes. And he may accommodate their wishes. He expects that the families of Oklahoma City bombing victims will make a push for closed-circuit television of his execution, just as they did for the trial. Should they succeed, McVeigh plans to go one step further.

"If they do that, I'm going to throw it back in their face. I'm going to demand they televise it nationally," he says. "I'm going to say, If you want to make a spectacle of it, I'm going to point out exactly what you are doing. What I'm going to do is contact a media outlet that has heavy money for lawyers, like a CBS *60 Minutes* or a CNN, [and tell them,] You guys fight the battle for me. If you want this exclusive film, you use your lawyers and fight it." Pointing to CBS's decision to air one of Dr. Jack Kevorkian's assisted suicides on national TV, McVeigh believes that one of them may do exactly that. He has already sent letters to the major networks, advising them of this possibility.

Amid all the tragic ironies that surround the Oklahoma City bombing, one of the most unsettling is the conclusion McVeigh has reached about the consequences of his act: he is convinced, he says, that federal agents have begun to back down from the deadly tactics used at Ruby Ridge and Waco as a direct result of the Murrah Building attack. And as evidence he points to the 1996 standoff between federal agents and the Montana Freemen, a militia group who claimed to have established a sovereign nation on 960 acres of land near Jordan, Montana.

In some ways, the standoff in Montana resembled the situation at Waco. The Freemen angered authorities by harassing local officials, refusing to pay taxes, writing rubber checks, and threatening the life of a federal judge. But after eighty-one days the Freemen's saga ended peacefully, with the surrender of twenty-three adults and four children.

From the start, the FBI seemed determined to bring the Freemen standoff to a nonviolent conclusion. There were no government armored vehicles rumbling around the Freemen's compound, and members of the FBI's

Hostage Rescue Team walked about in nonthreatening sneakers and slacks rather than Kevlar helmets and black military-style clothing. McVeigh followed every development in the case from his prison cell with enormous interest. "I'm convinced the Freemen would be dead if not for the Murrah Building bombing," he says.

Clinton R. Van Zandt, the former FBI agent who had tried without success to negotiate a peaceful end to the Waco standoff three years earlier, agrees with McVeigh, at least on that point. Retired from the FBI and working as a security consultant, Van Zandt feels that the government learned a painful lesson from the Oklahoma City bombing. In Van Zandt's words, the government realized that it must become a "velvet brick," not a battering ram. "What an absolute classic tragedy," Van Zandt had said soon after the conflagration at Waco. "What a total indictment of mankind's inability to communicate and relate, even though we have different religious or personal philosophies." While Van Zandt condemned the Oklahoma City bombing, he felt that Waco had started a war, and that McVeigh's bombing had been not only an escalation but a turning point in that war.

McVeigh says he has observed other signs that his bombing was having some effect on government policy. He does not believe it was pure coincidence that, four months after the Oklahoma City bombing, the government finally made amends for its actions at Ruby Ridge. It entered into a $3.1 million settlement with Randy Weaver and his surviving children; in exchange the Weavers dropped a $200 million civil suit they had filed against the government.

A continuing stream of revelations about the Waco standoff, which McVeigh continues to follow from prison, also heartened him. In 1999, six years after the incident, Danny O. Coulson, founder of the FBI's Hostage Rescue Team, publicly conceded that the FBI had fired two incendiary devices at Waco—an admission that came after years of government denials that agents used any pyrotechnic devices hours before storming the Branch Davidians' complex. Soon after Coulson went public, the Clinton administration appointed John Danforth, the respected former U.S. senator from Missouri, as special counsel to reexamine the Waco case.

McVeigh was disappointed on July 14, 2000, when a Texas jury found that the government was not responsible for the deaths and injuries at the Branch Davidian complex. A week later, Danforth issued a preliminary report; his investigators had also reached the conclusion that Koresh and his followers started the killer fires at Waco. "The tragedy at Waco rests with certain Branch Davidians and their leader David Koresh who shot and killed four [government] agents, wounded 20 others, shot at FBI agents trying to insert tear gas into the complex, burned down the complex, and shot at least 20 of their own people, including five children," Danforth said. He stressed that "what is remarkable is the overwhelming evidence exonerating the government from the charges made against it, and the lack of any real evidence to support the charges of bad acts. This lack of evidence is particularly remarkable in light of the widespread and persistent public belief that the government engaged in bad acts at Waco."

Still, McVeigh remains convinced that feds bore the true responsibility for the firestorm. And he was gratified to learn from news reports that President Clinton had come to regret that he did not prevent federal agents from storming the compound on April 19, 1993. The president told investigators in April 2000 that he had made a "terrible mistake" by allowing the Justice Department to go ahead with the attack after a fifty-one-day siege. "I gave in to the people at the Justice Department who were pleading to go in early," Clinton said, "and I felt personally responsible for what happened, and I still do."

On March 12, 2000, tens of millions of Americans witnessed McVeigh in conversation for the first time. He appeared in an extraordinary televised interview with Ed Bradley on *60 Minutes*. Bradley received permission to interview McVeigh in the Terre Haute prison; in an interview that consumed roughly two thirds of the broadcast, they spoke about McVeigh's politics, his feelings about Desert Storm, and his opinion that he did not receive a fair trial. But the interview conditions imposed by McVeigh prevented Bradley from asking the questions that most Americans wanted answered: *Did you bomb the Murrah Building? And if so, why?*

Bradley tried backing into the issue. When McVeigh ventured that American citizens have to be vigilant to keep their government under control, Bradley asked whether violence was the way to do that.

"If government is the teacher, violence would be an acceptable option," McVeigh answered. "What did we do to Sudan? What did we do to

Afghanistan? Belgrade? What are we doing with the death penalty? It appears they use violence as an option all the time."

Once again McVeigh showed no sign of remorse about the bombing. As he watched the interview from his home in Oklahoma City, Tom Kight—Frankie Merrell's stepfather—shook his head. "If only McVeigh knew how many people here would love to hear some expression of apology from him," Kight said. "That would mean a lot."

McVeigh's stubborn refusal to express regret has been echoed on television by a figure who had remained enigmatic throughout his trial: his mother. Suffering from psychiatric problems, Mickey Hill gave an interview to Tampa's WTSP-TV in December 1999. Her family cringed as Mickey compared the bombing deaths to the O. J. Simpson murder case, the World Trade Center bombing, and fatal air crashes. "Every bombing or shooting is a big case," she said. "Plane crashes—there's more people killed in a plane crash than was killed in Oklahoma. And yet these people think they're the only victims? I do feel sorry for them, but let's face it. This happened four and a half years ago. Let's get it out of our minds. Let's get it out of our lives." Her remarks offended many people in Oklahoma City and elsewhere.

McVeigh privately agreed with his mother's remarks, although he was well aware that she had enraged the public. He is surprised that he and his mother had reached such like-minded conclusions separately, since they have never discussed the issue. "Weird," he observes, "especially since I barely write her and I don't call." The temptation to link McVeigh's acts with his mother's history of erratic behavior strikes him as inevitable: "People on the outside will say 'See, he does think like his mother. It's genetically inherited. They're both psychos.' I know that's going to be the reaction."

His mother was involuntarily committed to mental hospitals three times after the bombing. She had begun telling people that she suspected the FBI might have been watching her family a full year before that fateful day in Oklahoma City. After the bombing, she would continue to claim that people were watching and following her—and that she was somehow under the protection of the CIA.

McVeigh watched all this helplessly, unable even to keep track of his mother's place of residence. He had first noticed odd behavior in his mother more than two years before the bombing. On a visit with her in Florida, he had noticed that she constantly pulled plugs from electrical outlets. At first, he thought she was trying to save electricity; only later did he realize that she was afraid of health dangers from electromagnetic fields. McVeigh now believes that her condition was probably accelerated by pressures of coping with his involvement with the bombing.

McVeigh likens the bombing's effects on his family to a kind of post-traumatic stress disorder—a condition he felt able to identify with. He is convinced that his participation in the Gulf War had stricken him with emotional aftershock—a belief sharpened in his mind, ironically, after reading about rescue workers at the Murrah Building who began seeking out self-destructive behavior after the event had passed. After returning home from the war, McVeigh reflected, he himself had plummeted into a self-destructive cycle—gambling himself into near-bankruptcy, even considering suicide. His own experience, he claims, helped him understand how some of those who had survived the bombing could later have floundered. It is a comparison likely to unsettle even the most hardheaded observers.

As Timothy McVeigh awaits his execution, he refuses to consider his actions through any lens but the single-minded one that casts him as a patriot. He clings to the position that his act was needed to right a faltering America.

"I bombed the Murrah Building," he flatly admits now. In a separate interview, he adds, "I like the phrase 'shot heard 'round the world,' and I don't think there's any doubt the Oklahoma City blast was heard around the world.

"A shrink might look at what I have to say and decide, 'He's a psychopath or sociopath. He has no respect for human life.' Far from that—I have great respect for human life. My decision to take human life at the Murrah Building—I did not do it for personal gain. I ease my mind in that . . . I did it for the larger good."

McVeigh clings stubbornly to a vision of himself as a crusader; in his final statement before execution, he says, he intends to invoke the text of "Invictus" by William Ernest Henley—a poem famous for the lines "I am the master of my fate / I am the captain of my soul." McVeigh noted especially a line from the third stanza—"Beyond this place of wrath and tears"—which he knew many would view as an apt description of Oklahoma City in the wake of the bombing. But he has yet to waver from his contention that the U.S.

government was becoming a bully that needed to be defied. "Once you bloody the bully's nose, and he knows he's going to be punched again," he said, "he's not coming back around."

But McVeigh refuses to accept the notion that, to millions of people around the world, he is the ultimate bully. That it was his act that shattered the lives of hundreds of innocent people, and for a moment shook America's confidence in its own security.

When Timothy McVeigh meets his own fate in the execution chamber, he will become the final casualty of the bombing at Oklahoma City.

Dusk

In the days following the McVeigh trial, an event occurred in Pendleton, New York, that caught the attention of the McDermott family, the McVeighs' long-time neighbors. In childhood, McVeigh had planted a peach tree on the border of the McDermotts' backyard. After McVeigh's trial ended in the spring of 1997, the tree suddenly filled with blossoms. In August, when the court imposed the death sentence, the tree's branches bore a full harvest of fruit, after years of dormancy. The sight of so many peaches brought tears to the eyes of Liz McDermott and her daughter, Mollie. Surely, they thought, this was some kind of sign of hope. For years Bill McVeigh had generously supplied her family with fresh produce from his garden. Now Liz McDermott decided it was her time to return the favor, and brought him a supply of peaches from the tree planted so long ago by his son. It was a rare opportunity to bestow upon the father the fruits of his son's childhood labors.

Then, two years later, in September 1999, a shaft of lightning ripped through the tree. Liz was distraught; it was as if heaven had taken back her sign of hope. Yet somehow the strange tree withstood the howling western

New York winter, and when the first spring of the new millennium appeared, the tree revived with it. Liz watched as buds began to appear on its branches, as its first green leaves opened up. And she waited with patience to see whether heaven could ever offer the same mercy to the hands that had planted it.

In Oklahoma City stands another tree, this one a symbol to thousands of people. Known as the Survivor Tree, it stands about 150 feet from where the Alfred P. Murrah Building once stood. Since April 19, 1995, the tree has become a living testament to the fragility of life and the tenacity of the people of Oklahoma.

The force of the blast from McVeigh's seven-thousand-pound bomb stripped the thirty-five-foot tree of most of its leaves. What the explosion's roaring concussion didn't take from the American elm's shady green canopy, the fire and the debris did. By any measure, the tree should have been incinerated in the parking lot across from the Murrah Building, where it was surrounded by cars and trucks that burst into flame after the explosion. And yet, battered but strong, it survived.

No one seemed to notice the tree in the mayhem immediately after the blast. There were so many more important tasks to attend to—the injured, the dying, and the dead. But as time passed, and the residents of Oklahoma City were given an opportunity to take stock of what had happened in the bombing, they noticed the tree's hearty trunk protruding from the asphalt parking lot.

In the spring of 1996 the first buds started bursting open on the tree; soon fresh green leaves faced up to the heavens and soaked up the Oklahoma sun. A gentle shade now touched the earth, so angrily scorched by fire and soaked by blood a year earlier. The tree suddenly became a symbol of life's endurance. Workers from a nursery in Clinton, Oklahoma, took small branches from the tree and grew young saplings to ensure that one day, when the original tree died, it could be replaced. Decades later, when that cutting had grown up and died, it would be replaced by another, keeping the legacy of the tree alive indefinitely. And seeds were collected from the tree and given to the families of the victims and survivors, so that each family might share in the blessings of the Survivor Tree.

When guidelines were drawn up for the Oklahoma City National Memorial to honor the living and deceased victims of the bombing, it was decided that the tree should be part of that tribute. On April 19, 2000, when the memorial opened, the tree stood in its midst, as living witness to the emotional ceremony. No longer isolated in a parking lot, the tree now stood on an overlook where visitors could gaze out on the memorial. Carved into a stone wall curving around the outlook were the words: THE SPIRIT OF THIS CITY AND THIS NATION WILL NOT BE DEFEATED; OUR DEEPLY ROOTED FAITH SUSTAINS US.

To the residents of Oklahoma City, especially the survivors of the bombing and the families of the victims, the memorial was a place where a hellish nightmare had been replaced with symbols of peace and human dignity. Many would come there at all hours of the day and night, just to sit and think.

From a strategic point beneath the Survivor Tree, visitors can look directly across what once was NW 5th Street to the Field of Empty Chairs, a structure placed on the exact spot where the government building once stood. Designed by Torrey and Hans Butzer, a young couple who focused all of their architectural training and talent to design the memorial, the 168 high-back bronze and stone chairs that form the heart of the memorial are designed to appear as though they are floating. Each chair, bearing the name of a victim, rests atop a boxed pedestal of glass that is illuminated at night, providing a symbol of hope even in darkness. The chairs are assembled in nine rows to represent the nine floors of the building; smaller chairs honor the nineteen children killed in the bombing, fifteen of them in the second row, corresponding to where the day-care center was located. The northeast corner of the field is framed by an original concrete wall from the Murrah Building, and the field's immediate perimeter is surrounded by pine trees. One day, it is expected, their height should reach ninety feet—the height of the original building.

At the east and west ends of the memorial are bronze gates for visitors to enter. But they are more than simple gates. They are double-faced walls, with winding ramps between them to provide a moment of transition, as if to let visitors know that they are about to tread on hallowed ground. Outside each wall closest to the streets are the somber words: WE COME HERE TO REMEMBER THOSE WHO WERE KILLED, THOSE WHO SURVIVED, AND THOSE

CHANGED FOREVER. MAY ALL WHO LEAVE HERE KNOW THE IMPACT OF VIO-
LENCE. MAY THIS MEMORIAL OFFER COMFORT, STRENGTH, PEACE, HOPE AND
SERENITY. The face of the east wall reads "9:01," the west "9:03"—the mo-
ments immediately before and after the bomb's detonation.

The Oklahoma City National Memorial stands as a somber yet vivid reminder of the act of one young man who was compelled to sacrifice American lives to his own vision of justice. Millions of words have been and will be
spent on Timothy McVeigh's act, but in the end the words of Richard
Williams, the former assistant manager of the Murrah Building, carry a simple grace:

"The bombing brought us to our knees, but we got back up," he said. "If
anything, it made us stronger."

As for Bill McVeigh, he found his own way to cope with his strange fate. In
the years after the bombing, he retired from his auto plant job; following his
late father's example, he threw himself full force into volunteer activities,
running bowling and golf tournaments for older retirees. When relatives of
bombing victims called on him, as they did with some frequency, he always
made himself available to talk, to commiserate. One of them was Bud Welch,
who had lost his twenty-three-year-old daughter, Julie Marie, in the blast.
Welch at first had desperately wanted revenge; for five weeks after the
bombing, all he could think was "just hang them." Then he remembered the
conversations he'd had with his daughter, and the opposition to the death
penalty the two had shared. Julie Marie had been outraged about the prolific
rate of executions in neighboring Texas; her father recalled her conviction
that the death penalty taught a lesson in hatred to the children of that state.

Welch never stopped missing his daughter, but with time he came to for-
give Timothy McVeigh and began a speaking tour against the death penalty,
addressing mainly Catholic church groups. The tour eventually brought him
to western New York, where Liz and Jack McDermott met him and arranged
a meeting with Bill McVeigh, their old neighbor. At the very dining room
table where Bill had helped the FBI build the death-penalty case against his
son, Bill and Jennifer McVeigh and Bud Welch shared their losses and
helped one another through the process of healing.

Welch would encounter Liz McDermott again in April 1999 at a conference in San Antonio, Texas, organized to help mobilize forces against the death penalty. Liz addressed the assembly, arguing that even Tim McVeigh, as a human being, did not deserve to die for his sins. After she spoke McDermott and Welch spoke again, this time about Bill McVeigh.

"I never felt closer to God than when I met Bill McVeigh," Welch told her. He was overwhelmed, he said, by the experience of finally encountering someone who he felt was an even bigger victim of the bombing than himself.

"When Bill McVeigh meets a stranger," Welch said, "he probably doesn't say he has a son. I can travel the world, bragging about how great my Julie Marie was. Bill McVeigh, for the rest of his life, wakes every morning with a noose around his neck, knowing that his son was convicted of killing a hundred and sixty-eight people."

Welch contends today that Timothy McVeigh's execution will bring peace to no one. "The day they take Timothy McVeigh from his cage for the purpose of killing him is not going to bring Julie Marie Welch back, and it will not bring peace to me or anyone else in America. God simply did not make us that way, to where we are going to get a feel-good from killing another human being," said Welch.

Bill McVeigh's own thoughts on the bombing have not wavered from the first moment he heard about it. "Tim," he said recently, "wasn't brought up to do that." If he could relive his fatherhood, he says, he would not change a thing. "I think we brought Tim up right. This is something that happened when he went in the service, as far as I can see. We were a close family." Though it would be easy to conclude that his wife's decision to split up the family had a formative influence on his son's character, Bill McVeigh refuses to make his ex-wife a scapegoat. "Mickey was a great mother," he says. "She cared for her kids."

Even today, there is much that Bill McVeigh loves about his son—this intelligent, outgoing young man who could always make a friend in a minute when Bill was so shy he could hardly speak. But he will forever be haunted by the question that goes unanswered: *Why Timmy? Why my son?*

The same imponderable question haunts those who lost sons, daughters, spouses, friends, and other loved ones when America's long-simmering tensions over gun rights and big government exploded in Oklahoma City.

Why?

APPENDIX A

The names of the 168 victims killed in the Oklahoma City bombing:

LUCIO ALEMAN, JR., 33, Oklahoma City;
Department of Transportation, engineer

TERESA ANTIONETTE ALEXANDER, 33, Oklahoma City;
Social Security Administration, visitor

RICHARD A. ALLEN, 46, Yukon;
Social Security Administration, claims representative

TED L. ALLEN, 48, Norman;
Department of Housing and Urban Development, urban planner

MISS BAYLEE ALMON, 1, Oklahoma City;
America's Kids day-care center

DIANE E. (HOLLINGSWORTH) ALTHOUSE, 45, Edmond;
Department of Housing and Urban Development, loan manager

REBECCA NEEDHAM ANDERSON, 37, Midwest City;
nurse, outside building

PAMELA CLEVELAND ARGO, 36, Oklahoma City;
Social Security Administration, visitor

SAUNDRA ("SANDY") G. AVERY, 34, Midwest City;
Social Security Administration, development clerk

PETER R. AVILLANOZA, 56, Oklahoma City;
Department of Housing and Urban Development,
director of fair housing and equal opportunity division

CALVIN BATTLE, 62, Oklahoma City;
Social Security Administration, visitor

PEOLA BATTLE, 56, Oklahoma City;
Social Security Administration, visitor

DANIELLE NICOLE BELL, 15 months, Oklahoma City;
America's Kids day-care center

OLETA C. BIDDY, 54, Tuttle;
Social Security Administration, claims representative

SHELLY D. TURNER BLAND, 25, Tuttle;
Drug Enforcement Administration, asset forfeiture specialist

ANDREA YVETTE BLANTON, 33, Oklahoma City;
Department of Housing and Urban Development, secretary

OLEN BURL BLOOMER, 61, Moore;
Department of Agriculture, budget assistant

ARMY SGT. 1ST CLASS LOLA RENE BOLDEN, 40, Birmingham, Ala.;
U.S. Army Recruiting Office, recruiter

JAMES E. BOLES, 50, Oklahoma City;
Department of Agriculture, administrative officer

MARK ALLEN BOLTE, 28, Oklahoma City;
Department of Transportation, engineer

CASANDRA KAY BOOKER, 25, Oklahoma City;
Social Security Administration, visitor

CAROL LOUISE BOWERS, 53, Yukon;
Social Security Administration, operations supervisor

PEACHLYN BRADLEY, 3, Oklahoma City;
Social Security Administration, visitor

WOODROW ("WOODY") CLIFFORD BRADY, 41, Oklahoma City;
Federal Employees Credit Union, visitor

CYNTHIA L. BROWN, 26, Oklahoma City;
Drug Enforcement Agency, special agent

PAUL GREGORY BEATTY BROXTERMAN, 42, Oklahoma City;
Inspector General's office,
Department of Housing and Urban Development, special agent

GABREON D. L. BRUCE, 3 months, Oklahoma City;
Social Security Administration, visitor

KIMBERLY RUTH BURGESS, 29, Midwest City;
Federal Employees Credit Union, administrative assistant to the
credit union president

DAVID NEIL BURKETT, 47, Oklahoma City;
Department of Housing and Urban Development, financial analyst

DONALD EARL BURNS, SR., 63, Oklahoma City;
Department of Housing and Urban Development, construction cost analyst

KAREN GIST CARR, 32, Midwest City;
U.S. Army Recruiting Office, civilian administrative assistant

MICHAEL J. CARRILLO, 44, Oklahoma City;
Department of Transportation, regional director

ZACKERY TAYLOR CHAVEZ, 3, Oklahoma City;
America's Kids day-care center

ROBERT N. CHIPMAN, 51, Edmond;
Oklahoma Water Resources Building, financial analyst

KIMBERLY KAY CLARK, 39, Oklahoma City;
Department of Housing and Urban Development, legal assistant

DR. MARGARET ("PEGGY") L. CLARK, 42, Chickasha;
Department of Agriculture, veterinary medical officer

ANTHONY CHRISTOPHER COOPER II, 2, Moore;
America's Kids day-care center

ANTONIO ANSARA COOPER, JR., 6 months, Midwest City;
America's Kids day-care center

DANA LEANNE BROWN COOPER, 24, Moore;
America's Kids day-care center, director

HARLEY RICHARD COTTINGHAM, JR., 46, Edmond;
Department of Defense Investigative Service, special agent

KIM R. COUSINS, 33, Midwest City;
Department of Housing and Urban Development, construction coordinator

AARON M. COVERDALE, 5, Oklahoma City;
America's Kids day-care center

ELIJAH S. COVERDALE, 2, Oklahoma City;
America's Kids day-care center

JACI RAE COYNE, 14 months, Moore;
America's Kids day-care center

KATHERINE LOUISE CREGAN, 60, Oklahoma City;
Social Security Administration, claims representative

RICHARD ("DICK") CUMMINS, 55, Mustang;
Department of Agriculture, senior investigator

STEVEN DOUGLAS CURRY, 44, Norman;
General Services Administration, inspector

BRENDA FAYE DANIELS, 42, Oklahoma City;
America's Kids day-care center, teacher

SGT. BENJAMIN LaRANZO DAVIS, 29, Edmond;
U.S. Marine Corps, operations clerk

DIANA LYNNE DAY, 38, Oklahoma City;
Department of Housing and Urban Development, program assistant

PETER L. DEMASTER, 44, Oklahoma City;
Department of Defense Investigative Service, special agent

CASTINE BROOKS HEARN DEVEROUX, 49, Oklahoma City;
Department of Housing and Urban Development, clerk

TYLOR SANTOI EAVES, 8 months, Midwest City;
America's Kids day-care center

ASHLEY MEGAN ECKLES, 4, Guthrie;
Social Security Administration, visitor

SUSAN JANE FERRELL, 37, Oklahoma City;
Department of Housing and Urban Development, attorney

CARROL ("CHIP") JUNE FIELDS, 48, Guthrie;
Drug Enforcement Administration, secretary

KATHY ANN FINLEY, 44, Yukon;
Federal Employees Credit Union, vice president of operations

JUDY J. (FROH) FISHER, 45, Oklahoma City;
Department of Housing and Urban Development, clerk

LINDA LOUISE FLORENCE, 43, Oklahoma City;
Department of Housing and Urban Development, secretary

DON FRITZLER, 64, Oklahoma City;
Social Security Administration, visitor

MARY ANNE FRITZLER, 57, Oklahoma City;
Social Security Administration, visitor

TEVIN D'AUNDRAE GARRETT, 16 months, Midwest City;
America's Kids day-care center

LAURA JANE GARRISON, 61, Oklahoma City;
Social Security Administration, visitor

JAMIE (FIALKOWSKI) GENZER, 32, Wellston;
Federal Employees Credit Union, loan officer

SHEILA R. GIGGER-DRIVER, 28,
and unborn infant GREGORY N. DRIVER II, Oklahoma City;
Federal Employees Credit Union, visitor

MARGARET BETTERTON GOODSON, 54, Oklahoma City;
Social Security Administration, claims representative

KEVIN ("LEE") GOTTSHALL II, 6 months, Norman;
America's Kids day-care center

ETHEL L. GRIFFIN, 55, Edmond;
Social Security Administration, claims representative

J. COLLEEN GUILES, 59, Oklahoma City;
Department of Housing and Urban Development, senior underwriter

MARINE CAPT. RANDOLPH A. GUZMAN, 28, Castro Valley, Calif.;
U.S. Marine Corps, executive officer

CHERYL E. HAMMON, 44, Oklahoma City;
Social Security Administration, visitor

RONALD VERNON HARDING, SR., 55, Oklahoma City;
Social Security Administration, claims representative

THOMAS LYNN HAWTHORNE, SR., 52, Choctaw;
Social Security Administration, visitor

DORIS ("ADELE") HIGGINBOTTOM, 44, Oklahoma City;
Department of Agriculture, purchasing agent

ANITA CHRISTINE HIGHTOWER, 27, Oklahoma City;
Job Corps, Athenian Building, secretary

THOMPSON EUGENE ("GENE") HODGES, JR., 54, Norman;
Department of Housing and Urban Development, evaluation supervisor

PEGGY LOUISE HOLLAND, 37, Oklahoma City;
U.S. Army Recruiting Office, civilian computer specialist

LINDA COLEEN HOUSLEY, 53, Oklahoma City;
Federal Employees Credit Union, loan officer

DR. GEORGE MICHAEL HOWARD, 45, Oklahoma City;
Department of Housing and Urban Development,
community development planning representative

WANDA LEE HOWELL, 34, Spencer;
America's Kids day-care center, teacher

ROBBIN ANN HUFF, 37,
and unborn infant AMBER DENISE HUFF, Bethany;
Federal Employees Credit Union, loan officer

JEAN NUTTING HURLBURT, 67, Oklahoma City;
Social Security Administration, visitor

DR. CHARLES E. HURLBURT, 73, Oklahoma City;
Social Security Administration, visitor

PAUL D. ICE, 42, Midwest City;
Customs Service, senior special agent

CHRISTI YOLANDA JENKINS, 32, Edmond;
Federal Employees Credit Union, teller

NORMA "JEAN" JOHNSON, 62, Oklahoma City;
Department of Defense Investigative Service, secretary

RAYMOND "LEE" JOHNSON, 59, Oklahoma City;
Social Security Administration, administrative clerk

LARRY JAMES JONES, 46, Yukon;
Department of Transportation, computer specialist

ALVIN J. JUSTES, 54, Oklahoma City;
Federal Employees Credit Union, visitor

BLAKE RYAN KENNEDY, 18 months, Amber;
America's Kids day-care center

CAROLE SUE KHALIL, 50, Oklahoma City;
Department of Agriculture, export document examiner

VALERIE JO KOELSCH, 33, Oklahoma City;
Federal Employees Credit Union, marketing director

ANN KREYMBORG, 57, Oklahoma City;
Department of Housing and Urban Development, loan manager

RONA LINN KUEHNER-CHAFEY, 35, Oklahoma City;
Drug Enforcement Administration, secretary

TERESA LEA TAYLOR LAUDERDALE, 41, Shawnee;
Department of Housing and Urban Development,
secretary to the director of the single-family division

MARY LEASURE-RENTIE, 39, Bethany;
Department of Housing and Urban Development,
organization personnel specialist

KATHY CAGLE LEINEN, 47, Oklahoma City;
Federal Employees Credit Union, collections officer

CARRIE ANN LENZ, 26,
and unborn infant MICHAEL JAMES LENZ III, Choctaw;
Drug Enforcement Administration, contract employee

DONALD RAY LEONARD, 50, Edmond;
Secret Service, special agent

AIRMAN 1ST CLASS LaKESHA RICHARDSON LEVY, 21, Midwest City;
Social Security Administration, visitor

DOMINIQUE RAVAE (JOHNSON) LONDON, 2, Oklahoma City;
America's Kids day-care center

RHETA BENDER LONG, 60, Oklahoma City;
Department of Agriculture, clerk

MICHAEL L. LOUDENSLAGER, 48, Harrah;
General Services Administration, planner-estimator

AURELIA DONNA LUSTER, 43, Guthrie;
Social Security Administration, visitor

ROBERT LEE LUSTER, JR., 45, Guthrie;
Social Security Administration, visitor

MICKEY B. MARONEY, 50, Oklahoma City;
Secret Service, special agent

JAMES K. MARTIN, 34, Oklahoma City;
Department of Transportation, engineer

REV. GILBERT X. MARTINEZ, 35, Oklahoma City;
Social Security Administration, visitor

JAMES A. McCARTHY II, 53, Edmond;
Department of Housing and Urban Development, director

KENNETH GLENN McCULLOUGH, 36, Edmond;
Drug Enforcement Administration, special agent

BETSY J. (BEEBE) McGONNELL, 47, Norman;
Department of Housing and Urban Development, loan manager

LINDA G. McKINNEY, 47, Oklahoma City;
Secret Service, office manager

AIRMAN 1ST CLASS CARTNEY J. McRAVEN, 19, Midwest City;
Social Security Administration, visitor

CLAUDE ARTHUR MEDEARIS, 41, Norman;
Customs Service, senior special agent

CLAUDETTE (DUKE) MEEK, 43, Oklahoma City;
Federal Employees Credit Union, vice president of financial services

FRANKIE ANN MERRELL, 23, Oklahoma City;
Federal Employees Credit Union, teller

DERWIN W. MILLER, 27, Oklahoma City;
Social Security Administration, claims examiner

EULA LEIGH MITCHELL, 64, Oklahoma City;
Social Security Administration, visitor

JOHN C. MOSS III, 50, Oklahoma City;
U.S. Army Recruiting Office, civilian chief of public affairs

RONOTA ANN NEWBERRY-WOODBRIDGE, 31, Edmond;
Department of Transportation, engineer

PATRICIA ANN NIX, 47, Edmond;
Department of Housing and Urban Development, housing specialist

JERRY LEE PARKER, 45, Norman;
Department of Transportation, engineer

JILL DIANE RANDOLPH, 27, Oklahoma City;
Federal Employees Credit Union, employee

MICHELLE A. REEDER, 33, Oklahoma City;
Department of Transportation, administrative assistant

TERRY SMITH REES, 41, Midwest City;
Department of Housing and Urban Development,
acting director of public housing

ANTONIO ("TONY") C. REYES, 55, Edmond;
Department of Housing and Urban Development,
fair housing equal opportunity specialist

KATHRYN ELIZABETH RIDLEY, 24, Oklahoma City;
parking lot, student reporting to Job Corps

TRUDY JEAN RIGNEY, 31, Midwest City;
Water Resources Building, draftsman

CLAUDINE RITTER, 48, Moore;
Federal Employees Credit Union, collections officer

CHRISTY ROSAS, 22, Moore;
Federal Employees Credit Union, receptionist

SONJA LYNN SANDERS, 27, Moore;
Federal Employees Credit Union, chief teller

LANNY LEE DAVID SCROGGINS, 46, Oklahoma City;
Department of Housing and Urban Development, auditor

KATHY LYNN SEIDL, 39, Shawnee;
Secret Service, investigative assistant

LEORA LEE SELLS, 57, Oklahoma City;
Department of Housing and Urban Development, legal secretary

KARAN HOWELL SHEPHERD, 27, Moore;
Federal Employees Credit Union, loan officer

CHASE DALTON SMITH, 3, Oklahoma City;
America's Kids day-care center

COLTON WADE SMITH, 2, Oklahoma City;
America's Kids day-care center

MASTER SGT. VICTORIA ("VICKEY") L. SOHN, 36, Moore;
U.S. Army Recruiting Office, recruiter

JOHN THOMAS STEWART, 51, Oklahoma City;
Department of Housing and Urban Development,
program operation director

DOLORES ("DEE") STRATTON, 51, Moore;
U.S. Army Recruiting Office, civilian personnel clerk

EMILIO TAPIA, 50, Oklahoma City;
Social Security Administration, visitor

VICTORIA JEANETTE TEXTER, 37, Oklahoma City;
Federal Employees Credit Union, VISA supervisor

CHARLOTTE ANDREA LEWIS THOMAS, 43, Oklahoma City;
Social Security Administration, service representative

MICHAEL GEORGE THOMPSON, 47, Yukon;
Social Security Administration, claims representative

VIRGINIA M. THOMPSON, 56, El Reno;
Federal Employees Credit Union, loan department receptionist

KAYLA MARIE TITSWORTH, 3, Junction City, Kan.;
U.S. Army Recruiting Office, visitor

RICK L. TOMLIN, 46, Piedmont;
Department of Transportation, program specialist

LaRUE A. TREANOR, 55, Guthrie;
Social Security Administration, visitor

LUTHER H. TREANOR, 61, Guthrie;
Social Security Administration, visitor

LARRY L. TURNER, 42, Oklahoma City;
Department of Defense Investigative Service, special agent

JULES A. VALDEZ, 51, Edmond;
Department of Housing and Urban Development,
Indian programs manager

JOHN KARL VAN ESS III, 67, Chickasha;
Department of Housing and Urban Development, appraiser

JOHNNY ALLEN WADE, 42, Edmond;
Department of Transportation, engineer

DAVID JACK WALKER, 54, Edmond;
Department of Housing and Urban Development, environmental specialist

ROBERT N. WALKER, JR., 52, Oklahoma City;
Social Security Administration, claims representative

WANDA LEE WATKINS, 49, Oklahoma City;
U.S. Army Recruiting Office, civilian clerk

MICHAEL D. WEAVER, 45, Edmond;
Department of Housing and Urban Development, attorney

JULIE MARIE WELCH, 23, Oklahoma City;
Social Security Administration, claims representative and interpreter

ROBERT G. WESTBERRY, 57, Bethany;
Department of Defense Investigative Service, senior agent in charge

ALAN G. WHICHER, 40, Edmond;
Secret Service, special agent in charge

JO ANN WHITTENBERG, 35, Oklahoma City;
Department of Housing and Urban Development, program assistant

FRANCES ("FRAN") ANN WILLIAMS, 48, Oklahoma City;
Department of Housing and Urban Development, secretary

SCOTT D. WILLIAMS, 24, Tuttle;
salesman for William E. Davis food wholesaler,
making a delivery to America's Kids day-care center

W. STEPHEN WILLIAMS, 42, Cashion;
Social Security Administration, operations supervisor

CLARENCE EUGENE WILSON, SR., 49, Oklahoma City;
Department of Housing and Urban Development, chief counsel

SHARON LOUISE WOOD-CHESTNUT, 47, Oklahoma City;
Social Security Administration, claims representative

TRESIA JO ("MATHES") WORTON, 28, Oklahoma City;
Federal Employees Credit Union, teller

JOHN A. YOUNGBLOOD, 52, Yukon;
Department of Transportation, special agent

APPENDIX B

On April 25, 2000, convicted Unabomber Theodore Kaczynski sent a letter to the authors of this book detailing his impressions of Timothy McVeigh. Its text—eleven pages in the handwritten original—is reproduced here in full.

I should begin by noting that the validity of my comments about McVeigh is limited by the fact that I didn't know him terribly well. We were often put in the outdoor rec yard together in separate wire-mesh cages, but I always spent most of the rec period running in a small oval, because of the restricted area of the cages and consequently I had only about 15 or 20 minutes of each rec period for talking with other inmates. Also, I was at first reluctant to become friendly with McVeigh because I thought (correctly) that any friendly relations between McVeigh and me would be reported to the media and I also thought (incorrectly, it seems) that such reports would lose me many supporters. But my reluctance very soon passed away: When you're confined with other people under the conditions that exist on this range of cells, you develop a sense of solidarity with them regardless of any differences or misgivings.

On a personal level I like McVeigh and I imagine that most people would like him. He was easily the most outgoing of all the inmates on our range of cells and had excellent social skills. He was considerate of others and knew how to deal with people effectively. He communicated somehow even with the inmates on the range of cells above ours, and, because he talked with more people, he always knew more about what was going on than anyone else on our range.

Another reason why he knew more about what was going on was that he was very observant. Up to a point, I can identify with this trait of McVeigh's. When you've lived in the woods for a while you get so that your senses are far more alert than those of a city person; you will hardly miss a footprint, or even a fragment of one, and the slightest sound, if it deviates from the pattern of sounds that you're expecting to hear at a given time and place, will catch your attention. But when I was away from the woods, or even when I was in my cabin or absorbed in some task, my senses tended to turn inward, so to speak, and the observant alertness was shut off. Here at the ADX, my senses and my mind are turned inward most of the time, so it struck me as remarkable that even in prison McVeigh remained alert and consistently took an interest in his surroundings.

It is my impression that McVeigh is very intelligent. He thinks seriously about the problems of our society, especially as they relate to the issue of individual freedom, and to the extent that he expressed his ideas to me they seemed rational and sensible. However, he discussed these matters with me only to a limited extent and I have no way of being sure that he does not have other ideas that he did not express to me and that I would not consider rational or sensible. I know almost nothing about McVeigh's opinions concerning the U.S. government or the events at Waco and Ruby Ridge. Someone sent me a transcript of his interview with 60 Minutes, but I haven't read it yet. Consequently, I have no way of knowing whether I would consider his opinion on these subjects to be rational or sensible.

McVeigh is considered to belong to the far right, and for that reason some people apparently assume that he has racist tendencies. But I saw no indication of this. On the contrary, he was on very friendly terms with the African-American inmates here and I never heard him make any remark that could have been considered even remotely racist. I do recall his mentioning that prior to the Gulf War, he and other soldiers were subjected to propaganda designed to make them hate the people they were going to fight, but when he arrived in the Persian Gulf area he discovered that the "enemies" he was supposed to kill were human beings just like himself, and he learned to respect their culture.

McVeigh told me of his idea (which I think may have significant merit) that certain rebellious elements on the American right and left respectively had more in common with one another than is commonly realized, and that the two groups ought to join forces. This led us to discuss, though only briefly, the question of what constitutes the "right." I pointed out that the word "right," in the political sense, was originally associated with authoritarianism, and I raised the question of why certain radically anti-authoritarian groups (such as the Montana Freemen) were lumped together with authoritarian factions as the "right." McVeigh explained that the American far right could be roughly divided into two branches, the fascist/racist branch, and the individualistic or freedom-loving branch which generally was not racist. He did not know why these two branches were lumped together as the "right," but he did suggest a criterion that could be used to distinguish left from right: the left (in America today) generally dislikes firearms, while the right tends to be attracted to firearms.

By this criterion McVeigh himself would have to be assigned to the right. He once asked me what kind of rifle I'd used for hunting in Montana, and I said I'd had a .22 and a .30–06. On a later occasion McVeigh mentioned that one of the advantages of a .30–06 was that one could get armor-piercing ammunition for it. I said, "So what would I need armor-piercing ammunition for?" In reply, McVeigh indicated that I might some day want to shoot at a tank. I didn't bother to argue with him, but if I'd considered it worth the trouble I could have given the obvious answer: that the chances that I would ever have occasion to shoot at a tank were very remote. I think McVeigh knew well that there was little likelihood that I would ever need to shoot at a tank—or that he would either, unless he rejoined the Army. My speculative interpretation is that McVeigh resembles many people on the right who are attracted to powerful weapons for their own sake and independently of any likelihood that they will ever have a practical use for them. Such people tend to invent excuses, often far-fetched ones, for acquiring weapons for which they have no real need.

But McVeigh did not fit the stereotype of the extreme right-wingers. I've already indicated that he spoke of respect for other people's cultures, and in doing so he sounded like a liberal. He certainly was not a mean or hostile person, and I wasn't aware of any indication that he was super patriotic. I suspect that he is an adventurer by nature, and America since the closing of the frontier has had little room for adventurers.

McVeigh never discussed the Oklahoma City bombing with me, nor did he ever make any admissions in my hearing. I know nothing about that case except what the media have said, so I'm not going to offer any opinion about whether McVeigh did what they say he did. However, assuming that the Oklahoma City bombing was intended as a protest against the U.S. government in general and against the government's actions at Waco in particular, I will say that I think the bombing was a bad action because it was unnecessarily inhumane.

A more effective protest could have been made with far less harm to innocent people. Most of the people who died at Oklahoma City were, I imagine, lower-level government employees—office help and the like—who were not even remotely responsible for objectionable government policies or for the events at Waco. If violence were to be used to express protest, it could have been used far more humanely, and at the same time more effectively, by being directed at the relatively small number of people who were personally responsible for the policies or actions to which the protesters objected. Such protest would have attracted just as much national attention as the Oklahoma City bombing and would have involved relatively little risk to innocent people. Moreover, the protest would have earned far more sympathy than the Oklahoma City bombing did, because it is safe to assume that many anti-government people who might have accepted violence that was more limited and carefully directed were repelled by the large loss of innocent life at Oklahoma City.

The media teach us to be horrified at the Oklahoma City bombing, but I won't have time to be horrified at it as long as there are greater horrors in the world that make it seem insignificant by comparison. Moreover, our politicians and our military kill people in far larger numbers than was done at Oklahoma City, and they do so for motives that are far more cold blooded and calculating. On orders from the president, a general will kill some thousands of people (usually including many civilians regardless of efforts to avoid such losses) without bothering to ask himself whether the killing is justified. He has to follow orders because his only other alternative would be to resign his commission, and naturally he would rather kill a few thousand people than spoil his career. The politicians and the media justify these actions with propaganda about "defending freedom." However, even if America were a free society (which it is not), most U.S. military action during at least the last couple of decades has not been necessary for the survival of American society but has been designed to protect relatively narrow economic or political interests or to boost the president's approval rating in the public-opinion polls.

The media portray the killing at Oklahoma City as a ghastly atrocity, but I remember how they cheered the U.S. action in the Gulf War just as they might have cheered for their favorite football team. The whole thing was treated as if it were a big game. I didn't see any sob stories about the death agonies of Iraqi soldiers or about their grieving families. It's easy to see the reason for the difference: America's little wars are designed to promote the interests of "the system," but violence at home is dangerous to the system, so the system's propaganda has to teach us the correspondingly correct attitudes toward such events. Yet I am much less repelled by powerless dissidents who kill a couple hundred because they think they have no other way to effectively state their protest, than I am by politicians and generals—people in positions of great power—who kill hundreds or thousands for the sake of cold calculated political and economic advantages.

You asked for my thoughts on the behavior of federal law enforcement officers. My personal experience suggests that federal law enforcement officers are neither honest nor competent, and that they often disobey their own rules.

I've found by experience that any communication with journalists is risky for one in my position. I'm taking the risk in this case mainly because I think that McVeigh would want me to help you in the way that I have. As I indicated near the beginning of this letter, when you're locked up with other people you develop a sense of solidarity with them in spite of any differences.

Sincerely yours, Ted Kaczynski.

SOURCE NOTES

The bulk of the new information included in the account of Timothy McVeigh's life given in these pages derives from the firsthand recollections of McVeigh himself, which he has contributed to this book freely and with no compensation or right of approval. Wherever possible his version has been checked against other sources, although in many instances—including, most dramatically, the account of McVeigh's final drive to Oklahoma City—McVeigh is the only possible firsthand source.

The authors conducted three major interview sessions with McVeigh. The first occurred over four consecutive days, May 6 through May 9, 1999, at the U.S. Penitentiary in Florence, Colorado, also known as the Supermax facility. The second three-day session began on January 14, resumed on January 17, and concluded on January 18, 2000, in the death-row unit at the U.S. Penitentiary, Terre Haute, Indiana. The third was a four-hour telephone interview on July 6, 2000, originating from Terre Haute's death row. We have conducted many shorter telephone interviews with McVeigh in the last several years, which continued up until weeks before the publication of this book. We have also exchanged hundreds of letters with McVeigh, who often responded in letters several pages in length, providing answers to follow-up questions and offering further detail on every aspect of his life.

Dawn

McVeigh discussed his actions and mind-set on the morning of April 19, 1995, during interviews at the Supermax prison in Colorado and at the federal death row in Terre Haute, Indiana. His descriptions of the truck and the timing of his drive to Oklahoma City are consistent with the allegations filed against him in the federal indictment of August 10, 1995.

1. The Boy Next Door

The opening quote comes from the first day of the four-day May 1999 interview with Timothy McVeigh. McVeigh provided a detailed account of his childhood during that interview. His parents, Bill McVeigh and Mickey Hill, supplied extensive information on their son's early years in many interviews. Both offered details about themselves and their courtship. A survey of back issues of the *Lockport Union Sun and Journal* and the *Niagara Gazette,* formerly the *Niagara Falls Gazette,* was also helpful. Bill McVeigh's and Mickey Hill's yearbooks from the former DeSales Catholic High School in Lockport also shed light on their late adolescence. A baby journal with extensive entries chronicling McVeigh's journey into toddler years and boyhood offered priceless snapshots of his formative life, including a contemporary survey of his frequent illnesses and childhood injuries. (Bill McVeigh has confirmed that Tim and his older sister, Patty, were frequently ill.)

McVeigh's boyhood friend Todd Carter gave an extensive interview explaining McVeigh's insistence on playing the role of the good guy and hero in their childhood games. Other neighbors shared their insights into McVeigh's youth; most notable were Liz and Jack McDermott of Meyer Road, confirming the observations of his parents. McVeigh's love of animals, which arguably was greater than his love for human beings, was detailed mainly in his own recollections, though his father confirmed his son's affection for house pets. McVeigh's lifelong hatred for bullies can be traced back to his boyhood, to incidents where he was picked on by youths either bigger or older than him. Art Braunscheidel, who with Bill McVeigh coached the youth baseball team McVeigh played for, confirmed witnessing one of the earliest incidents.

Both Bill McVeigh and Mickey Hill shared details of their faltering marriage, which ended in a 1986 divorce. Friends of the couple have said privately that Mickey Hill cheated on her husband, a claim she adamantly denies. McVeigh provided extensive details of his relationship with his paternal grandfather, Edward McVeigh. Interviews with McVeigh's sister Jennifer; his neighbor Mollie McDermott, the daughter of Liz and Jack McDermott; and Jean Hill Zanghi, the sister of Mickey Hill; as well as courtroom testimony given at McVeigh's trial by his childhood friend Vicki Hodge, also contributed to our portrait of McVeigh's early years.

2. Real World

As the story carried forth into his adolescence, McVeigh provided a more complete chronology of the experiences that began shaping his outlook on the world. Family and friends confirmed many of McVeigh's recollections, as did testimony offered at his trial. McVeigh, for the first time, offered his own explanation of how he came to read *The Turner Diaries* and other ultra-right-wing literature; the authors have read both the *Diaries* and *Unintended Consequences* in the course of their research. Liz and Jack McDermott confirmed McVeigh's interest in their basement fallout shelter. McVeigh provided details on his deep interest in the survivalist movement, prompted by his reading and his viewing of films including *Planet of the Apes* and *The Omega Man*. McVeigh also shed light on why he quit business school and sought a pistol permit to gain employment as an armed guard with Burke Armored Car after high school. Bill McVeigh confirmed a story involving a heated encounter McVeigh experienced with a neighbor while target-shooting in Bill McVeigh's Campbell Road backyard. This led to McVeigh's explanation of why he and an old high school friend purchased land in the Southern Tier for a shooting range and possible future construction of a bunker at the site in the town of Humphrey. Trial testimony and an interview with Burke supervisor Vincent Capparra confirmed McVeigh's work-related stories at Burke. McVeigh also explained how his job on an armored car in the inner city gave him his first exposure to racism. During this period, McVeigh offered a vivid picture of a moral dilemma he experienced one morning while on his way to work when a motorist struck a deer. McVeigh told of how he dispatched the animal after other stopped motorists refused the task. He did so fearing the police would find him and arrest him for shooting his pistol in a no-discharge zone. Following the advice of neighbors and his love of guns, McVeigh quit his job and enlisted in the Army.

3. "A Hundred Tim McVeighs"

Information on McVeigh's decision to join the Army, and his ensuing experience with recruiters, was drawn from interviews with McVeigh, Richard Drzyzga, and Bill McVeigh. Descriptions of Fort Benning and McVeigh's experiences there came from the public information office at Fort Benning, and interviews with McVeigh and William Dilly. Dilly, who roomed with McVeigh for more than a year, provided invaluable help with details about Fort Benning, Fort

Riley, and the Persian Gulf War. The controversy over the School of the Americas is detailed in a number of *New York Times* articles, including a May 2000 article by Steven Lee Myers entitled "Army to Overhaul School of Americas; Critics Unimpressed." Background on Fort Riley and its history came from the official Web site run by the Fort Riley public information office.

McVeigh's friendships with Nichols and Fortier were described in interviews with McVeigh and Dilly, as well as Fortier's extensive testimony in both the McVeigh and the Nichols trials. McVeigh's fascination with firearms and right-wing literature during his Army years was confirmed by a large number of sources, including McVeigh himself, and the court testimony of Army friends, including Fortier, Dilly, Albert Warnement, Royal Witcher, and Jose Rodriguez. His excellence at marksmanship was confirmed by his Army personnel record: a report rating his performance in late 1991 noted the perfect 1,000 he scored on a gunnery test in the Bradley fighting vehicle. Allen Smith, who served with McVeigh, spoke with amazement of his marksmanship at Fort Riley and in the Gulf War, as did several other soldiers in their court testimony.

4. War Hero

Interviews with Allen Smith, William Dilly, and defense-team psychiatrist John R. Smith confirmed McVeigh's feelings of distress after killing Iraqi soldiers. McVeigh's training experience in Germany and his Desert Storm experiences were discussed in interviews with McVeigh, Smith, and Dilly, and in the court testimony of Jesus Rodriguez, Sheffield Anderson, Bruce Williams, Royal Witcher, and Howard Ian Thompson. McVeigh also wrote about those experiences in letters to Vicki Hodge and Liz McDermott, which were made public during his trial. McVeigh's war experiences have also been detailed in the following articles: "The Good Soldier," by Jonathan Franklin, *Spin* magazine, April 1997; "Biography of Timothy McVeigh, Part II," by Lawrence W. Myers, *Media Bypass* magazine, March 1996; "An Ordinary Boy's Extraordinary Rage," by Dale Russakoff and Serge Kovaleski, *Washington Post*, July 2, 1995; and "John Doe No. 1—A Special Report: A Life of Solitude and Obsessions," by Robert D. McFadden, *New York Times*, May 4, 1995.

Information about battles and military strategy in the Gulf War came from war reports in the Associated Press, *Time,* and *Newsweek,* in addition to several books, including *The Army Times Book of Great Land Battles, From the Civil War to the Gulf War,* by Col. J. D. Morelock and edited by Walter J. Boyne, Berkley Books, 1994; *Desert Storm: The War in the Persian Gulf,* by the editors of *Time,* edited by Otto Friedrich, Little, Brown & Co., 1991; and, from a western New York perspective, *Hometown Heroes: Western New Yorkers in Desert Storm,* by Brian Meyer and Tom Connolly, WNY Wares Inc., 1991.

McVeigh's description of his washout at the Special Forces training camp was augmented by the previously mentioned articles in the *New York Times, Washington Post, Spin,* and *Media Bypass.* McFadden's article in the *New York Times* alleged that McVeigh also failed a psychological test at Camp McCall, which McVeigh vehemently denies; Army officials also denied this in a December 2000 interview.

5. Nothingness

In the May 1999 interviews, McVeigh described his nervous breakdown after leaving the Army and how it nearly led to suicide in Ed McVeigh's house. He cited several incidents of disappointment in employment after coming home from the Gulf War a decorated veteran. At one point during his reentry into civilian life, he described befriending a grown cougar called Cory while working the graveyard shift at the Buffalo Zoo as a security guard; zoo officials confirmed that a cougar by that name resided in the zoo during that period. Two letters to the editor of the *Lockport Union Sun and Journal,* published February 11, 1992, and March 10, 1992, reflect McVeigh's growing disenchantment with government and the American way of life. A third letter, written on February 16, 1992, to his congressman, Representative John J. LaFalce, registered McVeigh's concern over a Niagara Falls resident's arrest for possession of Mace. McVeigh came to see himself as a victim of reverse discrimination. Jack McDermott confirmed that he and McVeigh took civil service tests together.

Jean Hill Zanghi, McVeigh's maternal aunt, recalled his stops at her house in the Genesee Valley in the spring of 1992. Jennifer McVeigh confirmed her conversations with her brother about what was wrong with America. Bill McVeigh also recalled his son's antigovernment posturing. McVeigh's stories of visiting the Veterans Affairs Medical Center in Buffalo for medical treatment were confirmed by confidential government sources, who spoke on the condition that their names be withheld. Real estate transactions confirm McVeigh's sale of the land he had purchased for a shooting range in the town of Humphrey. Interviews with Carl E. Lebron, Jr., a security guard at Burns Security, confirm McVeigh's work stories. Court testimony from Brian Profic, a Burns security supervisor, also sheds light on McVeigh's political views.

Bill McVeigh confirmed that Terry Nichols and his wife, Marife, visited McVeigh in the latter part of 1992. In *By Blood Betrayed,* a 1995 book by Lana Padilla and Ron Delpit, Josh Nichols, Padilla's son with Terry Nichols, recalls McVeigh driving hazardously on a side trip to Niagara Falls. McVeigh confirmed the incident, though he differed in the assessment of his driving abilities. McVeigh's heavy gambling on football games was confirmed by Bill McVeigh. Liz McDermott and Mollie McDermott provided details of McVeigh's plans to leave western New York.

6. Kindred Spirits

In February 1993, McVeigh sent a letter to the U.S. Defense Department in response to its request for restitution of money overpaid him while in the Army. McVeigh confirmed in prison interviews that he was aware of the overpayments, but said he felt he deserved the extra money. McVeigh's March 1993 visit to Waco was chronicled in a March 30, 1993, college newspaper story by Michelle Rauch, a senior at Southern Methodist University—an article entered as evidence at McVeigh's trial. Until now, McVeigh has never spoken publicly of his confrontation with federal agents at Waco. Details of McVeigh's visits to Michael and Lori Fortier's home in Kingman, Arizona, are drawn from the Fortiers' trial testimony and McVeigh's own recollections. He also shared details on his brief excursion into the drug world, with Fortier serving as his guide. McVeigh's encounters with Arkansas ammunition dealer Roger E. Moore and Moore's partner Karen Anderson are based on their testimony given at the Terry Nichols trial, as well as McVeigh's own recollections.

Details of McVeigh's visits to the Nichols farm in Decker, Michigan, are gleaned from interviews with him and his letters. Impressions of McVeigh and accounts of his visits are based on interviews with James Nichols; Joyce (Nichols) Wilt; and friends and neighbors, including Philip G. Morawski, MariAnn T. Saenen, and Paul V. Izydorek. Accounts of court appearances by James and Terry Nichols on different proceedings against them are based on interviews with James Nichols and Sandusky (Michigan) Circuit Court Judge Donald Teeple. Details on Marife Nichols, the second wife of Terry Nichols, are taken from interviews with McVeigh and the Nichols family, and her trial testimony. James Nichols and his neighbors supplied details on the recreational bombs made at his farm. The account of McVeigh and James and Terry Nichols watching the burning of Waco on April 19, 1993, on the television in the Nichols farmhouse was based on interviews with McVeigh and James Nichols.

McVeigh spread the word about government actions at Waco in a number of media, including videos he compiled himself by cobbling together footage from other sources. Gary Steinberger, a supervisor at State Security, where McVeigh worked as a security guard in Arizona, testified that McVeigh brought a television and VCR to work to show him a tape in 1993.

McVeigh, in our interviews, offered his perspective on why his friendship with Roger Moore began to deteriorate. He also explained the reasons for the Moore robbery, and insisted that securing money to finance the bombing was not a motive. On October 20, 1993, he wrote his sister Jennifer a detailed letter regarding his near-suicide attempt at his grandfather's home in 1992. The letter also made allegations of government misconduct. McVeigh described his efforts to revive Marife Nichols's toddler son, Jason Torres Nichols, who suffocated on November 22, 1993, at the Decker, Michigan, farmhouse. James Nichols provided additional background information on the child's death. As with all of his letters to her, Jennifer McVeigh in interviews and trial testimony offered insights into her brother's state of mind around the time of the letter he wrote her on December 24, 1993. McVeigh's July 14, 1994, letter severing his friendship with childhood friend Steve Hodge was introduced as evidence at the trial of Terry Nichols. McVeigh's account of his trip to Area 51 in Roswell, New Mexico, later that summer is drawn from interviews with McVeigh.

7. "Won't Be Back Forever"

Congress's and President Clinton's legislative efforts to curb assault weaponry was a developing story for months in the spring and summer of 1994, before legislation was finally approved on September 13, 1994; in our interviews, McVeigh cited the assault-weapons ban as the latest catalyst in his impulse to move against the government. Aside from McVeigh's own statements expressing general outrage at the government over Waco, his anger is well chronicled in the trial testimony offered by Michael Fortier. McVeigh characterized Fortier's statements as accurate, with the caveat that Fortier sometimes distorted the truth to portray himself in the best possible light. Michael McGuire, Fortier's attorney, insisted his client was honest and did not distort facts.

McVeigh, in our interviews, insisted that he manipulated both Michael Fortier and Terry Nichols to assist him in carrying out his bombing plans and that his friends had no control over the truck or what time of day the bomb would be delivered. He refused to cite where Fortier was less than truthful, fearing that any such statements might move federal prosecutors to reverse their plea deal with Fortier. Attempts to interview Fortier were unsuccessful, though his mother, Irene Fortier, provided details about McVeigh and her son in a brief interview. Ila Hart, Fortier's mother-in-law, also spoke briefly, though she offered little insight into McVeigh and his connection to her family. McVeigh provided an in-depth explanation on how he went about selecting the Murrah Building as his target. His criteria involved the number of federal law-enforcement offices in a building, architectural design, and location.

Both McVeigh and Marife Nichols were interviewed regarding claims about their alleged sexual relationship.

Fortier's testimony regarding McVeigh's construction of a small prototype bomb he exploded in the desert outside Kingman follows the time period explosives were stolen from the Martin Marietta Aggregates quarry in Marion, Kansas. The burglary was discovered on Monday, October 3, 1994. McVeigh's comments on the burglary also match testimony offered by Allen "Bud" Radtke, a quarry blaster.

McVeigh, in our interviews, dismissed speculation that he had selected the

Murrah Building because he thought it was where the orders against Waco had originated, and that Bob Ricks, the FBI's chief spokesman at Waco, worked in the building. Ricks, though from Oklahoma City, had offices in a different building. Phone card calling records presented at trial back McVeigh's claims of calling different manufacturers in search of bomb components. Bill McVeigh and Linda Daigler confirmed McVeigh's account of the snowblower dispute in early November 1994. During that same visit, Andrea Peters confirmed in an interview, she received a letter McVeigh had hand-delivered to her parents' home in Alden, New York, asking her on a date.

McVeigh described his efforts to continue his campaign against the government by writing letters on his sister Jennifer's word processor, including one entitled "Constitutional Defenders" and a second headed "ATF Read." These letters were used as evidence against McVeigh at his trial. Carl Lebron confirmed that McVeigh visited him at the Calspan research facility the night of November 22, 1994. Federal law-enforcement officials have verified that they had rented out office space in the Calspan complex for a secret operation called Operation North Star.

Information on Terry Nichols's November 1994 visit to Las Vegas to see his son Josh appears in the testimony of Lana Padilla, Josh's mother, at Nichols's trial. *By Blood Betrayed* provided additional details on the visit, Nichols's departure for the Philippines on November 22, 1994, and events that unfolded upon his return in January 1995. Padilla's description of the sealed package appears in both her testimony and the book. She also confirmed the information in interviews.

McVeigh's attempt to meet with Steven Colbern, a customer of the American Assault Company, was detailed in testimony from the Nichols trial. McVeigh said in our interviews that he was intrigued by Colbern, but that a meeting between them never took place. McVeigh confirmed writing the letter to Colbern that was found attached to a power transmission tower; that letter eventually made its way into the hands of federal prosecutors.

On December 13, 1994, McVeigh mailed a letter to Andrea Peters, again trying to romantically endear himself to her; in an interview with the authors, Peters said she later turned the letter over to the FBI after McVeigh was arrested and charged in the bombing. McVeigh confirmed Michael Fortier's testimony that he had given Fortier guns stolen in the Moore robbery for him to resell. In both interviews and letters, McVeigh denied seeing a day-care center at the Murrah Building on the different occasions he cased it, including the time he and Fortier drove past it in December 1994. McVeigh's December 1994 car accident while transporting blasting caps in Christmas gift-wrapped boxes was confirmed in testimony given at Terry Nichols's trial by Kevin Nicholas, a farmhand at the Nichols farm in Decker, Michigan, and friend of McVeigh. Gwenda

Strider, the aunt of Nicholas's wife, Sheila, also confirmed in an interview that she received letters from McVeigh, including one on February 10, 1995, when he wrote her he could "rip the bastards' [federal agents'] heads off." Strider says she cannot recall what she had written him in a previous letter, which had prompted his correspondence to her.

Several of the letters McVeigh wrote his sister are crucial as well, including an earlier letter from Michigan written while he was staying with Kevin Nicholas in December 1994, in which he wrote that he was living a life on the run in case "someone is looking to shut me up." The letter warning that "something big is going to happen in the month of the Bull" was followed by a second asking if Jennifer had destroyed the first, as requested. Information about these letters was obtained from Jennifer McVeigh's court testimony, as well as interviews with her and law enforcement.

The text of letters between Roger Moore and Karen Anderson and McVeigh after the November 5, 1994, robbery was introduced at Terry Nichols's trial. Details of McVeigh's final weeks in Kingman and his frustration with the lack of support from Terry Nichols and Michael Fortier in helping to carry out his plans are based on interviews with McVeigh as well as on Michael and Lori Fortier's testimony. Terry Nichols, despite a number of efforts to contact him at a jail in Oklahoma City, where he was awaiting trial on state murder charges, has been unreachable for interviewing.

8. Ready to Kill

McVeigh's account of leaving Kingman, Arizona, and arriving in Kansas confirms and augments the findings of the criminal investigation, which produced the billing records of the Daryl Bridges calling card, motel bills, the Ryder truck rental agreement, and all-important eyewitness statements. The witnesses' courtroom testimony, until now, provided the most comprehensive chronology of McVeigh's whereabouts. Whenever possible, independent interviews were conducted with individuals who came in contact with McVeigh in Junction City, a location he knew well from his days at Fort Riley.

Independent reference to the April 16, 1995, Easter Sunday telephone call McVeigh made to Terry Nichols's home in Herington, Kansas, comes in Lana Padilla's book, *By Blood Betrayed*, in which Josh Nichols recalls hearing McVeigh's voice screaming through the phone at Nichols. McVeigh confirms that he was threatening Nichols in order to coerce his friend into driving down to Oklahoma City with him to park the getaway car.

On Tuesday, April 18, 1995, McVeigh mixed the bomb at Geary Lake with Terry Nichols, who McVeigh says worked under duress. McVeigh contributed details about the bomb's ingredients, and was quick to point out when government investigators erred in their description of the bomb components and dimensions. McVeigh volunteered that he was prepared to kill Geary Lake fisherman Richard Wahl and subdue the man's young son if they had come too close to the Ryder truck during the mixing of the explosives.

9. Ground Zero

McVeigh related his actions and thoughts on the drive to Oklahoma City, and on his delivery of the bomb, in a series of interviews and letters between May 1999 and December 2000. With one of the letters he sent to the authors from prison, he mailed a hand-drawn diagram showing the location where he left his bomb, and the resulting damage to the Murrah Building. In a later letter, he provided a map showing the escape route he took on foot, just after igniting the bomb and leaving the truck behind. The packet of articles McVeigh left in his getaway car was described by federal prosecutor Joseph Hartzler in his opening argument at McVeigh's trial, and in much greater detail by FBI Agent William Eppright during his testimony on April 28, 1997.

10. Body Count

Horrific stories of the carnage inflicted by the bombing were told in interviews by Richard Williams, assistant manager of the Murrah Building, and a number of other bombing victims, including Patti Hall. Vicki Hamm, a Murrah Building government employee who was actually a few blocks away at the time of the bombing, also provided many helpful insights, based on her own experiences and those of friends who were severely injured.

Marsha Kight, who lost her twenty-three-year-old daughter in the blast, Marsha's husband, H. Tom Kight, and other family members of bomb victims were also invaluable sources of information. Many of their stories are told in Marsha Kight's book, *Forever Changed: Remembering Oklahoma City, April 19, 1995,* published in 1998 by Prometheus Books. An organization headed by Ms. Kight, Families and Survivors United, and officials of the Oklahoma City National Memorial were tremendously helpful with details of the tragedy.

The events were further described by dozens of witnesses at the McVeigh and Nichols trials, including Helena Garrett, Daina Bradley, Florence Rogers, and Sue Hunt. Hartzler, fellow prosecutor Beth Wilkinson, and others provided more information in court statements. The *Oklahoman*'s vivid and compelling newspaper accounts of the bombing and its aftermath were also very helpful in providing background material. Hartzler provided additional information about the bombing during an interview in January 2001.

McVeigh's insistence that he was alone when he delivered the bomb, and other aspects of the crime and getaway he described to the authors, were mirrored by the accounts he had given to defense-team psychiatrist Dr. John R. Smith. We spent an emotional night interviewing Dr. Smith, at a restaurant and at the bombing memorial site, in July 2000.

Our description of Trooper Charles Hanger's arrest of McVeigh resulted from interviews with McVeigh and Hanger, in addition to Hanger's testimony at the McVeigh and Nichols trials. McVeigh, Hanger, and Noble County Sheriff Jerry R. Cook provided the information on the booking of McVeigh at the Noble County Jail.

11. "Timmy's All Over CNN"

The two days McVeigh spent relaxing in the Noble County Jail, while cops frantically searched the nation for a then-unknown bomber, were detailed in interviews with McVeigh and Sheriff Cook, with some assistance from Noble County District Attorney Mark Gibson. Numerous law-enforcement officials provided helpful information about the nationwide search for the bomber, among them former FBI agents Danny Coulson, Floyd Zimms, Bob Ricks, J. Gary DiLaura, Dean Naum, and Clinton Van Zandt, in addition to still-active FBI agents Paul Moskal and Danny A. Defenbaugh. Some of these agents, along with Sheriff Cook and McVeigh, provided information on the famous "Perry Walkout," which gave the world its first view of McVeigh in an orange jail suit. No law-enforcement official would confirm McVeigh's claims that agents showed him photos of dead children during a jail interrogation; nor would any police official confirm his claim that he was denied use of a bulletproof vest.

Details about federal agents' dealings with Bill McVeigh and other family members in the days after the bombing came from DiLaura, Naum, Moskal, and other police officials in the Buffalo area. These events were also described by Bill McVeigh, Jennifer McVeigh, Mickey Hill, Monsignor Paul Belzer, family friend Art Braunscheidel, and Joel Daniels, Jennifer McVeigh's attorney.

Oklahoma City lawyers John Coyle and Susan Otto confirmed some of what McVeigh told the authors about their representation of him in the early stages of the case, but refused to speak about privileged attorney-client discussions they had with McVeigh.

Information about the FBI's dealings with Terry and James Nichols in the days after the bombing came from FBI officials, court documents, and interviews with James Nichols. The arrest of Terry Nichols in Herington, Kansas, was described in court papers submitted by the FBI, including the nine-page statement Nichols gave on April 21, 1995, and in an interview with Barry Thacker, the former assistant police chief of Herington. Nichols's ex-wife, Lana Padilla, also described some of what was happening with the family at the time in her book and in interviews.

The items found at the Nichols home after his arrest were described by FBI agents in testimony at Nichols's trial in December 1997. Defense lawyer Michael Tigar denied that a drawing found in a trash can outside the home was a map of downtown Oklahoma City, or that it was drawn by Nichols.

12. Indicted

The charges against McVeigh and Nichols were laid out in an indictment handed up by a federal grand jury in Oklahoma City on August 10, 1995.

Background information on McVeigh's lead defense lawyer, Stephen Jones, came from the Web site operated by Jones's law firm, Jones & Wyatt, in Enid, Oklahoma, from the Court TV Web site, from a two-hour interview with Jones in Oklahoma City in July 2000, from a 40-minute phone interview in December 2000, and from *Others Unknown,* the book Jones and Peter Israel published in 1998. The book was published by PublicAffairs, a member of the Perseus Books Group. Some of the other attorneys involved in the defense case also offered their insights.

Jones's account of his dealings with McVeigh before, during, and after the trial came from his book, the two interviews, and articles published in newspapers, as noted in the text. Jones has forcefully and repeatedly denied that he did anything but his best for McVeigh, and he has repeatedly denied McVeigh's allegation that his "conspiracy theory" defense was motivated by his desire to author a successful book. "I have some regrets," Jones confided in our July 2000 interview. "But I don't feel hurt, not in comparison to the hurt felt by victims of the bomb. There might have been some brickbats in the press, but I didn't lose my leg, my arm, my wife, or my child, as many of the bomb victims did." Jones reiterated his contention that he was not to blame for any of the news leaks of McVeigh confessions, and said in December 2000 that he felt "stronger than ever" that a wider conspiracy was behind the bombing, though he said he could not elaborate. Jones added that many criminal defendants turn on their attorneys after losing a trial. "If Mr. McVeigh keeps criticizing me, I might end up as the governor of Oklahoma," Jones joked toward the end of the Oklahoma City interview. "If he says to everybody, 'Mr. Jones is a great attorney,' I have a problem."

Lead prosecutor Hartzler said he thought the defense team "did a fine job—they didn't have much to work with." He added, however, that he never saw so many news leaks from any defense team in seventeen years as a federal prosecutor.

Jones's theories about bombing conspiracies involving foreign terrorists and residents of Elohim City in Oklahoma were explained in his book, and in court papers filed with Judge Matsch on March 25, 1997. Matsch declined interview requests.

The Reverend Robert G. Millar, founder of Elohim City, denied the allegations in an interview with the authors, as did his daughter-in-law, Joan Millar, and McVeigh himself. Cate McCauley, former executive director of a citizens' committee that did its own extensive investigations of the bombing, told the authors in July 2000 that she did not believe the Elohim City story, or any of the other conspiracy theories. McCauley, one of the leading experts on conspiracy theories and all aspects of the bombing, spent thousands of hours investigating the crime. She is one of the few investigators who has communicated with both McVeigh and Terry Nichols's family since the bombing.

Information about McVeigh's voter registration in Niagara County was confirmed by a former county elections commissioner, Lucille Britt.

In interviews and letters, McVeigh provided his insights on *Unintended Consequences*, the book he now considers superior to *The Turner Diaries*.

13. "Oh, My God, He Did It"

Information on the unusual security precautions for the trial was provided in interviews with McVeigh, federal court officials, and law-enforcement officials, and in authoritative trial coverage in the *Rocky Mountain News* and the *Denver Post*. Biographical information on Judge Matsch and other key players in the trial came from the two Denver newspapers and the Court TV and CNN Web sites.

Jury selection was detailed in official court transcripts from March and April of 1997. The profiles of the twelve jurors came from articles on May 31, 1997, in the Associated Press and on June 2, 1997, in the *Denver Post*; these were verified by checking jury selection transcripts. Jury consultant Sandy Marks, in an interview with the authors, said he did not recall the courtroom coughing incident, insisting that "a lot of people" had colds and were coughing at various times during the McVeigh trial; McVeigh stands by the story. Marks added that, if McVeigh had any complaints about his performance as a jury consultant, he does not recall McVeigh ever mentioning them during the trial.

The authors attended portions of the Denver trial; other trial information came from the official court transcripts of statements made by lawyers, Judge Matsch, and the witnesses.

McVeigh provided his insights into the trial in numerous interviews and letters, and some of the trial observers—including the Kights and Jannie Coverdale—offered further observations on McVeigh's conduct during the proceedings.

Bill McVeigh, Jennifer McVeigh, and Mickey Hill were also interviewed about their appearances on the witness stand.

14. Murderers' Row

Interviews with McVeigh, U.S. Marshal Tina Lewis Rowe of Denver, and her chief deputy, Larry Homenick, described the helicopter flight from Denver to the Supermax prison in Florence, Colorado. McVeigh's claim that he was roughed up by guards when he was moved to the Supermax, and later to federal death row in Terre Haute, Indiana, were never confirmed by prison or law-enforcement officials; federal prison officials insist he was always treated fairly, but refuse to comment on McVeigh's specific claims. The authors were authorized to visit McVeigh at both prisons, but were not allowed to tour either prison. McVeigh's descriptions of prison life were offered in interviews at both facilities and in numerous letters. His friendship with convicted Unabomber Ted Kaczynski was described in McVeigh's interviews and in the eleven-page letter Kaczynski sent to the authors; that letter is reproduced in full in appendix B by Kaczynski's request, to avoid the risk of being quoted out of context.

McVeigh's description of his prison talk with Michael Fortier has not been confirmed by Fortier, who did not respond to requests for interviews the authors sought to arrange through his family. However, his mother, Irene Fortier, has said that her son told her he spoke with McVeigh at the Supermax. Prosecutor Joseph Hartzler, and Fortier's attorney, Mike McGuire, confirmed that Fortier told them he never spotted a day-care center in the Murrah Building.

Details of Mickey Hill's emotional problems after the bombing, and of her December 1999 television interview, were obtained in interviews with her and other family members.

INDEX